50
BEST PLACES
FLY FISHING THE NORTHEAST

BOB MALLARD

STONEFLY
PRESS

640 Clematis St. #588
West Palm Beach, FL 33402
FAX: 877-609-3814

For information about discounts on bulk purchases, or
to book the author for an engagement or demonstration,
please contact Stonefly Press at info@stoneflypress.com,
or visit us at Stoneflypress.com.

stoneflypress.com

Printed in the United States

19   18   17   16   15   1   2   3   4   5

Library of Congress Control Number: 2014944976

Stonefly Press

Publisher: Robert D. Clouse

Acquiring Editor: Robert D. Clouse

Managing Production Editor: Bill Bowers

Copy Editor: Bill Bowers

Proofreader: Eileen McNulty

Front Cover Photo: Covered bridge in Downsville, New York. Rich Strolis

*Back Cover Photo: Evan Bottcher on catch-and-release section of the
West Branch of the Ausable River. Hungry Trout Resort*

This book is dedicated to my wife, Diana,
for allowing me to live the dream.
Without her, I would still be stuck behind a desk,
doing work I didn't like, in a place
I didn't want to be.

Contents

Acknowledgments

THERE ARE MANY people I wish to thank for directly or indirectly helping to make this book possible. It is impossible to thank all of them personally. I am, however, very grateful to all of them. I wish to specifically thank the following:

First and foremost, to all of those—far too many to list here—who contributed chapters to this book; for adding some star power, and for providing a level of local knowledge and expertise unmatched in the Northeast, I extend my deepest gratitude. These contributors took time out of their busy schedules to make your time on the water a bit more productive. Please support them as they have you.

All of those—again, too many to list—who generously provided pictures in support of the chapters in the book. As they say, every picture tells a story, and every story needs a picture.

Brad Gage, New England Outdoors; for forwarding my name to Terry Gunn as a candidate to write the Maine chapter in his book, *50 Best Tailwaters to Fly Fish.*

Terry Gunn of Lees Ferry Anglers, for his words of encouragement and the suggestion that I do more writing. Had it not been for my involvement in Terry's book, *50 Best Tailwaters to Fly Fish*, this endeavor would never have happened.

Robert Clouse, publisher of Stonefly Press for taking a chance on a less-than-perfect candidate for the book. The publisher takes all the risks—the rest of us are just along for the ride. I appreciate that he was able to see what I brought to the table, not just what I didn't.

Thomas Ames, Jr., author of *Hatch Guide for New England Streams, Fishbugs,* and *Caddisflies: A Guide to Eastern Species for Anglers and Other Naturalists,* for introducing me to a national audience, and contributing the Foreword to the book.

Bradford Camps and Libby Camps for opening their businesses to me so I could collect the photographs I needed to support my Arctic char and brook trout pieces.

Fisheries advocates Ted Williams and Clinton "Bill" Townsend; for befriending me, educating me, and forever changing how I view fishing, fish, and the places that fish live.

Bud Hawkins, the first person I ever met who had a true passion for fly fishing. And for showing me how to tie my first fly—using fur brushed from his old pet cat, Ma.

Tom Ames, Tim Beckwith, Chris Major, Dave Martel, Jeff Moore, David Peress, John Vacca, Dave Wysocki, and the rest of the *old guys* whom I fish with on a fairly regular basis—and in some cases have done so for years. Here's hoping there are many more days on the water ahead for all of us.

Lou Beckwith, Steve Bowman, Kash Haley, Dan and Tom Harrison, Nate Hill, Travis Parlin, Nate Pease, Jack Rowbottom, Kris Thompson, and the rest of the *young guys* for being willing to fish with a guy old enough to be their father—you guys help keep me young, while reminding me just how old I actually am.

Tim Beckwith and family; for sharing Camp U-No with me. I caught my first trout on a fly there—a foot-long stocked rainbow from the Israel River that took a Gray Hackle fished dry, or however it happened to land, on a 7-foot 5-weight fiberglass Daiwa fly rod and Pflueger Medalist reel. I remember it like it was yesterday.

About the Author

BOB MALLARD has lived in the Northeast for over 50 years. He has called Massachusetts, New Hampshire, and Maine home. He has spent at least a decade living in each. Connecticut and Vermont were always just a day or weekend trip away. New Jersey, New York, and Pennsylvania were just a long weekend away. His career resulted in long-term projects in greater DC and New Jersey, giving him easy access to New York and Pennsylvania.

Bob is on the water more than a hundred days a year, and has been for as long as he can remember. He travels all over the country in search of trout. Bob has owned and operated Kennebec River Outfitters, a full-service fly shop in Madison, Maine, since 2001. He maintains an online fly-fishing forum associated with his business. He teaches fly tying, fly casting, knot tying, and fly fishing.

Bob has written about fly fishing, fly tying, and fisheries conservation extensively. He has covered tackle, technique, travel, fisheries management, and fisheries conservation. His work has appeared in newspapers, sporting publications, fly-fishing magazines, and books. This includes a stint as the writer of a monthly fly-fishing column, *The Technical Fly Fisherman*, in a regional sporting publication. His work has appeared in *Northwoods Sporting Journal, The Maine Sportsman, Fly Fishing New England, Eastern Fly Fishing, Flyfishing & Tying Journal, Fly Fish America, Fly Fisherman, Fly Tyer,* and *Angling Trade*. He had a trout on the cover of *Flyfishing & Tying Journal*.

Bob and his fly shop have been featured in newspapers including *The Wall Street Journal*, regional and national sporting and fly-fishing magazines, on local and regional television programs, a Maine Department of Tourism ad, and several books. Most recently, Bob contributed two chapters to a book on the country's best tailwater fisheries: *50 Best Tailwaters to Fly Fish*, by Terry and Wendy Gunn (Stonefly Press, 2013). Look for his next book from Stonefly Press, *25 Best Towns: Fly Fishing for Trout*, due out in late 2014 or early 2015.

Bob has been involved with several fisheries advocacy groups over the years. He has been a tireless advocate for Maine's wild and native salmonids, including testifying in front of legislative committees on behalf of never-stocked-over brook trout, self-sustaining brook trout, remote ponds, fishing regulations, Arctic char, and the use of live bait on wild salmonid waters. He was instrumental in simplifying the regulations associated with Maine's brook trout lakes and ponds, getting live bait and stocking off Maine's never-stocked trout ponds and Arctic char waters, and initiating Maine's float stocking program.

Bob Mallard. Joe Klementovich

Thomas Ames, Jr.

Foreword

WHY THE HECK should anyone pay the least bit of attention to one man's selection of the 50 best places to cast a fly in the Northeast? To answer that question, let me sketch you a portrait of the man behind the list. He is opinionated. He is impatient. He is painfully organized. But he is so well informed that he can courageously argue both sides of a question with equal conviction. He is a man I can trust to be good to his word and to be fully prepared for what lies ahead. If you are planning to spend your precious time and hard-earned money traveling to the destinations described in this book, you are going to want to trust Bob Mallard the way I do.

I have always figured that the best way to catch fish was to study and imitate the foods that they eat. Bob's flair for fly fishing comes from an understanding of something even more fundamental and, quite literally, deeper. He knows fish—especially trout. He knows where they will be, how they will behave under a given condition, how they will respond to changing conditions, and how they will react when presented with a fly. This is not easy knowledge to come by. I can study trout foods—mostly insects—in an aquarium or streamside, but what actually results in fish getting hooked begins deep under the water's surface where most of us can't see it. That's why Bob pulls fish out of places where most of us would not bother casting a line, using flies that match-the-hatch purists like me do not even carry.

The kind of fish sense that Bob possesses comes only from time on the water. He spends more time with a fly rod in his hand than anyone I know. I used to wonder how he could devote himself so single-mindedly and whole-heartedly to fishing until I realized that he treasures each fish hooked as a lesson in angling learned. Bob has caught some big lessons, and a lot of them, but has yet to satisfy either his appetite or his capacity for knowledge. We've fished together every year for at least the last dozen, and I'll begrudgingly admit to having learned a lot more from Bob than he has learned from me. He has shared what he has learned freely, and with all of the tenderness of a defensive tackle.

Bob has both an uncanny knack for choosing the right fly and a practiced and polished delivery, but when a trout chooses to ignore his fly, Bob will not waste too much time trying to change its mind with minor changes in pattern or presentation. He will make a radical change or simply move on to the next fish and then return the next hour, the next day, or the next year with a whole new strategy for capturing the missed one. Bob doesn't wait for things to happen, he makes them happen.

In his second life as a fly-shop owner, Bob applies the same painstaking attention to minutiae that brought him success in a career in information technology. He scrutinizes every piece of fishing tackle, every stitch and seam on a vest and pair of waders, every fly rod, line, and pattern, with the idea that landing the fish of a lifetime will ultimately depend on the performance of his gear. If an item is flawed, poorly designed, poorly manufactured, or otherwise substandard in any way, he will not sell it to a customer, and he certainly will not get caught using it himself.

Bob has chosen both the waters and the writers for this book with the same exacting standards. No starry-eyed romanticism, no nod to nostalgia for the sake of nostalgia, has clouded his judgment in making his selections. No storied past in and of itself will earn a river or stream a place in this book if it is flawed or substandard and can no longer support a healthy fishery. If it is accessible, well-regulated, and well-maintained, it probably made the cut. If it is deficient in any of these qualities, he will not waste his time, or yours, by including it.

Just think: if you live in the Northeast you will never have to sit in another crowded airline seat to get to a fishing destination. If you made a list of the great waters you have fished in your lifetime, would there be fifty? Here are fifty great fisheries you can visit within a day's drive of home. Here, too, are the resources you will need to make your trip worthwhile, including tips about where to and how to fish them, by expert anglers who know the water.

—THOMAS AMES, JR.

Thomas Ames, Jr. is the author of *Hatch Guide for New England Streams, Fishbugs, Caddisflies: A Guide to Eastern Species for Anglers* and *Other Naturalists,* and numerous articles on fly fishing.

Chris Major on the upper Saco River. Fly Fish America

Introduction

I ALWAYS KNEW I would someday be involved in writing a definitive guide to fly fishing in the Northeast. Over the years friends, associates, and peers encouraged me to take the plunge and write down what I knew. I started several times, but I never finished. I struggled with the format. Where-to guides come in many flavors, and I just did not know where I wanted to go with it. Sometimes there seemed to be too much information. Other times, too little. Sometimes there were glaring omissions. Other times, odd inclusions.

I wasn't interested in writing the kind of kiss-and-tell book that identifies specific pools to fish, where to park, and what fly to use. I was not sure that level of detail was necessary. I wanted to tell people where to go and why. I figured they would know—or figure out—what to do when they got there. Sure, some basic tackle and fly information was useful, but to try to delve into too deep a level of detail without consideration of the current weather, water levels, water temperatures, and so on, seemed futile, and worse, potentially misleading.

While working on Terry and Wendy Gunn's *50 Best Tailwaters to Fly Fish*, I realized that I had finally found a format that worked for me. In addition to telling the angler where to go and why, the book provides information about local fly shops, guides, lodging, and food that would be useful to the visiting angler. The book is not burdened with a level of minutiae that was as likely to be wrong as it was right. It did not cover waters for the sake of covering waters—there was no room for filler. It focused solely on the *best*.

Next was the author/editor vs. solo author approach used in the book. Tapping fly-shop personnel, working guides, lodge owners, and others to contribute chapters wherever possible would allow me to create a veritable all-star team of regional expertise. This would in turn increase the value of the information in the book, and make it more interesting to read. It would give me a chance to share the limelight with friends, acquaintances, peers, and even competitors. It would present a real challenge to try to pull it all together—far harder, in reality, than writing everything myself.

When the same publisher, Stonefly Press, contacted me about the possibility of writing a book about the Northeast, I jumped at the opportunity. Finally, a format that worked for me and a publisher who understood that more is not necessarily better, and that less detail is better than inaccurate detail. The folks at Stonefly Press have brought a fresh and modern view to the fly-fishing where-to book. They have breathed new life into a genre that had become a bit stale. They have set the bar higher than it has ever been set before. I commend them for helping to reinvent the fly-fishing where-to book.

Blueback Trout (Salvelinus alpinus oquassa).

Blueback trout. James Prosek

COMPRISED OF THE SIX New England states, plus New York, New Jersey, and Pennsylvania, the Northeast represents a relatively small part of the country from a geographic standpoint. No state ranks higher than 30th in the nation in regard to size. Six are among the 10 smallest—including the smallest, Rhode Island. Eight of the 9 are within the 20 smallest.

Conversely, four of the states are within the top 10 in the nation in regard to population. Six of the 10 most densely populated states are in the Northeast—including the top four, New Jersey, Rhode Island, Massachusetts, and Connecticut. Population densities range from a low of about 40 people per square mile in Maine to over 1,000 people per square mile in New Jersey. The Northeast is home to roughly 20 percent of the nation's population—and within a short drive of about another 10 percent.

The History

While the focus in regard to fly fishing has shifted west over the years, it is important to remember that the Northeast is where it all started. From the historic hotels and sporting camps of Maine, to the hallowed waters of the Catskills, to the fabled limestone creeks of Pennsylvania, the Northeast has a rich fly-fishing history.

The Northeast was a hotbed for early fly design. From Carrie Stevens and her fabled Grey Ghost streamer, to Bill Bennett and his groundbreaking Pontoon Hopper, to Theodore Gordon and his delicate Quill Gordon dry fly, much early fly innovation came from the Northeast. In recent years, tiers such as Fran Betters, Dick Talleur, Dick Stewart, David Klausmeyer, Don Bastian, Ed Muzzerol, and David Mac have been torch bearers for classic fly tying.

Many early fly-fishing tackle manufacturers came from the Northeast as well. From Orvis—founded on the banks of the Batten Kill in Vermont—to Thomas and Thomas in Massachusetts, to Cortland Line Company in New York, to outdoor giant L. L. Bean in Maine, to the numerous early bamboo rod shops scattered across the region, the Northeast accounted for much of the fly-fishing tackle available in the 19th and early 20th centuries.

The Northeast was also well represented on the literary front. From Arthur R. MacDougall, Jr., famous for creating the fictional character Dud Dean, to the classic writings of Alfred W. Miller—aka Sparse Grey Hackle—to the technical genius of Vince Marinaro, Charlie Fox, and Ed Koch, to the insightful writings of Ernie Schwiebert, to the conservation prose of Ted Williams, to entomology guru Thomas Ames, Jr., the Northeast has produced some of the most important and groundbreaking fly-fishing writing in history.

Then there is the celebrity. From the time when the first Atlantic salmon caught in Maine each season went to the president of the United States, to the local ramblings of baseball legend Ted Williams and his friend, sportscaster Curt Gowdy, to TV personality Gadabout Gaddis and his 1970s show, *The Flying Fisherman* (filmed on the banks of the Kennebec River in Maine), the Northeast has been highly visible in the world of fly fishing.

Finally are the ambassadors of the sport. From Cornelia "Fly Rod" Crosby (1854–1946)—Maine's first registered guide, to Leon Chandler of Cortland Line fame, to Leon Leonwood Bean of L.L. Bean fame, to George Harvey's Pennsylvania college teachings, to Cathy and Barry Beck's endless promotion of tackle and techniques, to Tom Ackerman and his resurrection of the classic *American Sportsman* show, the Northeast has always been at the forefront of fly-fishing promotion.

The Waters

The rivers, streams, brooks, and creeks of the Northeast can be divided into three primary categories—tailwater, freestone, and limestone. What constitutes a river, stream, brook, or creek is less clear. Some rivers are smaller than some streams. There is no identifiable characteristic that differentiates a stream from a brook. Most—but not all—creeks are either limestone or coastal.

A tailwater is a section of river downstream of a dam. Many expect tailwaters to be cold, clear, and rich in nutrients, with specific types of plant and insect life. Very few rivers in the Northeast fit this description. While some tailwaters in the Northeast have consistent and cold flows, many do not due to low dams, shallow impoundments, or mid-depth releases from high dams.

Most Northeast rivers are what would more accurately be referred to as freestone—even many that originate at a dam. On freestone rivers, the bottom is usually strewn with rocks and boulders of various sizes. Slower sections are often covered with sand and gravel—and even mud or silt. They tend to warm up as the season progresses. Flows are inconsistent and often unpredictable. This is the classic Northeast river.

The Northeast's streams and brooks are mostly freestone. There are, however, meadow streams, estuary brooks, and the aforementioned limestone creeks. Most freestone streams are relatively infertile and subject to radical flow changes. Many of these suffer from low water in the summer. Some get too warm to hold trout throughout the year. But many do hold trout—even wild trout.

Limestone creeks are to the Northeast what spring creeks are to the West. They get their water from underground springs. Limestone creeks are found primarily, but not exclusively, in Pennsylvania. They have consistent water temperatures and flows, and robust plant and insect life. They are as tough to fish as any waters in the country—and some would argue the toughest. If you can catch fish on a limestone creek, you can catch fish anywhere.

While not as popular with fly fishers as moving water, lakes, ponds, and reservoirs offer some unique, challenging, and fun opportunities for those willing to try them. Like the differences among rivers, streams, brooks, and creeks, the difference between lakes and ponds is murky at best. There are ponds that are larger than some lakes—so it is not a size issue.

Saltwater fly fishing in the Northeast is done offshore, in the surf, in estuaries, and on the flats. Like our tailwaters, our Northeast flats do not fit the classic definition. Thinking of saltwater flats conjures up images of white sand, turquoise water, and boats with poling platforms. While some flats in the Northeast fit that description to some degree, many do not. But they are beautiful nonetheless.

The Fish

The Northeast is home to myriad gamefish species. These include ten salmonids; largemouth and smallmouth bass; pickerel, pike, and muskellunge; carp; and stripers, bluefish, and false albacore in salt water. Fly fishers target them all, and they represent a level of diversity found in few if any other places in the country.

Five of the ten salmonids are native to the Northeast: brook trout, lake trout, landlocked (Atlantic) salmon, Atlan-

tic salmon, and Arctic char. The last two are some of the rarest salmonids in the country. Steelhead, along with king and coho salmon were introduced to the Great Lakes to create a sport fishery. Coho were also introduced to some coastal rivers in New Hampshire and Massachusetts, but never took hold. Rainbow and brown trout were introduced throughout the region, as they were elsewhere in the country.

While smallmouth and largemouth bass are native to the Northeast, the range of both species has expanded greatly over the years. But when it comes to fly fishing for bass in the Northeast, the smallmouth is king. The same can be said for pike and muskellunge in regard to range expansion. While neither has been pursued by fly fishers in the Northeast to the same extent as trout, salmon, and bass, they are caught on fly tackle.

The Fishing

When it comes to trout fishing, Connecticut, Massachusetts, New Jersey, and Rhode Island have done a lot with a little. While they do not have the number of quality fly fisheries the other states have, each can lay claim to some of the finest trout fishing in the Northeast. The first has some pike fishing, all have some smallmouth fishing, and all offer saltwater fishing for striped bass as well.

New Hampshire and Vermont are arguably the two most beautiful states in the Northeast. Both have diverse fly-fishing offerings. From trout to salmon to pike; from large rivers to small mountain streams, from large lakes to tiny ponds, these states offer something for everyone.

Maine boasts seven species of salmonids: brook trout, brown trout, rainbow trout, lake trout, landlocked salmon, Atlantic salmon, and Arctic char. It is the only state where the last two still exist, and has more wild and native salmonid water than any state in the Northeast. It is also a top smallmouth bass and striper destination.

New York has some of the most famous trout, salmon, and steelhead rivers in the Northeast. Plus it offers some of the finest smallmouth and striped bass fishing in the Northeast. When it comes to fly fishing, New York truly has it all.

Pennsylvania's Heritage Waters are some of the finest wild trout fisheries in the country. The state is home to the largest concentration of spring creeks—locally referred to as limestone creeks—east of the Mississippi. There are steelhead and smallmouth bass as well.

Access

Landowner rights and trespass are complicated issues. Some Northeast states have seen court battles related to trespass driven solely by angler access. Laws governing access have been subject to challenge, interpretation, and subsequent revision. Most fly fishers believe they have more legal rights in regard to access to water than they actually do.

Some water in the Northeast is public, some is not. Some water on public land is open to anglers, some is not. Some water on private land is open to anglers, some is not. Some of the fishing allowed on private land is voluntary, some is not. It is imperative that anglers understand the laws governing trespass to avoid conflicts with landowners and law enforcement.

Maine's Great Ponds Act guarantees access to waters larger than 10 acres for the purpose of fishing. This can, however, be restricted to walk-in and fly-in. Many states have *navigable water* laws associated with rivers and streams. The definition of navigable varies from state to state. This allows anglers access by foot or boat, as long as they enter on public property, and stay below the high-water mark. In some states, however, if the landowner owns both banks of the stream, he or she also owns the riverbed, and you cannot wade or even drop anchor without permission.

Unfortunately, as in many other parts of the country, some quality water is not open to the public. In many cases these are nonnavigable streams or small ponds. Some private land in the Northeast is restricted to pay-to-fish or even membership in exclusive clubs. While this situation is primarily found in Pennsylvania, it is not exclusive to Pennsylvania.

Great Fisheries

All fisheries go through peaks and valleys. Events such as floods, droughts, heatwaves, and harsh winters can all affect a fishery from one year to the next. Then there are the parasites and diseases that can change a fishery for decades—or longer. Invasive plants and fish can severely impact a fishery as well.

Regulatory changes usually—but not always—impact fisheries in a positive way. Eliminating the use of bait reduces harvest, and incidental mortality, and can help stop the spread of invasive minnows. Catch-and-release, slot limits, and creel reductions all result in fewer fish being harvested.

Fisheries can be quite resilient, especially great ones. They often respond well—and faster than most expect—to changes such as stricter regulations, habitat restoration, and reclamation. They can also rebound from what might look like a hopeless situation. One need look no further than the Madison River in Montana, which, after losing 90 percent of its wild rainbow trout at the peak of the whirling disease catastrophe, has once again become a marquee fishery.

While one fishery is down, another may be up. All fisheries have good years and bad years. Some fisheries can stay down for a decade, and then seemingly overnight rebound to the point where they were before they crashed. Some fisheries experience explosions for reasons no one quite understands. Some keep chugging along year after year, with little if any real noticeable change.

Striped bass populations are famous for peaks and valleys. After hitting rock bottom a few decades ago, the Northeast striper fishery rebounded to a point where people were coming from all over the country to enjoy it. But recent changes have some concerned again.

I suspect that all the fisheries that are currently down will eventually rebound. They are great fisheries, and great fisheries usually do come back. I also suspect some others will fall on hard times in the years to come. But they too will most likely come back. And in many cases, bad fishing on a great fishery is better than great fishing on a bad fishery.

The List

This book is about great fisheries, those that have been great for many years and will hopefully be great for years to come. I give consideration to infrastructure—lodging, food, boat launches, fly shops, guides, and so on. This makes a great fishery even better. I also give consideration to regulations, such as artificial lures only, fly fishing only, catch-and-release, and slot limits, which all help to improve the overall experience.

By far, the biggest challenge in writing this book was coming up with the list of waters. If the list was not solid, the book would suffer. There could be no glaring omissions. But there should be some surprises—regardless of whom I might upset.

I had to look at the waters in an objective and unbiased manner. This meant potentially leaving out waters I wanted to cover for professional reasons. In some cases, it meant omitting waters where friends, peers, and associates had a financial investment. In other cases, I would be directing anglers to a fishery that some people I know would rather I did not.

Each fishery had to be covered in a way that did it justice within the space available. To write about the Swift River in Massachusetts, and not write about the river below Route 9, would be a disservice at best. Conversely, trying to cover rivers as large and diverse as the Kennebec in Maine in just a few pages would present a challenge.

This book is about fly fishing. While fly fishing is often associated with trout, it is not exclusive to trout. While trout are often associated with moving water, they are not exclusive to moving water. As a result, this book is not exclusively about trout or moving water. It is, however, primarily about trout and moving water, as this is often the best, and most popular, fly fishing available in the Northeast.

The Northeast's primary saltwater species—striped bass or stripers—can be found up and down the coast. I have chosen a few destinations based on their overall quality and reliability.

Smallmouth bass are popular gamefish in the Northeast. In many areas they are the only game in town. They also offer season-long fishing in areas where the trout fishing falls off in the summer due to warm water. As such, they deserve a place in the book, and they get one. So do pike, which have gained in popularity over the last decade.

Last but not least, while clearly not as popular with today's fly fishers as moving water, lakes and ponds deserved to be covered to at least some degree. I looked at stillwaters across species, giving coverage wherever I felt it most warranted.

So this is how the list, and by default the book, came to be. I hope you enjoy what is presented and find the information useful for years to come.

Note that waters are presented from north to south and east to west by state, and then north to south and east to west within states. This was done to provide some level of geographic continuity so that readers could easily locate the waters closest to them, or closest to a given area.

A Quick Word on Infrastructure

In a sincere attempt to provide the reader with some level of help in regard to locating fly shops, outfitters, guides, lodging, and food, we have included some general contact information pertaining to each.

This is by no means an all-inclusive list, nor necessarily even a best-of list—just what was available to us at the time the book was written. Lack of inclusion does not imply anything about a given business—just that we were unable to include it due to space, access to accurate contact information, knowledge that it existed, or that we simply forgot it.

It is also important to note that businesses come and go—especially these days. Businesses that have been there for decades can close overnight and without warning. New businesses pop up to take their places. Addresses, phone numbers, websites, and email addresses can change as well. Businesses change hands. And like fisheries, businesses can go through good times and bad times.

Be sure to contact businesses ahead of time to make sure they will be there to serve you when you arrive. In addition, it never hurts to search around the Internet a bit to see if any new businesses have come to the area since the book was written, or were missed by the author, editor, or contributor, or were left out due to space limitations.

Below. Kennebago upper river moose. Rangeley Region Sport Shop
Overleaf. Bob Mallard on the Kennebago River. Diana Mallard

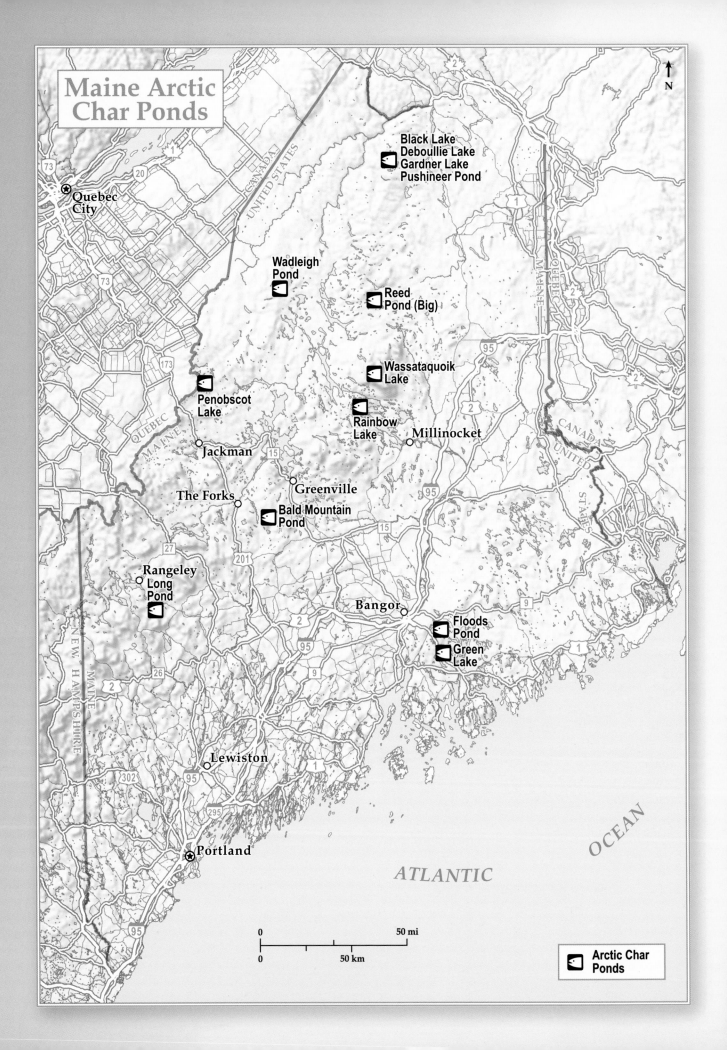

Maine Arctic Char Ponds

N

Black Lake
Deboullie Lake
Gardner Lake
Pushineer Pond

Quebec City

Wadleigh Pond

Reed Pond (Big)

Wassataquoik Lake

Penobscot Lake

Rainbow Lake

Millinocket

Jackman

Greenville

The Forks

Bald Mountain Pond

Rangeley Long Pond

Bangor

Floods Pond

Green Lake

Lewiston

NEW HAMPSHIRE

MAINE

QUEBEC

UNITED STATES

CANADA

Portland

ATLANTIC

OCEAN

0   50 mi

0   50 km

Arctic Char Ponds

1 · Maine Arctic Char Ponds

➤ **Location:** Central and Northern Maine, about a 2- to 3-hour ride from Bangor; a 3- to 4-hour ride from Portland; and a 4- to 5-hour ride from Boston, Massachusetts or Manchester, New Hampshire. Full-service airports are available in all four cities. Float plane pickup from lakes within an hour of Bangor can be arranged.

Maine is home to one of the rarest salmonids in the country—and by far the rarest salmonid in the Northeast. Formerly called blueback trout (and Sunapee trout in New Hampshire and Vermont), these fish are now collectively referred to as Arctic char. Self-sustaining native Arctic char are now extant in no more than 12 waters in the continental United States—all of which are in Maine. Two of these have recently suffered introductions of invasive baitfish, forcing costly reclamation efforts to restore the fisheries and preserve the unique genetics.

There are several other viable—albeit introduced—populations of Arctic char in Maine as well. A few more waters are rumored to have char, with no record of them ever having been stocked. Of the roughly 20 waters where native Arctic char still exist, have been introduced, or have been documented as having a presence, no more than 10 are places where you could reasonably expect to encounter one while fishing. The rest are long shots at best.

According to the Maine Department of Inland Fisheries & Wildlife, there are 14 lakes and ponds in the state that contain Arctic char. This encompasses nearly 10,000 acres of water. Twelve are considered relic—or native. Two are the result of introductions involving fish trapped from Floods Pond. Nine are classified as Principal Fisheries, meaning that an angler has a reasonable chance of catching an Arctic char there. There are no plans for the further expansion of char.

Green Lake near Acadia National Park is a unique case. It has what is classified as a native Arctic char population. It is also one of just four native landlocked salmon lakes in Maine—and the only one where char and landlocked salm-

on historically overlapped. Green Lake is a native rainbow smelt water as well. Smelt introductions have been responsible for the demise of Arctic char populations in other waters. The char in Green Lake are smaller than those found in other waters. This makes some question if they are not in fact dwarf Arctic char, which would make them arguably the rarest salmonids in the continental United States.

Big Reed Pond, in the northern part of the state, is ground zero for native char in Maine. The Nature Conservancy owns the land around this jewel of a pond, which also includes an

Big Reed Pond. Bob Mallard

equally rare stand of virgin, old-growth mixed forest. Unfortunately, Big Reed Pond was one of the two waters that recently succumbed to an introduction of invasive smelts. As part of a multi-agency effort that included The Nature Conservancy, Trout Unlimited, and the Maine Department of Inland Fisheries & Wildlife, along with support from local sporting camps, guides, and anglers, workers were able to trap char from the pond, isolate them in a hatchery, hatch and rear enough fish to use as seed stock, reclaim the pond, and successfully restore this invaluable population of rare fish, all while keeping the genetics intact.

One of the most intriguing things about Arctic char is that these rare and beautiful fish are found within a few short

Bradford Camps' Outback Camp on Big Reed Pond. Bob Mallard

hours of Boston and only an hour's flight from New York City. That this remnant of the Ice Age has survived this long is actually quite amazing. Equally astounding is where some of these char populations are found. Bald Mountain Pond in Somerset County is just over an hour north of the state capital in Augusta. Floods Pond is located on the outskirts of bustling Bangor. The former is open to fishing, the latter is closed to protect a public water supply.

Most of the remaining Arctic char waters are located in the northern part of the state. Almost all of them are found off a network of unmarked—and often unmaintained—dirt roads. Most are also outside the power grid. This means that gas, food, conventional lodging, and general supplies are often an hour or more away, and subject to business hours that are conducive to profitable commerce in rural areas. As is the case with regard to Maine's remote brook trout ponds, this can create something of a problem for the traveling angler.

Fortunately, there are a few traditional sporting camps that are located on, or near, char waters. This gives those seeking to fulfill a bucket list item (catching a rare and beautiful Arctic char) a place to base out of. These businesses offer lodging, food, guides, rental boats, and fly-in service, allowing the angler to focus on fishing rather than logistics. One sporting camp even maintains an outpost cabin on Big Reed Pond, which is now open to catch-and-release angling, and once again putting up wild native Arctic char to anglers willing to put in their time.

Fall arctic char from Big Reed Pond. Bradford Camps

If you think you can just show up at an Arctic char lake and catch fish, you are wrong. Arctic char are deepwater fish that come near the surface only at certain times of year: spring and fall. They can, however, be targeted with sinking lines at other times of year. Fishing for Arctic char is not a numbers game. It is a chance to catch a rare fish in a remote setting. It is a chance to do something that most fly fishers have never done, and never will do. It is a chance to do something truly special—hold a rare and beautiful remnant of the Ice Age in your hand for a fleeting moment.

After years of working to provide the level of protection due these rare fish, there have been several major breakthroughs. First was the so-called Heritage Char legislation. This prohibits the use of live bait on any native char water.

Trapped fall char. Maine Dept. of Inland Fisheries and Wildlife

It also prohibits stocking—with a provision for restoration stocking. Wisely, the Maine Department of Inland Fisheries & Wildlife removed bait of any sort from all but one native char water. They also extended the no-live-bait restriction to the tributaries of these waters. But we could still do more—like a statewide catch-and-release regulation. This would seem prudent when you consider what is at stake.

➤ **Tackle:** A 9-foot 5-weight rod with a floating line is your best bet for fishing dry flies out of a boat on most Arctic char lakes and ponds. If you plan on fishing subsurface—which you may have to do—a 9-foot 6-weight with a fast full-sinking line is your best option. Float tubers may want to consider a 9½- or 10-foot rod with a dry and sinking line as an alternative to carrying two rods—and to help keep your backcast out of the water. Leaders should be 9 to 15 feet and tapered to 4X or 5X for dries, and 6 to 7½ feet for wets—with fluorocarbon being your best bet for the latter. Flies should include leech patterns, classic Black-nosed Dace and Mickey Finn streamers; all stages of mayflies in gray, tan, and yellow in size 14, 12, and 8 to 6, respectively; size 14 caddis in a range of colors; and a few size 10 to 8 caddis in green or olive. You will also want to be sure to tap the fly shops and lodges for some local patterns.

BOB MALLARD has fly fished for over 35 years. He is a blogger, writer, and author; and has owned and operated Kennebec River Outfitters in Madison, Maine since 2001. His writing has been featured in newspapers, magazines, and books at the local, regional, and national levels. He has appeared on radio and television. Look for his upcoming books from Stonefly Press, *25 Best Towns: Fly Fishing for Trout* (winter 2014) and *50 Best Places: Fly Fishing for Brook Trout* (summer 2015). Bob is also a staff fly designer for Catch Fly Fishing. He can be reached at www .kennebecriveroutfitters.com, www.bobmallard.com, info@bobmallard.com, or 207-474-2500.

CLOSEST GUIDES/OUTFITTERS
Refer to Closest full-service lodges.

CLOSEST FULL-SERVICE LODGES
Bradford Camps
(Big Reed Pond Cabins)
Munsungan Lake, Maine
May–November 207-433-0660
December–April 207-746-7777
www.bradfordcamps.com
maine@bradfordcamps.com

Red River Camps
Island Pond, Maine
Deboullie Township
207-554-0420
www.redrivercamps.com
jen@redrivercamps.com

Penobscot Lake Lodge
Penobscot Lake, Maine
207-280-0280
www.penobscotlakelodge.com
PenobscotLake@aol.com

CLOSEST LODGING
Refer to Closest full-service lodges.

CLOSEST FOOD
Refer to Closest full-service lodges.

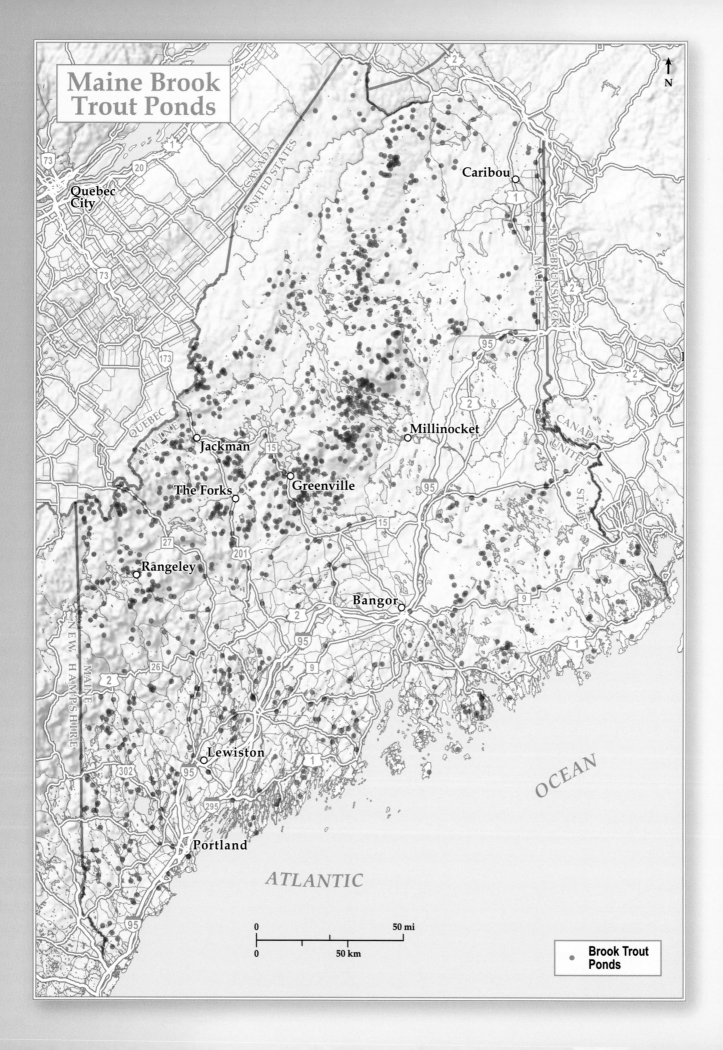

Maine Brook
Trout Ponds

N

Quebec
City

Caribou

Jackman

Millinocket

The Forks

Greenville

Rangeley

Bangor

Lewiston

Portland

OCEAN

ATLANTIC

QUEBEC

MAINE

NEW BRUNSWICK

CANADA

UNITED STATES

NEW HAMPSHIRE

0   50 mi

0   50 km

Brook Trout
Ponds

2 · Maine Brook Trout Ponds

➤ **Location:** Western, Central, and Northern Maine, about a 2- to 3-hour ride from Bangor, a 3- to 4-hour ride from Portland; and a 4- to 5-hour ride from Boston, Massachusetts or Manchester, New Hampshire. Full-service airports are available in all four cities. Float plane pickup from lakes within an hour of Bangor can be arranged.

Maine boasts one of the largest (if not *the* largest) inventories of pond-dwelling, self-sustaining native trout populations in the continental United States—in this case Eastern brook trout. There are more than 600 such waters scattered across the state. Roughly 325 have never been stocked. The rest have not been stocked in at least 25 years. This represents approximately 95 percent of the remaining self-sustaining native brook trout lakes and ponds in the country.

There are another 500 or so ponds in Maine that are stocked with brook trout. Many of these support strong populations of holdover fish. This brings the total number of brook trout ponds in Maine to roughly 1,100—far more than are found anywhere else in the country.

Approximately 175 of the brook trout ponds in Maine are classified as Remote by the Land Use Planning Commission. This means that there is no development—including permanent roads—within a half mile of the shoreline. In most cases, even unimproved roads have been blocked. These represent some of the most pristine brook trout ponds in the Northeast.

It would be impossible—and I believe a real disservice—to try to name just one of these ponds for the purposes of this book. In aggregate, they represent a fly-fishing resource unlike anything else found in the Northeast. In fact, they probably bring more anglers to Maine than all the rivers and streams put together. As a result, I have opted to cover them as a group.

The majority of Maine's best brook trout lakes and ponds are found in the western, central, and northern parts of the state. They are located off a network of unmarked, and often unmaintained, dirt roads. While many of these are located on private land managed for forestry, others are on public land such as sprawling Baxter State Park, private land owned by individuals such as philanthropist Roxanne Quimby, private land owned by conservation groups such as The Nature Conservancy, and conservation easements managed by groups such as the Appalachian Mountain Club.

Under Maine's Great Ponds Act, all lakes and ponds over 10 acres are open to the public for the purpose of fishing. This law guarantees overland access solely for fishing—all other activities fall under the standard laws governing trespass. This does not allow for vehicular access, or even unobstructed foot access. Landowners can—and do—gate their property wherever they see fit, often requiring a long walk to reach the water.

Bob Mallard hooked up on a remote pond. Thomas Ames, Jr.

Most of Maine's best brook trout lakes and ponds are located outside the power grid. Gas, food, lodging, and services are often in short supply. While this presents a certain logistical problem for the visiting fly fisherman, many of these waters are near traditional sporting camps that offer lodging, meals, guides, rental boats, and even float plane service. This is often the most convenient, and safest, way to take advantage of this wonderful resource.

Fishing Maine's brook trout lakes and ponds effectively requires some type of watercraft. Shorelines are lined with trees, and the bottoms are usually muddy, making wade fishing all but impossible. Float tubes, canoes, and small rowboats are often used. Some of the larger waters have boat launches. In many cases, it is the distance from the road that dictates what type of watercraft is needed. On many of the more remote waters, sporting camps maintain an inventory of rental boats.

Bob Mallard with spring-caught wild brookie. Libby Camps

Most of the better brook trout lakes and ponds in Maine contain only brook trout and a native minnow or two—usually some sort of dace. This lack of competition allows the brookies to prosper. This also adds to the uniqueness of these waters, as many brook trout ponds found elsewhere in the Northeast have succumbed to the introduction of one or more nonnative gamefish and/or baitfish.

Many of the best brook trout lakes and ponds are restricted to fly fishing only—some to artificial lures only. Many have some sort of a slot limit prohibiting, or restricting, the harvest of large fish. Bag limits are often restricted to just one or two fish per day—and in a few cases they are managed for catch-and-release.

Hatches on Maine's brook trout ponds start soon after ice-out and continue right into the fall. Mayflies, such as Black Quills and *Callibaetis*, come first. These are followed

Bob Mallard fishing a remote pond. Thomas Ames, Jr.

by caddis—including Giant Traveling Sedges. Then the often overlooked ants, beetles, dragonflies, and damsels. Next is the *Hexagenia*—the largest mayfly in the country—and as much an event as it is a hatch. The dry-fly season ends with an early fall midge hatch, which is also overlooked. Fish also feed on the ever-present leeches, minnows, scuds, and in some cases, crayfish. Early and late in the season—and in between hatches—brook trout can be caught by fishing scud, nymph, leech, and streamer patterns below the surface. In fact, this is probably the best way to target large fish—regardless of when, or what is going on at the surface.

The fish in Maine's brook trout ponds run from 6 to 20 inches. Most are somewhere in between. Ponds have either lots of small fish, a medium number of mixed-size fish, or a small number of large fish. This does not mean you cannot catch a large fish out of any water at any given time, just that the best way to catch big fish is to target waters that are known to hold big fish. Conversely, if you want lots of fish, head to a pond known for holding many fish.

Time at a traditional Maine sporting camp, with your days spent fishing on remote and undeveloped brook trout ponds, is an experience you will not soon forget. While there, you will likely hear the haunting cries of loons. You may encounter secretive goldeneyes and buffleheads, curious otters, territorial tail-slapping beavers, graceful deer, elusive black bears, and the king of the North Woods—the majestic, albeit ungainly, moose. As for the fish, most anglers will agree that there is nothing more beautiful than a wild Eastern brook trout.

➤ Tackle: A 9-foot 5-weight rod with a floating line is your best bet for fishing dry flies out of a boat on most Maine brook trout ponds. Anything lighter than a 5-weight will make it hard to cast larger flies such as *Hexagenia* imitations. As for rods shorter than 9 feet, this can make it hard to get the distance sometimes required to target a fish feeding away from the boat. If you plan to fish subsurface, a 9-foot 6-weight with one slow and one fast full-sinking line is your best option. Float tubers may want to consider a 9½- or 10-foot rod with a dry and sinking line as an alternative to carrying two rods—and to help keep your backcast out of the water. Leaders should be 9 to 15 feet and taper to 4X or 5X for dries, and 6 to 7½ feet for wets—with fluorocarbon being your best bet for the latter. Flies should include leech patterns, classic streamers such as Black-nosed Dace,

Fall brookie caught by Nate Pease. Travis Parlin

Mickey Finns, and Zonkers; all stages of mayflies in gray, tan, and yellow, in sizes 14, 12, and 8 to 6, respectively; size 14 caddis in a range of colors; and a few sizes 10 to 8 caddis in green or olive; all stages of midges in size 18 to 20; and a selection of dragonflies, damsels, ants, and beetles. Also you will want to be sure to tap the fly shops and lodges for some local patterns.

BOB MALLARD has fly fished for over 35 years. He is a blogger, writer, and author; and has owned and operated Kennebec River Outfitters in Madison, Maine since 2001. His writing has been featured in newspapers, magazines, and books at the local, regional, and national levels. He has appeared on radio and television. Look for his upcoming books from Stonefly Press, *25 Best Towns: Fly Fishing for Trout* (winter 2014) and *50 Best Places: Fly Fishing for Brook Trout* (summer 2015). Bob is also a staff fly designer for Catch Fly Fishing. He can be reached at www.kennebecriveroutfitters.com, www.bobmallard.com, info@bobmallard.com, or 207-474-2500.

CLOSEST FLY SHOPS

Kennebec River Outfitters
469 Lakewood Road
Madison, Maine 04950
207-474-2500
www.kennebecriveroutfitters.com
info@kennebecriveroutfitters.com

Rangeley Region Sport Shop
2529 Main Street
Rangeley, Maine 04970
207-864-5615
www.rangeleysportshop.com
rivertoridge@aol.com

Maine Guide Fly Shop
34 Moosehead Lake Road
Greenville, Maine 04441
207-695-2266
www.maineguideflyshop.com
info@maineguideflyshop.com

CLOSEST GUIDES/OUTFITTERS
Refer to Closest full-service lodges

CLOSEST FULL-SERVICE LODGES

Libby Camps
Millinocket Lake, Maine
207-435-8274
www.libbycamps.com
matt@libbycamps.com

Bradford Camps
Munsungan Lake, Maine
May–November: 207-433-0660
December–April: 207-746-7777
www.bradfordcamps.com
maine@bradfordcamps.com

Cobb's Pierce Pond Camps
Pierce Pond, Maine
207-628-2819

Red River Camps
Island Pond, Maine
Deboullie Township
207-554-0420
www.redrivercamps.com
jen@redrivercamps.com

Nahmakanta Lake Camps
Nahmakanta Lake, Maine
207-731-8888
www.nahmakanta.com
info@nahmakanta.com

CLOSEST LODGING
Refer to Closest full-service lodges

CLOSEST FOOD
Refer to Closest full-service lodges

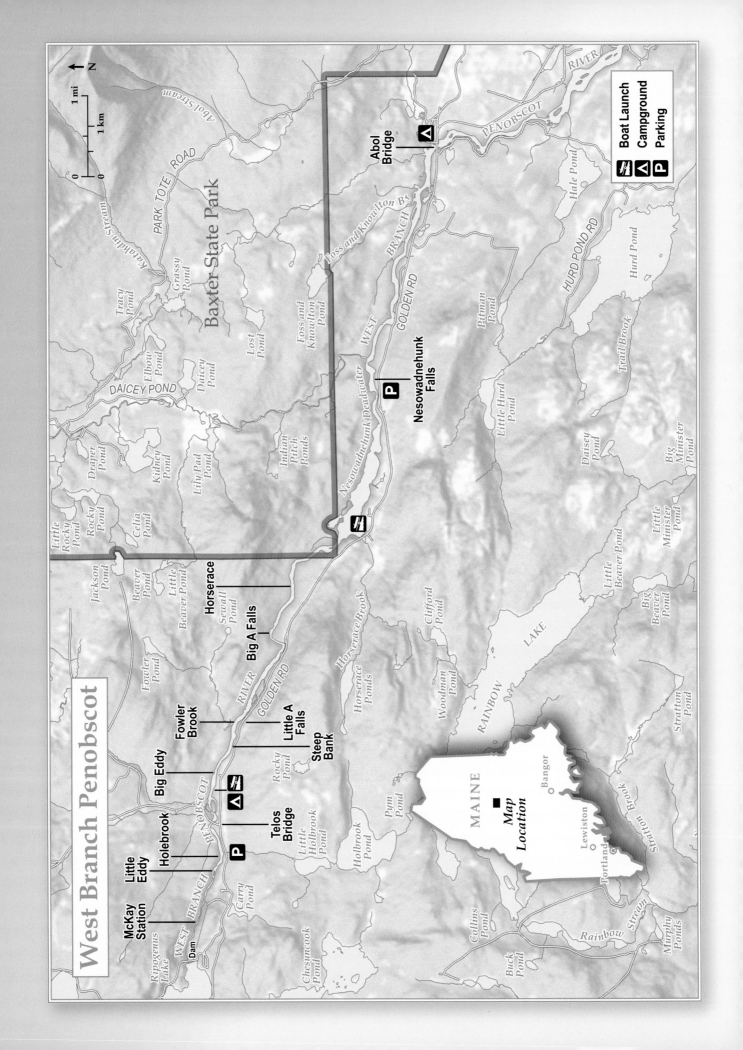

3 · West Branch Penobscot River

➤ **Location:** North-central Maine, about a 2-hour ride from Bangor, a 4-hour ride from Portland; and a 5½-hour ride from Boston, Massachusetts. Full-service airports are available in all three cities.

The West Branch Penobscot is the finest self-sustaining, river-dwelling landlocked Atlantic salmon fishery in Maine—and arguably the finest in the country. While not native to the river, landlocked salmon have thrived in the West Branch since their introduction in the late 1800s. This is due largely to an abundance of spawning habitat, a diverse forage base, and coolwater releases. The river also holds a significant population of wild native brook trout. However, salmon far outnumber the trout.

The West Branch flows 117 miles before emptying into the Penobscot River. It begins at Seboomook Lake northwest of Moosehead Lake. The river runs roughly 25 miles before entering Chesuncook Lake. Below the lake, it flows approximately 20 miles before entering Pemadumcook Chain of Lakes. It drops roughly 1,775 feet from its headwaters to Medway. The river was once host to runs of Atlantic salmon. This ended with the construction of a series of dams that blocked passage.

The West Branch has a rich history. It once served as a route of travel and reflection for author and naturalist Henry David Thoreau. His book *The Maine Woods* chronicles his exploration of the river and the Mount Katahdin region. The river also served as a conduit for "driving," the hazardous work of moving logs downstream to mills, which finally ended in the 1970s when trucking became the transportation mode of choice. The dangerous task of moving wood down the rough waters of the West Branch fell to teams of river drivers. Many lost their lives while working the river. Their tales live on around flickering campfires.

The land surrounding the West Branch is some of the most rugged and beautiful in the Northeast. The views are second to none. Maine's highest point, Mount Katahdin (5,269 feet) and other distant peaks in Baxter State Park are constantly in view. The area is home to a wide variety of wildlife including eagles, ospreys, mink, coyotes, beavers, otters, deer, and a large population of moose. The area is a popular destination for hiking, whitewater rafting, canoeing, and wildlife watching.

The West Branch is located west of Millinocket amid a vast working forest. The river corridor is protected by conservation easements that prohibit development. With the exception of a few private camps, two campgrounds, and a handful of rustic campsites, the West Branch looks much the way it did when Thoreau visited the area. Power and phone service end roughly 8 miles west of Millinocket. Access to the river is gained via the fabled Golden Road, a private road

Mount Katahdin from below Nesowadnehunk Falls. Maine River Guides

open to the public. Logging trucks have the right of way. Heed all warning signs, and park well off the road.

The West Branch is a large freestone river. Flows are controlled by McKay Power Station, roughly ¾ mile downstream of Ripogenus Dam. Between Ripogenus Dam and McKay Station, there is a short stretch of river with a natural flow regime. The average flow below McKay Station is between 2,200 and 3,200 cfs.

The roughly 10-mile section between McKay Station and Abol Bridge is the most popular with fly fishers—it offers the best fishing and access. The Golden Road parallels the river. From McKay to Big Eddy, the West Branch is a rugged

Greg Bostater with Ripogenus Gorge landlocked salmon. Seneca Love

river with Class III–V whitewater. Here the river is a series of drops, rapids, and runs, interrupted by deep pools and long tailouts. The Big Eddy is the most famous pool on the river. Below the eddy, the river widens into a series of riffles, runs, small rapids, and long pools before reaching Big Ambejackmockamus Falls. This begins a 2-mile stretch of Class III water known as Horserace, which terminates at Nesowadnehunk Deadwater. Below here is Class IV Nesowadnehunk Falls. Starting just downstream of the falls begins Abol Deadwater, which runs to Abol Bridge.

The river opens to fishing April 1. As a result of runoff, fishing does not pick up for several weeks. The best fishing runs from around Memorial Day through September, when the season ends. The section from Ripogenus Dam to the Telos Bridge is restricted to fly fishing only. There is a one-fish limit on salmon, with a minimum length of 26 inches. From Telos Bridge downstream to the red markers at the head of Pockwockamus Falls, tackle is restricted to single-hook artificial lures only. The limit on salmon is one fish. The mini-

mum length limit is 18 inches. From August 16 through September 30, the entire section is restricted to fly fishing only.

The average salmon on the West Branch runs between 12 and 16 inches. Fish between 18 and 20 inches are not uncommon. Fish over 20 inches are always a possibility. Brook trout average 8 to 12 inches. Trout up to 18 inches are possible, yet rare.

➤ **Hatches:** Salmon and trout on the West Branch feed on smelt, dace, insects, crayfish, eggs, and worms. Insects include mayflies, caddis, stoneflies, and midges. Fish will feed on sucker eggs in the spring, and on salmonid eggs in the fall. Smelt are the most important food source on the West Branch. They enter the upper river via Ripogenus Dam. The lower river gets a spawning run of smelt in the spring from Ambajejus Lake.

Mayfly hatches begin in late May, with Blue-winged Olives, Quill Gordons, and Hendricksons. Stoneflies start around Memorial Day, and run all season. There are Yellow Sallies, Goldens, and occasionally *Pteronarcys*. March Browns, Sulphurs, and Cahills hatch in June.

Caddis hatches start in June, continuing well into September. Netspinners, Zebra Caddis, and Great Autumn Sedges are all present. Caddis hatches can be epic at times.

The West Branch is a big, brawling river. It can be intimidating for the wading angler not familiar with the river. The river can be floated. This is, however, best left to expert rowers who are familiar with the river. The West Branch is a great dry-fly fishery. Early in the season, streamer fishing with smelt patterns can be outstanding. Nymph fishing can be productive as well. The West Branch represents classic landlocked salmon fishing at its finest.

Chris McMullen fishing the Cribwork. Maine River Guides

Landlocked salmon caught at Steep Bank Pool by Paul Korenkiewicz. Maine River Guides

➤ **Tackle:** A 9-foot 5-weight rod with a floating line is your best bet for the West Branch most of the time. If you want to fish streamers, a 9-foot 6-weight with a fast-sinking sink tip is your best option. Dry-fly fishing can be done with a 9-foot 4-weight, as you may need to drop to 6X to fish smaller patterns such as Blue-winged Olives effectively. While rods longer than 9 feet can work, especially for nymphing, rods shorter than 9 feet are not practical. Light-line switch rods can help wading anglers hit spots that are otherwise not reachable. Strike indicators should be large enough to float two flies and added weight. Flies should include smelt patterns, and all stages of mayflies, stoneflies, and caddis in a variety of sizes and colors.

GREG BOSTATER is a Registered Maine Guide. He owns and operates Maine River Guides, LLC. He can be reached at 207-749-1593, maineriver guides@gmail.com, or www.maineriverguides.com.

CLOSEST FLY SHOPS

Maine Guide Fly Shop
34 Moosehead Lake Road
Greenville, Maine 04441
207-695-2266
www.maineguideflyshop.com
info@maineguideflyshop.com

CLOSEST GUIDES/OUTFITTERS

Maine River Guides
131 Edwards Street
Portland, Maine 04102
207-749-1593
www.maineriverguides.com
maineriverguides@gmail.com

Penobscot Drift Boats
364 Hudson Road
Glenburn, Maine 04401
207-570-4235
www.penobscotdriftboats.com
ripgorge@hotmail.com

CLOSEST LODGING

Big Eddy Campground
Rustic Cabins and Tent Sites
207-350-1599
www.chewonki.org/vacations/vacations_big_eddy.asp
bigeddy@chewonki.org

Big Moose Inn
Millinocket Lake, Maine 04462
877-666-7346
www.bigmoosecabins.com
info@bigmoosecabins.com

Twin Pines Cabins
Fire Road 20 D
Millinocket, Maine 04462
800-634-7238
www.neoc.com

Allagash Gateway Campground & Cabins
Chesuncook Lake Road
Ripogenus Lake, Maine 04462
207-723-9215
www.allagashgatewaycamps.com
belinda@allagashgatewaycamps.com

CLOSEST RESTAURANTS

Fredericka's Restaurant
Fine Dining & Pub
Millinocket Lake, Maine 04462
877-666-7346
www.bigmoosecabins.com
info@bigmoosecabins.com

River Drivers Restaurant
Fine Dining & Pub
Fire Lane 20D
Millinocket, Maine 04462
207-723-8475
www.neoc.com
vacation@neoc.com

Scootic In Restaurant
70 Penobscot Avenue
Millinocket, Maine 04462
207-723-4566
www.scooticin.com

The Northern Restaurant
Abol Bridge Campground & Store
Millinocket, Maine 04462

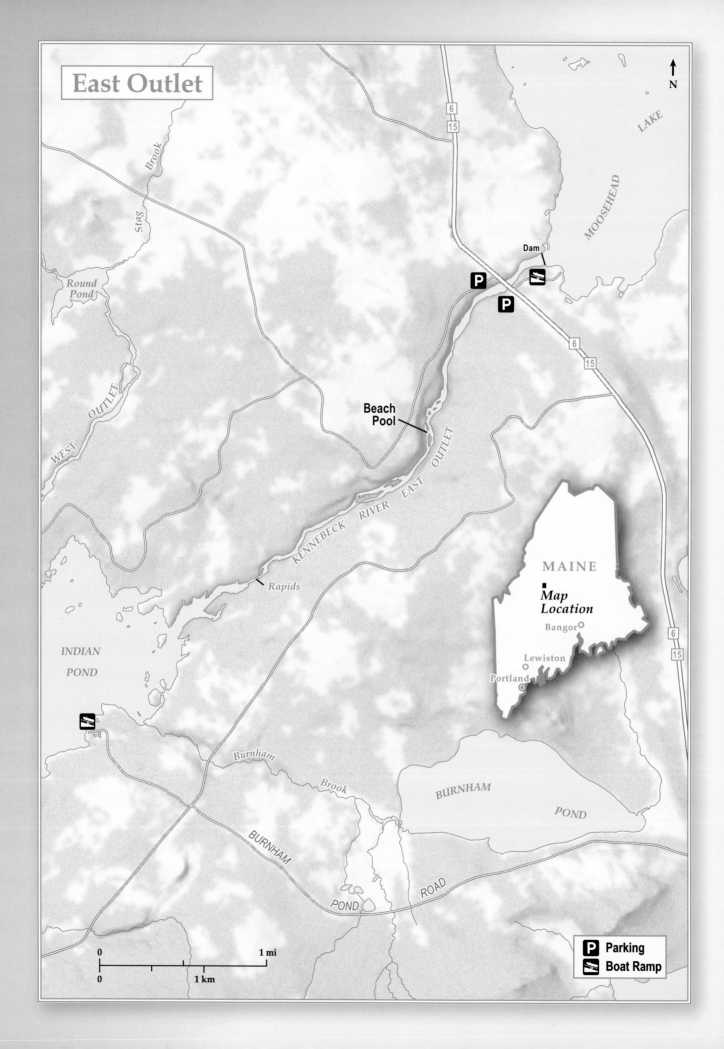

4 · East Outlet

➤ **Location:** Central Maine, about a 1½-hour ride from Bangor, a 3-hour ride from Portland; a 4½-hour ride from Boston, Massachusetts; and a 4-hour ride from Manchester, New Hampshire. Full-service airports are available in all four cities.

The East Outlet is a branch of the fabled Kennebec River. It is located 15 minutes northwest of the historic town of Greenville. The "Outlet," as it is called locally, originates at Moosehead Lake—the largest lake in Maine. Moosehead is a rare example of a body of water with two outlets. After exiting the big lake at a low dam, the Outlet travels roughly 3½ miles before emptying into Indian Pond. Dropping an average 25 feet per mile, the East Outlet is the polar opposite of its sluggish sibling to the west. Its swift current flows over large rocks, providing an ideal, oxygen-rich habitat favored by landlocked salmon. The East Outlet is considered one of the finest landlocked salmon fisheries in Maine.

Most of the land surrounding the East Outlet is designated Maine Public Preserved Land. This protects it from development and allows it to retain its wild character. It is home to one of the larger white-tailed deer wintering areas in the state. Moose and black bears are common. The East Outlet typifies northern Maine's (and the southern boreal forest's) ruggedly beautiful scenery and large-river angling for landlocked Atlantic salmon and eastern brook trout amid the musical sound of falling water. Conifers, ferns, and large granite rocks line its banks and river bottom.

Most anglers typically wade the first mile of river, fishing from the dam to what is known as the Spawning Beds. These areas can be reached from the highway and a dirt road that parallels the river to the north. The dirt road is best left to vehicles with good clearance and four-wheel drive. There is parking on either side of the river at the Route 6/15 bridge. There are several pull-outs along the dirt road. One ends at the Beach Pool. Below here access becomes more difficult, requiring a walk to reach the more remote sections down to the lake.

The best way to experience the East Outlet and cover the entire 3½ miles of river is by drift boat. Unlike many rivers where fish hold near the banks, in the Outlet salmon and trout can be just about anywhere. Midriver runs inaccessible to wading anglers often hold fish. Drift boats can be maneuvered into position and anchored in the river's swift current, giving access to fish that wading anglers never reach. When the water is high, driftboat anglers can continue to fish productively, while wading anglers have few options. It is, however, important to note that the East Outlet is not easy

Sluice Pool in Fall. Maine Guide Fly Shop

to float. It is a technical river with Class II and III rapids. As a result, it is best floated by expert rowers with an intimate knowledge of the river and its flow regime. This is a river where hiring a guide is always a good idea.

Flows in the East Outlet are generally consistent—at least in regard to the seasons. The lowest flows occur in the summer, late fall, and winter. High flows occur in the spring, late summer, and early fall. Flows below 1,200 cfs are considered low. Those in the 1,200–2,000 cfs range are considered medium. Flows above 2,000 cfs are considered high. Flows

Above. East Outlet Dam at Moosehead Lake. Fliesandfins.com

Left. Greg Bostater with fall brookie. Fliesandfins.com

above 3,000 cfs make fishing tough. Low flows are conducive to wading; high flows are not. The opposite applies to floating, because low flows are difficult to row. Medium flows are wadable and floatable, and usually offer the best fishing. Wading anglers should be vigilant, as the water can rise unexpectedly—and fast. Harris hydropower station at Indian Pond, water levels in Moosehead Lake, and heavy rains can all influence flows. Projected daily flows are posted in the parking area at the Route 6/15 bridge. There is also a toll-free flow information number: 800-557-3569. Wading staffs are highly recommended, as the riverbed is lined with slippery bowling ball–size rocks.

May through October is prime time on the Outlet. Fall typically produces the largest fish. The river is heavily stocked by the Maine Department of Inland Fisheries & Wildlife—the Outlet is one of the most heavily stocked stretches of river in the state. Fish are stocked in both spring and fall. There is some level of natural salmon reproduction. Artificial spawning beds have been built on the river. In the fall, large

salmon can be seen moving in and out of these beds, which are closed to fishing. There are also some resident brook trout. Trout and salmon enter the river from both Moosehead Lake and Indian Pond as well. There are also holdover fish. Trout average a foot long, though fish up to 16 inches are caught. Salmon average roughly the same, but some fish over 20 inches are caught every year.

➤ **Hatches:** Hatches on the East Outlet occur slightly later than those on the lower sections of the Kennebec. They are, however, both strong and predictable. Mayflies start in late May and run well into late June. They hatch intermittently in the summer and pick back up again in the late summer and early fall. Caddis overlap early mayfly hatches, peak in the late spring and summer, and continue into early fall. Blue-winged Olives can provide excellent dry-fly angling during overcast conditions. Stoneflies can hatch pretty much anytime, and classic streamer fishing for salmon in the spring and fall, and on overcast days, can be particularly productive.

➤ **Regulations:** The East Outlet is restricted to fly fishing only. It is catch-and-release from October 1 through April 30. From May 1 to September 30 there is a one-fish limit. The minimum length limit on trout and salmon is 14 inches. From November 1 through March 31, the lower section of the river (from the yellow markers at the tail end of Beach Pool to the red markers at Indian Pond) is closed to fishing.

As I mentioned in the beginning, the East Outlet represents classic landlocked salmon fishing at its finest. It is a unique fishery on a rugged and beautiful river in a remote and relatively undeveloped setting.

Fall landlocked salmon. Maine Guide Fly Shop

➤ **Tackle:** A 9-foot 5-weight rod with a floating line is your best bet for the East Outlet most of the time. If you want to fish streamers, a 9-foot 6-weight with a fast-sinking sink-tip is your best option. Dry-fly fishing is best done with a 9-foot 4-weight, as you may need to drop to 6X to effectively fish smaller patterns such as BWOs. While rods longer than 9 feet can work—especially for nymphing—rods shorter than 9 feet are not practical. Strike indicators should be large enough to float two flies and added weight. Flies should include smelt patterns and Woolly Buggers, and all stages of mayflies, stoneflies, and caddis in a variety of sizes and colors.

MIKE BUTLER guides out of Kennebec River Outfitters in Madison, Maine. He is also a nationally known maker of fine fish models, catch-and-release trophy carvings, and his signature weathervanes. He can be reached at 207-474-2500, info@kennebec riveroutfitters.com, or www.kennebecriveroutfitters .com for guiding; or for his fish carvings at www.MikeButlerFishCarver.com.

CLOSEST FLY SHOPS

Maine Guide Fly Shop
34 Moosehead Lake Road
Greenville, Maine 04441
207-695-2266
www.maineguideflyshop.com
info@maineguideflyshop.com

Kennebec River Outfitters
469 Lakewood Road
Madison, Maine 04950
207-474-2500
www.kennebecriveroutfitters.com
info@kennebecriveroutfitters.com

CLOSEST GUIDES AND OUTFITTERS

Maine River Guides
Portland, Maine
207-749-1593
www.maineriverguides.com
maineriverguides@gmail.com

Penobscot Drift Boats
Glenburn, Maine 04401
207-570-4235
www.penobscotdriftboats.com
ripgorge@hotmail.com

Northwoods Outfitters
5 Lily Bay Road
Greenville, Maine 04441
866-223-1380
www.maineoutfitter.com
info@maineoutfitter.com

CLOSEST LODGING

Moose Mountain Inn
314 Rockwood Road
Greenville, Maine 04441
800-792-1858
www.moosemountaininn.com
info@moosemountaininn.com

Wilsons on Moosehead Lake (cabins)
Route 15
Greenville Junction, Maine 04442
800-817-2549
www.wilsonsonmooseheadlake.com
info@wilsonsonmooseheadlake.com

CLOSEST LODGING

The Captain Sawyer House Bed & Breakfast
18 Lakeview Street
Greenville, Maine 04441
207-695-2369
www.captainsawyerhouse.com
info@captainsawyerhouse.com

Kineo View Motor Lodge
50 Overlook Drive
Greenville, Maine 04441
800-659-8439
www.kineoview.com
info@kineoview.com

CLOSEST RESTAURANTS

Blair Hill Inn
351 Lily Bay Road
Greenville, Maine 04441
207-695-0224
www.blairhill.com
info@blairhill.com

Black Frog (pub-style food)
17 Pritham Avenue
Greenville, Maine 04441
207-695-1100
www.theblackfrog.com

Kelly's Landing
West Cove, Moosehead Lake
Greenville, Maine 04441
207-695-4438
www.kellysatmoosehead.com
BradyKLanding@hotmail.com

Flatlanders (pub-style food)
36 Pritham Avenue
Greenville, Maine 04441
207-695-3373

Auntie M's (breakfast)
Lilly Bay Road
Greenville, Maine 04441
207-695-2238

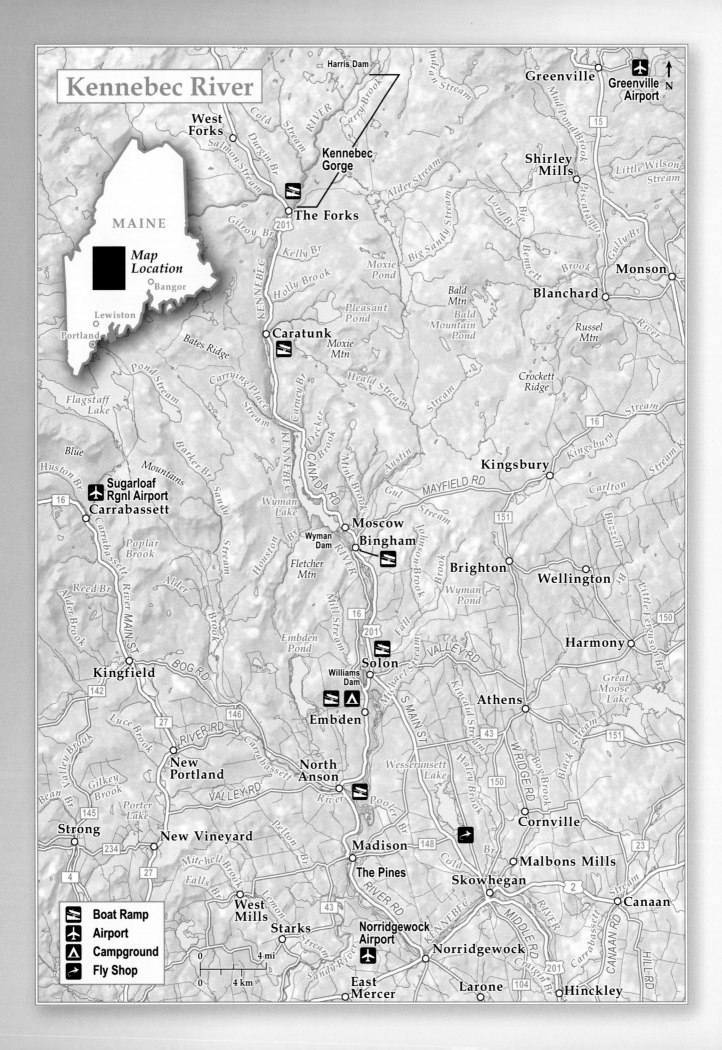

Kennebec River

MAINE

Map Location

Bangor

Lewiston

Portland

Harris Dam

Greenville
Greenville Airport

Shirley Mills

West Forks

Monson

Blanchard

The Forks

Kennebec Gorge

Russel Mtn

Crockett Ridge

Caratunk

Moxie Mtn

Bald Mtn

Bald Mountain Pond

Pleasant Pond

Moxie Pond

Kingsbury

MAYFIELD RD

Flagstaff Lake

Bates Ridge

Blue

Huston Br

Sugarloaf Rgnl Airport
Carrabassett

Poplar Brook

Wyman Lake

Moscow
Bingham

Brighton

Wellington

Harmony

Kingfield

Fletcher Mtn

Embden Pond

Solon

Athens

Great Moose Lake

Embden

Williams Dam

New Portland

North Anson

Wesserunsett Lake

Cornville

Strong

New Vineyard

Madison

The Pines

Malbons Mills

Skowhegan

Canaan

West Mills

Starks

Norridgewock Airport

Norridgewock

Larone

Hinckley

East Mercer

Legend

- Boat Ramp
- Airport
- Campground
- Fly Shop

0   4 mi

0   4 km

5 · Kennebec River

➤ **Location:** Central Maine, about a 1-hour ride from Bangor, a 2-hour ride from Portland, Maine; a 3½-hour ride from Boston, Massachusetts; and a 3½-hour ride from Manchester, New Hampshire. Full-service airports are available in all four cities.

The Kennebec Valley is rich in fly-fishing lore. Arthur R. Macdougall's fictional character Dud Dean, Maine Guide, plied his trade on the Kennebec River and surrounding waters during the golden age of sporting. Gadabout Gaddis, aka The Flying Fisherman, filmed his TV show in the 1960s and 1970s on the banks of the river—a small grass airport bears his name. The Kennebec was also the site of one of the first major dam removal projects in the country. The removal of Edwards Dam in Augusta opened up 17 miles of river to anadromous alewives, striped bass, sturgeon, and endangered Atlantic salmon.

The section of Kennebec of most interest to fly fishers lies between Harris Dam and Madison. Here the Kennebec is basically four rivers in one. In a stretch of roughly 50 miles—interrupted by several impoundments—there are four dams: Harris, Wyman, Williams, and Abnaki. Below each is a tailwater. Each tailwater is significantly different. The topography, size, flow regime, insect life, and even species of salmonids change.

Below Harris near The Forks, in what is called the Gorge, lies the most rugged and remote stretch of salmonid river in the Northeast. Best known for its whitewater rafting, it is also a great wild brook trout and landlocked salmon fishery. Brook trout can reach 18 inches. Salmon get even larger. Nowhere in the Northeast can you float a river while fly fishing for wild trout and salmon, and feel more remote.

The Wyman tailwater in Bingham is home to one of the few—and by far the finest—wild rainbow trout fisheries north of New York. Fish over 20 inches are encountered.

These are remnants of a stocking program that's been defunct for more than 30 years. There are also wild landlocked salmon and brook trout, with the former outnumbering the latter. Here the river meanders lazily through riffles, runs, and pools.

Below Williams Dam in Solon, the river is predominantly a stocked brown trout fishery. Brown trout over 20 inches are caught here. There are also wild landlocked salmon. Brook trout and rainbow trout are present as well. This section gives you the best chance at a four-species outing—referred to as

Diana Mallard fishing in Solon. Bob Mallard

the "Kennebec Slam." Not only is this a great dry-fly fishery, it is also the best streamer water on the river. A day in the bow of a drift boat throwing large streamers tight to the bank is your best way to catch a large brown trout here.

The Abnaki tailwater in Madison is a stocked brown trout fishery. Brook trout and salmon are also stocked. This is a wade fishery with no viable downriver access. It does, however, boast the strongest and most diverse hatches on the river. Here the river is made up of long riffles, runs, a few pools, and some large rapids.

John Vacca fishing below Wyman Dam. Bob Mallard

Bob Mallard with Kennebec Gorge brook trout. Chris Russell

Much of the Kennebec River can be accessed from Route 201, which parallels the river for much of its length. Public access is limited in some areas. There is, however, walk-in access at three bridges, some boat launches, a multiple-use trail on the east shore in Bingham, a small ball field in The Forks, The Pines in Madison, and several private businesses.

The Kennebec is a large river by any standards. In many places the river is 200 to 300 feet wide. The two middle tailwaters are braided, giving you more water than you can fish in a single outing. The three upper tailwaters average roughly 8 miles in length, the lower about 2 miles.

Flows in the Gorge are feast-or-famine. Low flows are in the 325 cfs range—mandated morning and evening fish flows—and high flows are in the 5,000+ cfs range. There are very few flows in between, as the water is reserved for power generation and whitewater rafting. Several feeder streams add to the flow and can impact this section during runoff. Wyman flows are similar to those at Harris. Low flows run at 1,000 to 1,200cfs. Power-generating flows run at 5,000 cfs or more. When there's no power generation, flows drop to 2,500 to 3,500 cfs. There is only one significant tributary, Austin Stream, less than a mile below the dam. After it rains, this can have a significant—but temporary—impact on the river. Below Williams and Abnaki, flows become more consistent. Flows usually run in the 3,000 to 4,000 cfs range and are not subject to the daily, and even hourly, changes experienced below the two upper tailwaters.

The Kennebec can be waded during low flows. It is tough to wade during high water. Fishing from a drift boat—or raft where appropriate—whenever possible is often the best way to fish regardless of flows. This allows you to cover more water. It also addresses some of the access issues noted above.

The three upper tailwaters are open from April 1 through October—the lower year-round. Prime time is May and June and September and October. In July and August fishing is best below Harris and Wyman Dams. All four tailwaters are restricted to artificial lures only. Below Wyman, Williams, and Abnaki there is a one-fish limit and a minimum length limit of 16 inches on rainbows, browns, and salmon. The limit on brook trout is 12 inches. Below Harris Dam there is a two-fish, 12-inch minimum on all trout and salmon.

The trout in the Kennebec feed on minnows and insects. The predominant minnows are sculpin, fallfish, and smelts—which are found only below the Harris and Wyman Dams. Insects include stoneflies, mayflies, and caddis. Hatches on the Kennebec are strong and predictable. Mayflies start in mid-May and run well into June. They hatch intermittently in the summer and pick up again in the early fall. Caddis overlap early mayfly hatches, peak in the late spring and summer, and continue into the fall. Stoneflies can hatch pretty much anytime.

Below Wyman, Williams, and Abnaki; the Kennebec is a classic dry-fly river. It is one of the few rivers in the area that offers season-long dry-fly fishing. Even in the heat of summer, most evenings will see a caddis hatch. Fish are also regularly caught on nymphs. On overcast days, fish will take streamers—including some of the largest trout.

Pteronacys.
Bob Mallard

➤ **Tackle:** A 9-foot 5-weight rod with a floating line is your best bet for the Kennebec River most of the time. If you want to fish streamers, a 9-foot 6-weight with a fast-sinking sink-tip is your best option. Dry-fly fishing is best done with a 9-foot 4-weight, as you may need to drop to 6X to effectively fish smaller patterns such as Blue-winged Olives. While rods longer than 9 feet can work, especially for nymphing, rods shorter than 9 feet are not practical. Strike indicators should be large enough to float two flies and added weight. Flies should include Woolly Buggers; sculpin and smelt patterns; and all stages of mayflies, stoneflies, and caddis in a variety of sizes and colors.

John Vacca with dry-fly caught rainbow. Bob Mallard

BOB MALLARD has fly fished for over 35 years. He is a blogger, writer, and author; and has owned and operated Kennebec River Outfitters in Madison, Maine since 2001. His writing has been featured in newspapers, magazines, and books at the local, regional, and national levels. He has appeared on radio and television. Look for his upcoming books from Stonefly Press, *25 Best Towns: Fly Fishing for Trout* (winter 2014) and *50 Best Places: Fly Fishing for Brook Trout* (summer 2015). Bob is also a staff fly designer for Catch Fly Fishing. He can be reached at www.kennebecriveroutfitters.com, www.bobmallard.com, info@bobmallard.com, or 207-474-2500.

CLOSEST FLY SHOPS

Kennebec River Outfitters
469 Lakewood Road
Madison, Maine 04950
207-474-2500
www.kennebecriveroutfitters.com
info@kennebecriveroutfitters.com

CLOSEST LODGING

Inn by the River (B&B)
Route 201
The Forks, Maine 04985
866-663-2181
www.innbytheriver.com
info@innbytheriver.com

The Evergreens Campground & Restaurant
Route 201A
Solon, Maine 04979
207-643-2324
www.evergreenscampground.com
info@evergreenscampground.com

Hawk's Nest Lodge
Route 201
West Forks, Maine 04985
207-663-2020
www.hawksnestlodge.com
info@hawksnestlodge.com

The Belmont Motel
273 Madison Avenue
Skowhegan, Maine 04976
800-235-6669
www.belmontmotel.com

CLOSEST RESTAURANTS

Heritage House Restaurant
(fine dining, reservations recommended)
182 Madison Avenue
Skowhegan, Maine 04976
207-474-5100
www.hhrestaurant.com
Hhrestaurant23@yahoo.com

Old Mill Pub
39 Water Street
Skowhegan, Maine 04976
207-474-6627
www.oldmillpub.net

Northern Outdoors
(pub-style lunch and dinner)
Route 201
The Forks, Maine 04985
800-725-7238
www.northernoutdoors.com

The Evergreens Campground & Restaurant
(dinner and breakfast buffet on weekends—see above)

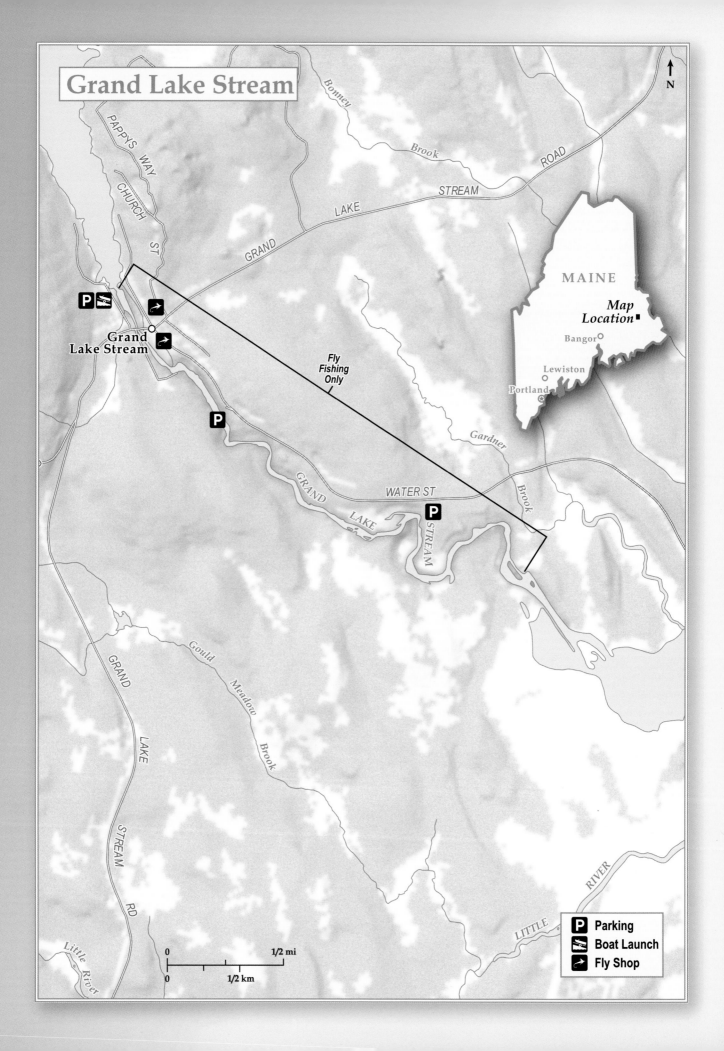

Grand Lake Stream

MAINE

Map Location ■

Bangor ○

Lewiston ○

Portland ⊕

PAPPY'S WAY

CHURCH ST

BONNEY BROOK

GRAND LAKE STREAM ROAD

P ⬞ ➤

Grand Lake Stream ○ ➤

P

Fly Fishing Only

GRAND LAKE

WATER ST

GARDNER BROOK

P

GRAND LAKE STREAM

GRAND LAKE STREAM RD

Gould Meadow Brook

Little River

LITTLE RIVER

0   1/2 mi
0   1/2 km

P Parking
⬞ Boat Launch
➤ Fly Shop

6 · Grand Lake Stream

➤ **Location:** Eastern Maine, about a 2-hour ride from Bangor and 4 hours from Portland. Full-service airports are available in both cities.

Long known for its fabled landlocked salmon fishing, Grand Lake Stream has been a popular destination with fly fishers since the mid-1800s. West Grand Lake—the headwaters of Grand Lake Stream—was home to one of only four native populations of landlocked salmon in the Lower 48, all of which are in Maine. The Grand Lake Stream fish hatchery program began in 1868, making it one of the longest-operating fish hatcheries in the country, where this strain of salmon is still raised today.

The community of Grand Lake Stream is well known for its guides, sporting camps, and the Grand Lake canoe, which has been used for more than a century to guide anglers on the large lakes in the region. Grand Lake Stream was the setting for the fictional characters in *The One-Eyed Poacher of Privilege* and game warden Tom Corn, charged with trying to outfox him. Edmund Ware Smith, whose short stories were published in *The New Yorker* magazine, created them in the 1940s.

Glaciers carved out the region during the last Ice Age, creating deep, crystal-clear lakes with shorelines dotted with large granite boulders, interspersed with fine sand and gravel beaches. Grand Lake Stream is also home to active faults, which intersect the stream in a couple of locations, creating significant waterfalls that make the stream difficult and dangerous to navigate with boats.

Grand Lake Stream is approximately 3 miles long. It runs between West Grand Lake and Big Lake. The upper stream is defined by deep clear pools interspersed with riffles and gentle rapids. Wading is generally easy here at most flows. The middle stream runs fast, with a steep elevation drop for roughly a mile. This section is fishable at lower flows only, and offers tremendous small pool and pocketwater fishing under the right conditions. There is usually less angling pressure in this area due to the tougher access and the fact that wading is more difficult here than in the upper pools.

The lower stream returns to its riffle-pool-run characteristics, with some pocketwater before it enters Big Lake.

A small dam at the outlet of West Grand Lake regulates the flows in Grand Lake Stream. Flows run from a low of 175 cfs to well over 1,000 cfs. Average flows are from 300–500 cfs. Lower flows allow access to some parts of the river that are otherwise difficult to reach. Higher flows—up to 1,000 cfs—allow fish to hold in areas where they otherwise could not. Suitable habitat is determined by the water levels as much as anything else. Salmon holding water changes as the flows change.

The open season on Grand Lake Stream runs from April 1 though October 20. The daily limit on salmon is one fish, with a minimum length of 14 inches. There is a brief catch-and-release season starting October 1. The stream has been fly-fishing-only since 1903.

Salmon move back into West Grand Lake when the water warms. Weatherby's

Fishing on Grand Lake Stream starts soon after ice-out. This can vary dramatically from year to year, but averages late April to early May. Once the ice is off the lakes, flows increase, drawing smelt from the lakes into the stream to spawn. Hungry after a long winter, salmon follow the smelt

Inset. Guide Kevin Winsor with male salmon. Weatherby's

Fall nymphing at the Picnic Pool. Weatherby's

into the stream and feed voraciously on them. White suckers enter the stream for their spawning run soon after the smelt. Salmon follow the suckers and feed heavily on the eggs as they drift in the current. After the spring spawning runs, salmon move upstream and settle into the pools and runs.

By midsummer in most years, the majority of salmon have moved back to West Grand Lake. However, in summers with high water and cool temperatures, the salmon stay in the stream longer—sometimes into August. By mid-Septem-

Fat spring female. Weatherby's

ber, the days are shorter, air temperatures drop, and the water cools. This triggers the annual salmon spawning run in the stream. Fall fish are typically much larger and heavier than spring fish, having fed on smelt all summer in the lake. They sport their bright autumn colors, with males displaying the pronounced kype that is typical of spawning salmon.

The later in the fall one fishes, the more fish can be found in the river. This starts in the upper pools, and spreads downstream from there. Fall fishing can be rewarding. However, it can be frustrating as well, as the salmon are not feeding aggressively and begin to exhibit territorial behavior. Many of the fish in the fall will be caught on smelt imitations, as they have been feeding on smelt in the lakes all summer. They will also take large, bright streamers that stimulate territorial strikes. Fish will still feed on caddis, stonefly, and mayfly nymphs. There are also some significant BWO hatches in September and October—if you have trouble hooking up, go smaller.

➤ **Hatches:** The first hatches begin in mid-May as Hendricksons and March Browns start to appear. This is followed by prolific caddis hatches starting in late May and running well into June. Mid-June to July finds the caddis tapering off, with stoneflies and Sulphurs taking over, followed by Blue-winged Olives into July. In late spring, terrestrials such as flying ants, dragonflies, and hoppers are present.

Access to Grand Lake Stream is good. From the dam to the village of Grand Lake Stream—a distance of approximately 1 mile—there are many private houses and camp lots, but public access exists in several locations. Below the village down to Big Lake—approximately 2 miles—the streambank is primarily public, with excellent access along unmarked footpaths following the stream to the lake. There are only a few private lots in this area, and one can easily wade around them.

Grand Lake Stream is the most famous landlocked salmon fishery in the country. Along with the Sebago, Green, and Sebec Lake systems, it is part of one of only four native landlocked salmon watersheds in the country. This is a unique and historically important fishery.

➤ **Tackle:** A 9-foot 5-weight rod with a floating line is your best bet for Grand Lake Stream most of the time. If you want to fish streamers, a 9-foot 6-weight with a fast-sinking line is your best option. Dry-fly fishing is best done with a 9-foot 4-weight, as you may need 6X tippet to effectively fish small patterns. While rods longer than 9 feet can work, especially for nymphing, rods shorter than 8½ feet are not practical. Strike indicators should be large enough to float two flies and added weight. Flies should include Woolly Buggers; smelt patterns; mayfly and stonefly nymphs and adults; all stages of caddis in a variety of sizes and colors; and egg patterns in the spring.

Tailout of the Dam Pool. Weatherby's

JEFF MCEVOY owns and operates Weatherby's in Grand Lake Stream. He is a Registered Master Maine Guide and can be booked through the lodge. He can be reached at 877-796-5558, info@weatherbys.com, or www.weatherbys.com.

CLOSEST FLY SHOPS

Weatherby's Fly Shop
3 Water Street
Grand Lake Stream, Maine 04637
877-796-5558
www.weatherbys.com
info@weatherbys.com

Pine Tree Store
3 Water Street
Grand Lake Stream, Maine 04637
207-796-5027
Pinetreestore@gmail.com

CLOSEST LODGING

Weatherby's (see above)

Bellmard Inn
86 Main Street
Princeton, Maine 04668
207-796-2261
bellmardinn@myfairpoint.net

Indian Rock Camps
3 Water Street
Grand Lake Stream, Maine 04637
800-498-2821
www.indianrockcamps.com
indianrockcamp@midmaine.com

Cobbscook Bay State Park
(tent and RV sites)
40 South Edmunds Road
Dennysville, Maine 04628
207-726-4412
www.maine.gov/doc/parks/

CLOSEST RESTAURANTS

Weatherby's (see above)
Pine Tree Store (see above)

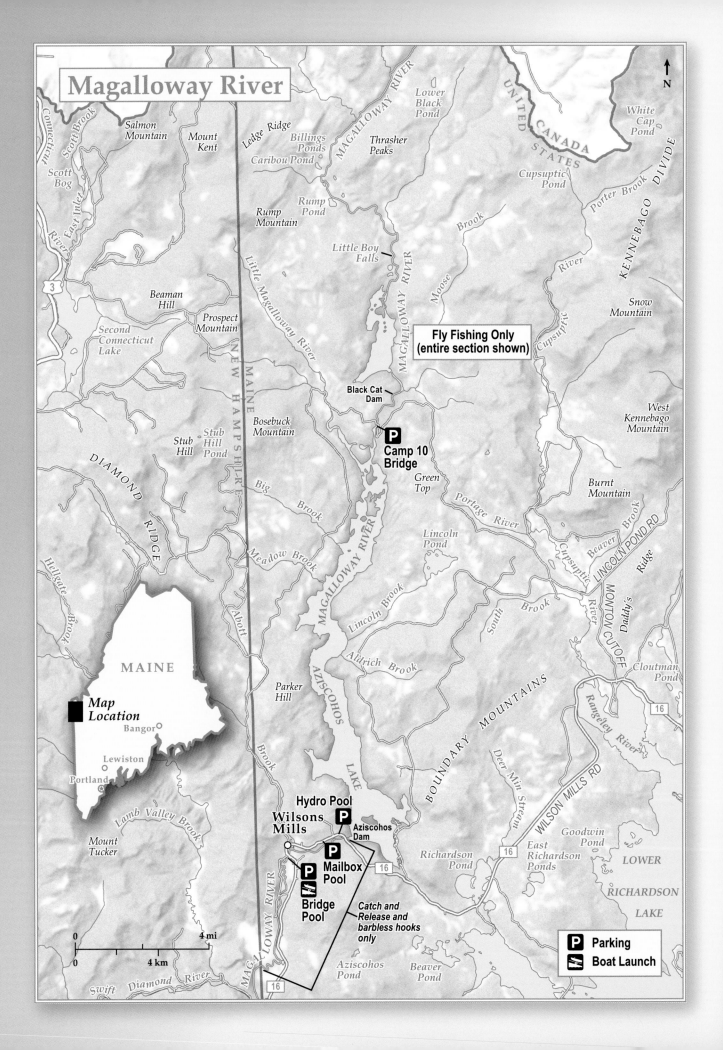

Magalloway River

Fly Fishing Only
(entire section shown)

Catch and
Release and
barbless hooks
only

P Parking
⛵ Boat Launch

0 _____ 4 mi
0 _____ 4 km

MAINE

**Map
Location**

Bangor ○
Lewiston ○
Portland ⊛

Connecticut River
Scott Brook
Salmon Mountain
Mount Kent
Ledge Ridge
Billings Ponds
Caribou Pond
Magalloway River
Lower Black Pond
Thrasher Peaks
UNITED STATES
CANADA
White Cap Pond
KENNEBAGO DIVIDE
Cupsuptic Pond
Porter Brook
Scott Bog
East Inlet River
3
Rump Pond
Rump Mountain
Little Boy Falls
Magalloway River
Moose Brook
River
Cupsuptic
Snow Mountain
Beaman Hill
Prospect Mountain
Little Magalloway River
NEW HAMPSHIRE
MAINE
Bosebuck Mountain
Black Cat Dam
P
Camp 10 Bridge
Green Top
West Kennebago Mountain
Stub Hill
Stub Hill Pond
Big Brook
Lincoln Pond
Portage River
South Brook
Cupsuptic River
Beaver Brook
LINCOLN POND RD
Burnt Mountain
DIAMOND RIDGE
Meadow Brook
Abott
Lincoln Brook
Aldrich Brook
MONTON CUTOFF
Daddy's Ridge
Cloutman Pond
Hellgate Brook
Mount Tucker
Parker Hill
AZISCOHOS
BOUNDARY MOUNTAINS
Rangeley River
16
LAKE
Deer Min Stream
WILSON MILLS RD
Goodwin Pond
Lamb Valley Brook
Brook
Hydro Pool
P
Wilsons Mills
Aziscohos Dam
P
16
Richardson Pond
East Richardson Ponds
LOWER
Mailbox Pool
P
⛵
Bridge Pool
MAGALLOWAY RIVER
16
Aziscohos Pond
Beaver Pond
RICHARDSON LAKE
Swift Diamond River

➤ **Location:** Northwestern Maine, about a 3-hour ride from Portland and Bangor; a 3-hour ride from Manchester, New Hampshire; and a 4-hour ride from Boston, Massachusetts. Full-service airports are available in all four cities.

Sometimes overlooked in regional guidebooks, the Magalloway River is by any rational definition one of the two finest native Eastern brook trout rivers in the country. Brook trout here are measured in pounds, not inches. Nonnative landlocked Atlantic salmon are also present. These, too, can grow to trophy sizes. All trout and salmon in the river are wild—there is no stocking.

The Magalloway is rich in history and lore. Roughly 10,000 years ago, Paleoindians camped along its banks below what is now Aziscohos Lake. Here they hunted herds of migrating caribou. Metallak, "The Lone Indian of the Magalloway," hunted, trapped, fished, and guided the area. A pond and a mountain just over the border in New Hampshire were named after him. Parmachenee Lake was named after his daughter—said to be a beautiful young woman. President Eisenhower fished the river in 1955. A plaque on the bank commemorates his visit.

The Magalloway River is divided into three sections: upper, middle, and lower. The river is nearly 30 miles long, not including two lakes. Each section is different in regard to topography, size, flow, and the fishery itself.

The upper Magalloway originates from springs along the Canadian border. Several small tributaries converge to form the river, which flows into 2½-mile-long Parmachenee Lake. This section winds its way through thousands of acres of private timber company land. Access is via a network of logging roads, but is restricted by several locked gates—unless you are a camp owner, or a guest at the nearby sporting lodge. Here the Magalloway is a small freestone river with riffles, runs, and pools. Brook trout and salmon in the 6- to 12-inch range are plentiful. Larger fish ranging from 16 to 20 inches

migrate upstream from the lake in the spring, fall, and after a heavy rain. These fish will stay in the river until the flow drops, or the water becomes too warm.

Below Parmachenee Lake, at the remnants of Black Cat Dam, begins the middle Magalloway. Here, the river runs for roughly 1½ miles before entering 15-mile-long Aziscohos Lake. The river here is roughly 30 to 40 feet across in most places. Access can be gained via boat or from dirt roads on the east and west shores of the lake. Like the upper river, flow levels and water temperatures fluctuate greatly throughout the season. Smelt enter the river from the lake soon after ice-

Spring morning on Mailbox Pool. Pond in the River Guide Service

out on their annual spawning run. This brings brook trout and salmon into the river in search of an easy meal. After that, suckers move up from the lake to spawn. Trout and salmon follow them to gorge on their eggs.

The Lower Magalloway begins below Aziscohos Lake. Here the river drops nearly 250 feet in elevation in less than a mile. This stretch of river is a tailwater, with coldwater releases throughout the year. This allows for consistent fishing

Fishing above the power station. Pond in the River Guide Service

through even the warmest months. Most of the flow from the lake is diverted into a power-generating facility that releases water roughly ¼ mile downstream from the dam. The section between the dam and the power station is a series of falls, plunge pools, and pocketwater that does hold some fish. However, the best fishing starts downstream of the power station. Downstream at Wilsons Mills, the Magalloway changes from a rugged freestone river to a meandering meadow stream. From there it flows toward its termination at Umbagog Lake, near the Maine–New Hampshire border. Brook trout outnumber salmon in this section. They run from 12 to 16 inches. Trout over 18 inches are caught on a fairly regular basis. Landlocked salmon range from 12 to 16 inches, with fish over 20 inches sometimes taken. Fishing usually starts by the April 1 season opener. The fishing drops off for a week or two during spring runoff. Hatches are similar to those upriver, but occur a couple weeks earlier on the lower river.

Jake Borgeson with spring brook trout.
Pond in the River Guide Service

Flows on the middle and upper Magalloway River run between 50 and 150 cfs. Flows on the lower river typically run in the 300–600 cfs range. All sections are subject to spikes during ice-out and after rainstorms. Scheduled whitewater releases on the lower river in the summer run from 900–1,200 cfs. The entire river is wadable—albeit not always easily. Occasionally, boats and canoes are used in large pools, and where the river enters the lakes.

➤ **Hatches:** The trout and salmon in the Magalloway feed on insects, baitfish, crayfish, leeches, and fish eggs. Insects include mayflies, caddis, stoneflies, midges, and aquatic worms. The primary baitfish species is smelt (during both the seasonal spawning runs and intermittently through the season as they slip through the dam) as well as sculpins, and dace. The first major insect hatches—Quill Gordons and Hendrickons—occur in early to mid-May. Stoneflies hatch in the late spring and early summer, with Yellow Sallies and the larger Golden Stones. Caddis hatches start in mid- to late May, and continue through September.

Fish in the Magalloway are very migratory. They tend to congregate in certain places at specific times of year. Hiring a guide—at least for your first trip—is never a bad idea. A guide can show you the safest places to cross the river, where the fish are at any given time, and the best flies to use. This is most important to the traveling angler who has a limited amount of time to fish.

➤ **Regulations:** The Magalloway River is restricted to fly fishing only. Above Aziscohos Lake, all brook trout less than 6 inches and longer than 12 inches must be released at once. This helps protect the larger fish. There is a two-fish limit on brook trout. Below Aziscohos Lake, it is catch-and release on brook trout, with barbless hooks required. Salmon are managed under a one-fish, 14-inch-minimum-length restriction. The river is open from April 1 through the end of September. Starting August 15 and running through the end of the season, all brook trout and salmon must be released.

If big wild brook trout in moving water are what you are looking for, the Magalloway River is one of the best places to find them.

➤ **Tackle:** A 9-foot 5-weight rod with a floating line is the best all-around choice for most sections of the Magalloway River. A sink-tip can be helpful on the middle and lower sections if you wish to fish streamers. Lighter 3- or 4-weight rods can be used effectively in the upper river at certain times of the year. Fluorocarbon leaders and tippet are important on the lower river, as fish see a lot of flies, but it is not necessary on the middle and upper river. Large strike indicators are

Large fall spawn male brookie. Pond in the River Guide Service

KRIS THOMPSON resides in the Rangeley area—including maintaining a home on the lower Magalloway. He is co-owner of Pond In The River Guide Service in Rangeley, Maine. Kris is a Registered Maine Guide and has guided the Magalloway River for more than 15 years. He can be reached at 207-864-9140, info@rangeleyfly fishing.com, or www.rangeleyflyfishing.com.

needed to fish a pair of flies, and sufficient weight to get the flies down quickly in the fast-moving water. Flies should include smelt, minnow, and sculpin streamer patterns; mayfly and stonefly dries and nymphs; all stages of caddis in varying sizes and colors; as well as egg and worm patterns.

CLOSEST FLY SHOPS

Rangeley Region Sport Shop
2529 Main Street
Rangeley, Maine 04970
207-864-5615
www.rangeleysportshop.com
rivertoridge@aol.com

CLOSEST GUIDES/OUTFITTERS

Pond In The River Guide Service
Rangeley, Maine 04970
207-864-9140
www.rangeleyflyfishing.com
info@rangeleyflyfishing.com

CLOSEST LODGING

Pleasant Street Inn Bed & Breakfast
104 Pleasant Street
Rangeley, Maine 04970
207-864-5916
www.pleasantstreetinnbb.com
info@pleasantstreetinnbb.com

Bosebuck Mountain Camps (rustic cabins)
2013 Parmachenee Road
Lynchtown, Maine 04970
207-670-0013
bosebuck@bosebuck.com
www.bosebuck.com

Morton & Furbish (vacation rentals)
2478 Main Street
Rangeley, Maine 04970
855-218-4882
www.rangeleyrentals.com
vacation-planner@rangeleyrentals.com

The Rangeley Inn
Rooms
2443 Main Street
Rangeley, Maine 04970
207-864-3341
www.therangeleyinn.com
reservations@TheRangeleyInn.com

Country Club Inn
56 Country Club Road
P.O. Box 680
Rangeley, Maine 04970
207-864-3831
www.countryclubinnrangeley.com
ccinn1@myfairpoint.net

CLOSEST RESTAURANTS

Parkside & Main
(lunch and dinner menu, full bar)
2520 Main Street
Rangeley, Maine 04970
207-864-3774

Loon Lodge (fine dining)
16 Pickford Road
Rangeley, Maine 04970
207-864-5666
www.loonlodgeme.com
info@loonlodgeme.com

The Rangeley Tavern
Rustic Cuisine & Light Fare
2443 Main Street
Rangeley, Maine 04970
207-864-3341
www.therangeleyinn.com
reservations@TheRangeleyInn.com

Thai Blossom Express (eat-in/takeout)
2473 Main Street
Rangeley, Maine 04970
207-864-9035

Moosely Bagels/Scoops
(breakfast, lunch, ice cream; food and coffee to go)
2588 Main Street
Rangeley, Maine 04970
207-864-5955

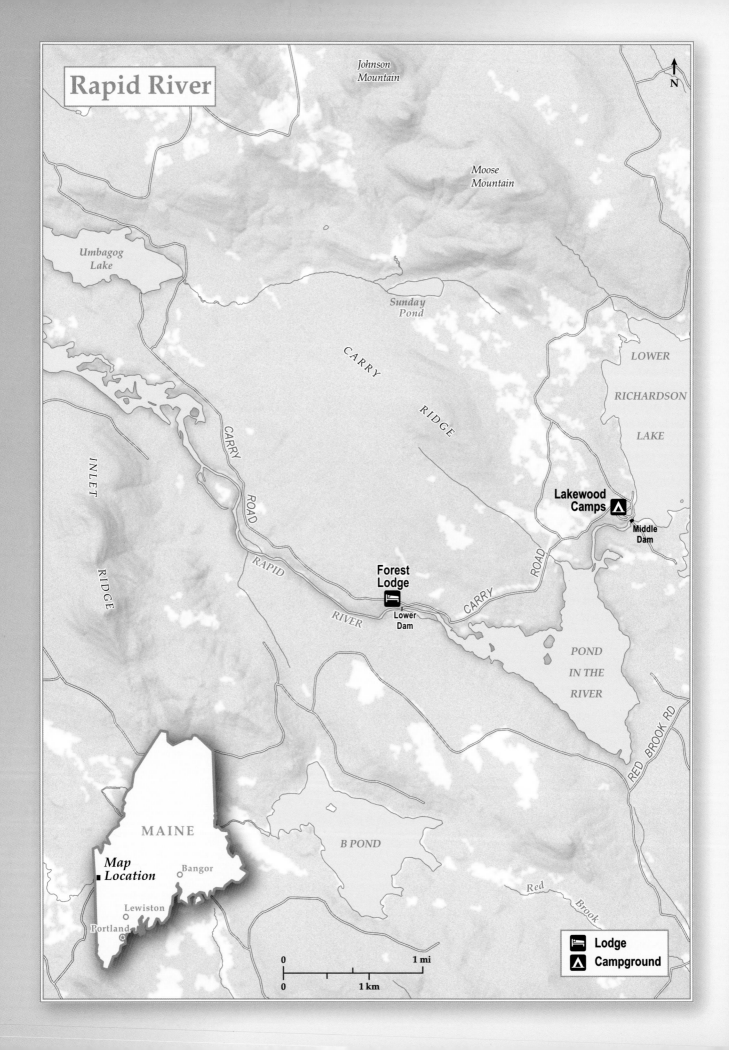

8 · Rapid River

➤ **Location:** Northwest Maine, about a 3-hour ride from Portland and Bangor; a 3-hour ride from Manchester, New Hampshire; and a 4-hour ride from Boston, Massachusetts. Full-service airports are available in all four cities.

The Rapid River is a true treasure—and the nation's finest wild native Eastern brook trout fishery. It offers fly fishers the best chance of catching a 5-pound wild brook trout of any river in the United States. The Rapid is rich in fly-fishing lore and history. Several classic streamers such as Carrie Stevens's Grey Ghost and Herb Welch's Black Ghost were developed not far from the river. Louise Dickinson Rich wrote several books while living along the Rapid. Her most famous, *We Took to the Woods*, was written at Lower Dam, once a working log drive dam, recently demolished and memorialized by a plaque at its site. This section has some of the best brook trout water on the river.

Located in the rugged Western Mountains near the New Hampshire border, the Rapid connects Lower Richardson Lake and Umbagog Lake. The total length of the river, including a small pond, is approximately 5 miles. The river drops 800 feet in elevation between the two large lakes. The Rapid is surrounded by a mixed hardwood deciduous forest. It is protected by a conservation easement that prohibits any new development or logging within 165 feet of the river. There is very little development on the river, which allows for a true wilderness experience. There are a few rustic cabins, no power or phone service, and only dirt roads leading to the river. Access is restricted by locked gates and requires a walk of 20 to 45 minutes. Vehicle access is allowed only if you are staying at one of the sporting camps, or hiring a guide.

Regulated for fly fishing only, barbless hooks, and catch-and-release, the brook trout fishery has prospered. In addition to brook trout, there are landlocked salmon. They are regulated under a three-fish, 12-inch-minimum rule. The brook trout are native; the salmon were introduced in the late 19th century.

Middle Dam, the headwaters of the Rapid, controls the river flow, which averages between 300 and 800 cfs. Flows can run as highs as 5,000 cfs during high-water periods, such as spring runoff, ice-out, or after a heavy rain. Roughly a mile below Middle Dam, the river flows into aptly named Pond in the River. This is a 500-acre natural pond, and serves as a summer refuge for trout and salmon. Below Pond in the River, the Rapid flows for another couple of miles before ending at Lake Umbagog on the Maine–New Hampshire border.

Hedgehog Pool on the lower river. Pond in the River Guide Service

The Rapid is dominated by pocketwater, runs, and pools for most of its length. Most of the river is easily accessible via an informal trail network and dirt roads. It is best fished wading, as boating can be difficult due to the numerous technical drops and boulder fields. The use of canoes and small boats can, however, help you gain access to out-of-the-way spots you cannot cast to.

The Rapid River's season runs from April 1 to September 30. Pond in the River is closed to all fishing From July 1 through August to protect fish that seek refuge from the warm river water. The brook trout spawning area above Lower Dam closes to all fishing after September 15. Peak fishing

Above. First Current Pool. Bob Mallard
Inset. Kris Thompson with large male brookie. Pond in the River Guide Service

is generally May through June, and again in September. The Rapid can fish well in the early spring, even with ice on the lakes, very cold water in the river, and snow on the ground. Summers can be warm, and fishing slows as the fish seek thermal refuge.

Brook trout in the Rapid River average between 12 and 15 inches long. There are a good number of fish in the 16- to 20-inch range, with brookies over 20 inches always a possibility. Landlocked salmon run slightly smaller, averaging 12 to 14 inches. There are many salmon in the 15- to 20-inch range. This combination of two uniquely New England species and the number of fish over 20 inches makes the Rapid a true trophy river.

Trout and salmon in the Rapid take advantage of a variety of food sources. These include smelt, dace, sculpins, crayfish, insects, and fish eggs. Insects include stoneflies, caddis, mayflies, and dragonflies. Brook trout and salmon feed heavily on sucker eggs in the early spring, starting when the water temperatures reach roughly 50 degrees. Smelt are also a very important spring food source. Smelt spawn in the Rapid before the suckers do, drawing large trout into the river to feed.

➤ **Hatches:** Hatches on the Rapid are rarely epic, but they are consistent and predictable. In spring, Blue-winged Olives and Hendricksons dominate. Caddis show up later in the spring, and hatch periodically until fall. Stoneflies will hatch from spring to early fall. Dragonflies can be seen crawling out of the water in the late spring to hatch. This triggers large fish to feed voraciously while they are available.

Many different methods of fly fishing are effective on the Rapid River. Among the most productive is nymphing. This provides consistent action throughout the season. Streamer fishing is a great way to catch large fish in the spring when smelt are abundant. During the fall spawning period, trout and salmon become territorial, and attractor streamers work well. Trout and salmon will feed on the surface when there is a hatch.

By most definitions, the Rapid River is the premier brook trout river in the country. The brook trout here also represent a rare wild and native fishery. If catching a trophy wild native Eastern brook trout is on your list of things to do, there is no better place to do it than the Rapid River in Rangeley, Maine.

Kris Thompson with landlocked salmon.

➤ **Tackle:** A 9-foot 5-weight rod with a floating line is the best all-around choice for most sections of the Rapid River. A sink-tip can be helpful if you wish to fish streamers. Fluorocarbon leaders and tippet are important, as fish see a lot of flies. Large strike indicators are needed to fish a pair of flies and sufficient weight to get the flies down quickly in the fast-moving water. Flies should include smelt, minnow, and sculpin streamer patterns; mayfly and stonefly dries and nymphs; all stages of caddis in varying sizes and colors; as well as eggs and worm patterns.

KASH J. HALEY resides in Rangeley, Maine. He is co-owner of Pond In The River Guide Service in Rangeley. Kash is a Registered Maine Guide and has guided the Rapid River for almost 15 years. He also owns Parkside & Main Restaurant in downtown Rangeley. He can be reached at 207-864-2147, info@rangeley flyfishing.com, or www.rangeleyflyfishing.com.

CLOSEST FLY SHOPS

Rangeley Region Sport Shop
2529 Main Street
Rangeley, Maine 04970
207-864-5615
www.rangeleysportshop.com
rivertoridge@aol.com

CLOSEST GUIDES/OUTFITTERS

Pond in the River Guide Service
Rangeley, Maine 04970
207-864-2147
www.rangeleyflyfishing.com
info@rangeleyflyfishing.com

CLOSEST LODGING

The Rangeley Inn
Rooms
2443 Main Street
Rangeley, Maine 04970
207-864-3341
www.therangeleyinn.com
reservations@TheRangeleyInn.com

Country Club Inn
56 Country Club Road
P.O. Box 680
Rangeley, Maine 04970
207-864-3831
www.countryclubinnrangeley.com
ccinn1@myfairpoint.net

Pleasant Street Inn B&B
104 Pleasant Street
Rangeley, Maine 04970
207-864-5916
www.pleasantstreetinnbb.com
info@pleasantstreetinnbb.com

Pond in the River Apartment & Cabin
Rangeley, Maine 04970
207-864-2147
www.rangeleyflyfishing.com
info@rangeleyflyfishing.com

CLOSEST RESTAURANTS

Parkside & Main
(lunch and dinner menu, full bar)
2520 Main Street
Rangeley, Maine 04970
207-864-3774

Loon Lodge Inn (gourmet dining)
16 Pickford Road
Rangeley, Maine 04970
207-864-5666
info@loonlodgeme.com
www.loonlodgeme.com

The Rangeley Tavern
Rustic Cuisine & Light Fare
2443 Main Street
Rangeley, Maine 04970
207-864-3341
www.therangeleyinn.com
reservations@TheRangeleyInn.com

Thai Blossom Express (eat-in/takeout)
2473 Main Street
Rangeley, Maine 04970
207-864-9035

Moosely Bagels/Scoops
(breakfast, lunch, ice cream, and food and coffee to go)
2588 Main Street
Rangeley, Maine 04970
207-864-5955

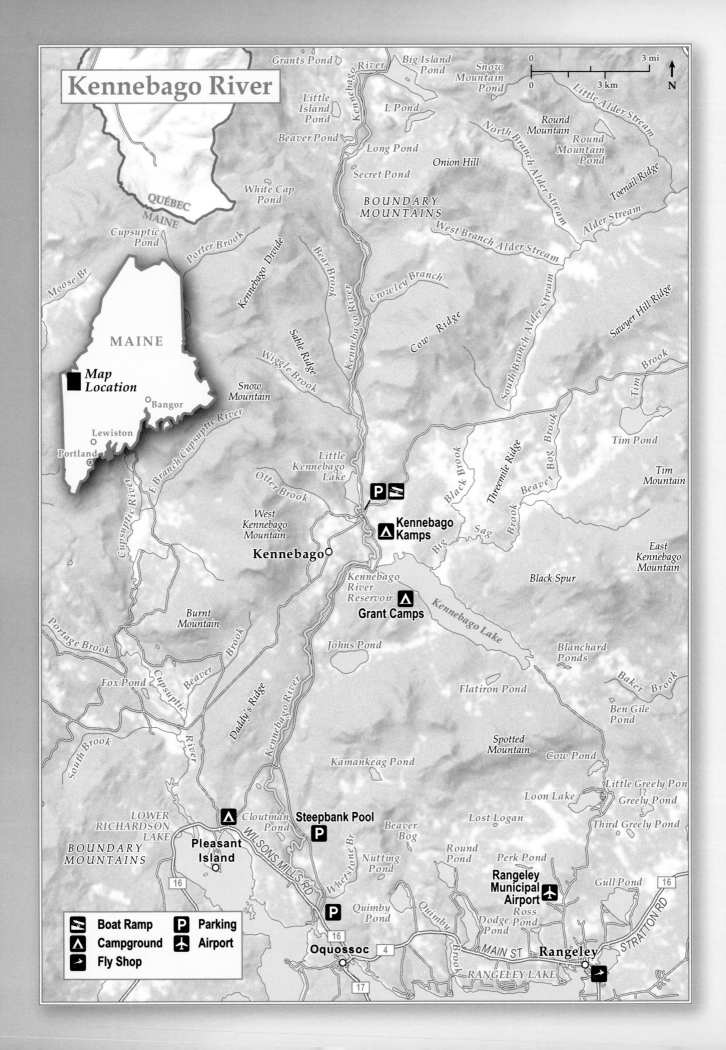

Kennebago River

QUÉBEC
MAINE

MAINE

Map
Location

Bangor

Lewiston

Portland

Grants Pond

Little
Island
Pond

Beaver Pond

White Cap
Pond

Cupsuptic
Pond

Moose Br

Porter Brook

Kennebago Divide

Sable Ridge

Wiggle Brook

Snow
Mountain

E Branch Cupsuptic River

Cupsuptic River

Portage Brook

Fox Pond

South Brook

Beaver Brook

Cupsuptic River

Daddy's Ridge

Burnt
Mountain

West
Kennebago
Mountain

Otter Brook

Little
Kennebago
Lake

Kennebago

LOWER
RICHARDSON
LAKE

BOUNDARY
MOUNTAINS

Pleasant
Island

Cloutman
Pond

WILSONS MILLS RD

16

Whetstone Br

Kennebago River

Johns Pond

Kamankeag Pond

Steepbank Pool

Beaver
Bog

Nutting
Pond

Quimby Pond

16

Oquossoc

4

17

Kennebago
River
Reservoir

Grant Camps

Kennebago Kamps

Kennebago
River

Big

Sag

Brook

Black Brook

Threemile Ridge

Beaver Bog Brook

L Pond

Kennebago River

Big Island
Pond

Snow
Mountain
Pond

BOUNDARY
MOUNTAINS

Long Pond

Secret Pond

Onion Hill

North Branch Alder Stream

West Branch Alder Stream

South Branch Alder Stream

Crowley Branch

Cow Ridge

Round
Mountain

Round
Mountain
Pond

Little Alder Stream

Toenail Ridge

Alder Stream

Sawyer Hill Ridge

Tim Brook

Tim Pond

Tim
Mountain

East
Kennebago
Mountain

Black Spur

Blanchard
Ponds

Flatiron Pond

Spotted
Mountain

Cow Pond

Loon Lake

Lost Logan

Round
Pond

Quimby Brook

Dodge
Pond

Ross Pond

Perk Pond

Rangeley
Municipal
Airport

MAIN ST

RANGELEY LAKE

Baker Brook

Ben Gile
Pond

Little Greely Pon

Greely Pond

Third Greely Pond

Gull Pond

16

Rangeley

STRATTON RD

0 ____ 3 mi
0 ____ 3 km

N

Legend

- ⚓ Boat Ramp
- ⛺ Campground
- 🎣 Fly Shop
- 🅿 Parking
- ✈ Airport

9 · Kennebago River

➤ **Location:** Northwestern Maine, about a 3-hour ride from Portland and Bangor; a 3-hour ride from Manchester, New Hampshire; and a 4-hour ride from Boston, Massachusetts. Full-service airports are available in all four cities.

The Rangeley Lakes Region is rich in history and lore, and the Kennebago River is part of the reason. In the 1860s, word began to spread about the giant brook trout that inhabited the waters of this wild and remote corner of New England. In 1868, the Oquossoc Anglers Association was founded at the mouth of the Kennebago River, and fly-fishing exploration of the river began. Ed Grant founded Grant's Kennebago Camps on Kennebago Lake in 1906. The camps are still in operation today.

Kennebago is the name of a tribe of Native Americans who inhabited the area around Kennebago Lake. It translates to "people of the land of sweet flowing waters." They were the first to recognize the commercial potential of the area, guiding sportsmen from Boston and New York.

The Kennebago begins at Big Island Pond along the Maine–Quebec border. The river is roughly 25 miles long. It is a diverse mix of slow, meandering stretches, short riffles, and pocketwater. Several miles below Big Island Pond, the river is interrupted by Long Pond. From there it flows roughly 8 miles before entering Little Kennebago Lake. A couple of miles after exiting Little Kennebago, the river is joined by the outlet of Kennebago Lake—the largest fly-fishing-only lake in Maine. From here the Kennebago flows unbroken for roughly 8 miles before terminating at Mooselookmeguntic Lake. Both Kennebago and Little Kennebago Lakes offer outstanding fishing for brook trout and the occasional landlocked salmon. Kennebago Lake is gated against public access. Little Kennebago Lake is accessible to the general public. The latter is restricted to nonmotorized boats only.

The Kennebago is divided into four sections. The first, and least fished, is between Big Island Pond and Little Kennebago Lake. This section has a resident population of brook trout. The second is from Little Kennebago Lake to Kennebago Lake. Most of the fish here come from the two lakes. The third section is from Kennebago Lake to the bridge on Kennebago River Road. Fish from Mooselookmeguntic Lake reach the lower end of this section. There are also resident brook trout. The last section is from the bridge to Mooselookmeguntic Lake—including fabled Steep Bank Pool. Large brook trout move up into the river from the lake in late May and again in early fall. Landlocked salmon move in soon after the brook trout.

There is good public access to the Kennebago between Steep Bank Pool and Mooselookmeguntic Lake. A gate just above Steep Bank prevents motorized traffic. You can, how

Fall fishing on middle river. Diana Mallard

ever, fish above Steep Bank if you walk, or have permission to go beyond the gate, usually associated with stays at one of the sporting camps. From Steep Bank to Kennebago Lake, the river is mostly riffles, fast water, pocketwater, and pools. Many fly fishers do use the road for walk-in access. This section provides a level of solitude not found on the easy-to-access water downstream of the gate. Fishing can be quite good in this section—possibly the best on the river.

Fall brook trout. Tim Ervin

Upper river. Rangeley Region Sport Shop

You can also access the river by vehicle from the bridge located just below Little Kennebago Lake. From here you can fish down to the outlet of Kennebago Lake. This section is mostly riffles and runs. It also warms up quickly in the spring, resulting in the fish moving back into the lakes.

The Kennebago is a wild fishery. The brook trout are native. The landlocked salmon are introduced. There is no stocking on the river. The Kennebago strain of brook trout is, however, used by the Maine Department of Inland Fisheries and Wildlife as brood stock for stocking programs elsewhere—a testimony to the strength of the genetics of these fish. Brook trout average 10 to 12 inches. However, fish over 4 pounds are caught in the Kennebago. They are as beautiful as any brook trout found anywhere. Fall fish demonstrate the vibrant colors, pronounced kype, and humped backs that make wild brook trout some of the—if not *the*—most beautiful fish in the world. Salmon average 12 to 16 inches, with much larger fish encountered. Fishing in the spring when fresh salmon have entered the river from the Mooselookmeguntic Lake can be very rewarding. Like all salmon, these fish usually go airborne immediately after they are hooked.

➤ Hatches: Trout and salmon in the Kennebago gorge themselves on spawning smelt as soon as the ice goes off the lakes. As the water warms, insects become more active and fish will switch their focus to them. Caddis—green or olive—and Hendricksons are the predominant hatches in the spring. Black stoneflies, dragonflies, and ants can provide food for the fish as well. Tan-colored caddis are the most consistent hatch, and extend through most of the summer.

Streamers can be fished effectively on the Kennebago in the spring and again in the fall. Spring streamers should im-

itate smelt—fall streamers should be of the attractor variety. Streamers can also be effective in the deeper pools and when the river is running high or off-colored. Dry-fly fishing can be effective during a hatch, and when using attractors or terrestrials. As is often the case, when the fish are not looking up, and refuse streamers, nymphing is your best bet.

➤ Regulations: The Kennebago River is open to fishing from April 1 through September 30. The river and its tributaries are restricted to fly fishing only. There is a two-fish limit on trout. The minimum length limit is 10 inches; only one fish may be larger than 12 inches. The limit on salmon is one fish. The river is catch-and-release after August 15. The tributaries are closed to fishing after August 15. One short section of the river closes September 15 to protect spawning fish.

The Kennebago is one of the top three native brook trout rivers in the country. The other two, Rapid and Magalloway, are within striking distance. The Kennebago should be near the top of every fly fisher's list of places to go.

The Logans. Tim Ervin

➤ **Tackle:** A 9-foot 5-weight rod with a floating line is the best all-around choice for most sections of the Kennebago River. A 9-foot 6-weight with a sink-tip or full sinking line can be helpful on the middle and lower sections if you wish to fish streamers. Lighter rods in the 4-weight range can be used effectively in the upper river at certain times of the year. Large strike indicators are needed to fish a pair of flies and sufficient weight to get the flies down quickly in the fast-moving water in the lower river. Flies should include smelt, minnow, and sculpin streamer patterns; mayfly and stonefly dries and nymphs; all stages of caddis in varying sizes and colors; as well as egg patterns.

BRETT DAMM is a Master Maine Guide. He owns and operates Rangeley Region Sport Shop and River To Ridge Guide Service. He can be reached at 207-864-5615, rivertoridge@aol.com, or www.rangeleysportshop.com.

CLOSEST FLY SHOPS

Rangeley Region Sport Shop
2529 Main Street
Rangeley, Maine 04970
207-864-5615
www.rangeleysportshop.com
rivertoridge@aol.com

CLOSEST GUIDES AND OUTFITTERS

Pond In The River Guide Service
Rangeley, Maine 04970
207-864-9140
www.rangeleyflyfishing.com
info@rangeleyflyfishing.com

CLOSEST LODGING

Grant's Kennebago Camps
PO Box 786
Rangeley, Maine 04970
800-633-4815
www.grantscamps.com
grantscamps@gmail.com

Kennebago River Kamps
PO Box 677
Rangeley, Maine 04970
207-864-2402
www.krkamps.com
rhammond42@myfairpoint.net

Rangeley Saddleback Inn
2303 Main Street
Rangeley, Maine 04970
207-864-3434
www.rangeleysaddlebackinn.com
info@rangeleysaddlebackinn.com

North Country Inn Bed and Breakfast
2541 Main Street
Rangeley, Maine 04970
207-864-2440
www.northcountrybb.com
info@northcountrybb.com

The Rangeley Inn
Rooms
2443 Main Street
Rangeley, Maine 04970
207-864-3341
www.therangeleyinn.com
reservations@TheRangeleyInn.com

CLOSEST RESTAURANTS

Parkside & Main
(lunch and dinner menu, full bar)
2520 Main Street
Rangeley, Maine 04970
207-864-3774

The Red Onion Restaurant
Maine Street
Rangeley, Maine 04970
207-864-5022
www.rangeleyredonion.com
rangeleyredonion@myfairpoint.net

The Farmhouse Inn
2057 Main Street
Rangeley, Maine 04970
207-864-5805

The Rangeley Tavern
Rustic Cuisine & Light Fare
2443 Main Street
Rangeley, Maine 04970
207-864-3341
www.therangeleyinn.com
reservations@TheRangeleyInn.com

Moosely Bagels/Scoops
(breakfast, lunch, ice cream,
and food/coffee to go)
2588 Main Street
Rangeley, Maine 04970
207-864-5955

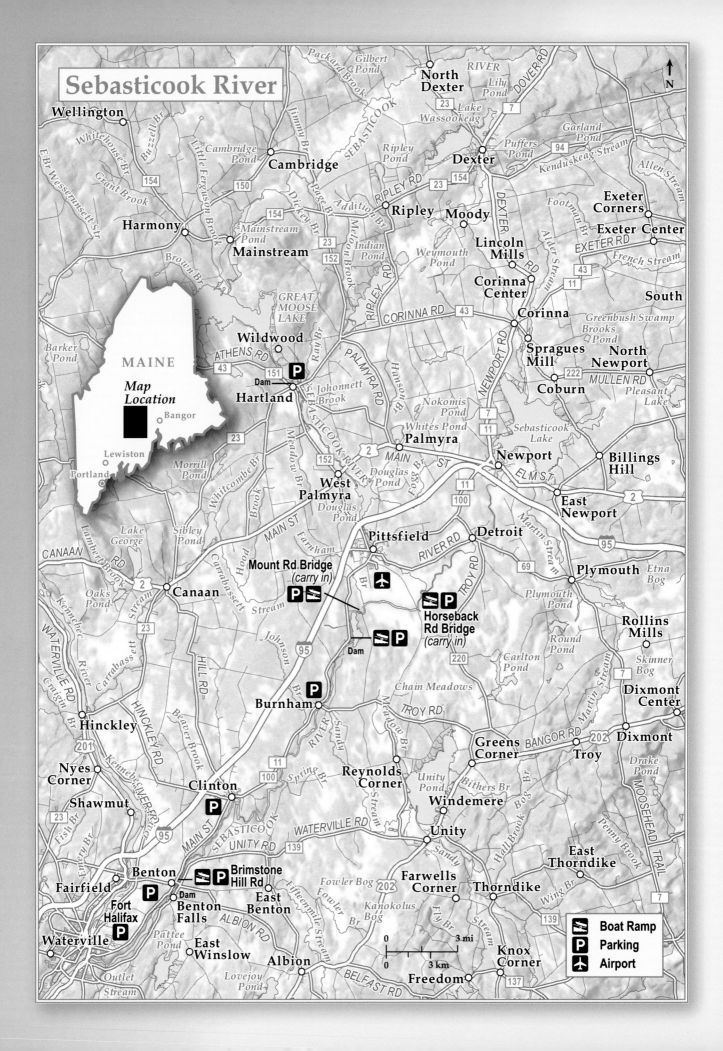

10 · Sebasticook River *(bass)*

➤ **Location:** Central Maine, about a 1-hour ride from Bangor, a 2-hour ride from Portland; a 3½-hour ride from Boston, Massachusetts; and a 3½-hour ride from Manchester, New Hampshire. Full-service airports are available in all four cities.

"For years I've fished for smallmouth bass in Maine's ponds, lakes, streams, and rivers. My all-time favorite is the Sebasticook River—I try to go back every year."
— *Lefty Kreh*

From its humble beginnings at Great Moose Pond in the central Maine town of North Dexter, the Sebasticook River makes a slow and lazy course roughly 45 miles through the small towns of Burnham, Pittsfield, and Benton, before terminating at the Kennebec River at historic Fort Halifax in Winslow. Its tannic waters transition from shallow riffles, deep pools, and small impoundments, as it drains approximately 985 square miles of low-lying forests, swamps, and farmland. A hydroelectric station located on the lower end of the river at Benton Falls is the only dam left between there and the Atlantic Ocean, roughly 60 miles away.

While the Sebasticook River may not be as well-known as many waters in this book, it has a much deeper history in regard to fishing than most could ever imagine. In fact, the river is the site of the oldest known fish weir in North America. This submerged wooden structure predates the pyramids of Egypt.

The Sebasticook River was in the national news when the Fort Halifax Dam in Winslow became the second dam in Maine to be slated for removal in support of fish passage. As part of a 50-year relicensing agreement, the owners of the 492-foot-wide, 29-foot-high, early 20th century hydroelectric dam were required to provide safe passage through the dam for anadromous fish such as American shad, alewives, blueback herring, striped bass, sturgeon, and endangered Atlantic salmon. However, because of the dam's marginal electricity generation capacity, they chose to remove the structure rather than install a costly fish ladder. After a short court battle involving impoundment shorefront owners who were opposed to its removal, the dam was finally breached in July 2008. This marked the first time in 170 years that fish had unobstructed access from the Atlantic Ocean to the town of Benton.

My first experience with the Sebasticook came late one summer in the mid-1980s while I was driving back to college. Armed with a fiberglass fly rod, Pflueger Medalist reel, a pair of shorts with the pockets full of deer-hair poppers, and an old pair of wading sneakers, I hooked and lost more hard-fighting, acrobatic smallmouth bass than I was able to

Slow water section. King Montgomery

land. From that day on, I became enamored with the Sebasticook's high numbers of large fish and the fast fishing action. I spent the rest of that fishing season migrating between college classes and the river—while exploring every foot of its dark waters. This river was one of the reasons that my college career took 5½ years as opposed to the planned 4 years.

River grass. King Montgomery

Inset above. Smallie with streamer. King Montgomery

I returned to the Sebasticook River in the mid-1990s to film footage for the designers of the Banjo Minnow fishing lure. While filming, I was again amazed by the numbers of smallmouth we encountered. My past obsession with the river was rekindled and, as I had when in college, I returned to the river the next day. This time I benefited by having spent the previous 5 years honing my skills as a professional fishing guide. I arrived equipped with a float tube, breathable waders, a modern fly rod and reel, and the memory of the fast action I had enjoyed the day before with the white Banjo Minnow. The smallmouth attacked my large white streamers with an almost angry aggression. It became obvious that this river was something truly special. The Sebasticook became a regular destination for me when guiding my smallmouth clients.

Fishing the Sebasticook for smallmouth bass is relatively easy for the first-time angler. Access is available at nearly all river crossings, allowing you to fish short, slow-moving sections with carry-on boats. The river has sections of moving water and short riffles that can produce fast action under the right conditions. As with most fisheries, it is always a good bet to try fishing directly below the dams, where allowed. There is a small boat launch above the Benton Falls dam. This gives anglers motorboat access to roughly 4 miles of impoundment. Guides on the river utilize jet boats, canoes, and drift boats to gain access to the most productive water. Taking advantage of local knowledge can help you eliminate a lot of mediocre water, while giving you a better chance at hooking one of the river's trophy-size smallmouth.

The Sebasticook receives a fall run of sea-run alewives. This can produce frenzied feeding of schooled-up bass. My per-

Lefty Kreh with smallmouth bass. King Montgomery

sonal best smallmouth, measuring 23 inches, came during one of these feeding blitzes. Bass were staged up in deep water below a long riffle and were making slashing runs up into the shallows as they chased young alewives getting ready to return to the ocean. One or more bass would rush upriver until their backs were out of water, pushing the small fish back against the current. All I needed to do was make my streamer look like a stunned alewife with a simple up-and-across dead drift. This typically resulted in a hit as soon as the fly started to make its swing over the deeper water.

Chances are this is the first time you have heard of the Sebasticook River. It does not have a long and storied history as a sport fishery, unlike many of the waters covered in this book. However, as evident by the ancient fish weir, it does have a much older history as a subsistence fishery than many others. And as my dad says, pay attention to what older generations have to say, you just might learn something. As for it being Lefty Kreh's favorite Maine smallmouth fishery, is there a more valid modern stamp of approval than this? I don't believe so.

➤ Tackle: A 9-foot, 7- or 8-weight rod with a floating line is your best bet for the Sebasticook River most of the time. If the water is high, or the fish are deep, a fast-sinking sink-tip is your best option. Flies should include Woolly Buggers and other leech patterns; sculpin patterns; light-colored streamers that imitate juvenile alewives, shad, white perch, and shiners; and a few crayfish imitations.

CHRIS RUSSELL owns and operates Kennebec River Angler in Caratunk, Maine. He can be reached at 207-672-3408 or www.kennebecriverangler.com.

CLOSEST FLY SHOPS
Kennebec River Outfitters
469 Lakewood Road
Madison, Maine 04950
207-474-2500
www.kennebecriveroutfitters.com
info@kennebecriveroutfitters.com

CLOSEST GUIDES/OUTFITTERS
Kennebec River Angler
111 Main Street
Caratunk, Maine 04925
207-672-3408
www.kennebecriverangler.com
info@kennebecriverangler.com

CLOSEST LODGING
Comfort Inn & Suites
332 Main Street
Waterville, Maine 04903
207-873-2777
www.comfortinn.com

Best Western Plus
Waterville Grand Hotel
375 Main Street
Waterville, Maine 04903
207-873-0111

CLOSEST RESTAURANTS
Lobster Trap
21 Bay Street
Winslow, Maine 04901
207-872-0529
www.lobstertrap-seafood.com
jh@lobstertrap-seafood.com

Mirakuya Sushi & Hibachi Grill
150 Kennedy Memorial Drive
Waterville, Maine 04901
207-616-0088

Cacciatores
29 Upper Main Street
Fairfield, Maine 04937
207-872-9700

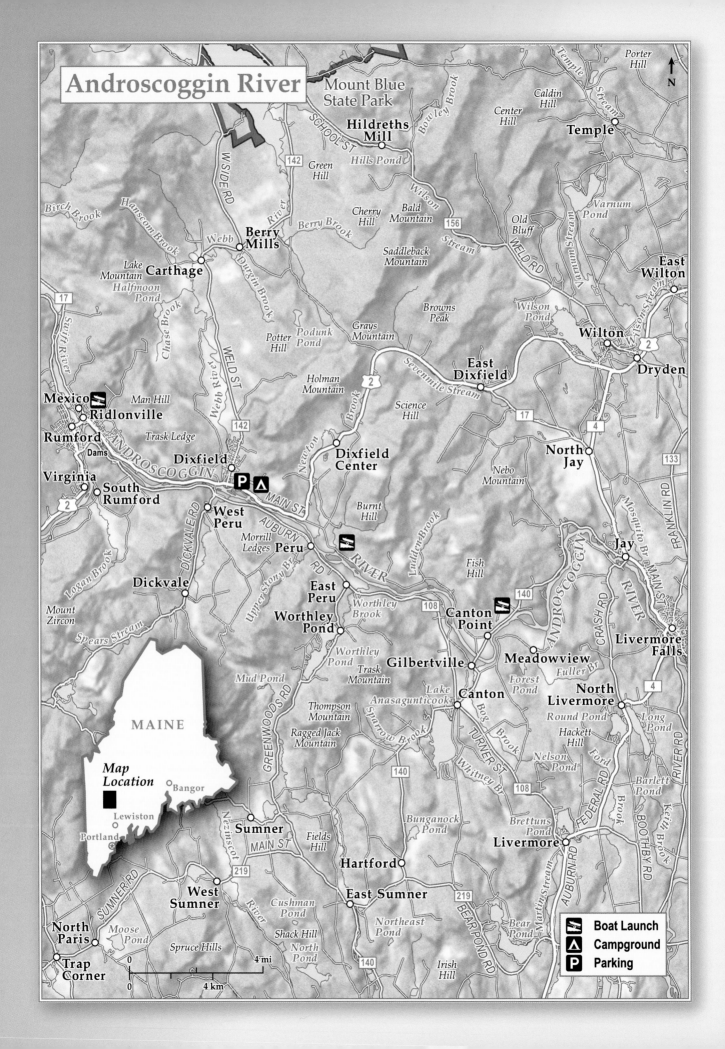

11 · Androscoggin River, Maine *(bass)*

➤ **Location:** Southwestern Maine, about a 2-hour ride from Portland, a 1-hour ride from Augusta; a 3-hour ride from Boston, Massachusetts; and a 3-hour ride from Manchester, New Hampshire. Full-service airports are available in all four cities.

The Androscoggin River is named after an Abenaki tribe who depended on the river for food and transportation for thousands of years. This 178-mile-long superhighway provided access from the Atlantic Ocean to the heavily forested and game-rich regions of Maine, New Hamshire, and Canada. The Andro, as it is called, was navigable by ocean-going boats upriver to Brunswick, Maine. The 1,500-foot drop from source to sea is the steepest of the major rivers in Maine, and provided water power during the Industrial Revolution, allowing timber, paper, shoe, and textile manufacturing industries to flourish.

Due to escalating water pollution, the Andro became ground zero for the Clean Water Act of 1972. Championed by United States Senator and Rumford, Maine native Edmund Muskie, this legislation reversed national water degradation trends by requiring water quality standards that met fishable and swimmable objectives. Today, the entire length of the Andro in Maine supports smallmouth bass, and in many sections they truly thrive.

The Androscoggin is the third-largest river in Maine, where it runs approximately 125 miles and drains roughly 2,730 square miles. The Androscoggin enters western Maine from New Hampshire at the Shelburne, NH–Gilead, Maine border. The river flows east from Gilead to Jay, then south toward Brunswick before emptying into Merrymeeting Bay.

Fly fishers seeking smallmouth bass target the section between Rumford and Jay due to the water quality, aesthetics,

topography, fishing consistency, and the availability of access for both wading and boating anglers. In this stretch, river users will find a mix of quick water and gently flowing flat water. The average flow rate is roughly 3,800 cubic feet per second. Flows are controlled by the dams in Rumford. Public access is via a series of hand carry and trailer boat launches, picnic spots, parks, feeder streams, and conservation areas. These sites are located along a network of primary and secondary roads that parallel the river for most of its length in Maine.

Dixfield, Maine. Mike Stillman

The Androscoggin River between Pennacook Falls in Rumford and the Riley Dam in Jay is one of the finest smallmouth bass fisheries in Maine—and in fact, the entire Northeast. It is a favorite of smallmouth connoisseur Lefty Kreh, who fishes it almost annually. Fast fishing and trophy smallmouth are available in this uncrowded section of river. The variety of depths and wide range of structural features such as boulder gardens, rock cribs, log piles, and bridge abutments, as well as the multitude of islands and fishable channels, make for phenomenal smallmouth habitat in this stretch of water. Access to this portion of the Andro begins just below the confluence with the Swift River, at the Town of Mexico public boat launch. This put-in is directly across

Riffle water. King Montgomery

Ray Stillman. Mike Stillman

the river from a large paper mill complex. Despite this industrial and somewhat urban beginning, the Andro quickly reverts to rural tree-lined fields and farmland, and provides an amazing level of seclusion when you consider where you are. This section of river is quite consistent in width and contains a series of gentle rips, which easily accommodate small boats in all but the lowest flows.

About 5 miles downstream from Mexico, the river passes under a set of bridges in Dixfield. Dixfield is a classic small New England town. Just downstream from the bridges, the Webb River enters from the north (left). Negotiations are underway to install a much-needed public boat ramp at this location. From the Dixfield bridges down to the Verso hand-carry boat access site, the river flows approximately 4½ miles, dotted by a series of uninhabited islands and multiple side channels, all of which are runnable during normal flows. It would take many years to fully explore this section

Nate Morse with large bass. Nate Morse

of river. Here the river has a sandy bottom, with small-mouth-friendly boulders, log structures, ledges, and feeder streams. Eagle and osprey sightings are common here. As you approach the Verso access from above, at about the 4-mile mark, be sure to stay in the left channel of the island just below the very prominent boulder garden.

Just a little over 2 miles downstream from the Verso public access, you will pass under a set of electric power lines that cross the river. Looking left, you will see a small sandy beach, which makes a great lunch site or place to get out and stretch. During low water, about a mile downriver from the sandy beach, you may have to drag your boat partway through a shallow riffle that covers the entire width of the river. The Andro soon deepens, and you will start to encounter a series of rock cribs formerly used to control log drives. Motorized boats with shallow drafts can usually come upstream to where the rock cribs begin. These rock cribs are veritable smallmouth factories. Fish them hard, but don't neglect the other somewhat featureless segments of the river. Sometimes smallmouth bass have favorite lies that are not always apparent from the river's surface.

About 6 miles down from the Verso put-in, you will encounter the recently refurbished Canton bridge. Just after the bridge, the river turns sharply left, and the lighting conditions change. This can lead to dramatic changes in fishing action. If the fishing slows, be ready to change techniques, flies, and depths. The 2-mile section of river from the Canton bridge to the Dory Road boat launch features rock cribs, log structure, sections of steep banks, and feeder streams. From the Dory Road boat launch to the Riley Dam, the river is a 2-mile-long, windy, and gradually deepening slow-water impoundment.

The Androscoggin River is open to fishing year-round. Smallmouth average 10 to 12 inches. Fish up to 16 inches are common, and much larger fish are caught. The middle Androscoggin in Maine offers a feeling of seclusion in an attrac-

Bonnie Holden, Bob Duport, and Lefty Kreh. King Montgomery

tive rural setting. It is one of the premier smallmouth fisheries in the Northeast. It is also an underutilized resource, providing a level of solitude not often found in a fishery of its caliber.

➤ Tackle: A 7-foot, 11-inch (tournament-legal) to 9-foot 7-weight rod with a floating line is the single choice for the Androscoggin most of the time. If you prefer a lighter action, a 5-weight or 6-weight rod can be used as well. To help fish streamers deep, a 10- to 15-foot, fast-sinking sink-tip or full-sinking line is your best option. Floating lines should be designed for turning over large flies. Specialty big game leaders 9 feet long and 8-pound test are your best bet for the flies generally used. Surface flies should include poppers, hair bugs, grasshoppers, foam ants, terrestrials, floating baitfish, and mice. For streamers, consider Deceivers, Clousers, Woolly Buggers, and crayfish, leech, and sculpin imitations.

BOB DIONNE owns and operates Aardvark Outfitters in Vienna, Maine. He is a registered Maine Guide and FFF-certified casting instructor. Bob can be reached at 207-491-7643 or aardvark.bob@gmail.com.

CLOSEST FLY SHOPS

Sun Valley Sports
129 Sunday River Road
Bethel, Maine 04217
877-851-7533
www.sunvalleysports.com
svs@sunvalleysports.com

CLOSEST GUIDES/OUTFITTERS

Aardvark Outfitters
Vienna, Maine 04360
207-491-7643
aardvark.bob@gmail.com

Marty DiMuzio
525 Kimball Pond Road
New Sharon, Maine 04955
207-778-4144
marty.d51@gmail.com

CLOSEST LODGING

Wilson Lake Inn
183 Lake Road
Wilton, Maine 04294
www.wilsonlakeinn.com
info@wilsonlakeinn.com

Comfort Inn
1026 U.S. 2
Wilton, Maine 04294
207-645-5155
www.comfortinn.com

CLOSEST RESTAURANTS

Calzolaio Pasta Company
248 Main Street, Suite 1
Wilton, Maine 04294
207-645-9500
www.calzolaiopasta.com
info@calzolaiopasta.com

Kawanhee Inn & Restaurant
12 Anne's Way
Weld, Maine 04285
207-585-2000
www.maineinn.net
info@maineinn.net

LaFleur's Restaurant
224 Main Street
Jay, Maine 04239
207-897-2117

Mill Street Café
1 Mill Street
Jay, Maine 04239
207-645-7570
www.mill-st-cafe.com

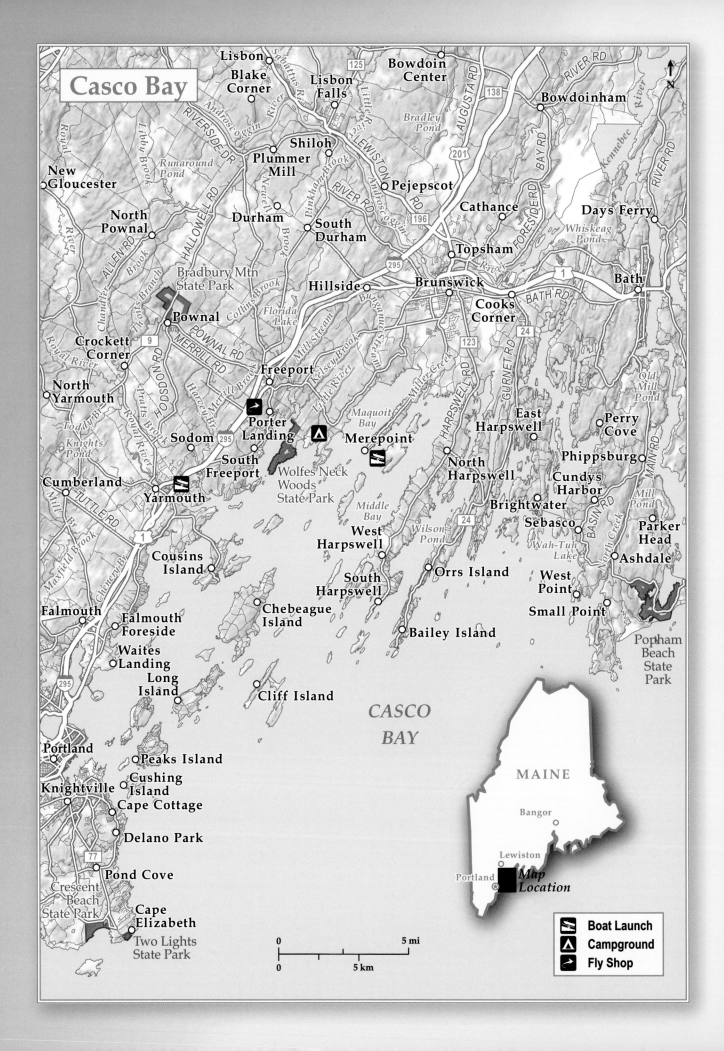

Casco Bay

Lisbon
Blake
Corner
Lisbon
Falls
Bowdoin
Center
Bowdoinham

Sabattus River
125
River Rd
138
Augusta Rd
River Rd
Little River
Lewiston Rd
Bradley Pond

New
Gloucester

North
Pownal

Shiloh
Plummer
Mill
Durham
South
Durham
Pejepscot
Cathance
Days Ferry
201
Topsham
Whiskeag Pond

Libby Brook
Runaround Pond
Riverside Dr
Androscoggin River
Pinkham Brook
Newell Brook
River Rd
196
Androscoggin River
Foreside Rd
Bay Rd
Kennebec River

Bradbury Mtn
State Park

Hillside
Brunswick
Bath

Pownal
9
Crockett
Corner

Allen Rd
Chandler Brook
Collins Brook
Florida Lake
Mill Stream
Bunganuc Stream
Androscoggin River
295
1
Bath Rd

Cooks
Corner
24

North
Yarmouth

Freeport
123
East
Harpswell
Perry
Cove

Pownal Rd
Merrill Rd
Hodgson Rd
Harvey Br
Merrill Brook
Kelsey Brook
Little River
Miller Creek
Harpswell Rd
Gurnet Rd
Old Mill Pond

Sodom
295
Porter
Landing
Maquoit
Bay
Merepoint
North
Harpswell
Phippsburg

Royal River
Pratts Brook
Toddy Br
South
Freeport
Wolfes Neck
Woods
State Park
Wilson Pond
24
Brightwater
Cundys
Harbor
Sebasco
Basin Rd
Mill Pond
Parker
Head

Cumberland
Yarmouth
Middle
Bay
West
Harpswell
Orrs Island
Wah-Tuh Lake
North Creek
Ashdale

Knights Pond
Mill Br
Tuttle Rd
Maxfield Brook
Chenery Br

West
Point
Small Point

Cousins
Island
South
Harpswell

1
Falmouth
Falmouth
Foreside
Chebeague
Island
Bailey Island
Popham
Beach
State Park

Waites
Landing
Long
Island

Portland
Cliff Island
**CASCO
BAY**

295
Peaks Island
Cushing
Island

Knightville
Cape Cottage

MAINE

Delano Park
Bangor

77
Pond Cove
Lewiston
Portland
*Map
Location*

Crescent
Beach
State Park
Cape
Elizabeth
Two Lights
State Park

0   5 mi

0   5 km

| Boat Launch |
| Campground |
| Fly Shop |

12 · Casco Bay (stripers)

➤ **Location:** Southern Maine, about a half-hour ride from Portland or a 1½-hour ride from Bangor, Maine; a 2-hour ride from Boston, Massachusetts; and a 2-hour ride from Manchester, New Hampshire. Full-service airports are available in all four cities.

When most people think of the Maine coast, they think of a rugged shoreline where evergreen forests push right up to the ocean; waves crashing the rocky shores; lighthouses, lobster boats, and quaint seaside villages; and seafood restaurants, takeout stands, and general stores. They do not think of sand beaches, with manicured lawns pushing up against the shoreline; calm, shallow water lapping gently against the beach; yacht clubs, flats boats, and large luxury homes; and sushi bars, coffee shops, and pubs.

The Casco Bay region near Portland fits the description of the latter, not the former. It looks more like Cape Cod than Bar Harbor. It feels more like Massachusetts than Maine. Those who take a closer look will see what actually lies within this beautiful setting. From tourist-friendly Freeport—the town that L.L. Bean built—to bustling Portland, they will find an opportunity to sight fish for striped bass—or stripers—and bluefish—or blues—in shallow water, in a modern and cosmopolitan setting.

Casco Bay is located on the northern end of the striped bass migration. This results in fewer fish than in places such as Montauk, New York. It also presents a unique flats-fishing opportunity where individual fish rather than schools of fish are targeted. While fewer fish migrate this far north, those that do call these waters home for the season. Fish in Casco Bay remain active even during the heat of the summer. Cool water temperatures and greatly fluctuating tides keep things interesting.

As early as mid- to late May, fly fishing near the mouths of rivers starts to turn on. However, this early season fishing can be spotty, and restricted to just a handful of locations. This is due to the fact that the stripers and bluefish are following baitfish such as alewives and river herring that are here to use rivers such as the Presumpscot and Royal for spawning. Once the baitfish have moved upstream, the stripers and blues begin to congregate on the flats to feed. This generally runs from mid-June through the end of September.

Southern New England's hot summer weather helps the fishing in Casco Bay. While the Red Sox and Yankees are

Dawn on a Casco Bay cove. Bob Mallard

slugging it out in July and August in the oppressive heat of downtown Boston, stripers and blues move north in search of cooler water. At this time, Casco Bay will see some of the largest fish of the season. Stripers move into the shallows at this time, in search of crabs, baby lobsters, and grass shrimp. These, along with the ever-present baitfish, keep them interested and localized.

The flats of Casco Bay experience a 7- to 10-foot tide swing. Expansive mud flats are exposed at low tide. Entire coves go dry. Others become a series of small, shallow channels. Things get really interesting, really quickly, if you do not know the area. You need to know the escape routes to keep your boat from being left high and dry. This also helps you understand the movements of the fish. As the tide drops, fish utilize these same routes to get back to deeper water. This concentrates them for a brief period of time. Targeting stripers in these tight confines is a true challenge.

When you arrive at the flats of Casco Bay at first light, the water looks more like a lake than the ocean. The glassy surface shows every disturbance. Ducks glide along quietly, shorebirds soar overhead looking for a meal, the occasional seal shows its head and takes a quick look around, and schools of bait dimple the surface. You move toward any nervous water you see, in search of feeding stripers and blues. Schools of bait are dispersed by unseen predators. The tranquility is suddenly interrupted by the slash of a feeding striped bass. You quietly move from fish to fish, making every cast count.

As the flats drain off, large fish can be seen pushing through the shallows as they head back to deeper water. You position the boat to intercept them. These fish are on alert. They are looking for an easy meal before being forced back to deep water where food is harder to obtain. They dart around in deliberate movements trying to find bait. You cast as they pass—sometimes right under the boat. You drop back with the water, looking for other areas to cover while you still can.

Like most flats species, stripers move around as tides change. Some set up in feeding lanes in shallow water. Others stage just outside the flats, near structure or current. Others—the most challenging—use the light-colored sand flats to hunt for small crabs, sand shrimp, and sand eels. These fish are as wary as any permit found in the Florida Keys. At this time, you will see large stripers pushing along the bottom, stirring up clouds of sand, and darting away at the first sign of trouble.

Fly fishing on the Casco Bay flats is a game of patience. It is more like hunting than fishing. You are usually casting to specific targets. Blind casts are reserved for when your guide senses there are fish around—usually because he or she has seen them there before. You will be told what direction, and how far to cast. Long, quick, and precise casts can really help here. You will be instructed to strip, pause, slow down, or speed up. From his perch above you, your guide can see things that you cannot.

The diversity of fly fishing found in Casco Bay rivals that found anywhere. As you enter Maine, the signs read Welcome to Vacationland. When you arrive in the Casco Bay area, you will quickly understand why. The cobblestone streets of the historic Old Port section of Portland are lined with restaurants, coffee shops, and pubs. Anchored by the L.L. Bean flagship store, Freeport, to the north, is arguably the most vibrant seaside community in Maine, its dozens of outlet stores drawing people from all over the Northeast.

➤ Tackle: A 9-foot 8-weight or 9-weight rod with an intermediate line is your best bet for Casco Bay most of the time. Seven-weight rods can be used for smaller patterns in shallow water. Ten-weight rods can be used for fishing deep and

Above. Kesley Gallagher with large striper.
Coastal Fly Angler

Left. Mike Roy releases a striper.
Coastal Fly Angler

Capt. Eric Wallace and Mike Bradley with first fly-caught striper. Bob Mallard

with larger flies. If you want to fish deeper, a 300- to 350-grain sinking-tip line is your best option. Full-sinking lines can be used when fishing very deep. Poppers are best fished on a floating line. Flies should include Clousers, Deceivers, sand eel patterns, and crabs in a variety of sizes and colors. Large featherwing—referred to as "hollow"—streamers work very well in shallower water.

CAPT. ERIC WALLACE owns and operates Coastal Fly Angler in Freeport, Maine. He guides in Maine and Florida. He is also an accomplished saltwater fly tier. Eric can be reached at 207-671-4330, eric@coastalfl angler.com, or www.coastalflyangler.com.

CLOSEST FLY SHOPS

L.L. Bean
95 Main Street
Freeport, Maine 04033
877-755-2326
www.llbean.com

The Tackle Shop
61 India Street
Portland, Maine 04101
207-773-3474
www.thetackleshop.net
deastman1974@gmail.com

Eldredge Bros. Fly Shop
1480 U.S. 1
Cape Neddick, Maine 03902
207-363-9269
www.eldredgeflyshop.com

CLOSEST GUIDES/OUTFITTERS

Coastal Fly Angler
Capt. Eric Wallace
Freeport, Maine 04032
207-671-4330
www.coastalflyangler.com
eric@coastalflyangler.com

CLOSEST LODGING

Harraseeket Inn
162 Main Street
Freeport, Maine 04032
800-342-6423
www.harraseeketinn.com
Harraseeke@aol.com

Maple Hill Bed & Breakfast
18 Maple Avenue
Freeport, Maine 04032
800-867-0478
www.maplehillbedandbreakfast.com
info@maplehillbedandbreakfast.com

Down-East Village
705 U.S. 1
Yarmouth, Maine 04096
800-782-9338
www.downeastvillage.com
info@downeastvillage.com

Casco Bay Inn
107 U.S. 1
Freeport, Maine 04032
800-570-4970
www.cascobayinn.com
innkeeper@cascobayinn.com

CLOSEST RESTAURANTS

Harraseeket Inn
162 Main Street
Freeport, Maine 04032
800-342-6423
www.harraseeketinn.com
Harraseeke@aol.com

Royal River Grillhouse
106 Lafayette Street
Yarmouth, Maine 04096
207-846-1226
www.royalrivergrillhouse.com
royalrivergrillhouse@gmail.com

Buck's Naked BBQ
568 U.S. 1
Freeport, Maine 04032
207-865-0600
www.bucksnaked-bbq.com

Miyake
468 Fore Street
Portland, Maine 04101
207-871-9170
www.miyakerestaurants.com

Angler on the upper river. New Hampshire Fish and Game

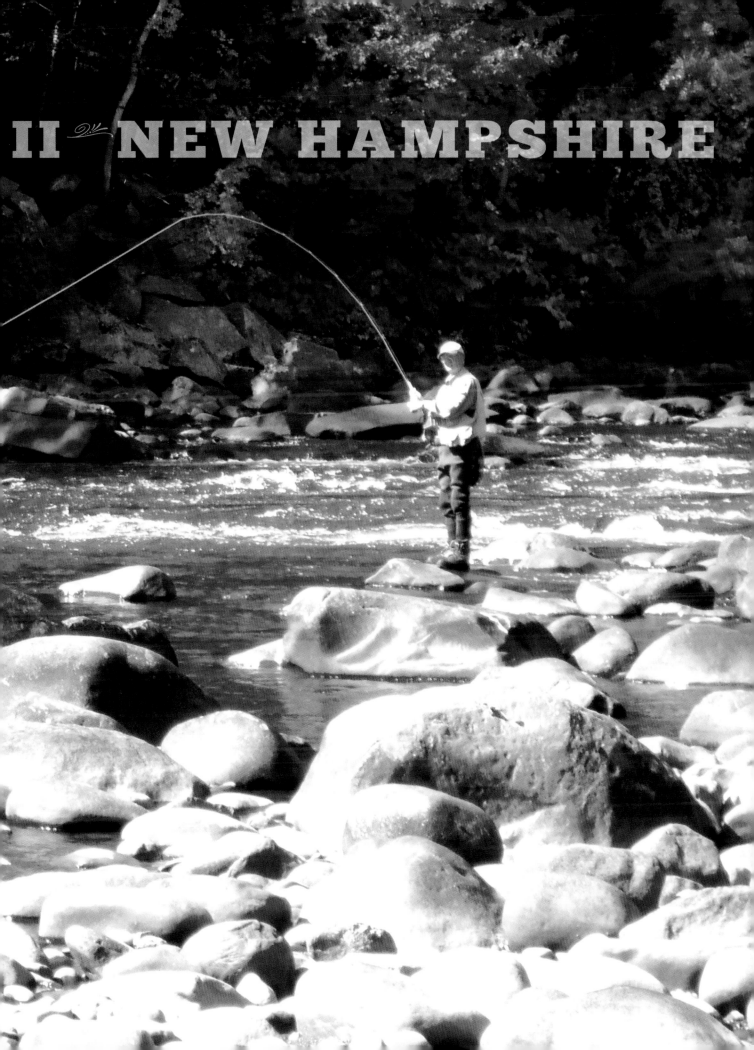

II · NEW HAMPSHIRE

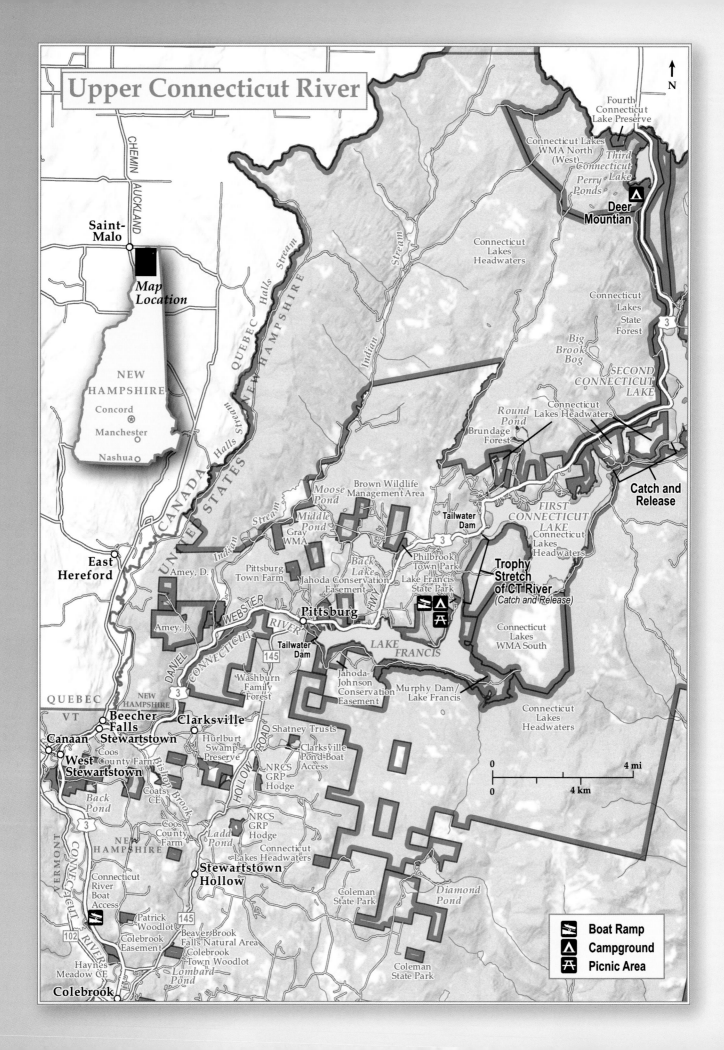

Upper Connecticut River

Saint-Malo

Map Location

NEW HAMPSHIRE

Concord

Manchester

Nashua

CHEMIN AUCKLAND

QUEBEC

Halls Stream

Halls Stream

NEW HAMPSHIRE

Indian Stream

CANADA

UNITED STATES

Indian Stream

East Hereford

Amey, D.

Amey, J.

DANIEL WEBSTER

CONNECTICUT RIVER

Moose Pond

Middle Pond

Gray WMA

Pittsburg Town Farm

Jahoda Conservation Easement

Back Lake

Brown Wildlife Management Area

Tailwater Dam

3

Philbrook Town Park

Lake Francis State Park

Trophy Stretch of CT River
(Catch and Release)

Fourth Connecticut Lake Preserve

Connecticut Lakes WMA North (West)

Third Connecticut Lake

Perry Ponds

Deer Mountian

Connecticut Lakes Headwaters

Connecticut Lakes State Forest

Big Brook Bog

SECOND CONNECTICUT LAKE

Round Pond

Brundage Forest

Connecticut Lakes Headwaters

Catch and Release

FIRST CONNECTICUT LAKE

Connecticut Lakes Headwaters

Connecticut Lakes WMA South

145

Tailwater Dam

Pittsburg

HWY

LAKE FRANCIS

Jahoda-Johnson Conservation Easement

Murphy Dam/ Lake Francis

Connecticut Lakes Headwaters

QUEBEC
VT

NEW HAMPSHIRE

Beecher Falls

Canaan

Stewartstown

West Stewartstown

3

Washburn Family Forest

Hurlburt Swamp Preserve

HOLLOW ROAD

Shatney Trusts

Clarksville Pond Boat Access

Clarksville

Coos County Farm

Coats CE

Bishop Brook

Coos County Farm

Ladd Pond

NRCS GRP Hodge

NRCS GRP Hodge

Connecticut Lakes Headwaters

Coleman State Park

Diamond Pond

VERMONT

Back Pond

3

NEW HAMPSHIRE

Stewartstown Hollow

Connecticut River Boat Access

102

CONNECTICUT RIVER

145

Patrick Woodlot

Colebrook Easement

Haynes Meadow CE

Beaver Brook Falls Natural Area

Colebrook Town Woodlot

Lombard Pond

Coleman State Park

Colebrook

	Boat Ramp
▲	Campground
🏕	Picnic Area

0   4 mi

0   4 km

N

13 · Connecticut River

➤ Location: Northern New Hampshire, about a 4½-hour ride from Boston or Portland, Maine, and a 3½-hour ride from Manchester, New Hampshire. Full-service airports are available in all three cities.

The headwaters of the Connecticut River begin in extreme northern New Hampshire at Fourth Connecticut Lake, in the town of Pittsburg, just a few hundred yards from the U.S.–Canadian border. From this tiny pond, at 2,660 feet elevation, the river begins its 407-mile journey to Long Island Sound. As the river flows south, it passes through a chain of deep, cold bodies of water known as the Connecticut Lakes. Dams below First Connecticut Lake and Lake Francis keep river temps cold right through the summer.

Indian Stream, a tributary to the Connecticut River below Lake Francis in Pittsburg, was once the site of the Republic of Indian Stream. This small community of just a few hundred citizens, with its own government and constitution, was extant in the early to mid-1830s. The existence of this independent republic was due to a border dispute—or more accurately, a lack of clarity—between Canada and the United States. The republic ceased to operate in 1835, when it was occupied by the New Hampshire Militia. The area was first settled under a land grant from King Philip, or Metacom, son of the famous Wampanoag sachem Massasoit. This adds to its already colorful history.

The Upper Connecticut River has three very different sections of interest to anglers. From below Second Connecticut Lake dam to First Lake, the river is small. This 2½-mile stretch is roughly 15 to 20 feet wide, with average stream flows between 60 and 90 cfs. Home to wild landlocked salmon and brook trout, this freestone section features riffles, pools, and a unique pond area where Dry Brook enters

the river. A recently opened section, the Cohos Trail, gives anglers good access. While small brook trout and salmon populate the river year-round, salmon come into the lower section in the spring to feed on spawning smelt. In the fall, large salmon return to this area of river to spawn, providing anglers with an opportunity to catch fish in the 15- to 22-inch range. Here, the regulations are fly fishing only and catch-and-release, from the dam downstream to the bridge on Magalloway Road. From the bridge to Green's Point on

Trophy stretch above the Jury Box pool. Tim Savard

First Connecticut Lake, it's fly fishing only, with a two-fish, 15-inch minimum length limit on salmon; and a two-fish limit on brook trout with no length limit.

Spring fishing is best done with streamers or nymphs. Spawning salmon in the fall will chase quickly retrieved streamers and small wets, as well as dead-drifted caddis dries. Small brook trout and salmon will take terrestrials, attractors, and other dry flies all summer.

Below the dam at First Connecticut Lake is the popular Trophy Stretch of the Connecticut River. The river widens here, with average summer flows of between 150 and 300 cfs.

The riffles, runs, and pools here are easily waded. The consistent releases from the dam provide cold water for trout and salmon. Conservation easements ensure angler access to this nearly 2-mile stretch of river. The river here has brook trout, brown trout, and rainbow trout, along with landlocked salmon. Trout and salmon are present throughout the summer, with large salmon entering the river in the spring to feed on smelts, and in the fall, during their annual spawning run. Famous pools such as Judge's, Doc's, Junction, and Bridge fish well throughout the season. These pools can be fished with nymphs, dries, and streamers. Fly-fishing-only regulations are in effect in this section. There is a daily limit of two fish. Trout must be over 12 inches, and salmon must be over 15. It is, however, rare to see anyone keep a fish here.

The dam at Lake Francis, the last in the chain of lakes, is a bottom-release structure that provides cold water for the river below. Water temperatures rarely exceed 50 degrees. This keeps the river cold enough for trout for roughly 30 miles. Typical flows in this stretch of river range from 300 to 600 cfs. There are no special regulations on this section, and bag limits for trout are five fish, or 5 pounds, whichever comes first. Walk-in access is easy here, as the river parallels U.S. Route 3 south through Pittsburg and Clarksville. Below the bridge, in West Stewartstown, the river begins to widen and access becomes more difficult for wading anglers. While some wade-fishing opportunities exist, the river here is best floated. There are numerous boat launches offering several different float-trip options. The river widens and slows as it works its way toward Colebrook and Columbia. Steep cutbanks and deep pools are the norm, with just a couple of Class II rapids to negotiate along the way. This section can produce some excellent dry-fly fishing when fish are looking up. Streamers cast to the bank and stripped back quickly can do the trick when fish are not looking up, or on overcast days, during high-water periods, or when the river is running off-colored.

➤ Hatches: Hatches usually start on the Connecticut sometime around mid-May. On warmer overcast afternoons you may find salmon rising to Blue-winged Olives in the upper section below Magalloway Bridge. Caddis and mayflies start to appear in early June on all sections. Caddis are the prevalent insects on the Upper Connecticut. It is not unusual to bring fish to the surface with a well-presented Elk-hair, even without a hatch. Late June and early July bring more mayflies, caddis, and stoneflies, in particular Little Yellow Sallies, while late August and September evenings bring the arrival of large stoneflies. Small Blue-winged Olives and caddis dominate the lower section of the Connecticut. During the last two weeks of August, a prolific hatch of Cinnamon Flying Ants occurs in the Colebrook and Columbia area.

Brook trout from the trophy stretch in the Judges Pool. Tim Savard

The Upper Connecticut River is located in a rugged, unspoiled region teeming with fish and wildlife. Moose sightings are common. That this is within just a few short hours of Boston is actually quite amazing.

➤ Tackle: A 9-foot 5-weight rod with a floating line is your best bet for the Connecticut River most of the time. If you want to fish streamers, a 9-foot 6-weight with a fast-sinking sink-tip is your best option. Dry-fly fishing is best done with a 9-foot 4-weight, as you may need to drop to 6X to effectively fish smaller patterns such as BWOs. While rods longer than 9 feet can work, especially for nymphing, rods shorter than 9 feet are not practical. Strike indicators should be large enough to float two flies and added weight. Fluorocarbon tippet is recommended. Flies should include Woolly Buggers, sculpin and smelt patterns, and all stages of mayflies, stoneflies, and caddis in a variety of sizes and colors.

TIM SAVARD and his wife Lisa are the former owners of Lopstick Lodge and Cabins and Lopstick Outfitters in Pittsburg, New Hampshire. An accomplished photographer, rod builder, and fly tier, Tim has fished the Upper Connecticut River for more than 30 years, 16 as a fly-fishing guide. Tim and Lisa have fished extensively in the American West, New Brunswick, and Central America. After 22 years of living the dream, they are retiring to their cabin on Rock Creek in Montana.

CLOSEST FLY SHOPS
Lopstick Outfitters
First Connecticut Lake
45 Stewart Young Road
Pittsburg, New Hampshire 03592
800-538-6659
www.cabinsatlopstick.com
lopstick@gmail.com

CLOSEST GUIDES/OUTFITTERS
Northern Rivers Guide Service
Tall Timber Lodge and Cabins
609 Beach Road
Pittsburg, New Hampshire 03592
800-835-6343
www.talltimber.com
jhowe@wildblue.net

Osprey Adventures
Columbia, New Hampshire 03576
603-922-3800
www.ospreyfishingadventures.com

CLOSEST LODGING
Cabins at Lopstick
First Connecticut Lake
45 Stewart Young Road
Pittsburg, New Hampshire 03592
800-538-6659
www.cabinsatlopstick.com
lopstick@gmail.com

Tall Timber Lodge and Cabins
609 Beach Road
Pittsburg, New Hampshire 03592
800-835-6343
www.talltimber.com
vacation@talltimber.com

CLOSEST RESTAURANTS
Rainbow Grille & Tavern
609 Beach Road
Pittsburg, New Hampshire 03592
603-538-9556
www.rainbowgrille.com
vacation@talltimber.com

Buck Rub Pizza Pub
Main Street
Pittsburg, New Hampshire 03592
603-538-6935
www.buckrubpub.com
buckrub@mindspring.com

Dube's Pit Stop
Breakfast and Lunch
Main Street
Pittsburg, New Hampshire 03592
603-538-9944

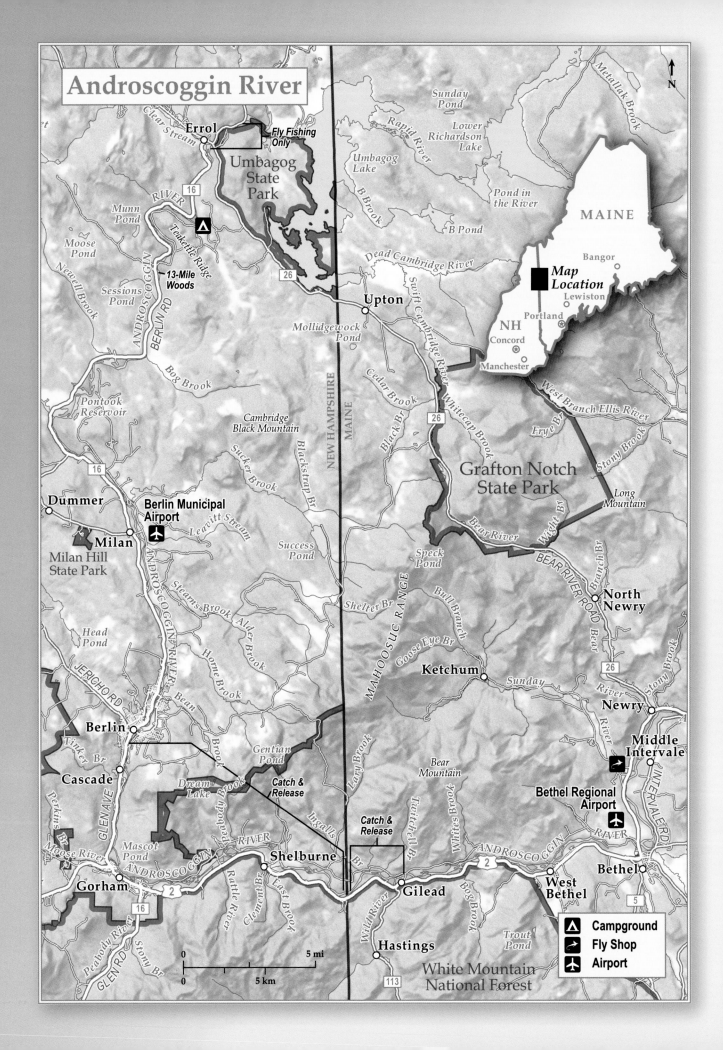

14 · Androscoggin River *(trout)*

➤ **Location:** Northern New Hampshire into western Maine, about 3 hours from Manchester; 2½ hours from Portland, Maine; and 3½ hours from Boston, Massachusetts. Full-service airports are available in all three cities.

The Androscoggin River begins at Lake Umbagog in Errol, New Hampshire. Named after an Abenaki tribe, the river runs approximately 50 miles before crossing into Maine. Within Maine there is another 8 or so miles of quality trout water. Below here fishing is limited to the mouths of coldwater tributaries. Along with the Connecticut, Kennebec, Merrimack, Penobscot, and Saco Rivers, the Androscoggin is one of the largest watersheds in New England.

The Andro, as it is called locally, is a large river. With classic riffles, runs, and pools, it is a great river to fly fish. In most areas the river is large enough for floating—and this is often the best way to fish it. The river can, however, be waded and public access is very good. From its densely forested 13 Mile Woods, to pastoral farmlands, to views of towering Mount Washington—the highest point in New England—in its lower reaches, the Androscoggin is also a beautiful river.

Several sections of the Androscoggin warrant the attention of fly fishers. They are accessible from Route 16 between Errol and Gorham, New Hampshire; and Route 2 between Gorham and Bethel, Maine. First is Errol Dam to Bragg Bay—a section of less than a mile. This is the lone fly-fishing-only section on the river. The next is Bragg Bay to Pontook Reservoir—including the fabled 13 Mile Woods. At over 20 miles, the section from Sawmill Dam in Berlin to the Maine border is the longest stretch of catch-and-release water in New England. The last is from the New Hampshire border to Bethel, Maine—this includes a stretch of catch-and-release water from the New Hampshire border to Gilead, Maine.

The section of the Androscoggin below Errol Dam, known for its large landlocked salmon and brook trout, is very popular with fly anglers. People come from all over the Northeast to fish here. Brown and rainbow trout are also present.

Between Mollidgewock Campground and Seven Islands Bridge—the 13 Mile Woods—the Androscoggin is ideally suited for drift boat fishing. This area is very lightly developed and known for its large brown, rainbow, and brook trout.

From Berlin and the Maine border, feeder streams such as Moose River and Peabody River provide cold water to the Androscoggin. This section is not stocked, and the fish are mostly wild. Rainbow trout, brown trout, and brook trout are all present. Some large fish are encountered here.

Between the New Hampshire border and Bethel, Maine, the Androscoggin picks up one of its largest tributaries—the Wild River. The confluence is located within a catch-and-release section and is popular with wade-in anglers. This is

Below Wild River in Gilead, Maine. Luke Gray

also a popular float fishery. This section boasts rainbows, browns, and some brook trout, including some large ones.

The best time to fish the Androscoggin is between mid-May and mid-July, and again from Labor Day until late fall—or where applicable, when the season closes. In late July and August, anglers should focus their efforts on early mornings

Thirteen Mile Woods in Errol, New Hampshire. Bill Barnhardt

New Hampshire brook trout. Ken Hastings

and late evenings. Midsummer days are best left to other recreationists such as canoers, kayakers, and tubers.

Ideal flows for fishing the Androscoggin are from 1,500 to 3,500 cfs. Below 1,500 cfs, while the river can be easily waded, floaters will have difficulty negotiating the rocks and gravel bars. Above 3,500 cfs, wading can become both difficult and dangerous. Float fishers may have difficulty holding an anchor at these high levels as well.

The Androscoggin is one of the best-known trout rivers in New England—and for good reason. It offers fly fishers a variety of conditions, multiple species, solid hatches, good public access, and some truly large fish in a beautiful setting. From Errol, New Hampshire to Bethel, Maine, most of the river supports trout. Next time you are in the area, give it a try.

➤ **Regulations:** The Androscoggin is open from January 1 through October 15 from Errol to Berlin, New Hampshire. Below Berlin—and into Maine—it is open year-round. From Errol Dam to Brag Bay, the river is restricted to fly fishing only. From Berlin to the Maine border, the river is restricted to artificial lures only and barbless hooks. Below Errol Dam there is a two-fish limit on trout and salmon, with a 12-inch and 15-inch minimum length limit, respectively. From Bragg Bay to Berlin, the limit on trout is 5 fish or 5 pounds—whichever comes first. From Berlin to Gilead, Maine, the river is catch-and-release. Below Gilead it has a one-fish limit and a slot limit that protects fish between 16 and 20 inches. The water covered in this chapter crosses state lines. From Umbagog Lake to Shelburne, a New Hampshire license is required. From there down, a Maine license is required.

➤ **Hatches:** Caddis are the most common insects on the Androscoggin. They start hatching in late May and continue throughout the summer and into the fall. Most evenings see a hatch. Mayflies are also present—including Blue-winged Olives, Sulphurs, and Hendricksons. Hendricksons hatch in late May and run for a week or so. Sulphurs hatch on and off all spring. Blue-winged Olives can be found anytime, but especially in the fall. Stoneflies are also very important. Fish gorge themselves on them when they are available. The river also has a solid baitfish population which includes sculpin, fallfish, and dace.

The upper Androscoggin is famous for its Alderfly, or Zebra Caddis, hatch, which occurs in late June. It usually starts around the third week of June, and runs for approximately 2 weeks. This large, mottled-winged caddis is a beautiful insect. During the hatch, caddis will swarm around the alders that overhang the river—hence the name Alderfly. At this time, trout and salmon—including large ones—can be caught on dry flies.

Nymph fishing is arguably the most effective way to catch trout on the Androscoggin. Two-fly rigs under an indicator, in conjunction with the right amount of weight, are best. Dry-dropper rigs work as well. The Androscoggin is also a good streamer river—especially when fishing from a boat. In

Dennis Fay with New Hampshire brook trout. Ed Hermaneau

addition, the Andro offers some very good dry-fly fishing—it gets good hatches, and fish feed on the surface eagerly during these times.

➤ **Tackle:** A 9-foot 5-weight rod with a floating line is your best bet for the Androscoggin most of the time. If you want to fish streamers, a 9-foot 6-weight with a fast-sinking tip is your best option. Dry-fly fishing is best done with a 9-foot 4-weight, as you may need to drop to 6X to effectively fish smaller patterns such as BWOs. While rods longer than 9 feet can work, especially for nymphing, rods shorter than 9 feet are not practical. Strike indicators should be large enough to float two flies and added weight. Flies should include Woolly Buggers and sculpin imitations, and all stages of mayflies, stoneflies, and caddis in a variety of sizes and colors.

JON HOWE owns and operates Northern Rivers Guide Service at Tall Timber Lodge in Pittsburg, New Hampshire. He has guided for more than 20 years, and runs both wade and float trips. Jon also worked at North Country Angler in North Conway, New Hampshire. He can be reached at 800-835-6343, jhowe@wildblue.net, or www.talltimber.com.

CLOSEST FLY SHOPS

L.L. Cote
7 Main Street
Errol, New Hampshire 03579
800-287-7700
www.llcote.com

North Country Angler
2888 White Mountain Highway
North Conway, New Hampshire 03860
603-356-6000
www.northcountryangler.com
shop@northcountryangler.com

Sun Valley Sports
129 Sunday River Road
Bethel, Maine 04217
207-824-7533
www.sunvalleysports.com
svs@sunvalleysports.com

CLOSEST GUIDES/OUTFITTERS

Northern Rivers Guide Service
Tall Timber Lodge and Cabins
609 Beach Road
Pittsburg, New Hampshire 03592
800-835-6343
www.talltimber.com
jhowe@wildblue.net

Hill Country Guide Service
Conway, New Hampshire 03818
508-498-1304
www.whitemountainflyfishing.com
info@whitemountainflyfishing.com

Osprey Fishing Adventures
Colebrook, New Hampshire 03576
603-922-3800
www.ospreyfishingadventures.com
ospreynh@wildblue.net

Locke Mountain Guide Service
Newry, Maine 04261
207-381-7322
www.lockemountainguideservice.com
lockemoutainguide@gmail.com

CLOSEST LODGING

Tall Timber Lodge and Cabins
609 Beach Road
Pittsburg, New Hampshire 03592
800-835-6343
www.talltimber.com
vacation@talltimber.com

Errol Motel
Route 26
Errol, New Hampshire 03579
603-482-3256
www.Errol-Motel.com

Town and Country Inn
20 State Route 2
Gorham, New Hampshire 03581
603-466-3315
www.townandcountryinn.com
info@townandcountryinn.com

Philbrook Farm Inn
Rooms & Cottages
881 North Road
Shelburne, New Hampshire 03581
603-466-3831
www.philbrookfarminn.com

River View Resort
Route 2
Bethel, Maine 04217
207-824-2808
www.riverviewresort.com
info@riverviewresort.com

CLOSEST RESTAURANTS

Hawg Trawf
Pub Style Lunch & Dinner
39 Colebrook Road
Errol, New Hampshire 03579
603-482-3665
hawg.trawf@yahoo.com

Bull Moose Restaurant and Lounge
Family Style Lunch & Dinner
Route 26
Cambridge, New Hampshire 03579
603-482-3856
www.bullmoosenh.com
Info@bullmoosenh.com

Libby's Bistro & SAALT Pub
Fine Dining
115 Main Street
Gorham, New Hampshire 03581
603-466-5330
www.libbysbistro.org

Rooster's Roadhouse
159 Mayville Road Route 2
Bethel, Maine 04217
207-824-0309
www.roostersroadhouse.com
roostersroadhouse2004@yahoo.com

Cho Sun
Japanese & Korean Cuisine
141 Main Street
Bethel, Maine 04217
207-824-7370
www.chosunrestaurant.com
lanechosun@hotmail.com

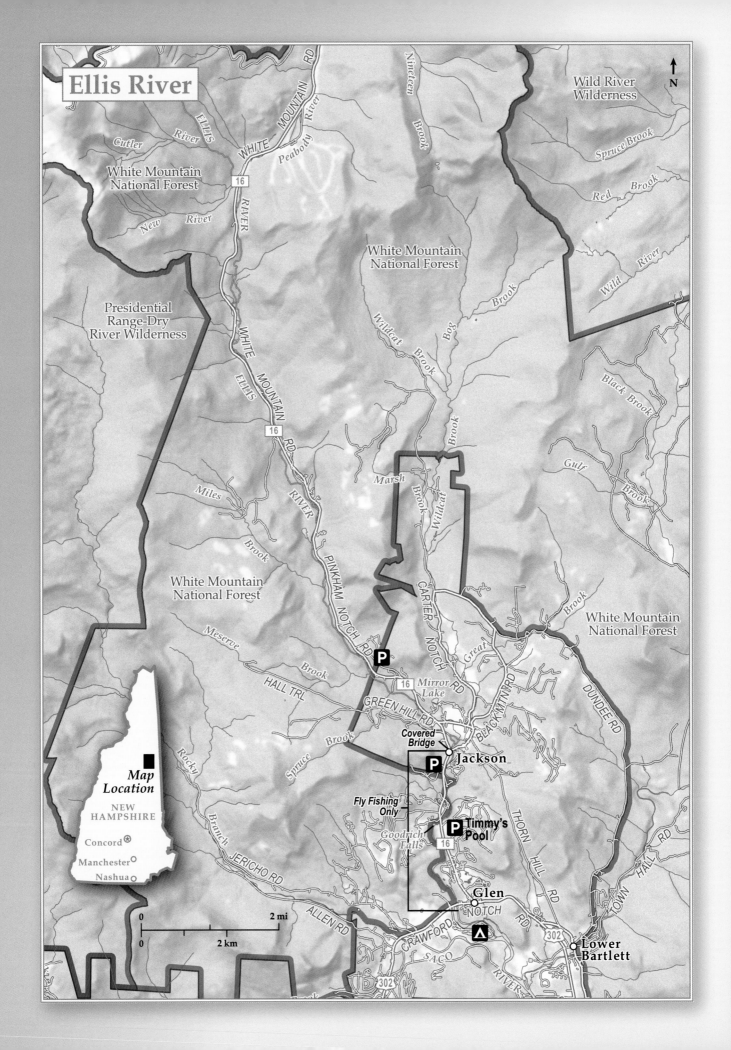

➤ **Location:** White Mountains of Northeastern New Hampshire, a 3½-hour drive from Boston, Massachusetts, and a 1½-hour drive from Portland, Maine. Full-service airports are available in both cities.

The Ellis River has long been a popular destination with fly fishers. Emanating from the famous, remote, hike-in ski trails of Mount Washington—the highest point in New England—the Ellis River was a favorite fishing spot of well-known Appalachian Mountain Club hut master Joe Dodge. Since Joe's time, the Ellis has been the choice of anglers seeking swift, gin-clear water.

The Ellis is a beautiful river. It begins at approximately 4,600 feet above sea level near the famous Tuckerman and Huntington Ravines of rugged Mount Washington. From here it runs roughly 17 miles and descends over 4,000 feet before terminating at the Saco River in Glen. The Ellis is joined by the Cutler River at 2,400 feet, and the New River at just over 2,000 feet. Below here it parallels Route 16, tumbles over the 60-foot Glen Ellis Falls, and continues its steep descent. This stretch, which extends to Jackson village, is the quintessential New England mountain stream. Mica-flecked granite boulders glisten under the stream's crystal-clear flow. The water teems with brightly colored brook trout.

While the upper reaches drop through staircase rapids and plunge pools as the Ellis weaves its way through Pinkham Notch, it changes to peaceful glides before entering Jackson Village. The fish found here are primarily wild brook trout ranging from 4 to 8 inches, with some stocked brook trout up to 12 inches mixed in.

While the upper river is popular with small-stream enthusiasts, most fly fishers focus their efforts on the fly-fishing-only section on the lower river. This section begins at the famous Honeymoon Covered Bridge in Jackson and extends down to the train trestle just downstream of the Route 302 bridge in Glen. Below here is a short stretch of unregulated water. Here the Ellis is a medium-size freestone river. There are large pools and boulder-strewn runs. This includes the

well-known Timmy's Pool, located where Route 16 crosses the river. This section contains both wild brook trout and stocked rainbow trout. Fish average a foot in length, with trout to 18 inches common. Fish larger than this are caught each year. There are few places in New England where fish this large are caught in water this small.

Fish in the Ellis start feeding when the blackflies start biting. Most years this begins around Memorial Day. With the exception of unusually warm years, the fly-fishing-only section remains productive throughout the summer. The upper section of the river fishes best during the dog days of summer, when trout seek out its coldwater refuge. While some rivers, like the nearby Saco, fish well at high flows, the Ellis does not. I prefer to fish the river at flows below 50 cfs. I find that fishing becomes less productive when the flow exceeds

Bob Mallard below Goodrich Falls. Diana Mallard

50 cfs. Fortunately, when the river does come up, it comes down just as fast. When it drops, the fish are eager to make up for lost time.

➤ **Regulations:** The Ellis River is restricted to fly fishing only from the Honeymoon Covered Bridge in Jackson and downstream to the train trestle just below the Route 302 bridge in Glen. The fishing season on the Ellis closes October 15.

Upper river pocket water. Fly Fish America
Inset. Upper river brook trout. Hill Country Guide Service

➤ **Hatches:** The Ellis has a wide variety of forage for fish. A seine will reveal a diverse selection of caddis, mayfly, and stonefly nymphs. Starting in late May or early June, the first hatches are Green Caddis, Gray Drake mayflies, and dark midges. On colder days, with no hatches, Woolly Buggers and Muddler Minnows will produce fish. As June progresses, Grey Fox (Cahill) mayflies, Yellow Sally stoneflies, and Tan Caddis become important. Some years, one insect seems more predominant than others, while in other years, they are of equal importance.

With July comes terrestrial season. On bright sunny days, trout will take well-presented ant and beetle patterns. This time of the year sees sporadic hatches of Golden Stoneflies and Pale Evening Duns. While these not as prolific as on some other rivers, there are often enough stones to get the trout looking up. At the first sign of stones, I quickly switch to a large Stimulator or some other stonefly imitation. Fished through the faster runs and riffles, these will result in aggres-

sive takes. Be sure to downsize your tippet, as I have seen more than one angler break off an exploding rainbow trout on the hook-set. At these times, look for Pale Evening Duns to come off just before dark. Low-profile patterns such as Klinkhammers and Compara-duns work best.

The Ellis is also a very good nymphing river. This can be done using an indicator or a dry-dropper combination.

By late August, flying ants become the insects of choice. Swarms of ants begin showing up in the last two weeks of August and can last until late September. They can be sporadic and of varying levels of intensity. But when the ant drop is strong, every fish in the river will be looking up. Chocolate-colored ants with white to gray wings in sizes 18 to 22 and cinnamon- to honey-colored ants in sizes 14 to 18 are your best bets. Ants can appear at any time of the day. Typically the larger females arrive before the smaller males. Look for large, slow pools, as this is where the fish will congregate to take advantage of this late summer feast. If you do not get strikes right away, be patient—your impostor has many real ants to compete with.

September can provide challenging dry-fly fishing with small Blue-winged Olives and midges. The trout have been well educated by this time of the year, and catching them presents a real challenge. At this time, light leaders and tippets are a must.

During the last few weeks of the season, the brook trout begin their prespawn activity and can become difficult to find.

If you are looking for a classic medium-size freestone river with the potential for catching a large trout, the middle and lower Ellis is a good place to try. For those looking for a small-stream experience, the upper river and its tributaries provide miles of solitude and wild native brook trout.

➤ **Tackle:** A 9-foot 5-weight rod with a floating line is your best bet for the lower Ellis. If you want to fish streamers, a 9-foot 6-weight with a sinking sink tip is your best option. Dry-fly fishing is best done with a 9-foot 4-weight as you may need to drop to 6X to effectively fish smaller patterns such as Blue-winged Olives. Rods longer than 9 feet can work, especially for nymphing. Shorter, 6- to 7½-foot, rods in 2- to 4-weight are a good idea in for the upper river. Strike indicators should be large enough to float two flies and added weight. Flies should include Woolly Buggers, sculpin patterns; and all stages of mayflies, stoneflies, and caddis in a variety of sizes and colors.

Two anglers fish Goodrich Falls. North Country Angler

NATE HILL asked for a fly rod for Christmas when he was 11 years old so that he could fish the Ellis River. He has fished the river ever since and guided on it for the past 6 years. He has a passion for finding wild trout waters in and around the Mount Washington Valley. He owns and operates Hill Country Guide Service in Conway, New Hampshire and can be reached at 508-498-1304, www.whitemountainfly fishing.com, or nate@whitemountainflyfishing.com.

CLOSEST FLY SHOPS

North Country Angler
2888 White Mountain Highway
North Conway, New Hampshire 03860
603-356-6000
www.northcountryangler.com
shop@northcountryangler.com

CLOSEST GUIDES/OUTFITTERS

Hill Country Guide Service
208 Quint Street
Conway, New Hampshire 03818
508-498-1304
www.whitemountainflyfishing.com
nate@whitemountainflyfishing.com

CLOSEST LODGING

RiverWood Inn (rooms & suites)
49 Main Street
Jackson, New Hampshire 03846
603-383-6666
www.riverwoodinn-jackson.com
innkeepers@riverwood-jackson.com

Nordic Village Resort
Route 16
Jackson, New Hampshire 03846
603-383-9101
www.nordicvillage.com
res@nordicvillage.com

Stonehurst Manor (rooms, suites, and condos)
3351 White Mountain Highway
North Conway, New Hampshire 03860
800-525-9100
www.stonehurstmanor.com
smanor@aol.com

North Conway Mountain Inn
2114 White Mountain Highway
North Conway, New Hampshire 03860
800-319-4405
www.northconwaymountaininn.com

The Bartlett Inn
Bed & Breakfast, Cabins
1477 U.S. Route 302
Bartlett, New Hampshire 03812
800-292-2353
www.bartlettinn.com
stay@bartlettinn.com

CLOSEST RESTAURANTS

Delaney's Hole In The Wall
(pub-style food and sushi)
2966 White Mountain Highway
North Conway, New Hampshire 03860
603-356-7776
www.delaneys.com
delaneys@delaneys.com

Stonehurst Manor (see above)

Thompson House Eatery
193 Main Street
Jackson, New Hampshire 03846
603-383-9341
www.thompsonhouseeatery.com

Red Fox Bar & Grille
(full menu and breakfast buffet)
Route 16
Jackson, New Hampshire 03846
603-383-4949
www.redfoxpub.com

The Shannon Door Restaurant & Pub
Route 16
Jackson, NH 03846
603-383-4211
www.shannondoor.com
nbean@roadrunner.com

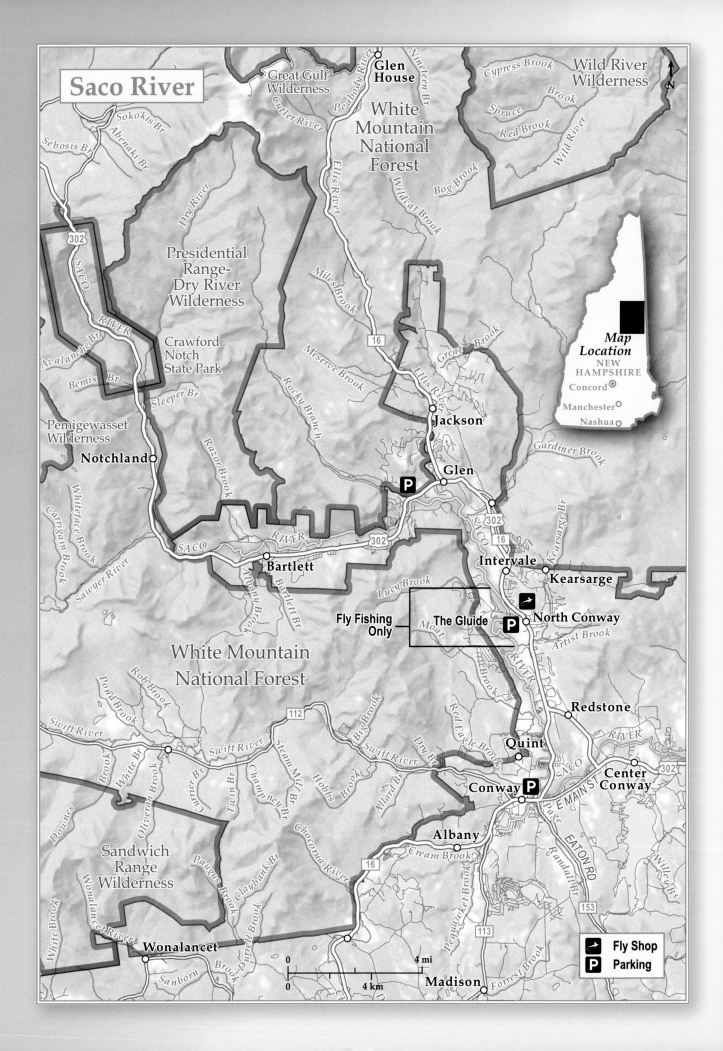

16 · Saco River

➤ **Location:** Northeast New Hampshire, about a 3-hour ride from Boston, Massachusetts; about a 1½-hour ride from Portland, Maine and Manchester, New Hampshire. Full-service airports are available in all three cities.

The Saco River has long been a destination for artists, writers, and anglers. In the 1800s, landscape artists came to the area to capture the beauty of the Saco Valley, giving rise to the White Mountain School of Art. Benjamin Champney, a New Hampshire native, is considered by many to be the founder of the movement. Today you can still recognize the locations of many of his paintings, as the valley has changed little. John Greenleaf Whittier and Nathanial Hawthorne traveled extensively in the White Mountains and strived to capture their mystery and legend in prose and poetry. Over the centuries, anglers have also come to the Valley in search of the quality trout fishing.

The Saco begins in historic Crawford Notch. From its source at tiny Saco Lake to the Maine border, it drops 1,500 feet in elevation in just 40 miles. Within New Hampshire, the watershed is roughly 427 square miles. Eighty percent of it is within the White Mountain National Forest. For much of its upper reaches, Route 302 parallels the river. This is one of New Hampshire's most scenic drives. The upper river flows through a beautiful and rugged valley, which includes the historic Willey House. Across from this is the only dam—a tiny structure—on the Saco within New Hampshire.

The upper river is a small mountain stream. Here you will find wild brook trout. The Dry River and Sawyer River empty into the Saco in this section. Both hold brook trout for those willing to hike. The Sawyer Ponds at the headwaters of the Sawyer River is a popular fishing destination as well. Below here, the Rocky Branch and Ellis River enter the Saco. The former is a good wild brook trout stream. The latter is one of the area's finest trout fisheries. The last major tributary is the East Branch, also an excellent brook trout fishery.

The portion of the Saco of most interesting to fly fishers is the fly-fishing-only section in North Conway. This begins at Lucy Brook and ends at Mill Brook, also called Artist Falls Brook. This section is less than 3 miles long, but offers some of the best fishing in the area. It can be accessed from First Bridge in North Conway. The river here is much wider than the boulder-strewn mountain creek found upstream. Mostly short gravel riffs and long glides, the river is bordered by forest and farmland. To the west are the Moat Mountains. To the east is Cranmore Mountain. Despite the bustling tourist-town of North Conway, the river feels quite remote.

Chris Major above The Glide. Fly Fish America

The Saco River is heavily stocked by New Hampshire Fish and Game and the local Trout Unlimited chapter, Saco Valley Anglers. Some fish hold over. Brook trout, rainbow trout, and brown trout are all present. The river is known for its large browns. Specimens over 18 inches are always possible, and fish much larger have been caught. There are also some huge rainbows in the 2-foot range.

Below Mill Brook, access becomes a problem for walk-in fishermen. However, it is possible to canoe this section.

Above. Photo courtesy of Fly Fish America

Inset. Nate Hill with large brown trout.
Milan Krainchich

Much of the river is quite shallow, but there are some very deep pools worth casting a line into.

In Conway, the Swift River enters the Saco from the west. The Swift River rises in Kancamagus Notch and follows Route 112, known as the Kancamagus Highway—the most famous scenic drive in New England. The Swift is a quality trout stream in its own right. The confluence of these two rivers is one of the best sections to fish. After that, the river swings east and heads to the Maine border and its journey to the sea. There are some deep pools in this section that hold some large trout and are worth exploring.

The best time to fish the Saco is June and July, and then again in September through the end of the season in mid-October. Before Memorial Day, the river is generally running high as a result of snowmelt. Fishing slows down during August due to low flows and warm water.

➤ **Regulations:** The Saco River is restricted to fly fishing only from Lucy Brook to Mill Brook. Above and below this stretch it is open under general rules.

➤ **Hatches:** The most important hatch on the Saco is the Gray Drake (*Siphlonurus*), beginning the last week of May and running through mid-July. Most size 12 Red Quill patterns will work. The evening spinner fall is the most important stage of the hatch. Duns are rarely seen, for reasons that are unclear. Anglers familiar with the river fish late. At times the spinner fall is delayed until morning. A masking hatch of *Mirus* spinners will sometimes come off at the same time. The *Mirus* are closely related, but differ in color, having a yellow abdomen with dark bands and a distinctive chocolate brown secondary wing. It is important to have both patterns with you. The fall brings some Blue-winged Olives.

Fish can also be caught on the Saco using terrestrials. This is especially true in late spring, summer, and early fall. Hoppers, ants, and crickets cast tight to the bank, around structure, and near midriver seams can produce action. Streamer fishing can be productive as well. Like terrestrials, they are best fished near structure and tight to the bank where the fish are hiding during the day. Nymphing is always possible, but not usually your best bet.

➤ **Tackle:** A 9-foot 5-weight rod with a floating line is your best bet for the lower Saco River. Shorter and lighter rods can be used on the upper river. If you want to fish streamers, a 9-foot 6-weight with a fast-sinking sink-tip is your best option. Dry-fly fishing is best done with a 9-foot 4-weight, as you may need to drop to 6X to effectively fish smaller patterns such as BWOs. Flies should include Woolly Buggers, sculpin patterns, and all stages of mayflies, stoneflies, and caddis in a variety of sizes and colors.

The town of North Conway is a gateway to the White Mountains, and by most definitions the premier rural New England tourist destination. In the late spring and summer, the Saco is best fished in the early morning or late in the day. This helps you avoid the inevitable recreationists who also use the river. This is also important due to the fact that the river runs gin-clear and the trout are easily spooked.

Many anglers pass by the Saco en route to more famous destinations such as the Connecticut Lakes in northern New Hampshire, or the Rangeley Region of Maine. They have no idea what they are missing!

Bob Mallard with spring brook trout. Chris Major

BILL THOMPSON, along with his wife Janet, owns North Country Angler in North Conway, New Hampshire. They have fished the Saco for over 30 years. Both are licensed New Hampshire guides. They have fished extensively in the Western United States and Canada. Bill writes a weekly column on fly fishing for the *Conway Daily Sun,* and a monthly column for the *New Hampshire/Vermont Outdoor Gazette.* Bill has also written articles for *Fly Tying* and *Fly Tyer* magazines. He can be reached at 603-256-6000 or www.northcountryangler.com.

CLOSEST FLY SHOPS
North Country Angler
2888 White Mountain Highway
North Conway, New Hampshire 03860
603-356-6000
www.northcountryangler.com
shop@northcountryangler.com

CLOSEST GUIDES/OUTFITTERS
Hill Country Guide Service
208 Quint Street
Conway, New Hampshire 03860
508-498-1304
www.whitemountainflyfishing.com
nate@whitemountainflyfishing.com

CLOSEST LODGING
Stonehurst Manor
3351 White Mountain Highway
North Conway, New Hampshire 03860
800-525-9100
www.stonehurstmanor.com
smanor@aol.com

North Conway Mountain Inn
2114 White Mountain Highway
North Conway, New Hampshire 03860
800-319-4405
www.northconwaymountaininn.com

Nereledge Inn Bed & Breakfast
94 River Road
North Conway, New Hampshire 03860
603-356-2831
www.nereledgeinn.com

The Bartlett Inn
Bed & Breakfast, Cabins
1477 U.S. Route 302
Bartlett, New Hampshire 03812
800-292-2353
www.bartlettinn.com
stay@bartlettinn.com

Nordic Village Resort
Route 16
Jackson, New Hampshire 03846
603-383-9101
nordicvillage.com
res@nordicvillage.com

CLOSEST RESTAURANTS
Delaney's Hole In The Wall
(pub-style food and sushi)
2966 White Mountain Highway
North Conway, New Hampshire 03860
603-356-7776
www.delaneys.com
delaneys@delaneys.com

Stonehurst Manor (see above)

Moat Mountain Smoke House and Brewing Company (pub-style food)
3378 White Mountain Highway
North Conway, New Hampshire 03860
603-356-6381
www.moatmountain.com
info@moatmountain.com

May Kelly's Cottage
Irish Pub
Route 16
North Conway, New Hampshire 03860

Taste of Thai
27 Seavey Street
North Conway, New Hampshire 03860
www.tasteofthai.com

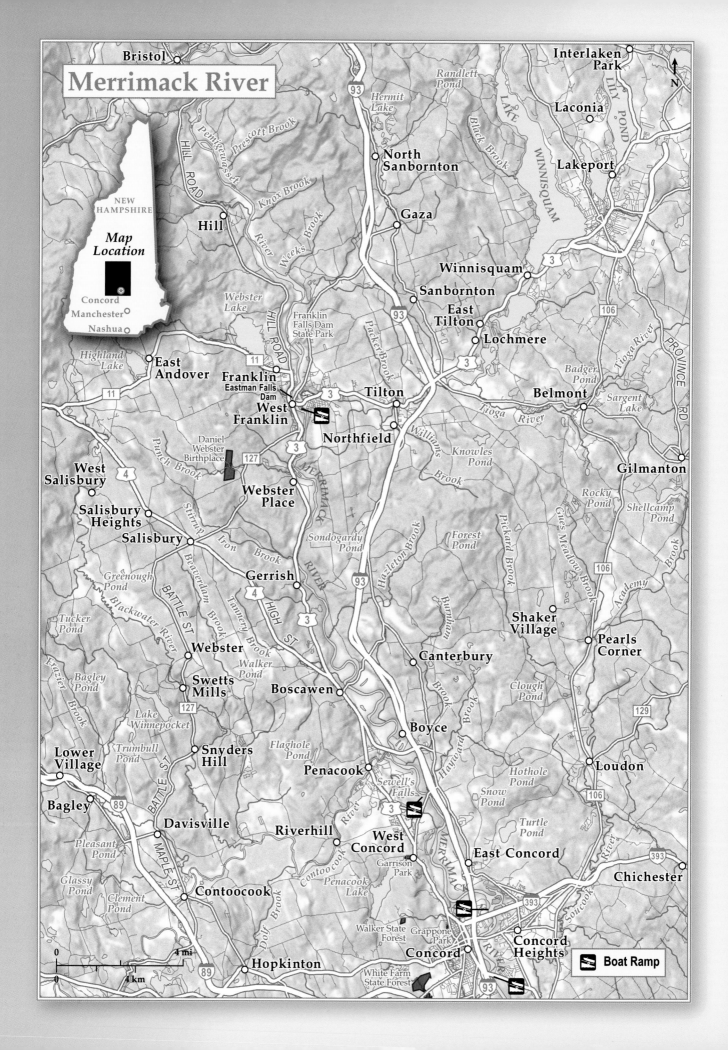

17 · Merrimack River *(Atlantic salmon)*

➤ **Location:** Central New Hampshire, less than an hour from Manchester an hour from Boston, Massachusetts; and 2-hour ride from Portland, Maine. Full-service airports are available in all three cities.

The Northeast was once home to large runs of anadromous Atlantic salmon. Adult salmon returned from the sea annually to spawn in their natal rivers in Massachusetts, New Hampshire, Vermont, and Maine. Some showed up elsewhere under what is called genetic drift—nature's way of maintaining genetic diversity. These salmon helped feed the indigenous populations for countless generations, and provided a critical food supply for the early European settlers.

States such as Maine relied heavily on Atlantic salmon. The salmon brought fly fishermen from all over the country to Maine. Celebrities such as baseball legend Ted Williams and his friend, sportscaster Curt Gowdy, came to Maine just to fish for Atlantic salmon. Salmon clubs—complete with their own clubhouses—were built on banks of rivers such as the Penobscot. For years, the first Atlantic salmon caught each season in Maine went to the President of the United States.

That was before the Northeast's Atlantic salmon population crashed due to dams, pollution, and overharvest by commercial driftnetters. Since then, Atlantic salmon have been listed under the Endangered Species Act. What started with restrictions on the seven Downeast Maine salmon rivers has expanded to include the Penobscot River, and more recently the Kennebec River and Androscoggin River in Maine. Other rivers have been closed to the taking, and even targeting, of salmon as well.

Contrary to popular belief, you can still fly fish for Atlantic salmon in the Northeast—at least in some form, and for now. Thanks to a cooperative effort between the New Hampshire Fish and Game department and the United States Fish and Wildlife Service, with help from local Trout Unlimited chapters, brood stock salmon raised in a federal hatchery in Nashua, New Hampshire, and used in the Merrimack River restoration program are tagged and released into the upper river for anglers to enjoy. While technically classified as endangered, Atlantic salmon released into the Merrimack River can be legally targeted under a special permit system. The money raised by the program is used to help fund Atlantic salmon restoration efforts. The fishery is open year-round, with anglers allowed to keep one fish a day and up to five fish per season.

The Merrimack River brood stock Atlantic salmon program has been in existence since 1993. During this time fly fishers have come to the river for that all-too-rare opportunity to legally catch the king of fish without going to Canada, Scandinavia, or Russia; and within an hour of Boston, Massachusetts and just 30 minutes from Manchester and

Angler on the upper river. New Hampshire Fish and Game

Concord, New Hampshire. Approximately 1,500 salmon a year are stocked into the Merrimack—750 in the spring and 750 in the fall. They average 18 to 30 inches long and 5 to 12 pounds, with fish up to 15 pounds thrown in from time to time. While the long-term future of the program is unclear due to low returns, it should continue—albeit possibly with reduced numbers—through at least 2015. After that, you can expect there will still be a few fish hanging around from previous stockings.

Steve Bowman with spring salmon. New Hampshire Fish and Game

Stocking the upper river. New Hampshire Fish and Game

Other than the tags affixed at the hatchery before release, the Atlantic salmon caught on the Merrimack River look like any other salmon you will encounter. Males demonstrate the pronounced kype on the lower jaw that makes this fish so recognizable. Takes are often jolting, followed by long runs and epic jumps—and no fish caught in fresh water jumps like an Atlantic salmon.

➤ **Regulations:** Several areas on the river are restricted to catch-and-release. Between October 1 and March 31, all fish must be released, regardless where you are. The lower Pemigewasset River—which becomes the Merrimack River—and its tributaries are restricted to fly fishing only. Many anglers practice voluntary catch-and-release. Be sure to check with the New Hampshire Fish and Game department for current regulations and seasons.

Fishing for Atlantic salmon is different than fishing for trout. You cannot muscle them in, you must bow to the jump, and you must let them run—usually well into your backing. The Atlantic salmon in the Merrimack River can be caught using conventional salmon tackle and flies. Traditional Atlantic salmon angling protocol and ethics found in other salmon waters apply on the Merrimack as well. This includes pool rotations, respecting another angler's raise, reeling in when someone has a fish on, and so on. You should read up on this before you go, to avoid unnecessary conflicts with other anglers.

This chapter is dedicated to Clinton "Bill" Townsend of Canaan, Maine, for his selfless and tireless efforts to protect and preserve this magnificent gamefish.

The Merrimack is a large river. It can, however, be waded. Many anglers fish from a boat—this helps reach fish that are unavailable to wading anglers. Local fly shops, New Hampshire Fish and Game, Merrimack Valley Chapter of Trout Unlimited, and several local fly-fishing websites can provide you with up-to-date information and conditions.

Unfortunately, Atlantic salmon restoration efforts on the Connecticut River in Connecticut and Massachusetts have been recently discontinued due to poor returns. New Hampshire's focus is on the Merrimack—and it too is at risk of being shut down. The average returns on the Merrimack have been roughly 120 fish per year. The goal is 300 per year. However, 2011 saw a record return of more than 400 fish—let's hope this is a trend.

The situations on the Saco, Androscoggin, and Kennebec rivers in Maine are similar to that found in the Merrimack. The seven Downeast rivers in Maine have their own hurdles, such as pesticides, dewatering, and a changing climate. The Penobscot River in Maine is faring a little better—and as a result, represents ground zero in regard to the preservation of wild Atlantic salmon in the Northeastern United States.

With any luck, this magnificent gamefish—the king of fish—will once again swim the great rivers of the Northeast in numbers large enough to allow for general fly-fishing seasons. That is the goal of ongoing restoration efforts and the programs that support them. Until then, consider going to the Merrimack River in New Hamp-

Matthew Carpenter with brood fish. New Hampshire Fish and Game

shire to try to catch one of these spectacular fish, and to see exactly what is at stake here.

➤ **Tackle:** A 9- to 10-foot 8-weight or 9-weight rod with floating line is a good outfit for the Merrimack River. If the water is running high or the fish are not looking up—which is often the case—a full-sinking or sink-tip line is a good idea. Sinking lines should be of the fast-sink variety. Sink-tip lines should have a long tip—15 feet or more, and also be fast-sinking. Reels should hold 200 or more yards of backing. Flies should include an assortment of traditional Atlantic salmon flies, steelhead patterns, and large streamers and Woolly Buggers in chartreuse.

BOB MALLARD has fly fished for over 35 years. He is a blogger, writer, and author; and has owned and operated Kennebec River Outfitters in Madison, Maine since 2001. His writing has been featured in newspapers, magazines, and books at the local, regional, and national levels. He has appeared on radio and television. Look for his upcoming books from Stonefly Press, *25 Best Towns: Fly Fishing for Trout* (winter 2014) and *50 Best Places: Fly Fishing for Brook Trout* (summer 2015). Bob is also a staff fly designer for Catch Fly Fishing. He can be reached at www. kennebecriveroutfitters.com, www.bobmallard.com, info@bobmallard.com, or 207-474-2500.

CLOSEST FLY SHOPS:

Stone River Outfitters
132 Bedford Center Road
Bedford, New Hampshire 03110
800-331-8558
www.stoneriveroutfitters.com
sales@stoneriveroutfitters.com

Opechee Trading Post
13 Opechee Street
Laconia, New Hampshire 03246
603-524-0908
www.opecheetradingpost.com
jim@opecheetradingpost.com

CLOSEST GUIDES/OUTFITTERS:

Ugly Duck's Guide Service
Wolfeboro, New Hampshire 03894
603-393-3636
www.uglyducksrodcare.com
uglyducks@hotmail.com

CLOSEST LODGING:

Cheney House Bed & Breakfast
82 Highland Street
Ashland, New Hampshire 03217
603-968-4499
www.cheneyhouse.com
info@cheneyhouse.com

The Common Man Inn & Spa
231 Main Street
Plymouth, New Hampshire 03264
603-536-2200
www.thecmaninn.com
info@thecmaninn.com

Belmore Courts (cabins)
7 Belmore Court Drive
Bristol, New Hampshire 03222
978-531-5262
www.belmorecourts.com
belmorecourts@aol.com

Baker River Campground
56 Campground Road
Rumney, New Hampshire 03266
603-786-9707
www.bakerrivercampground.com
bakerriver@bakerrivercampground.com

CLOSEST RESTAURANTS:

Steaks & Seafood South (casual dining)
11 South Main Street
Concord, NH New Hampshire 03303
603-856-7925
www.magicfoodsrestaurantgroup.com/
osteaks

Moritomo Japanese Restaurant and Sushi
32 Fort Eddy Road
Concord, New Hampshire 03301
603-224-8363
www.moritomonh.com
info@moritomo.com

The Homestead Restaurant and Tavern
(casual dining)
1567 Summer Street
Bristol, New Hampshire 03222
603-744-2022
www.homesteadnh.com
nate@homesteadnh.com

Heritage Farm Pancake House (breakfast)
16 Parker Hill Road
Sanbornton, New Hampshire 03269
603-524-5400
www.heritagefarmpancakehouse.com

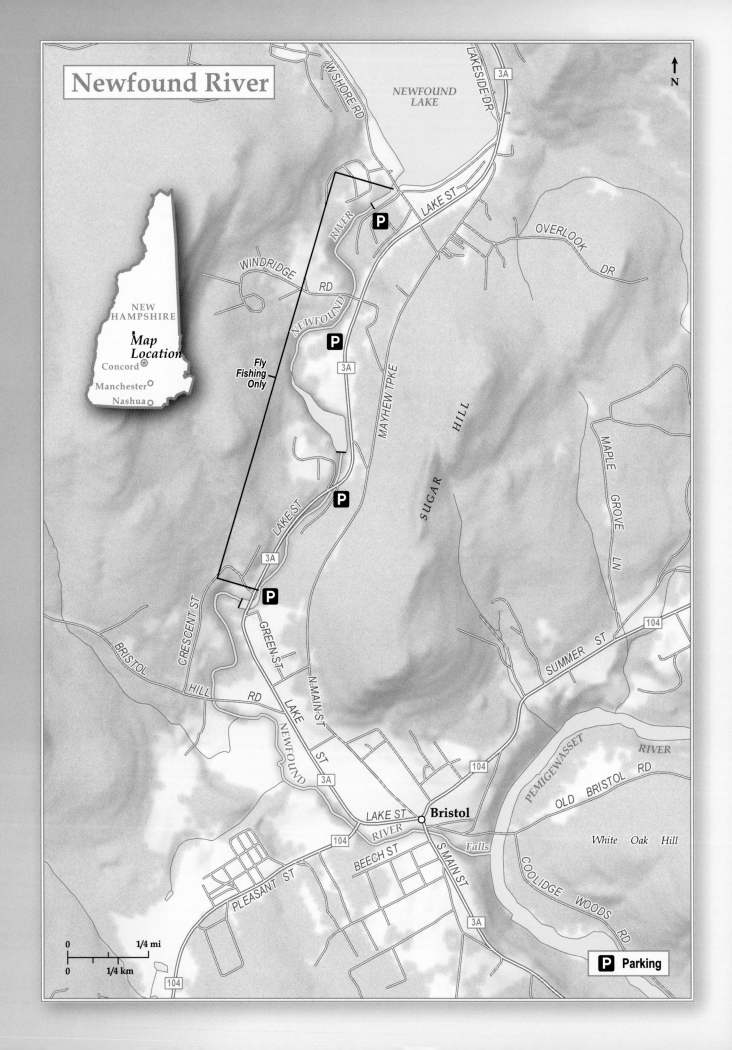

Newfound River

NEWFOUND LAKE

N

W SHORE RD

LAKESIDE DR

3A

LAKE ST

OVERLOOK DR

RIVER

P

NEW HAMPSHIRE

Map Location

Concord ⊛

Manchester ○

Nashua ○

WINDRIDGE

RD

NEWFOUND

P

Fly Fishing Only

3A

MAYHEW TPKE

SUGAR HILL

MAPLE GROVE LN

P

LAKE ST

3A

P

104

SUMMER ST

P

CRESCENT ST

BRISTOL HILL RD

GREEN ST

N MAIN ST

LAKE NEWFOUND ST

3A

104

PEMIGEWASSET RIVER

OLD BRISTOL RD

COOLIDGE WOODS RD

White Oak Hill

LAKE ST RIVER

Bristol

104

BEECH ST

S MAIN ST

Falls

PLEASANT ST

3A

0   1/4 mi

0   1/4 km

104

P Parking

18 · Newfound River

➤ **Location:** Central New Hampshire, about a 1-hour ride from Manchester; and a 2-hour ride from Boston, Massachusetts and Portland, Maine. Full-service airports are available in all three cities.

When I first started working at author Bob Mallard's fly shop, I noticed that 4 of the 16 fish pictures on the wall came from a river I did not recognize. After several attempts to pry the name from him, he finally came clean—the Newfound River in Bristol, New Hampshire. When I asked why so many large fish came from that one river, he replied, "Because it is one of the best trophy trout fisheries in New England." A decade later I moved from Maine to New Hampshire. I found myself just a short ride from the Newfound. Within a couple of months, I was fishing the Newfound almost exclusively. Since then the river has accounted for some of the largest rainbow trout of my life. Bob was right—it is one of the best trophy trout fisheries in New England.

The Newfound River flows from Newfound Lake. Both have a long history of salmonid fishing. The lake is a 4,100-acre jewel, considered one of the cleanest in the region. Fed by at least eight springs, it remains clear and cold even in the warmest months. Its icy 180-foot depths provide refuge for salmon and trout. The Newfound is a small freestone river—even by Northeast standards. Water flows are fairly consistent, with fall and winter levels around 150–300 cfs. The river is susceptible to spikes, which can top 1,500 cfs. In the early spring, the lake begins to shed its ice. At this time levels will increase, making wading difficult. But it is this increase that draws fish from the lake and into the river.

A couple of hundred yards below the lake is a small dam. This is one of the few structures you will encounter on the upper river. From here the river is a series of riffles, runs, and pools. Roughly a mile below the dam is a now-dry small impoundment at the site of a small defunct dam. Below here, the Newfound winds its way under the road, and behind houses and stores, on its way to its termination at the Pemigewasset River. Just before ending, it plunges over a waterfall, making it impossible for fish to move up from the larger river. The section of most interest to the fly fishers is from the lake to just below the old dam. After that the river becomes a bit urbanized and in some cases, hard to access.

While in the lake, trout and salmon gorge themselves on smelt. Once in the river, they feed primarily on insects—

Steve Bowman on upper river in winter. Michelle Bowman

mayflies, caddis, midges, and stoneflies. Hellgrammites are also present. Fish eggs are available in both the spring and fall. Baitfish such as dace, fallfish, and sculpins are found in the river as well as the lake. Rainbows average 15 inches, with many fish in the 16- to 18-inch range. Fish over 18 inches are caught on a regular basis. Fish over 20 inches are possible. One picture on the wall shows a rainbow that goes over 20 inches. The state record rainbow, nearly 16 pounds, was caught in the Pemigewasset River just below its confluence

Dam at outlet of Newfound Lake. Steve Bowman

The Newfound is a wading river. It is too small to float—even in high water. There is an informal trail network along the upper river. A paved bike path parallels the river in some areas. In other areas, the road—or even the sidewalk—are close enough to provide access to the river.

If you are looking for fall, winter, and early spring fishing for rainbows and landlocked salmon that are measured in pounds, not inches, the Newfound River is one of your best options.

➤ **Regulations:** Fishing season on the Newfound runs from January 1 to October 31. The river is restricted to fly fishing only. From January 1 to March 31 there is a two-fish limit on trout—no salmon may be kept. From April 1 to September 30, there is a combined two-fish limit on trout and salmon. From October 1 to October 31, it is catch-and-release on trout and salmon, with a barbless-hooks-only restriction. There is no length limit on trout, and a 15-inch minimum length limit on salmon.

➤ **Hatches:** While the Newfound River is not known for dry-fly fishing, fish do feed on the surface under certain conditions. A slight change in the water temperature caused by the sun can trigger a midday midge hatch—even in the dead of winter. This will bring fish to the surface. Early fall sees midday Blue-winged Olive hatches. Evening caddis hatches in the spring are always possible. Fish are also occasionally caught on small terrestrials such as ants and beetles.

Nymphing produces the most consistent results on the Newfound. Both strike indicator and Euro-style techniques work. The latter is best left to the faster runs, while the former will work in the slower, deeper runs and pools. Exceptions are immediately after the season opens, first thing in the morning, and right after a rain. In these cases, dead drifting large leech patterns, or swinging streamers, can produce fish—albeit in fewer numbers.

➤ **Tackle:** A 9-foot 5-weight rod with a floating line is your best bet for the Newfound River most of the time. If you want to fish streamers, a 9-foot 6-weight with a sink-tip line is your best option. Rods longer than 9 feet can work for nymphing—especially Euro style. Rods shorter than 9 feet are not practical. Fluorocarbon tippet is important when the water is

with the Newfound. It is likely this fish was a drop-down from the Newfound. Landlocked salmon average slightly smaller, but can exceed 22 inches. Bob's largest salmon ever—25 inches—came from this river. Brook trout are occasionally caught in the Newfound. These fish are typical stream-size brook trout in the 8- to 10-inch range. Lake trout will occasionally enter the river from the lake above. Lakers up to 10 pounds have been reported.

The Newfound River is an excellent spring and fall fishery—and arguably the best winter trout fishery in New England. Summer is usually too warm and low to offer reliable fishing. But any spike in the water, at any time of year, can draw a fresh batch of fish into the river. Even so, a few fish stay in the river all summer. The upper section of the Newfound has some excellent runs and pools. This is where the fish congregate. The shallow riffles between the runs and pools rarely hold fish. Anglers should concentrate their efforts on the deeper, slower sections.

Steve Bowman with large winter rainbow trout. Michelle Bowman

Jack Rowbottom below dam. Steve Bowman

clear. Medium-size strike indicators and small split-shot are best. Flies should include midge larvae; and caddis, mayfly, and stonefly nymphs in a variety of sizes—from #22 for the former to #8 for the latter—and colors. Streamers should include Bunny Leeches and sculpin and smelt imitations.

STEVE BOWMAN owns and operates Ugly Duck's Rod Care Products and Ugly Duck's Guide Service. He is a licensed New Hampshire fishing guide. He has worked for Lees Ferry Angler in Marble Canyon, Arizona; and Kennebec River Outfitters in Madison, Maine. He can be reached at 603-393-3636, ugly ducks@hotmail.com, or www.facebook.com/pages/Ugly-Ducks-Rod-Care-Products.

CLOSEST FLY SHOPS

Opechee Trading Post
13 Opechee Street
Laconia, New Hampshire 03246
603-524-0908
www.opecheetradingpost.com
jim@opecheetradingpost.com

Stone River Outfitters
132 Bedford Center Road
Bedford, New Hampshire 03110
800-331-8558
www.stoneriveroutfitters.com
sales@stoneriveroutfitters.com

CLOSEST GUIDES/OUTFITTERS

Ugly Duck's Guide Service
Wolfeboro, New Hampshire 03894
603-393-3636
www.uglyducksrodcare.com
uglyducks@hotmail.com

CLOSEST LODGING

A Newfound Bed and Breakfast
94 Mandi Lane
Bristol, New Hampshire 03222
603-744-3442
www.ANewfoundBnB.com
Sondra@ANewfoundBnB.com

The Common Man Inn & Spa
231 Main Street
Plymouth, New Hampshire 03264
603-536-2200
www.thecmaninn.com
info@thecmaninn.com

Davidson's Countryside Campground
100 Schofield Rd
Bristol, New Hampshire 03222
603-744-2403
www.davidsonscamp.com
davidsons@metrocast.net

CLOSEST RESTAURANTS

Steaks & Seafood South
11 South Main Street
Concord, New Hampshire 03303
603-856-7925
www.magicfoodsrestaurantgroup.com/osteaks

Moritomo Japanese Restaurant and Sushi
32 Fort Eddy Road
Concord, New Hampshire 03301
603-224-8363
www.moritomonh.com
info@moritomo.com

The Homestead Restaurant and Tavern
(casual dining)
1567 Summer Street
Bristol, New Hampshire 03222
603-744-2022
www.homesteadnh.com
nate@homesteadnh.com

Heritage Farm Pancake House (breakfast)
16 Parker Hill Road
Sanbornton, New Hampshire 03269
603-524-5400
www.heritagefarmpancakehouse.com

Bob Mallard on the Batten Kill River. Diana Mallard

III VERMONT

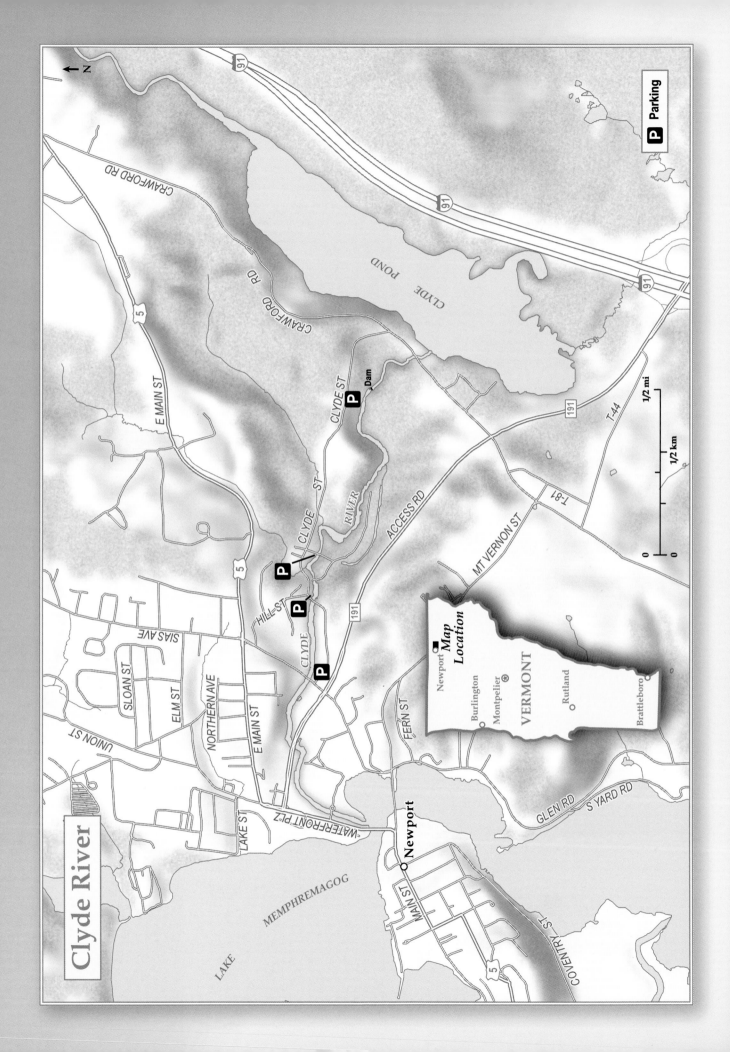

Clyde River

N

91

CRAWFORD RD

5

E MAIN ST

CRAWFORD RD

CLYDE POND

91

91

CLYDE ST

Dam

P

CLYDE ST

CLYDE   RIVER

191

T-44

1/2 mi

1/2 km

0   0

P

CLYDE

HILL ST

P

ACCESS RD

191

MT VERNON ST

T-81

SIAS AVE

SLOAN ST

ELM ST

NORTHERN AVE

E MAIN ST

UNION ST

P

CLYDE

FERN ST

Map Location

Newport

VERMONT

Burlington

Montpelier ®

Rutland

Brattleboro

GLEN RD   S YARD RD

LAKE ST

WATERFRONT PLZ

Newport

MAIN ST

MEMPHREMAGOG

LAKE

5

COVENTRY ST

19 · Clyde River

➤ **Location:** Northern Vermont, about a 2-hour ride from Burlington; a 1½-hour ride from Montpelier; a 2½-hour ride from Manchester, New Hampshire; and a 3½-hour ride from Boston, Massachusetts. Full-service airports are available in all four cities.

Originating at the outflow of Island Pond in northeast Vermont, the Clyde River flows more than 30 miles before emptying into Lake Memphremagog, in the city of Newport. The slow, meandering upper and middle reaches of the Clyde offer angling opportunities for brook, brown, and rainbow trout. However, it is the famed salmon run on the lower ½ mile or so of river that draws fly fishers each spring and fall.

The Clyde was home to some of the last known Atlantic salmon in New England that made their way to the Atlantic Ocean following the Ice Age. The receding ice left most of these formerly anadromous fish stranded in deep, coldwater lakes. However, by way of the St. Lawrence River, Clyde River salmon made their way to the sea, until dams blocked their passage.

In the early 1900s, anglers traveled by train from all over the Northeast for a chance at the Clyde's tackle-busting salmon. Fish up to 10 pounds were caught. For close to 50 years, the Clyde River salmon fishery was a large part of the economy of Newport. This ended when a diversion dam dewatered the lower ½ mile of river, virtually wiping out the Clyde's salmon fishery. With landlocked salmon, lake trout, brown trout, walleye, and steelhead unable to spawn in the river, a once-booming fishery was lost, and the local economy began to crumble.

In August 1996, after a long legal battle between the Citizens Utility power company and Vermont's Northeast Kingdom Chapter of Trout Unlimited, removal of Citizens Utility #11 dam began. Thanks to the efforts of local citizens and Trout Unlimited, landlocked salmon and other species were able to reach spawning habitat that had been inaccessible for more than 30 years.

Today the Clyde offers outstanding opportunities for fly fishers, as fish enter the river on their spring and fall migrations. Fly fishers focus their efforts on the lower portion of the river, from the Great Bay Hydro Dam below Clyde Pond to Lake Memphremagog. This relatively small piece of water can be broken down into several sections, all with their own unique characteristics.

Upper river. Bob Shannon, Fly Rod Shop

The upper section begins downstream of the Great Bay Hydro Dam and continues approximately ¼ mile to just below the site of the former diversion dam. This can be accessed via the parking area at the hydro facility on Clyde Street. Studded boots and wading staffs are recommended. The river drops steadily here, with fast pocketwater and a couple of large pools near the site of the former dam. The next section is referred to locally as the Jungle. This begins just below the old dam site, and runs approximately ¼ mile. This section is best accessed via the footbridge parking

Fall on the upper Clyde. Stephanie Garguilo

dor is one of the most beautiful sites a fly angler can witness. Please note that local anglers often frown upon nymphing for salmon on their spawning beds. The preferred method is to look for aggressive fish willing to chase a streamer. This becomes increasingly important as the fall run goes on.

In collaboration with Vermont Fish & Wildlife, Great Bay Hydro Company installed a "trap & truck" system at the spillover dam below Clyde Pond. Here salmon are trapped, tagged, recorded, and trucked a few miles upstream, to prime spawning habitat. To date, only a small percentage of fish trucked upstream have returned to Lake Memphremagog. It is believed that many have taken up residence in Lake Salem.

Ideal flows on the Clyde run from roughly 80–350 cfs. Because of the river's small size, low water can be difficult to fish due to the fact that the fish can easily see you. The Clyde River and its banks can be difficult for wading anglers to navigate, so fly fishers should exercise caution when making their way around. It should be noted that it is rarely necessary to stand in this river and fish—most angling can be done from the bank.

Salmon on the Clyde River average approximately 14 to 17 inches. However, fish over 20 inches are common. In addition to salmon, the lower Clyde also receives notable runs of walleye, smallmouth bass, steelhead, lake trout, brown trout, and rock bass.

➤ **Regulations:** From the downstream edge of the bridge on Clyde Street, the river is open to fishing from the second Saturday in April through October 31. Above that, the season opens May 11. From October 1 through October 31, the river is restricted to catch-and-release and fly fishing only. From the season opener to the last day of September, the limit is two fish, with a 17-inch maximum length limit. Note that felt soles are not legal in Vermont. In addition, lead weights must weigh ½ ounce or less.

Large fall run of landlocked salmon. Bob Shannon, Fly Rod Shop

area on Clyde Street, and offers a mix of pocketwater and plunge pools.

The section from the downstream edge of the Jungle to the Clyde Street bridge is well known for its two primary pools, Halfmoon and Pumphouse. Both offer deep runs with long tailouts, and serve as staging areas for migrating fish. Halfmoon is best accessed via the footbridge parking area. Pumphouse has a small access site on Clyde Street. The lower section, accessed via a Vermont Fish & Wildlife parking area on Clyde Street, begins at the downstream edge of the Clyde Street bridge, and runs to the lake. This section is relatively shallow and very slow-moving, making it challenging to fish.

Shortly after ice-out, salmon follow schools of baitfish such as smelt and emerald shiners into the Clyde to feed. The spring run ends when water temperatures reach the upper 50s to low 60s. At this time, the salmon retreat back to the lake.

The fall run is a spawning migration. It begins in late summer or early fall, depending on conditions. Acrobatic, bright, fresh salmon going airborne amid a backdrop of fall splen-

Timothy S. Hayes with landlocked salmon. Peter LaRou

➤ **Hatches:** Notable hatches on the Clyde are Hendricksons, stoneflies, and Tan Caddis in the spring. In the fall, caddis and tiny Blue-winged Olives often fill the air.

➤ **Tackle:** A 9-foot 5-weight rod with a floating line will work on the Clyde River most of the time. Longer rods can be helpful for nymphing. Lighter rods in the 4-weight range can be good for dry-fly fishing. If you want to fish streamers, a 9-foot 6-weight with a fast-sinking sink-tip is your best option. Fluorocarbon leaders and tippets are recommended. Strike indicators should be large enough to float two flies and added weight. Flies should include minnow and smelt imitations; attractor streamers; sculpin imitations; San Juan Worms; and all stages of mayflies, stoneflies, and caddis in a variety of sizes and colors.

CHRIS LYNCH manages the Green Mountain Troutfitters fly shop and guide service in Jeffersonville, Vermont. He is also a licensed guide in New York State, the founder of Green Mountain Fly Fishing Camp for kids, and cofounder of Lake Champlain's exclusive catch-photo-release tournament for fly anglers, the Ditch Pickle Classic. He can be reached at 800-495-4271, chris@gmtrout .com, or www.gmtrout.com.

CLOSEST FLY SHOPS:

Green Mountain Troutfitters
233 Mill Street
Jeffersonville, Vermont 05464
802-644-2214
www.gmtrout.com
Gmtvermont@gmail.com

The Fly Rod Shop
2703 Waterbury Road
Stowe, Vermont 05672
802-252-7346
www.flyrodshop.com
angler@flyrodshop.com

CLOSEST LODGING:

Newport City Motel
444 East Main Street
Newport, Vermont 05855
802-334-6558
www.newportcitymotel.net
ncmmotel@myfairpoint.net

Water's Edge B&B
324 Wishing Well Avenue
Newport, Vermont 05855
802-334-1840
www.watersedgebnb.com

Pepins Motel
4537 U.S. Route 5
Newport, Vermont 05855
802-334-8080

Little Gnesta Bed & Breakfast
115 Prospect Street
Newport, Vermont 05855
802-334-3438
www.littlegnesta.com
ruth@littlegnesta.com

CLOSEST RESTAURANTS:

The East Side Restaurant & Pub
47 Landing Street
Newport, Vermont 05855
802-334-2340
www.eastsiderestaurant.net

Le Belvedere Restaurant
100 Main Street
Newport, Vermont 05855
802-487-9147
www.lebelvedererestaurant.com
lebelvedere11@hotmail.com

Lago Trattoria
95 Main Street
Newport, Vermont 05855
802-334-8222
www.lagatrattoria.com
laga.trattoria@yahoo.com

Baan Thai Cuisine
158 Main Street
Newport, Vermont 05855
802-334-8833
www.facebook.com/baanthaivt

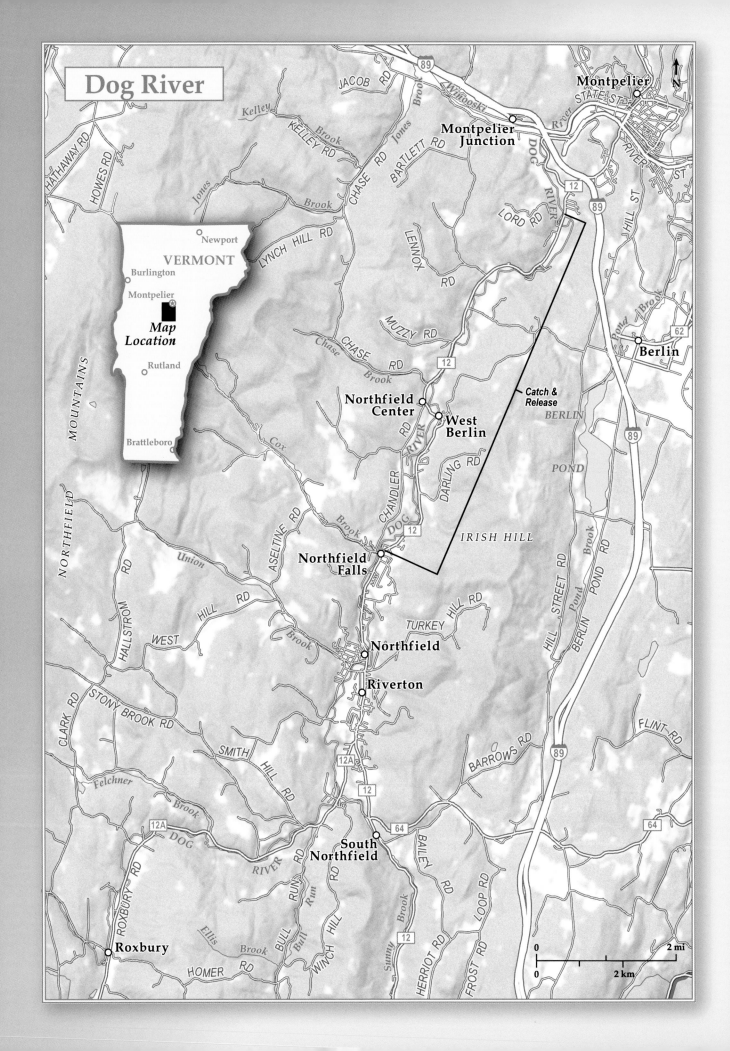

20 · Dog River

➤ **Location:** Central Vermont, about a 1-hour ride from Burlington; a 2-hour ride from Manchester, New Hampshire; a 3-hour ride from Hartford, Connecticut; and a 3-hour ride from Boston, Massachusetts. Full-service airports are available in all four cities.

The Dog River originates in the town of Roxbury, Vermont. It flows north approximately 20 miles through the pastoral villages of Northfield and Berlin before terminating at the Winooski River in Montpelier—the state capital. The major tributaries of the Dog River include Felchner Brook, Bull Run, Stoney Brook, Sunny Brook, Union Brook, Cox Brook, and Chase Brook. The river supports a self-sustaining population of native brook trout in its upper reaches. It also has wild rainbow trout and brown trout. This affords the fly fisher the opportunity to catch Vermont's trout grand slam.

One advantage to fishing the Dog River is that there are a lot of other things to do in the area. You do not have to travel far to enjoy some of Vermont's finest New England charm. Montpelier is just up the road. Its gold-domed capitol building was built in 1859. The Vermont Historical Society is just a short walk from the capitol building. The town of Warren—just a few miles away—is home of Sugarbush and Mad River Ski areas. Twenty minutes north on Vermont's historic Route 100, you will find the village of Stowe—home to the state's highest peak, Mount Mansfield, and Stowe Mountain Resort. These areas offer a plethora of summer activities, from farmers markets, to antique car shows, to small specialty retail shops. The famous Ben & Jerry's ice cream factory in Waterbury is Vermont's number-one summer attraction.

The Dog River is considered one of the state's most productive wild trout streams. The river has been managed as a wild trout fishery since 1992. Though this is a small river even by New England standards, observant anglers traveling north along Vermont's scenic Route 12 cannot help but be tempted by its riffles, runs, and deep aqua-green pools. The Dog River experienced an unsettling decline in trout populations in the early 2000s.

➤ **Regulations:** The state of Vermont's Fish & Wildlife Board and the Fish & Wildlife Department took an extraordinary proactive action in 2010, by imposing catch-and-release on certain sections of the river. This includes the area located between Northfield Falls in Northfield and the Junc-

tion Road Bridge in Montpelier. Tackle is restricted to artificial flies and lures only. This was done to try to restore the population of wild trout. The results have been fast and noticeable. This temporary emergency catch-and-release restriction is scheduled to expire at the end of the 2015 fishing season. At that time the Fish & Wildlife Board and the Fish & Wildlife Department intend to review the situation and decide, based on scientific data, whether to continue with the catch-and-release. Let's hope they do.

➤ **Hatches:** Fishing on the Dog River begins on the second Saturday in April—the standard season opener. Those venturing into central Vermont at this time may find the fishing a bit challenging. Water temperatures begin to warm and start to produce hatches between the 1st and 15th of May. This is

Swinging spring streamers on the Dog. Bob Shannon, Fly Rod Shop

somewhat dependent on how quickly winter loosens its grip on the Vermont mountains. Some of my fondest memories of dry-fly fishing in Vermont go back to the early 1980s, when the spring Hendrickson hatch begins on the lower reaches of the Dog River. Many a large rainbow and brown trout were more than willing to rise to an imitation of one of the river's best early-season midday hatches. Even though the Dog consistently produces some of Vermont's best river-resident trout year after year, they do not come easy. Many anglers

Left. Releasing a wild brown trout. Bob Shannon, Fly Rod Shop

are left scratching their heads as they search through their fly boxes trying to find the right pattern to try to fool rising trout in its gin-clear pools.

As summer takes hold in the Green Mountains of Vermont, fly anglers will have their best luck during the early-morning hatches and the late-evening spinner falls. By July, fly fishers can enjoy the ultimate challenge of dry-fly fishing for wary, sipping trout with small Tricos on long, light, fluorocarbon leaders. This is as much stalking as it is fishing. Those anglers fishing later in the day should be prepared to come off the river with the aid of a headlamp, if they want to take advantage of the peak of the evening spinner fall. Leaving the river while you can still hear the sound of trout slurping spinners off the surface can be tough to take. One of the best trophy trout the Dog put up, in my guiding career, was caught by a client who was willing to stay on the river long after dark. Midsummer night fishing for trophy trout is well known to central Vermont fly fishers.

During August, fly fishers can catch trout on the Dog with terrestrials. Some of the best fishing of the summer months is done with imitations of the large, farm-field grasshoppers that tempt the trout along every bend of river. In the mid- to late afternoon, flying ants are known to blanket the surface of the river right up until the first frost of fall.

As the days shorten and cooler temperatures arrive in September and October, hatches and feeding activity are strongest during the middle of the day. The river is open to fishing through the end of October. Those who appreciate

New England's fall foliage will be amazed by the brilliance of colors that surround this watershed. Small Blue-winged Olives produce most of the late-season dry-fly fishing. But this is also the time of year that I pull out my sink-tip line, and start targeting the Dog River brown trout with large conventional and articulated streamer patterns. Prespawn browns are measured in pounds, not inches, so make sure to bring your camera to capture what could be some of the best fishing and scenery Vermont rivers have to offer.

The Dog River is a small body of water known for large fish. It is also a beautiful river located in a beautiful place. What more could you ask for?

➤ Tackle: A 9-foot 5-weight rod with a floating line is your best bet for the Dog River most of the time. If you want to fish streamers, a 9-foot 6-weight with a fast sinking sink tip is your best option. Dry-fly fishing is best done with a 9-foot 4-weight, as you may need to drop to 6X to effectively fish smaller patterns such as Blue-winged Olives. While rods longer than 9 feet can work, especially for nymphing, rods shorter than 9 feet are not practical. Fluorocarbon leaders and tippet are a good idea, due to the clear water. Strike indicators should be large enough to float two flies and added weight, yet small enough to detect subtle takes. Flies should include Woolly Buggers and sculpin patterns, and all stages of mayflies, stoneflies, and caddis in a variety of sizes and colors.

90

Large, wild brown trout. Bob Shannon, Fly Rod Shop

BOB SHANNON owns and operates The Fly Rod Shop and Fly Fish Vermont guide service in Stowe, Vermont. Bob has guided in Vermont, New York, New Hampshire, Montana, Canada, and the Caribbean. He has also taught fly fishing at Johnson State College in Johnson, Vermont for the last two decades. Bob is a member of the St. Croix Pro Staff and an ambassador for Simms Fishing Products.

CLOSEST FLY SHOPS

The Fly Rod Shop
2703 Waterbury Road
Stowe, Vermont 05672
802-252-7346
www.flyrodshop.com
angler@flyrodshop.com

Green Mountain Troutfitters
233 Mill Street
Jeffersonville, Vermont 05464
802-644-2214
www.gmtrout.com
Gmtvermont@gmail.com

Middlebury Mountaineer
2 Park Street
Middlebury, Vermont 05753
802-388-7245
www.mmvt.com
info@mmvt.com

CLOSEST GUIDES/OUTFITTERS

Stream and Brook Fly Fishing
160 South Pleasant Street
Middlebury, Vermont 05753
802-989-3510
www.streamandbrook.com
brian.cadoret@gmail.com

CLOSEST LODGING

Capitol Plaza Hotel & Conference Center
100 State Street
Montpelier, Vermont 05602
802-223-5252
www.capitolplaza.com

The Pitcher Inn
275 Main Street
Warren, Vermont 05674
802-496-6350
www.pitcherinn.com
info@pitcherinn.com

Stowe Cabins in the Woods
513 Cabin Lane
Waterbury Center, Vermont 05677
802-244-8533
www.stowecabins.comm
stay@stowecabins.com

The Econo Lodge
101 Northfield Street
Montpelier, Vermont 05602
802-223-5258
www.econolodge.com

CLOSEST RESTAURANTS

New England Culinary Institute's NECI on Main
118 Main Street
Montpelier, Vermont 05602
802-223-3188
WWW.NECI.EDU

The Pitcher Inn
275 Main Street
Warren, VT
802-496-6350
www.pitcherinn.com
info@pitcherinn.com

J. Morgan's Steakhouse
Capitol Plaza Hotel & Conference Center
100 State Street
Montpelier, Vermont 05602
802-223-5222
www.capitolplaza.com

The Knotty Shamrock Irish Pub
21 East Street
Northfield, Vermont 05663
802-485-4857
www.knottyshamrock.com
manager@knottyshamrock.com

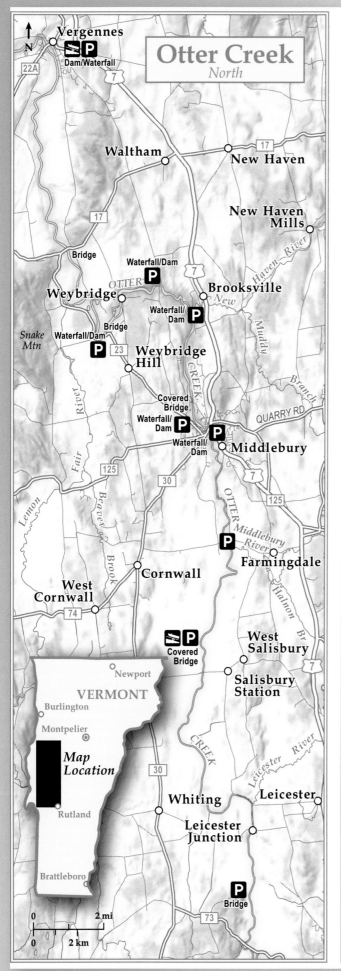

21 · Otter Creek

➤ **Location:** West-central Vermont, about a 1-hour ride from Burlington; a 2½-hour ride from Albany, New York; a 3-hour ride from Manchester, New Hampshire; and a 3½-hour ride from Boston, Massachusetts. Full-service airports are available in all four cities.

There is nothing like stripping an 8-inch streamer as fast as you can with a water wolf chasing it. If you like casting large flies to big pike, Otter Creek is the place for you. Regulars consider a 24-inch pike small, a 30-inch pike a good one, a 36-inch pike somewhat common, and pike over 40 inches always a possibility. Even small pike provide excitement with their hard hits and reckless behavior. I once read that northern pike (*Esox lucius*) are the fastest freshwater fish, capable of short bursts of up to 35 mph. Henry David Thoreau described the pike as the "swiftest, wariest and most ravenous of fish." In 25 years fishing Otter Creek, there have been many times I have seen a 30-inch pike try to eat the fish I was playing. Few, if any, rivers in the Northeast can match Otter Creek in regard to the quantity and size of its pike.

Otter Creek is known as the "Indian Road" and played an important role in settling Vermont. It is the longest river in the state, at 112 miles. It terminates at Lake Champlain. Otter Creek is a tiny stream when it flows out of Emerald Lake in East Dorset. It is still fairly small as it goes through Danby and Wallingford. By the time Otter flows into Rutland, it is a big river.

Vermont Fish & Wildlife, along with other state and federal agencies and private organizations, has been working to ensure that the future of Otter Creek is bright, and that it will continue to provide critical habitat for a variety of fish and wildlife. When asked about Otter Creek and its northern pike population, Department of Fisheries Biologist Shawn Good explained the important role Otter Creek plays in providing fish and wildlife habitat, protecting water quality, and reducing the impacts of flooding.

Otter Creek is a slow, meandering stream flowing through a wide valley. Its fertile soil was highly desirable for farming at the turn of the 20th century. Farmers ditched and drained the lands along Otter Creek to convert floodplain to farmland. This negatively impacted the river, along with the fish and wildlife it supported. Floodplains improve quality and flood attenuation. As water fills the floodplain, its velocity slows. As the water spreads out, and velocity decreases outside the river channel, silt and sediment drop out of the water. This helps keeps silt and sediment out of Lake Champlain. This is also why floodplains are so fertile. The ancillary

Otter Creek in Middlebury, Vermont. Brian Cadoret, Stream & Brook Fly Fishing

benefit is that floodplains act as important spawning habitat for northern pike and a wide variety of minnow species. Waterfowl use the flooded land for nesting. Ditching and draining of floodplains to create farmland diverts flood water back into the river; reduces spawning habitat; and interrupts fish egg deposition, hatching, and development.

The Wetland Reserve Program involves Vermont Fish & Wildlife, along with a number of other groups such as the U.S Fish & Wildlife Service, Natural Resources Conserva-

Above. Where Middlebury River dumps into Otter Creek. Brian Cadoret, Stream & Brook Fly Fishing

Inset. Brian Cadoret with 36" pike. Brian Cadoret, Stream & Brook Fly Fishing

tion Service, and Ducks Unlimited. The Pomainville Wild-life Management Area in Pittsford is the most high-profile project they have completed to date. This project has helped restore water quality and fish and wildlife habitat along Ot-ter Creek. It has been especially beneficial in regard to pro-viding critical northern pike spawning habitat and juvenile nursery areas.

There is a set of falls below Rutland called Proctor Falls—or Sutherland Falls. The stretch of river between these two falls offers great fishing, with limited angling pressure. The best way to access this section is by using a boat you can carry up steep banks, such as a canoe or kayak. Otter Creek flows unobstructed from Proctor Falls to Middlebury Falls. This 30-mile stretch of river is prime big-pike water. Here the creek flows under many covered bridges; through farm-lands and swamps; and past the towns of Pittsford, Brandon, Leicester, Sudbury, Salisbury, and Cornwall. Dirt roads par-allel and cross the river. There are many spots where you can launch a small boat, or fish from shore. Logjams can make the river impassible. Fly fishers must be prepared to carry their boats over or around them.

From Middlebury to Vergennes Falls is about 15 miles. Fishing here is excellent. There are several dams and wa-terfalls in this section. There are boat portage trails around them. Miles of river here barely get fished, which allows the pike to grow very large. There is 7 miles of stream between Vergennes Falls and Lake Champlain. This section falls un-der Lake Champlain regulations. Depending on the time of year, you can catch pike, musky, gar, carp, bowfin, bass, wall-eye, and trout.

From Center Falls in Rutland down to Lake Champlain, Otter Creek is open to fishing year-round. The rest of the creek opens the second Saturday in April and closes October 31. Upper Otter Creek contains mostly trout. There are tro-phy trout in lower Otter Creek. Seemingly endless numbers of smallmouth bass are always willing to chase a fly. Howev-er, in Otter Creek, northern pike rule the river. Otter Creek is truly a trophy fishery in regard to northern pike. However, the only way to guarantee its future is for people to realize the importance of riparian protection, conservation, and resto-ration. Catch-and-release, along with proper fish handling, is a key part of this.

Water levels in Otter Creek vary greatly. In the spring, and after rain, the creek runs bank to bank. In midsummer, the river is low and the clay banks are steep. Access is good on the creek. Fly fishers should focus on structure, deep cor-

Ken Capsey
with flies.
Brian Price

ners, and anywhere water enters the creek. Baitfish congregate in these spots, and the pike are there looking for an easy meal. When large pike are feeding, you'll often see minnows jumping out of the water to elude them.

Otter Creek is well worth traveling to. It offers a broad range of conditions for fly fishers looking for large fish. And to top all this off, it has brewery named after it!

➤ Tackle: A 9- to 10-foot, 8-weight fly rod with a floating line is your best bet for pike on Otter Creek. A sinking line can help in the deeper pools. Flies should be 6 to 10 inches long, in red/white, orange/white, chartreuse, and yellow. Perch patterns can work especially well. Wire leaders and tippet should be in the 12- to 20-pound-test range.

BRIAN "LUG" CADORET is the co-owner of Stream and Brook Fly Fishing guide service in Middlebury, Vermont. He spends over 150 days a year on the water and has a passion for trophy browns, pike, and steelhead. Brian is active in conservation and youth outreach. He can be reached at 802-989-3510, www.streamandbrook.com, or brian.cadoret@gmail.com.

CLOSEST FLY SHOPS
Middlebury Mountaineer
2 Park Street
Middlebury, Vermont 05753
802-388-7245
www.mmvt.com
info@mmvt.com

CLOSEST GUIDES/OUTFITTERS
Stream and Brook Fly Fishing
160 South Pleasant Street
Middlebury, Vermont 05753
802-989-3510
www.streamandbrook.com
brian.cadoret@gmail.com

CLOSEST LODGING
The Inn on the Green
71 So. Pleasant Street
Middlebury, Vermont 05753
888-244-7512
www.innonthegreen.com
reservations@innonthegreen.com

Middlebury Inn
14 Court Square
Middlebury, Vermont 05753
802-388-4961
www.middleburyinn.com
reservations@middleburyinn.com

Swift House Inn
25 Stewart Lane
Middlebury, Vermont 05753
866-388-9925
www.swifthouseinn.com
info@swifthouseinn.com

Waybury Inn & Pub
457 East Main Street
East Middlebury, Vermont 05740
802-388-4015
www.wayburyinn.com
info@wayburyinn.com

CLOSEST RESTAURANTS
Jessica's Restaurant (fine dining)
Swift House Inn
25 Stewart Lane
Middlebury, Vermont 05753
802-388-9925
www.jessicasvermont.com
info@swifthouseinn.com

Otter Creek Brewing
793 Exchange Street
Middlebury, Vermont 05753
802-388-0727
www.ottercreekbrewing.com
info@ottercreekbrewing.com

Two Brothers Tavern
86 Main Street
Middlebury, Vermont 05753
802-388-0002
www.twobrotherstavern.com
info@twobrotherstavern.com

Fire and Ice
26 Seymour Street
Middlebury, Vermont 05753
802-388-7166
www.fireandicerestaurant.com

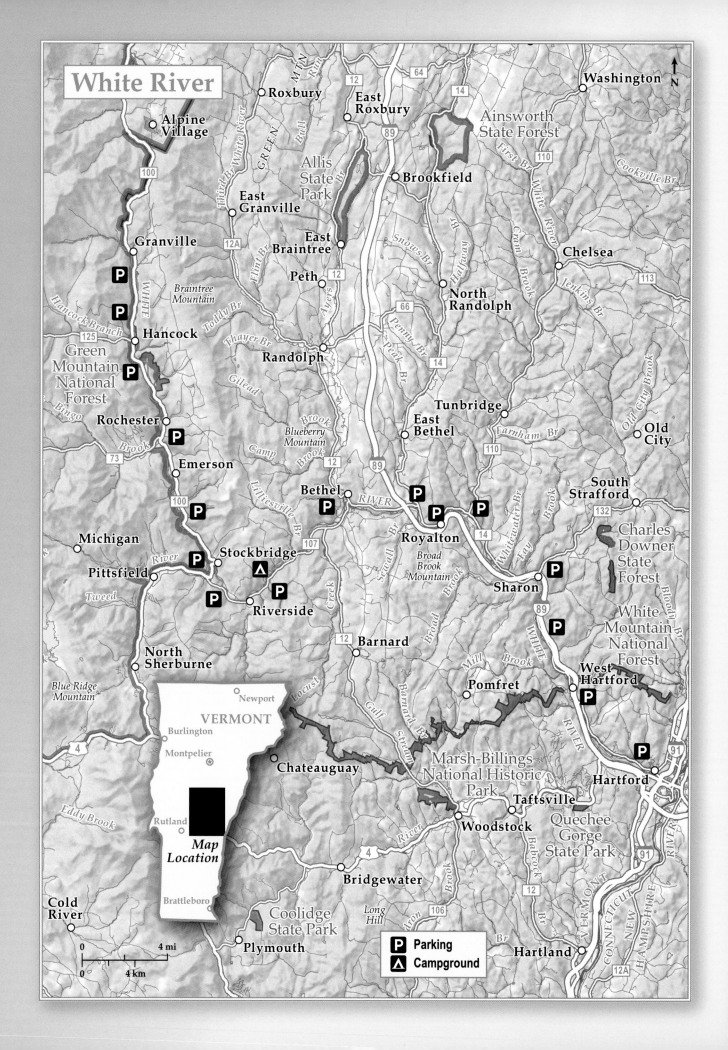

22 · White River

➤ Location: East-central Vermont, about a 1-hour ride from Burlington; a 2½-hour ride from Boston, Massachusetts; and a 2½-hour ride from Albany, New York. Full-service airports are available in all three cities.

The White River has long been an important part of Vermont's heritage. From its origin deep in the Green Mountain National Forest to its confluence with the fabled Connecticut River at White River Junction, the river provided access to the central part of the state since long before European settlers arrived.

The river was also critical spawning habitat for once-prolific runs of Atlantic salmon. These fish journeyed nearly 200 miles up the Connecticut River from the Atlantic Ocean to spawn in the clear, cold water and gravel runs of the White River. These salmon were a critical food source for indigenous tribes and early European settlers. As a result of damming and pollution—industrial, agricultural, municipal, and residential—the runs have been greatly reduced. Today Atlantic salmon are on the endangered species list. Sadly, efforts to restore this magnificent fish to the Connecticut River system have been suspended recently due to poor returns.

The White River is the largest undammed river in Vermont. It is roughly 55 miles long and drains an area of over 700 square miles—50,000 acres of which is located within the Green Mountain National Forest. The river drops more than 2,000 feet in elevation from its genesis in the Green Mountain National Forest to its termination at the Connecticut River. It has three branches: First, Second, and Third. Each branch flows from the north into the main stem, supplying the river with cool mountain water throughout the season. Countless named and unnamed tributaries wind their way into the main stem and its branches. These elements combine to make the White River one of Vermont's finest and most diverse trout fisheries.

Today the White River is home to brown, rainbow, and brook trout. The former two are introduced. The latter are native. There are both wild and stocked fish present. The river has something to offer everyone. From its remote plunge pools and backcountry brook trout, to its large pocketwater,

to its deep runs and pools inhabited by large fish, it is truly a diverse watershed.

The White River can be divided into three major sections: the upper valley from Granville to the confluence with the Tweed River; from the Tweed River to Bethel; and from Bethel to its confluence with the Connecticut River in White River Junction. Each has a unique topography.

Throughout the upper section, dozens of small streams drain into the river from the mountains. Many of these hold populations of wild brook trout. Some are home to popula-

White River in late autumn in Stockbridge. Jesse Haller

tions of wild rainbow trout. There are brown trout present as well. Trout range from 6 to 12 inches, with much larger fish always a possibility. Between Granville and its confluence with the Tweed River, the White River runs through a scenic and lightly developed valley. The river here parallels Route 100. This is quintessential Vermont. The low gradient here offers an abundance of riffle water with occasional deep bends and pools. The river here ranges from just a few feet wide to close to 40 feet where it picks up the Hancock Branch, West Branch, and Tweed River.

Starting at its confluence with the Tweed River, the White quickly begins a dramatic change in topography as the gradient steepens. Here much larger boulders, ledges, and deeper

Above. Alex MacDonald with rainbow trout, South Royalton, Vermont. Jesse Haller

Right. Jake Whitcomb fights a fish near Royalton. Stream and Brook Fly Fishing

pools are found. The steeper gradient creates great pocketwater and many deep pools. Probing the depths of these pools stretches the demands on anglers, but can produce some very large trout. The highly oxygenated nature of the river as it flows through Stockbridge and Gaysville offers some of the best trout habitat. Most of the fish in this section are rainbows between 8 and 14 inches. There is a mix of wild and stocked fish.

As you approach Bethel, the White River slows and picks up the Third Branch. The upper portion of this section is primarily freestone. However, large ledges begin to appear that create what look like bottomless pools and back eddies. The gin-clear water allows you to peer deep into the pools. In some places you can actually see the fish holding. Most of this stretch offers great conditions for fly fishing. Several large tributaries join the river as it continues its journey to the Connecticut River. This section is heavily stocked with rainbow trout. The average fish is between 8 and 14 inches. Much larger fish haunt this stretch as well, including some that top the 20-inch mark. This section also has smallmouth bass, some reaching 4 to 5 pounds. Access is plentiful along this stretch and can be found off Route 14, which has two exits off Interstate 89.

The White River is very conducive to wading. It is also large enough to facilitate float fishing along much of its length. However, water levels can vary significantly throughout the year, making floating all but impossible, and even dangerous, in some sections. Launch infrastructure is also somewhat limited. As a result, hiring a guide to take you down the river is never a bad idea.

➤ **Regulations:** While a portion of the upper White River is managed for general-law fishing, the nearly 30-mile stretch starting at the Route 107 bridge in Bethel and extending to the confluence with the Connecticut River is open year-round. From November through March it is restricted to artificial lures only and catch-and-release. The season in the general-law stretch runs from the second Saturday in April through October.

➤ **Hatches:** The White River has a diverse insect population. Mayflies, stoneflies, and caddis are all present. Hatches are not, however, what would be called "strong" and would be better described as sporadic. The best hatches occur from May into midsummer, and again in the fall. The grassy banks can offer good terrestrial fishing in the summer months. Being prepared for all types of conditions is recommended, as predicting what the day may bring is never easy. There are substantial baitfish and crayfish populations as well. This makes the river a good place to fish streamers.

➤ **Tackle:** A 9-foot 5-weight rod with a floating line is your best bet for the White River most of the time. If you want to fish streamers, a 9-foot 6-weight with a fast-sinking sink-tip is your best option. Dry-fly fishing is best done with a 9-foot 4-weight, as you may need to drop to 6X to effectively fish smaller patterns such as Blue-winged Olives. While rods longer than 9 feet can work, especially for nymphing, rods shorter than 9 feet are not practical. Strike indicators should be large enough to float two flies and added weight. Flies should include Woolly Buggers; sculpin and smelt patterns; and all stages of mayflies, stoneflies, and caddis in a variety of sizes and colors.

Sutton Doria holds a brown trout caught on a streamer near Sharon, Vermont. Jesse Haller

JESSE G. HALLER is the manager and lead guide for Middlebury Mountaineer/Green Mountain Adventures. He spent nearly a decade guiding in Colorado before moving to Vermont. He has fished and guided for multiple gamefish species all over the country. Jesse is an Ambassador for Simms Fishing Products. He is the current president of the New Haven River Anglers Association. He is also the founder and two-time pro division champion of the Otter Creek Classic. He can be reached at 802-388-7245 or jesse@mmvt.com.

CLOSEST FLY SHOPS

Middlebury Mountaineer
Green Mountain Adventures
2 Park Street
Middlebury, Vermont 05753 (802-388-7245)
www.mmvt.com
info@mmvt.com

Upper Valley Outfitters
69 Hanover Street
Lebanon, New Hampshire 03766
603-727-9305
www.uppervalleyoutfitters.com
steve@uppervalleyoutfitters.com

CLOSEST GUIDES/OUTFITTERS

Vermont Trout Bum
71 Arnold Mountain Road
Stockbridge, Vermont 05772 (802-234-5281)
www.vttroutbum.com
mstedina@vttroutbum.com

Green Mountain Ghillie
White River Junction, Vermont
802-291-0859
www.greenmountainghillie.com
artrafus@gmail.com

CLOSEST LODGING

Inn on the Green
71 South Pleasant Street
Middlebury, Vermont 05753 (802-388-7512)
www.innonthegreen.com
reservations@innonthegreen.com

Liberty Hill Farm
511 Liberty Hill
Rochester, Vermont 05767 (802-767-3926)
www.libertyhillfarm.com
beth@libertyhillfarm.com

Huntington House Inn
19 Huntington Place
Rochester, Vermont 05767 (802-767-9140)
www.huntingtonhouseinn.com

White River Valley Campground
40 Bridge Street
Gaysville, Vermont 05746 (802-234-9115)
www.whiterivervalleycamping.com

Twin Farms
452 Royalton Turnpike
Barnard, Vermont 05031 (800-894-6327)
www.twinfarms.com
info@twinfarms.com

The Quechee Inn at Marshland Farm
1119 Quechee Main Street
Quechee, Vermont 05059 (802-295-3133)
www.quecheeinn.com

CLOSEST RESTAURANTS

The Quechee Inn at Marshland Farm
1119 Quechee Main Street
Quechee, Vermont 05059 (802-295-3133)
www.quecheeinn.com

Jessica's Restaurant
Swift House Inn
25 Stewart Lane
Middlebury, Vermont 05753 (802-388-9925)
www.jessicasvermont.com
info@swifthouseinn.com

School Street Bistro
13 School Street
Rochester, Vermont 05767 (802-767-3126)
www.facebook.com/SchoolStreetBistroVt

Harrington House
88 North Road
Bethel, Vermont 05032 (802-392-8034)
www.harringtonhouseinn.com
rick@harringtonhouseinn.com

Black Krim
21 Merchants Row
Randolph, Vermont 05061 (802-728-6776)
www.blackkrimtavern.blogspot.com

Worthy Burger (pub-style food)
56 Rainbow Street
South Royalton, Vermont 05068
802-763-2575
www.worthyburger.com
info@worthyburger.com

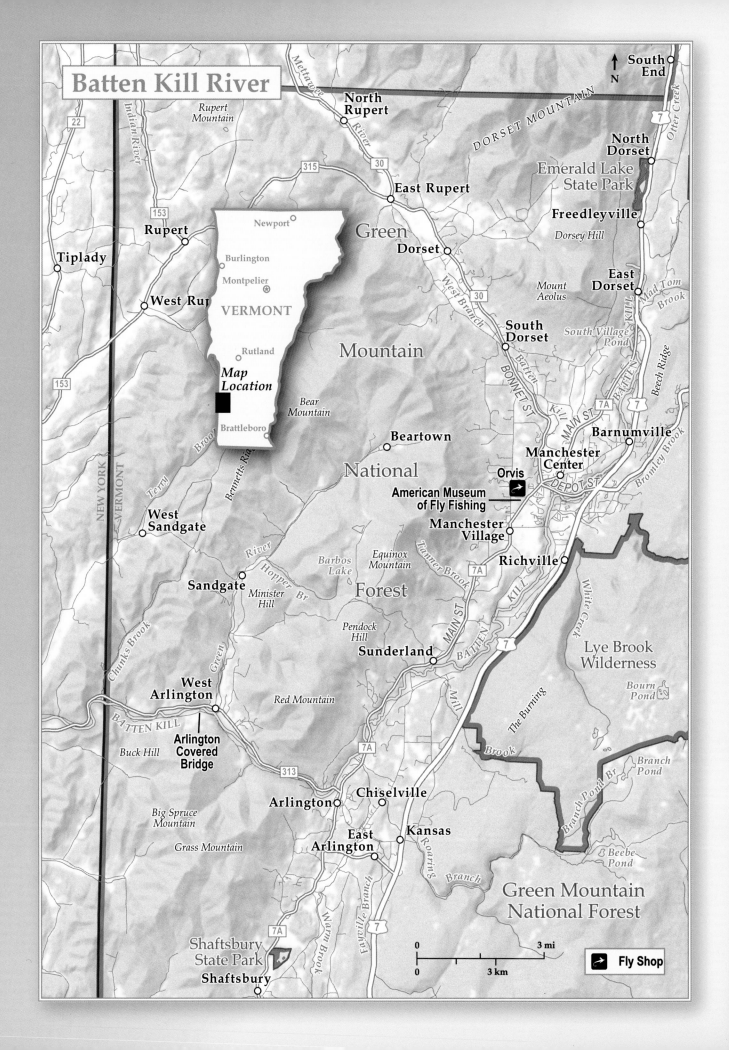

23 · Batten Kill River

➤ **Location:** Southwestern Vermont, about a 1-hour ride from Albany, New York; a 2½-hour ride from Burlington, Vermont; a 3½-hour ride from Boston, Massachusetts; and a 2½-hour ride from Manchester, New Hampshire. Full-service airports are available in all four cities.

The Batten Kill in Vermont is arguably the most famous trout river in New England—and also one of the most famous trout rivers in the Northeast. Its reputation as a premier trout fishery is both longstanding and nationally known. Most fly fishers have at least heard of the Batten Kill. Many have read about it. The Batten Kill is to Vermont what Letort Spring Run is to Pennsylvania, and the Madison is to Montana.

In the mid-1850s, Charles F. Orvis founded his retail namesake on the banks of the Batten Kill in the town of Manchester, Vermont. His fly rods and reels soon became popular with anglers near and far. In the mid-1960s, the business was purchased by the Perkins family, who still own it today. Now a veritable retail giant, Orvis is to the town of Manchester what L.L. Bean is to the town of Freeport, Maine. Fly-fishing legend Lee Wulff (1905–1991) also called the Batten Kill home for a time, residing on its banks just over the border in New York.

Today, Manchester is a four-season tourist destination. Anchored by the Orvis flagship store, the area boasts a lodging, restaurant, and shopping infrastructure that rivals anything found in rural New England. It is also the home of the American Museum of Fly Fishing. As a result, the Batten Kill is that rare fly-fishing destination where a fly fisher can take their non-fly fishing significant other, or the entire family—there truly is something for everyone here.

Nestled in the foothills of southwest Vermont's Green Mountain, the Batten Kill is the quintessential New England freestone trout river. Its idyllic rural setting represents what most people think of when they envision classic New England. Sprawling dairy farms, rustic covered bridges, and

small white country churches add to the natural beauty of the river, valley, and surrounding hills.

The Batten Kill runs roughly 25 miles from its source in Vermont to the New York border. There is another 25 miles of river within New York. As is the case with many rivers in the Northeast, major roads parallel the river for much of its course. However, once in the riverbed, you get the feeling you are farther away from civilization than you actually are, achieving the illusion of seclusion.

The upper Batten Kill gets much of its water from underground springs and mountain streams. This keeps the temperatures cool even during the warmest of months. It is a brown trout and brook trout fishery. The state of Vermont

Covered bridge in Arlington, Vermont. Diana Mallard

discontinued stocking on the river in the 1970s—brown trout first, followed by brook trout, and all stocking was stopped by 1975. Today it is a wild trout fishery. While the brook trout are your typical small but beautiful stream-size fish, brown trout can grow to rather impressive sizes. Brook trout run 8 to 10 inches, while the brown trout average slightly larger.

Like many great rivers, the Batten Kill has seen its ups and downs. Several factors, including overharvest and habitat degradation, led to a decline in the fishery in the early

1990s. In fact, some would call it a crash. Fish numbers—primarily browns—plummeted. Entire year classes of fish were missing. There were reports of diminished hatches. The decline in fish numbers was most likely due to exploitation and habitat degradation. Loss of canopy, bank erosion, siltation, and other factors all contributed. The loss of insects was most likely caused by the habitat degradation and, oddly enough, improvements made to municipal infrastructure implemented to help clean up the river.

After numerous studies to determine what had happened to the fishery, a plan was adopted in early 2007 to restore the Batten Kill and manage the wild trout. The plan included habitat restoration and imposing catch-and-release restrictions on the lower river. The plan also called for restoring the fish populations without the aid of stocking—a wise move. These efforts have yielded positive results, with increases in numbers of both small and large fish. This proves once again that great rivers are resilient—we just need to protect them.

➤ **Regulations:** The Batten Kill is open to fishing from the second Saturday in April through the end of October. It is currently regulated for catch-and-release, from the New York border to Manchester. Above Manchester, the limit is 12 fish, of which only 6 can be brown trout or rainbow trout. There is no minimum length limit here. All methods of angling—fly, spin, and bait—are allowed on the Batten Kill, both above and below Manchester.

The Batten Kill is once again a wild brook trout and brown trout fishery. Brook trout numbers are strong, and brown trout numbers are improving. After 5-plus years of catch-and-release, there are some very large brown trout lurking in the river. Some are caught on dry flies. However, if you really want to catch trophy brown trout you need to target them. This means fishing during low-light conditions—including early-morning and high-water periods—and forgoing more productive dry-fly fishing in favor of what is often slow streamer fishing.

➤ **Hatches:** The hatches on the Batten Kill are typical of those found in most Northeast freestone rivers. Mayflies, caddis, and stoneflies are all found. Mayflies include the classic early spring Hendrickson. There are Tricos in the Batten Kill—not as common in the Northeast as you might think. Hatches start in late April to mid-May, depending on weather, and run throughout the season. Terrestrials are also present in the summer months, with hoppers, crickets, beetles, and ants all present. There are also sculpins and several minnow species in the river.

So, is the Batten Kill still worth fishing? The short answer is absolutely yes—it is a great river in a beautiful setting. While public land is scarce, access is very good thanks to generous landowners who share their property with the masses. You can fish for wild brook trout and brown trout that are as challenging as any you will find. It also puts you in a place that is rich in fly-fishing history—and like other famous fisheries, it just feels different. And as I wrote in the beginning of the book, bad fishing on a great fishery is better than great fishing on a bad fishery.

➤ **Tackle:** A 9-foot 5-weight rod with a floating line is your best bet for the Batten Kill most of the time. If you want to fish streamers, a sink-tip is a good idea. Dry-fly fishing is

Left. Spring fishing on the Batten Kill. Alec Underwood

Inset. Wild brown trout. Alec Underwood

best done with a 9-foot 4-weight, as you may need to drop to 6X to effectively fish smaller patterns such as Blue-winged Olives. While rods longer than 9 feet can work, especially for nymphing, rods shorter than 9 feet are only practical in the upper reaches. Strike indicators should be large enough to float two flies and added weight. Leaders and tippet should be between 3X and 6X. Flies should include Woolly Buggers, sculpin patterns; and all stages of mayflies, stoneflies, and caddis in a variety of sizes and colors.

Wild brown trout. Tyler Atkins

BOB MALLARD has fly fished for over 35 years. He is a blogger, writer, and author; and has owned and operated Kennebec River Outfitters in Madison, Maine since 2001. His writing has been featured in newspapers, magazines, and books at the local, regional, and national levels. He has appeared on radio and television. Look for his upcoming books from Stonefly Press, *25 Best Towns: Fly Fishing for Trout* (winter 2014) and *50 Best Places: Fly Fishing for Brook Trout* (summer 2015). Bob is also a staff fly designer for Catch Fly Fishing. He can be reached at www.kennebecriveroutfitters.com, www.bobmallard.com, info@bobmallard.com, or 207-474-2500.

CLOSEST FLY SHOPS

Orvis
4180 Main Street, Historic Route 7A
Manchester, Vermont 05255
802-362-3750
www.orvis.com

The Reel Angler
302 Depot Street
Manchester Center, Vermont 05255
802-362-0883
www.thereelangler.com

CLOSEST GUIDES/OUTFITTERS

Taconic Guide Service
Manchester, Vermont 05255
802-688-4304
www.taconicguideservice.com
vtangler@live.com

Chuck Kashner's Guide Service
Wells, Vermont
802-287-4000
www.vermontfishingtrips.com
cdkashner@gmail.com

Peter Basta Guide Service & Outfitter
Dorset, Vermont 05251
802-867-4103
www.vtflyfishingguide.com
peterbastavt@gmail.com

CLOSEST LODGING

The Arlington Inn
3904 Route 7A
Arlington, Vermont 05250
802-375-6532
www.arlingtoninn.com
stay@arlingtoninn.com

Equinox Resort
3567 Main Street Route 7A
Manchester Village, Vermont 05254
800-362-4747
www.equinoxresort.com

Casablanca Motel (cabins)
5927 Main Street, Historic Route 7A
Manchester Center, Vermont 05255
800-254-2145
www.casablancamotel.com
casablancamotelVT@gmail.com

North Shire Lodge (cabins)
97 Main Street
Manchester, Vermont 05254
888-339-2336
www.northshirelodge.com
stay@northshirelodge.com

CLOSEST RESTAURANTS

Mulligans of Manchester
Route 7A
Manchester, Vermont 05254
802-362-3663
www.mulligans-vt.com
mulligansmanchester@gmail.com

Seasons Restaurant
4566 Main Street
Manchester Center, Vermont 05255
802-362-7272
www.seasonsvt.com
seasonsvt@gmail.com

Bistro Henry
Gourmet Dining
1942 Depot Street (Route 11/30)
Manchester Center, Vermont 05255
802-362-4982
www.bistrohenry.com
info@bistrohenry.com

Ye Olde Tavern
5183 Main Street
Manchester Center, Vermont 05255
802-362-0611
www.yeoldetavern.net
1790@yeoldetavern.net

IV · NEW YORK

Getting away from the crowds. Art Salomon

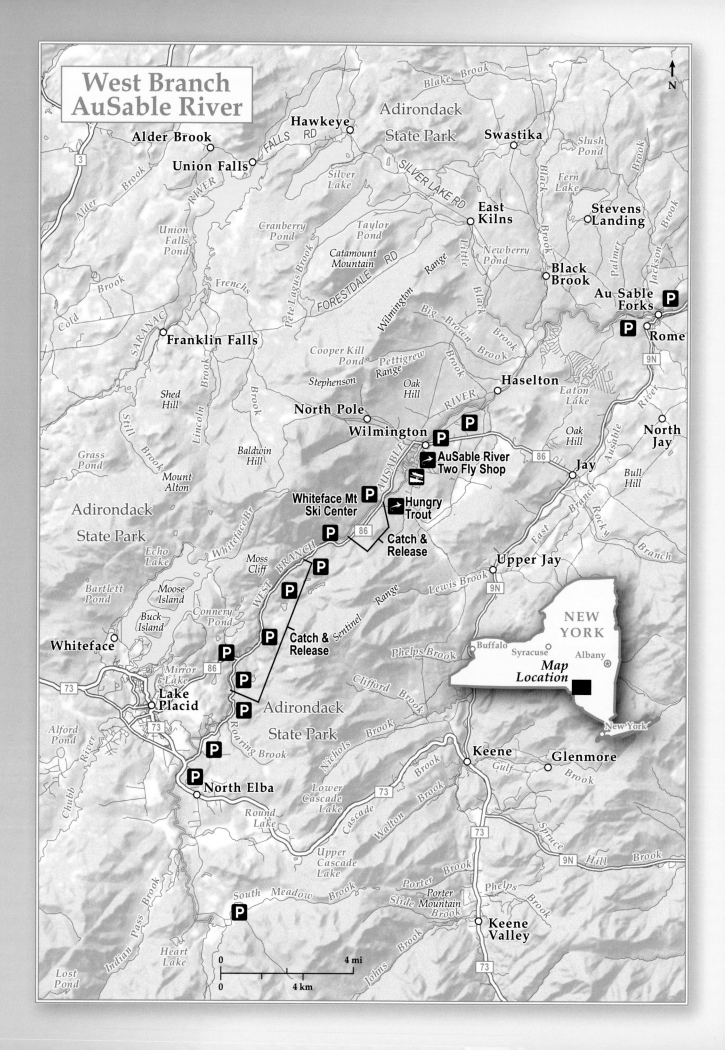

24 · West Branch Ausable River

➤ **Location:** Northeast New York, about a 5-hour ride from New York City; a 2½-hour ride from Albany, New York; a 2½-hour ride from Burlington, Vermont; and a 2-hour ride from Montreal, Quebec. Full-service airports are available in all four cities.

The West Branch of the Ausable River begins in the Adirondack Mountains High Peaks region, at 4,000 feet above sea level. Its headwaters are near Lake Placid, the site of two Winter Olympics. The river flows for roughly 30 miles before merging with the East Branch to form the Ausable proper. The latter terminates at Lake Champlain.

The Ausable River is considered one of the finest trout streams in the East. It is a freestone river known for prolific hatches and great fly fishing. There are native brook trout, along with rainbow trout and brown trout. It is also one of the most scenic rivers in the East.

The Ausable is rich in fly-fishing tradition. It was home to the renowned Francis Betters—a member of the Fly Fishing Hall of Fame—who invented the Ausable Wulff, the Haystack, and the Usual, fly patterns still used today. Born in 1931, Betters fished the Ausable with his father, an Adirondack guide, and his friends, including Red Wilbur and Ray Bergman, who authored the classic fishing guide *Trout* in 1938. For almost five decades, anglers visiting the Adirondacks stopped by Mr. Betters's Adirondack Sport Shop. His passing in 2009 was a heartfelt loss to the community.

The Ausable has diverse habitat, with waterfalls, deep pools, riffles, runs, pocketwater, and slow glides. The river is clean and rich in minerals. It is well-oxygenated as a result of the numerous springs and feeder streams. These also help maintain cool temperatures throughout the season. A heavy canopy of trees borders most of the stream, providing shelter from the sun, and good habitat for insects. The streambed consists of sand, gravel, rocks, and boulders, which provides ideal habitat for trout and insects.

The section most popular with fly fishers begins at the Olympic Ski Jumping Complex in Lake Placid. The river here is small, cold, boulder-strewn, and well-shaded. It requires a hike to reach the water. East of Lake Placid, the river is predominantly slow water with deep bends, undercut banks, long runs, riffles, and a sand and gravel bottom. There is 4½ miles of catch-and-release water, starting near Holcomb Pond Brook and ending at the Notch. This section is a mix of slow water, deep bends, and undercut banks. There is some pocketwater at the upper end. Access is easy, with several parking areas next to the river.

Between the Notch and Wilmington—a section of roughly 4 miles—there is a 1-mile stretch of catch-and-release water. This is classic pocketwater. The river drops approximately 130 feet in elevation in this section, and the bottom is littered

Below Fran Betters Pool. John Ruff, Ruff Waters Fly Fishing

with rocks and boulders. Fishing this section requires good wading skills. The fish here tuck themselves in around the many boulders, making it difficult to get to them.

Below the Flume Bridge is a short section of public water before the river runs into Lake Everest. The Flume pool is a popular spot for cliff jumpers during July and August. If you can get there when no one is swimming, there is a good chance you might hook a large trout from the depths of the pool. It is best to fish the lake by canoe or float tube. The lake is approximately 2 miles long and offers anglers tranquility and good evening topwater action.

107

Above. Evan Bottcher on catch-and-release section. Hungry Trout Resort
Inset. Evan Bottcher releasing a brown trout. Steve Uwe Reiss

From the dam below the lake downstream for a distance of 10 miles is some of the best fly-fishing water on the river. The first 2 miles is mostly pocketwater, fast water, and pools. This area receives less pressure than the catch-and-release water, due to the fact that it is more remote and requires a hike to reach it.

Below the Lewis Bridge is 4 miles of private water. There is a Public Fishing Rights access trail that provides access to the Bush Country stretch. This stretch is the most remote on the river. There is outstanding pocketwater where the fishing can be quite rewarding. The last stretch is in the Town of Ausable Forks, where the pocketwater continues for 1 mile before the river ends at its confluence with the East Branch.

Much of the West Branch of the Ausable is located on state land. There are Public Fishing Rights access sites in many areas. Access along most of the river is ample and easy

The West Branch of the Ausable near North Elba. Alec Underwood

to locate. The river is between 40 and 60 feet wide. Flows run in the 300–800 cfs range. The West Branch is a wading river.

➤ **Regulations:** Fishing season runs from April 1 to October 15. The catch-and-release sections are open year-round. The river is usually fishable by Opening Day. By mid-May, fishing is in full swing.

After a midsummer drop-off due to warm water, fishing picks up again in late August, and gets better until the season closes. The best times to fish are early May to mid-July, and late August to the end of the season.

➤ **Hatches:** Hendricksons hatch in early May, and can last from 10 to 14 days. Next come March Browns, Blue-winged Olives, and Sulphurs, which hatch through June. The most famous hatch is the Green Drake. Anglers come from all over for this hatch. The hatch starts in early to mid-June, and usually lasts a week to 10 days. There are almost continuous hatches of caddis and stoneflies during the season. This is part of the reason the West Branch of the Ausable is considered one of the finest trout streams in the East.

The Ausable is a classic dry-fly river. The hatches are strong and diverse. Trout will often feed on the surface even when there is no hatch. They will take attractors skittered on the surface. Early in the season, on overcast days, and during high-water periods, trout will take streamers. The fish will also take nymphs.

If you like to mix some breathtaking scenery and angling history with great fly fishing, the West Branch of the Ausable is a great place to visit.

➤ **Tackle:** A 9-foot 5-weight rod with a floating line is your best bet for the West Branch Ausable most of the time. Rods lighter than this can be used for dry-fly fishing. Longer rods up to 10 feet are good choices for nymphing. You can often use shorter rods in the 7- to 8-foot range in the upper river. Fluorocarbon leaders and tippets are always a good idea for nymphing. Strike indicators should be large enough to float two flies and added weight. Flies should include streamer patterns; a selection of mayflies in various sizes, colors, and life stages; stonefly nymphs; attractors; and all stages of caddis in a variety of sizes and colors.

TOM CONWAY owns and operates Ausable River Two Fly Shop in Wilmington, New York. He can be reached at 518-946-3474, tom@ausablerivertwo flyshop.com, or www.ausablerivertwoflyshop.com.

CLOSEST FLY SHOPS

Ausable River Two Fly Shop
5698 NYS Route 86
Wilmington, New York 12997
518-946-3474
www.ausablerivertwoflyshop.com
tom@ausablerivertwoflyshop.com

Hungry Trout Resort and Fly Shop
5239 NYS Route 86
Wilmington, New York 12997
518-946-2217
www.hungrytrout.com
info@hungrytrout.com

Wiley's Flies
1179 Route 86
Ray Brook, New York 12977
518-891-1829
www.wileysflies.com
vince@wileysflies.com

CLOSEST GUIDES/OUTFITTERS

Ruff Waters Fly Fishing
828 Springfield Road
Wilmington, New York 12997
518-524-3732
www.ruffwatersflyfishing.com
john@ruffwatersflyfishing.com

CLOSEST LODGING

Hungry Trout Resort and Fly Shop
(see above)

Wilderness Inn II
(rustic cabins)
5481 NYS Route 86
Wilmington, New York 12997
518-946-2391
www.wildernessinnadk.com
WildernessInnAdk@yahoo.com

Mountain Brook Lodge
NYS Route 86
Wilmington, New York 12997
518-946-2262
www.mountainbrooklodge.com
mtbrook@frontiernet.net

Trout Landing Cottage
(house rental)
977 Springfield Road
Wilmington, New York 12997
866-235-9655
www.adirondackholiday.com/rooms/class/
trout-landing-cottage.htm
adirondack.holiday@yahoo.com

North Pole Resorts
(motel/RV sites/camping)
5644 NYS Route 86
Wilmington, New York 12997
518-946-7733
www.northpoleresorts.com
info@northpoleresorts.com

CLOSEST RESTAURANTS

Hungry Trout Restaurant (fine dining)
5722 NYS Route 86
Wilmington, New York 12997
518-946-2217
www.hungrytrout.com
info@hungrytrout.com

R.F. McDougall's Pub (pub-style food, full bar)
5239 NYS Route 86
Wilmington, New York 12997
518-946-2219
www.hungrytrout.com
info@hungrytrout.com

Lake Placid Pub & Brewery
813 Mirror Lake Drive
Lake Placid, New York 12946
518-523-3813
www.ubuale.com

Wilderness Inn II Restaurant
(gourmet dining)
5481 NYS Route 86
Wilmington, New York 12997
518-946-2391
www.wildernessinnadk.com
WildernessInnAdk@yahoo.com

Up The Creek
(breakfast, lunch, and food/coffee to go)
5549 NYS Route 86
Wilmington, New York 12997
518-946-2013
www.tgostore.com/restaurant.html

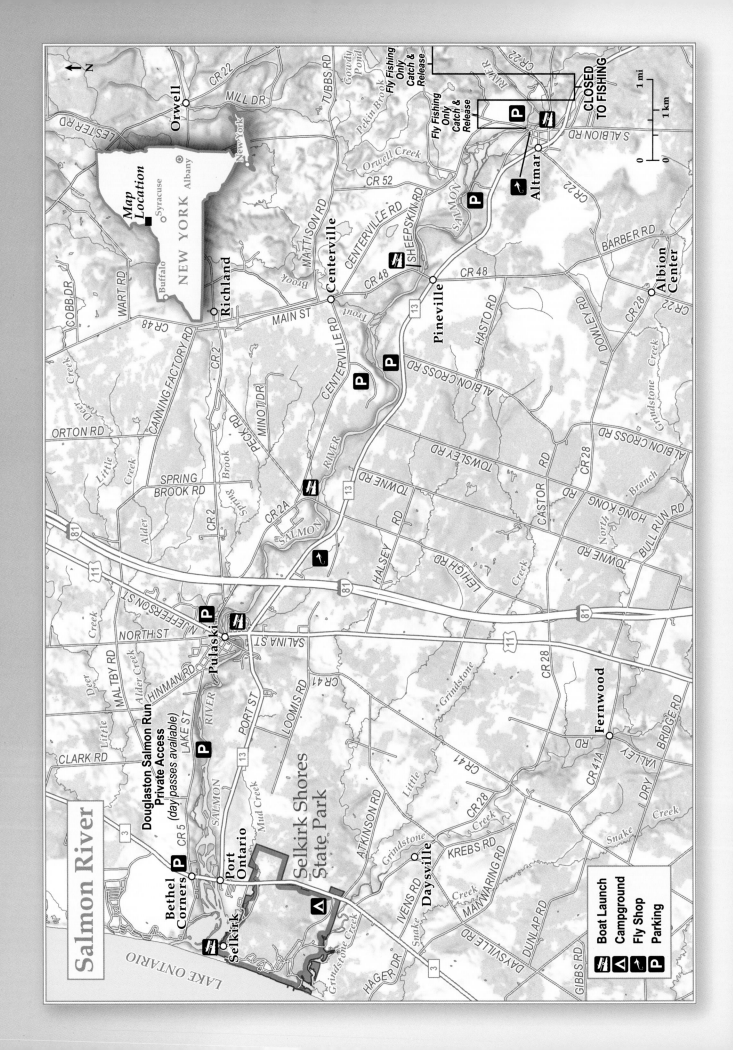

Salmon River

N

LAKE ONTARIO

Orwell

New York

Map Location

NEW YORK

Syracuse   Albany
Buffalo

Richland

Centerville

Pineville

Altmar

Albion Center

Fly Fishing Only
Catch & Release

Fly Fishing Only
Catch & Release

CLOSED TO FISHING

Pulaski

Port Ontario

Selkirk

Bethel Corners

Daysville

Fernwood

Selkirk Shores State Park

Douglaston Salmon Run
Private Access
(day passes available)

Roads and labels:
LESTER RD, CR 22, MILL DR, TUBBS RD, Gowdy Pond, Pekin Brook, RIVER, CR 22, S ALBION RD, CR 22, BARBER RD, CR 28, Orwell Creek, CR 52, SHEEPSKIN RD, SALMON, CR 48, CR 48, CENTERVILLE RD, MATTISON RD, Trout Brook, MAIN ST, CENTERVILLE RD, 13, HASTO RD, DOWLEY RD, Grindstone Creek, ALBION CROSS RD, CANNING FACTORY RD, CR 48, CR 2, PECK RD, MINOT DR, RIVER, TOWNE RD, CASTOR RD, ALBION CROSS RD, HONG KONG, CR 28, BULL RUN RD, North Branch, ORTON RD, Little Creek, Deer Creek, SPRING BROOK RD, Spring Brook, CR 2A, CR 2A, SALMON, 13, TOWNE RD, HALSEY RD, LEHIGH RD, Creek, 81, 81, 11, 81, 11, CR 28, Grindstone, Fernwood, COBB DR, WART RD, CLARK RD, Little Deer Creek, MALTBY RD, Alder Creek, NORTH ST, JEFFERSON ST, SALINA ST, HINMAN RD, RIVER, LAKE ST, PORT ST, LOOMIS RD, CR 41, ATKINSON RD, IVENS RD, Little Creek, CR 28, KREBS RD, Grindstone Creek, MANWARING RD, DUNLAP RD, Snake Creek, DRY Creek, DAYSVILLE RD, GIBBS RD, VALLEY RD, CR 41A, BRIDGE RD, SALMON, Mud Creek, HAGER DR, 3, 3, CR 5

Legend:
Boat Launch
Campground
Fly Shop
Parking

1 mi
1 km
0   1 km
0

➤ **Location:** West-central New York, about a ½-hour ride from Syracuse, a 2½-hour ride from Albany, a 4½-hour ride from New York City; and a 4½-hour ride from Philadelphia. Full-service airports are available in all four cities.

The Salmon River is home to one of the most robust and diverse trout and salmon fisheries the country. It is that rare place where you can catch Pacific and Atlantic salmon, steelhead, brown trout, and rainbow trout. The Salmon holds the Great Lakes record for king salmon. This fish tipped the scales at 47 pounds, 13 ounces. It also holds the world record for coho salmon—a 33-pound, 4-ounce specimen. That this fishery is within a half day's drive of many of the largest cities in the eastern United States makes it even more amazing. It is truly a fly fisher's paradise.

The section of the most interest to fly anglers lies between the Route 3 bridge in Port Ontario and the dam at the lower Salmon River Reservoir near Altmar. The Salmon can be separated into three different sections: upper, lower, and middle.

The lower section begins upstream of the Route 3 bridge. Here the river enters an estuary where salmonids stage before making their spawning migration in late August and early September. This section continues upstream through the village of Pulaski to the County Route 2A bridge. Here the Salmon is a very fast-moving river. Water flows through cuts in the bedrock. This is classic pocketwater, perfect for nymphing. Studded boots are a good idea here. While difficult to wade, this stretch of river can be extremely rewarding. When fresh fish enter the river, this is where you'll find them.

The first 2½ miles upstream of the Route 3 bridge is owned by Douglaston Salmon Run. It is open to the public under a fee system. The number of anglers is restricted. This gives guests the opportunity to pursue their passion in a safe and monitored environment for a modest fee. This area is home

to some fantastic pools and the famous Meadow Run, which is the first place fresh fish stop to rest when they migrate out of the estuary. Fresh-run salmon and trout are aggressive. They eagerly take flies. This is a great place to nymph or swing large streamers to fresh fish.

The middle section lies between County Route 2A bridge and County Route 48 bridge in Pineville. This section features some of the most remote water on the river, as well as some of the most productive, for those willing to walk. This is popular with driftboat anglers for the same reason. This section features transition water, with many large holes perfect for resting salmon. Browns and steelhead will also

Late summer sunrise over the famous Meadow Run in Douglaston Salmon Run. Garrett Brancy

winter here. Due to light angling pressure, fish in the middle section will strike a well-presented swung fly aggressively. Nymphing is very productive here.

Beginning at the County Route 48 bridge, the upper section runs to just below the dam at the lower Salmon River Reservoir in Altmar. This section contains most of the spawning habitat utilized by trout and salmon, as well as some of the best wintering holes for trout. Because of its

Garrett Brancy with winter steelhead from Douglaston Salmon Run. Garrett Brancy

distance from the lake, fishing here starts a few weeks after the first pods of salmon enter the river. Good angling continues through mid-April. After this, steelhead begin to migrate back to Lake Ontario. There are two fly-fishing-only areas in this section. They are separated by the Salmon River Fish Hatchery. The lower area begins upstream of the County Route 52 bridge in Altmar and ends ½ mile below the hatchery. The upper area begins ½ mile above the hatchery and ends ½ mile below the lower reservoir dam.

The Salmon River offers 17 miles of fishable water. Most of this is easily accessed from designated fishermen's parking areas. Many are located off NYS Route 13, which runs south of the river. The 2½ miles of private water can be accessed from the Douglaston Salmon Run office and parking area located on County Route 5. Walk-in and driftboat access is also available at the Route 52, 48, and 2A bridges; as well as several spots within Pulaski. There is another boat launch at Pine Grove in Selkirk Shores State Park. This provides access to the estuary and Lake Ontario.

Water levels can change daily on the Salmon River. Releases from the Light House Hill Dam can alter the flow at any time. Anglers should check the water level before wading. Flows are controlled by Brookfield Renewable Power. A release schedule can be found on the company's website at www.brookfieldrenewable.com. Typical flows range from 185–750 cfs. These are safe for wading. Flows of 500 cfs or more are required for floating. Releases of 750–2,000 cfs require that wading anglers use caution. Flows over 2,000 cfs are not conducive to wading.

The Salmon is open year-round to fishing. Peak salmon season is from September through mid-October. Steelhead, browns, and rainbows usually show up in early October. Brown trout spawn in November—this is the best time to catch trophy browns. Steelhead and rainbow trout fishing is also good in November. Some years, the steelhead fishing beats the brown trout fishing. Fresh steelhead and rainbows migrate into the river throughout the winter. Spawning occurs near the beginning of April. This is the best time to fish for steelhead. Post-spawn steelhead provide fly fishers with one last shot at fish as they return to the lake. Skamania, or summer-run, steelhead and Atlantic salmon move into the river starting in early May. These offer some of the most challenging fishing of the year.

Salmon River fish feed heavily on eggs and decaying salmon. Minnows and aquatic invertebrates are important foods in the winter and spring. This includes several species of dace and fallfish. Crayfish are also present. Insects include stoneflies, caddis, and mayflies. Hellgrammites and aquatic worms are present as well.

The Salmon River is the premier salmon and steelhead fishery in the East. It is also a trophy brown trout and rainbow trout fishery. It is an amazing resource located in an area easily reached by the masses.

➤ Tackle: A 9- to 10-foot 8-weight rod with a floating line is your best option for the Salmon River. Heavier rods are recommended if you are targeting Pacific salmon. Lighter rods are recommended for brown trout. Reels should have a smooth and reliable drag system, and 150 or more yards of backing. Spey rods are often used here, as are switch rods. You should have an adequate supply of split-shot in a variety of sizes. Indicators should be large. Leaders and tippets in the 0X–5X range are recommended. Fluorocarbon is always a good idea. Flies should include egg patterns, Bunny Leeches, Flesh Flies, and Woolly Buggers, along with stonefly and caddis nymphs in a variety of sizes and colors.

Sutton Doria with steelhead. Brian Cadoret

Doug Auyer hoists a monster king salmon. *Garrett Brancy*

GARRETT BRANCY manages Douglaston Salmon Run in Pulaski, New York. He can be reached at 315-298-6672, www.douglastonsalmonrun.com, or fish@douglastonsalmonrun.com.

CLOSEST FLY SHOPS

Whitaker's Sports Store
3707 NYS 13
Pulaski, New York 13142
315-298-6162
www.whitakers.com
feedback@whitakers.com

Troutfitter
3008 Erie Boulevard East
Syracuse, New York 13224
315-446-2047
syrtroutfitter@yahoo.com

Fat Nancy's Tackle & Fly Shop
3750 NYS 13
Pulaski, New York 13142
315-298-4051
www.fatnancystackle.com

Malinda's Fly and Tackle Shop
3 Pulaski Street
Altmar, New York 13302
315-298-2993

CLOSEST GUIDES/OUTFITTERS

Captain Adrian LaSorte Guide Service
33 Riverside Drive
Binghamton, New York 13903
607-427-7335
www.fishadrian.com
tightlines@fishadrian.com

Paul's Guide Service
Pulaski, New York 13142
315-298-3949
www.paulsguideservice.com
paul@paulsguideservice.com

Jay Peck Guides
4786 Ridge Road West
Spencerport, New York 14559
585-233-0436
www.jaypeckguides.com
jaypeckguides@gmail.com

CLOSEST LODGING

Douglaston Salmon Run
(streamside lodges, limited access/private water)
301 County Route 5
Pulaski, New York 13142
315-298-6672
www.douglastonsalmonrun.com
fish@douglastonsalmonrun.com

1880 House Bed & Breakfast
1 South Jefferson Street
Pulaski, New York 13142
315-298-6088
www.1800house.com
lynn1880@ix.netcom.com

Whitaker's Motel
3707 NYS 13
Pulaski, New York 13142
315-298-6162
www.whitakers.com
feedback@whitakers.com

The Schoolhouse Inn
29 Pulaski Street
Altmar, New York 13302
315-298-4371
www.theschoolhouseinn.net
info@theschoolhouseinn.net

Double Eagle Lodge
3268 New York 13
Pulaski, New York 13142
315-298-3326
www.doubleeaglelodge.com

CLOSEST RESTAURANTS

RiverHouse Restaurant (fine dining)
4818 Salina Street
Pulaski, New York 13142
315-509-4281
www.riverhouserestaurant.net
riverhouserestaurant@yahoo.com

Eddy's Place
3866 NYS 13
Pulaski, New York 13142
315-298-7538
www.eddysplacerestaurant.com
eddysplacepulaski@gmail.com

LD'S Alehouse
4861 North Jefferson Street
Pulaski, New York 13142
315-509-4234

Brandy's Sunrise Restaurant (breakfast)
7627 NYS Route 3
Pulaski, New York 13142
315-298-7774

Ponderosa Steakhouse
3734 New York 13
Pulaski, New York 13142
315-298-4883
www.ponderosasteakhouses.com

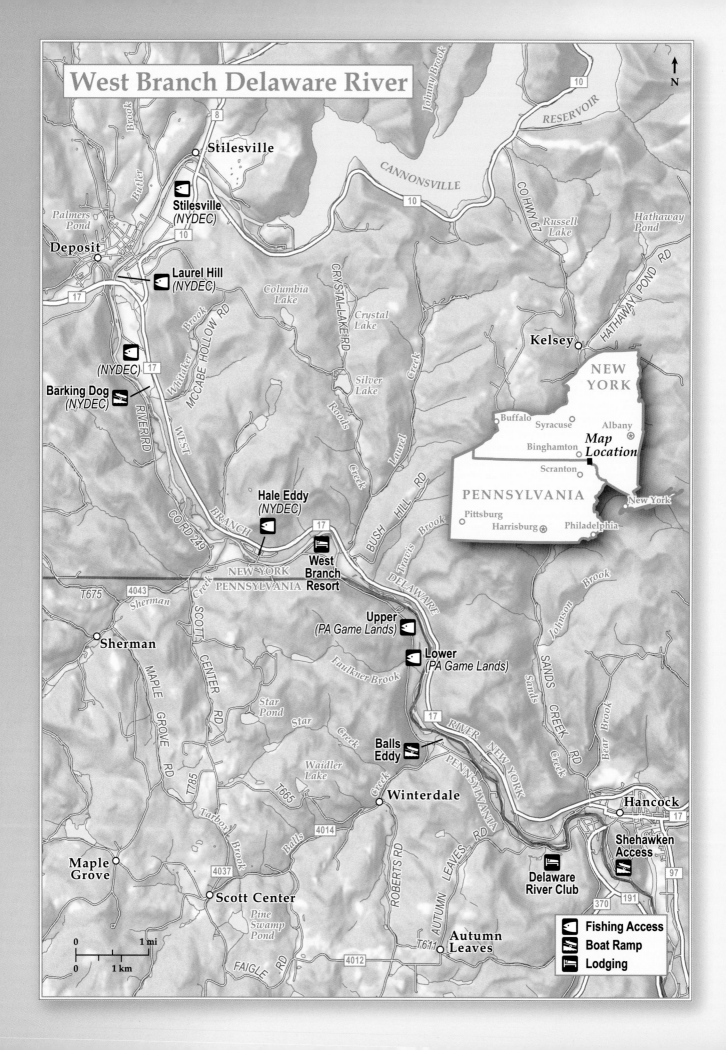

West Branch Delaware River

N

Stilesville

Stilesville
(NYDEC)

Palmers
Pond

Deposit

Laurel Hill
(NYDEC)

(NYDEC)

Barking Dog
(NYDEC)

Columbia
Lake

Crystal
Lake

Silver
Lake

Kelsey

NEW
YORK

Russell
Lake

Hathaway
Pond

CANNONSVILLE

RESERVOIR

Buffalo   Syracuse   Albany

Map
Location

Binghamton

Scranton

PENNSYLVANIA

New York

Pittsburg

Harrisburg   Philadelphia

Hale Eddy
(NYDEC)

West
Branch
Resort

Upper
(PA Game Lands)

Lower
(PA Game Lands)

Sherman

Star
Pond

Star

Creek

Balls
Eddy

Waidler
Lake

Winterdale

Hancock

Shehawken
Access

Delaware
River Club

Maple
Grove

Scott Center

Pine
Swamp
Pond

Autumn
Leaves

	Fishing Access
	Boat Ramp
	Lodging

0   1 mi

0   1 km

26 · West Branch Delaware River

➤ **Location:** Southeastern New York about a 1½-hour ride from New York City; a 2-hour ride from Newark, New Jersey; a 3-hour ride from Hartford, Connecticut; and a 4-hour ride from Boston, Massachusetts. Full-service airports are available in all four cities.

The West Branch of the Delaware River is considered one of the finest wild trout fisheries east of the Mississippi. It is located on the western edge of the Catskill Mountains—the birthplace of American dry-fly fishing. Some of the most notable names in fly fishing called the Catskills home. Theodore Gordon and Joan and Lee Wulff are just a few of the well-known anglers who fished these legendary waters. This region is home to some of the finest trout rivers in the country.

The West Branch is one of several tailwaters in the area created when the state built reservoirs in the mid-1960s to supply drinking water to New York City. Cannonsville Dam was constructed on the lower West Branch in the town of Deposit. This created Cannonsville Reservoir—a roughly 30-mile-long impoundment. The reservoir has a maximum capacity of 95.7 billion gallons.

The upper West Branch above the reservoir flows through farmland which has a negative effect

Cole's Riffle in July. John Miller

on the reservoir due to siltation. This makes it less desirable as drinking water. Compared to the other six area dams, the West Branch generally has the best flow regime. The releases from Cannonsville are mainly used to keep the salt water from encroaching up from Delaware Bay.

The section of West Branch below Cannonsville Dam is the most popular with fly fishers, thanks to the season-long coldwater releases. This section extends roughly 11 miles to the confluence with the East Branch, near the town of Hancock. It has some of the highest fish counts of any trout river east of the Rocky Mountains. Both brown trout and rainbow trout are present. In the spring, approximately 80 percent of the trout in the West Branch are brown trout. The remaining are mostly rainbows, with the occasional brook trout. As the main stem Delaware warms, rainbows migrate up into the West Branch, seeking colder water.

The West Branch is a large river. It is, however, conducive to wading. It is also ideal for floating. When the level drops below 500 cfs, floating becomes difficult. The upper section of the river is braided, due to several large islands and the side channels they create. These side channels are accessible to wading anglers during high-water periods. Trout will move into these to avoid the strong currents when the river gets over 1,000 cfs.

Water releases from Cannonsville fluctuate throughout the fishing season. They are dictated by three important factors. The first is how much water is in the reservoir. If the reservoir level drops, the amount of water released will go down. If the level is stable, releases will go up. When the reservoir reaches capacity, or overflows, the dam operators will siphon some water off. The dam helps buffer the river from runoff after rain. Even when it does get high or murky, you can usually move upriver toward the dam and find clear water.

Public access on the West Branch is very good. There are several parking areas in the catch-and-release section in New York, and several farther downstream on the Pennsylvania side, in what is known as the Gamelands. There is also ample driftboat infrastructure. There is a formal state boat ramp located every 2 to 4 miles along the West Branch. The boat ramps allow anglers and guides to float different sections of the river, depending on hatches and water conditions.

From New York State Route 17 downstream approximately 2 miles, the river is managed for catch-and-release. This section is known for hatches that go right into the late summer. This is due to its proximity to the dam. Even during low-water periods, the river will start the day in the low 40s and peak during the midday hours in the mid-50s. This holds true even when outside temperatures climb into the 80s and above.

Brown trout average over a foot long. Fish between 16 and 18 inches are fairly common. Fish up to 24 inches are not uncommon. Fish up to 30 inches have been caught. Rainbow trout in the Delaware system generally do not get much bigger than 20 inches. Compared to the brown trout, the rainbows grow quickly, but do not live as long. The few brook trout present in the system are usually found near the mouths of feeder streams along the West Branch.

➤ **Regulations:** The upper West Branch in located in New York. The lower half of the river forms the border of New York and Pennsylvania. A New York license is required for fishing the upper section. Either a New York or Pennsylvania license is valid on the lower section. The upper section of the river is open to fishing from April 1 through October 15. It closes in the fall to protect spawning brown trout. Rainbow trout spawn in the spring and utilize the tributaries, not the main river. The section forming the New York–Pennsylvania line is open to fishing year-round.

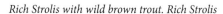

Rich Strolis with wild brown trout. Rich Strolis

Cole Elmandorf with large wild brown trout.
Zachary Anderson

➤ **Hatches:** Trout in the West Branch feed on the prolific insects throughout the spring and summer. Many of the trout caught on the West Branch are taken on dry flies. It is one of the finest dry-fly fisheries in the region.

Mayfly and caddis hatches are very prolific on the West Branch as a result of the cold, clean water. The timing of the hatches is pretty consistent with the other rivers in the area, and well before those found in parts of New England. Hatches can be expedited or delayed due to weather patterns. Hatches are usually in full swing by mid-April, and run through October. Trout on the West Branch are notoriously wary, and low-profile patterns such as emergers and Compara-duns are often required to fool them.

The reservoir is full of alewives. When it overflows, these 4- to 7-inch baitfish spill into the river and offer some excellent streamer fishing. Trout will take streamers at other times as well. Nymphing can be very productive, especially before, after, and between hatches.

➤ **Tackle:** A 9-foot 5-weight rod with a floating line is your best bet for the West Branch of the Delaware. A 9-foot 6-weight or 7-weight is a good option for streamer fishing from a boat. Dry-fly fishing is best done with a 9-foot 4-weight, as you may need to drop to 6X to effectively fish smaller patterns such as BWOs. While rods longer than 9 feet can work, especially for nymphing, rods shorter than 9 feet are not practical. Strike indicators should be large enough to float two flies and added weight. Flies should include Woolly Buggers and sculpin patterns; and all stages of mayflies, stoneflies, and caddis in a variety of sizes and colors.

John Miller in no-kill section in July. John Miller

BEN SHEARD works for West Branch Resort in Hancock, New York. He can be reached at 800-201-2557, www.westbranchresort.com, or orders@westbranchresort.com.

CLOSEST FLY SHOPS

West Branch Resort
150 Faulkner Road
Hancock, New York 13783
800-201-2557
www.westbranchresort.com
reservations@westbranchresort.com

Border Water Outfitters
159 East Main Street
Hancock, New York 13783
607-637-4296
www.borderwateroutfitters.com
bwo@hancock.net

Delaware River Club
1228 Winterdale Road
Starlight, Pennsylvania 18461
570-635-5880
www.thedelawareriverclub.com
flyfish@thedelawareriverclub.com

Baxter House River Outfitters
2012 Old Route 17
Roscoe, New York 12776
607-290-4022
www.baxterhouse.net
bhoutfitters@aol.comm

CLOSEST GUIDES/OUTFITTERS

Cross Current Guide Service & Outfitters
100 Laurel Acres Road
Milford, Pennsylvania 18337
914-475-6779
www.crosscurrentguideservice.com
crosscurrent@optonline.net

East Branch Outfitters
1471 Peas Eddy Road
Hancock, New York 13783
607-637-5451
www.eastbranchoutfitters.com
info@eastbranchoutfitters.com

CLOSEST LODGING

West Branch Resort
150 Faulkner Road
Hancock, New York 13783
800-201-2557
www.westbranchresort.com
reservations@westbranchresort.com

Delaware River Club
1228 Winterdale Road
Starlight, Pennsylvania 18461
570-635-5880
www.thedelawareriverclub.com
flyfish@thedelawareriverclub.com

Smith's Colonial Motel
23085 New York 97
Hancock, New York 13783
607-637-2985
www.smithscolonialmotel.com

Capra Inn
521 West Main Street
Hancock, New York 13783
607-637-1600

CLOSEST RESTAURANTS

River Run Restaurant
150 Faulkner Road
Hancock, New York 13783
607-467-5533
www.westbranchresort.com
reservations@westbranchresort.com

Koo Koose Grille
129 Front Street
Deposit, New York 13754
607-235-2817
www.kookoosegrille.com

Lydia's Crosstown Tavern
6031 Hancock Highway
Starlight, Pennsylvania 18461
570-635-5926
www.facebook.com/pages/Lydias-Cross-town-Tavern

Spiro's Countryside Restaurant
179 Rockland Road
Roscoe New York, 12776
607-498-4419
www.spiroscountryside.com
comments@spiroscountryside.com

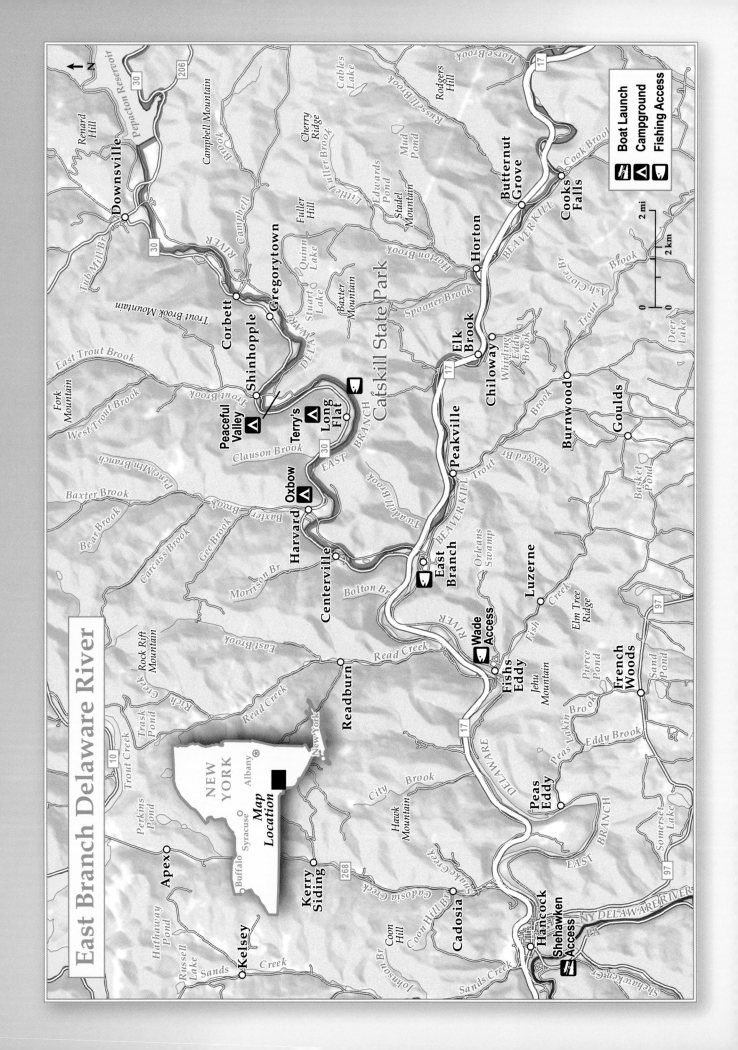

➤ **Location:** Central New York, about 2 hours from New York City, a 2½-hour ride from Newark, New Jersey; and a 4-hour ride from Boston, Massachusetts. Full-service airports are available in all three cities.

In 1955, Pepacton Reservoir was built on the East Branch of the Delaware River. It became New York City's largest reservoir, at 5,763 surface acres with a capacity of 140.2 billion gallons of water. After the reservoir was completed, coldwater releases, which average roughly 40 degrees, created the perfect environment for trout and the insects they feed on.

The East Branch of the Delaware is one of two rivers that combine to form the Delaware River. The East Branch is approximately 75 miles long from its source to its confluence with the West Branch of the Delaware in Hancock, New York. From its source in Grand Gorge, New York, the river winds its way along the western edge of Catskill Park, draining an area of roughly 371 square miles.

The section of the East Branch that is of most interest to fly fishers is between the dam in Downsville and the confluence with the West Branch in Hancock. This section is roughly 33 miles. Over its course, the river offers everything you can expect in a great fishery. The diversity of water is excellent. The insect hatches are reliable and prolific. The river also has high fish numbers and a good population of large fish.

The first section, from Downsville downstream to the town of East Branch, is about 16 miles long. This is the area most influenced by the coldwater releases from Pepacton Reservoir. Anglers are often surprised to find that the river here resembles a large spring creek. In this section, the river meanders through a beautiful valley with terrain that varies from steep forested slopes of cherry and hemlock to fields planted with corn and other crops.

The river averages 75 to 150 feet wide here. It is slow and flat throughout most of its course. There is very little riffle water, and pocketwater is nonexistent. The river here is mostly slow runs, short riffles, and deep pools. The bottom is primarily gravel and silt in the runs, while some of the larger pools are filled with large boulders and ledges. Aquatic vegetation is found throughout this section. For most of the year this section is subject to low, gentle flows and is generally a wader-friendly stretch of river.

The upper East Branch is home to wild brook trout, wild and stocked brown trout, and wild rainbows. Brown trout are the predominant fish by a large margin. Most fish will be in the 12- to 14-inch range. Fish 18 inches and larger are

Covered bridge in Downsville, New York. Rich Strolis

common. This section is known to produce some truly large browns, with stories of monster fish encountered during high-water periods and at night. Insect hatches are excellent.

➤ **Hatches:** Hatches start in early April, run through the summer, and continue right up until the season closes in

Upper East Branch. Baxter House River Outfitters

streambed supports heavy populations of mayflies, caddis, and stoneflies. Blizzardlike caddis hatches are often encountered. There are days when mayfly spinners will cover the decks of the drift boat.

Anglers will find a good mix of brown and rainbow trout throughout the lower East Branch. Most of the fish here are wild, as this section has not been stocked in years. Unlike the upper river, rainbow trout are much more numerous than brown trout. The riffles and pocketwater make excellent habitat for rainbows. Most rainbows will average 15 inches or less, but larger fish are relatively common. In recent years, the river has seen a significant increase in the number of rainbows over 20 inches—with some up to 2 feet long. The brown trout here take advantage of the large river and grow to rather impressive sizes.

Trout in the lower section of the East Branch are more opportunistic in regard to what they eat than those that are found in the tailwater farther upstream. The lower river is a great place to spend an afternoon prospecting the riffle water with large attractor-style dry flies, streamers, Woolly Buggers, and nymphs.

Overall, the East Branch of the Delaware offers the fly fisher a vast array of fishing opportunities throughout the season. It is a river that offers an intimate wading experience in its upper reaches, and big-water driftboat adventure downstream. What more could you ask for?

➤ **Tackle:** A 9-foot 5-weight rod with a floating line is your best bet for the East Branch of the Delaware. A 9-foot 6-weight or 7-weight is a good option for streamer fishing from a boat. Dry-fly fishing is best done with a 9-foot 4-weight, as you may need to drop to 6X to effectively fish smaller

Nice rainbow trout. Baxter House River Outfitters

mid-October. All the insects known to inhabit Catskill waters can be found here, but a few hatches are truly spectacular. These include the early-season Hendricksons, the giant Green and Brown Drakes, and the summer Sulphurs.

This section of river offers very consistent conditions, with match-the-hatch dry-fly fishing available for roughly eight months of the year. From the fly fisher's point of view, this section of river is among the most challenging. Anglers who regularly fish this stretch understand that patience, accurate casts, and a good knowledge of insects are critical. It is for these reasons that anglers are drawn back to this section of river year after year.

The lower section of the East Branch extends from East Branch downstream to Hancock, where the river meets the West Branch to form the main stem of the Delaware River. At the beginning of this section, the Beaverkill River enters the East Branch and changes its character dramatically. Here the river doubles in size. This section is dominated by fast runs, riffles, pocketwater, and long, deep pools that are more commonly found in steeper-gradient freestone rivers. Anglers will find a varied bottom in this section. Some areas have small stones that allow for easy wading. Other areas are strewn with large boulders and ledges, and are difficult to wade. This represents the classic Northeast freestone river.

In the upper reaches of the lower East Branch, the river begins to lose the coldwater influence from Pepacton Reservoir. Fishing conditions on this section are somewhat dependent on rainfall and cool weather. In most years, this section does not fish well during the hot summer months of July and August. Fly fishers will find prolific insect hatches throughout the season on this section. The diversity of water and

Brown trout caught on March Brown. Baxter House River Outfitters

KEN TUTALO owns and operates Baxter House River Outfitters in Roscoe, New York. He has fished the waters of the Upper Delaware region for over 35 years. During winter, Ken demonstrates fly tying and gives seminars on fly fishing the Upper Delaware River system at the regional fly-fishing shows. He publishes a daily fishing report on his website (www.baxterhouse .net) from April through November. He has also appeared on fly-fishing DVDs and on television. Ken can be reached at 607-348-7497, or bhoutfitters@aol.com.

patterns such as BWOs. While rods longer than 9 feet can work, especially for nymphing, rods shorter than 9 feet are not practical. Strike indicators should be large enough to float two flies and added weight. Flies should include Woolly Buggers; sculpin patterns; and all stages of mayflies, stoneflies, and caddis in a variety of sizes and colors.

CLOSEST FLY SHOPS

Baxter House River Outfitters
2012 Old Route 17
Roscoe, New York 12776
607-290-4022
www.baxterhouse.net
bhoutfitters@aol.com

Border Water Outfitters
159 East Main Street
Hancock, New York 13783
607-637-4296
www.borderwateroutfitters.com
bwo@hancock.net

Delaware River Club
1228 Winterdale Road
Starlight, Pennsylvania 18461
570-635-5880
www.thedelawareriverclub.com
flyfish@thedelawareriverclub.com

West Branch Resort
150 Faulkner Road
Hancock, New York 13783
800-201-2557
www.westbranchresort.com
reservations@westbranchresort.com

CLOSEST GUIDES/OUTFITTERS

Cross Current Guide Service & Outfitters
100 Laurel Acres Road
Milford, Pennsylvania 18337
914-475-6779
www.crosscurrentguideservice.com
crosscurrent@optonline.net

East Branch Outfitters
1471 Peas Eddy Road
Hancock, New York 13783
607-637-5451
www.eastbranchoutfitters.com
info@eastbranchoutfitters.com

CLOSEST LODGING

Baxter House River Outfitters
2012 Old Route 17
Roscoe, New York 12776
607-290-4022
www.baxterhouse.net
bhoutfitters@aol.com

West Branch Resort
150 Faulkner Road
Hancock, New York 13783
800-201-2557
www.westbranchresort.com
reservations@westbranchresort.com

Delaware River Club
1228 Winterdale Road
Starlight, Pennsylvania 18461
570-635-5880
www.thedelawareriverclub.com
flyfish@thedelawareriverclub.com

Downsville Motel
6964 River Road
Downsville, New York 13755
607-363-7575
www.downsvillemotel.com

Reynolds House
1394 Old Route 17
Roscoe, New York 12776
607-498-4422
www.reynoldshouseinn.com

CLOSEST RESTAURANTS

Riverside Café
16624 County Highway 17
Roscoe, New York 12776
607-498-5305
www.riversidecafeandlodge.com

Roscoe Diner
1908 Old Route 17
Roscoe, New York 12776
607-498-4405
www.theroscoediner.com

Raimondo's Restaurant & Pizzeria
Stewart Avenue
Roscoe, New York 12776
607-498-4702

River Run Restaurant
150 Faulkner Road
Hancock, New York 13783
607-467-5533
www.westbranchresort.com
reservations@westbranchresort.com

Rockland House
159 Rockland Road
Roscoe, New York 12776
607-498-4240
www.rocklandhouse.com

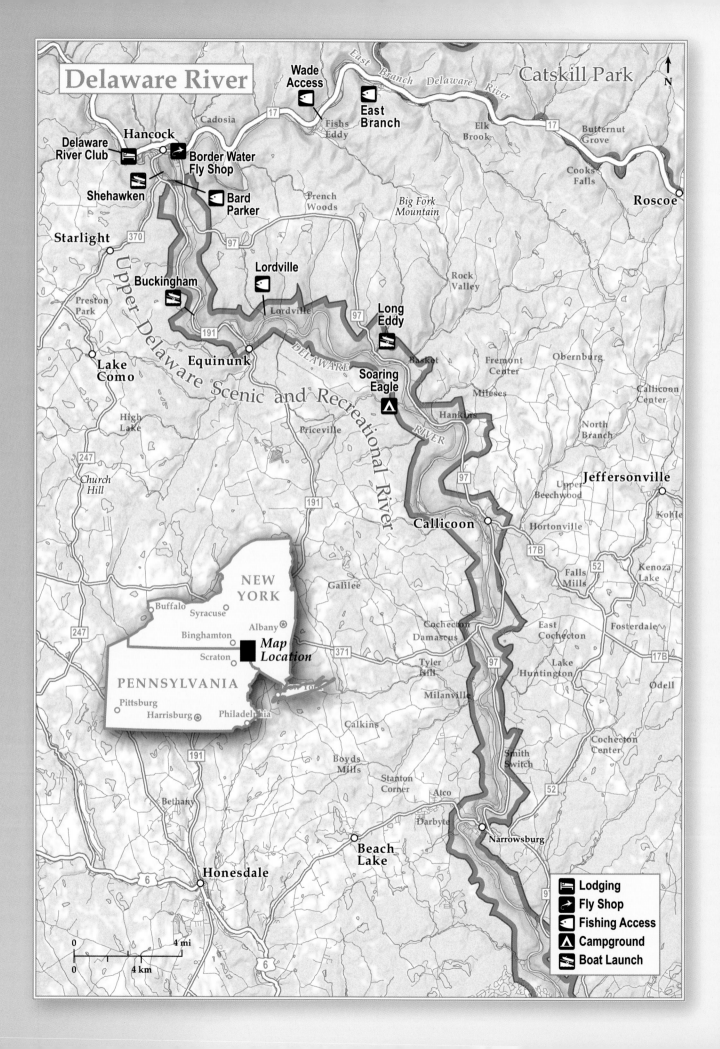

Delaware River

Catskill Park

Wade Access

East Branch

Fishs Eddy

Cadosia

17

Roscoe

Cooks Falls

Butternut Grove

Elk Brook

Hancock

Delaware River Club

Border Water Fly Shop

Shehawken

Bard Parker

French Woods

Big Fork Mountain

Rock Valley

Starlight

370

97

Buckingham

Lordville

Lordville

Long Eddy

97

Basket

Fremont Center

Obernburg

Callicoon Center

191

Equinunk

DELAWARE

Soaring Eagle

Hankins

Mileses

North Branch

Preston Park

Lake Como

High Lake

247

Church Hill

RIVER

Jeffersonville

Upper Beechwood

Kohle

Priceville

191

Hortonville

17B

Galilee

Callicoon

Falls Mills

52

Kenoza Lake

NEW YORK

Buffalo

Syracuse

Albany ⊛

Binghamton

Scraton

Map Location

371

Cochecton Damascus

East Cochecton

Fosterdale

17B

Lake Huntington

Odell

PENNSYLVANIA

Pittsburg

Harrisburg ⊛

Philadelphia

Tyler Hill

97

Cochecton Center

Milanville

Calkins

Boyds Mills

Stanton Corner

Smith Switch

52

Atco

Bethany

Darbyte

Narrowsburg

191

Beach Lake

Honesdale

6

6

0   4 mi

0   4 km

	Lodging
	Fly Shop
	Fishing Access
	Campground
	Boat Launch

28 · Delaware River

➤ **Location:** Southeastern New York/northeastern Pennsylvania, about a 2-hour ride from New York City and Newark, New Jersey; a 3-hour ride from Hartford, Connecticut; and a 4-hour ride from Boston, Massachusetts. Full-service airports are available in all four cities.

The East Branch and West Branch of the Delaware River converge just south of the village of Hancock, New York. This *Shehawken,* a Delaware Indian word meaning "wedding of the waters," denotes the beginning of the fabled Delaware River. The river is known locally as the "Big D." It is also called the crown jewel of the Delaware system, well regarded as one of the finest dry-fly fisheries in the country.

The Delaware River drains an area of 14,119 square miles. It flows roughly 420 miles to its termination at Delaware Bay. Along with the East and West Branches, it represents 388 miles of flowing river. It is one of just 19 Great Waters recognized by America's Great Waters Coalition. The average flow at its termination is 11,550 cubic feet per second (cfs).

In the early 1600s, an East India Company expedition led by Henry Hudson visited the Delaware. This led to the founding of a Dutch colony. The river was known as the South River at the time. What is now referred to as the Hudson River was called the North River. When the English forced out the Dutch in the mid-1660s, they took control of the area. It was at this time that the river was named the Delaware in honor of Sir Thomas West, 3rd Baron De La Warr, the Virginia colony's first governor.

Fed by the twin tailwaters of the East and West Branches, the first 12 miles of the Delaware remain cool enough to be conducive to trout year-round. Trout range extends downstream from Hancock to Narrowsburg during the springtime months. The Delaware is a large freestone river with classic riffle-run-pool structure that provides a perfect habitat for the wild rainbow and brown trout, as well as myriad aquatic insects.

The rainbow trout in the Delaware are the hardest-fighting members of their species found outside Alaska or Russia. It is not unusual to have a fish in the 14- to 16-inch range take you well into your backing, and with ease. Fish larger than that—some up to 24 inches—will test even the most seasoned fly fisher. According to local legend, these fish are the result of a train breaking down near Callicoon while transporting fingerlings from the McCloud River in California to

Lower mainstem Delaware River, mid-May. John Miller

a hatchery in Cold Spring. With no refrigeration in the train, the biologist in charge threw the rapidly expiring fingerlings into Callicoon Creek, a major tributary of the Delaware. Finding thermal refuge in the river, these fish soon established a small self-sustaining population. When the reservoirs were built in the 1960s, the population exploded due to the increased coldwater habitat. Having been in the system for generations, these fish have adapted to the river, moving from the riffles into the slower pools to feed.

Left. Christine Bogdanowicz with brown trout. Steve Bogdanowicz
Above. Shad fly hatch on lower mainstem.

While the rainbows are truly unique, the Delaware is best known for its wild brown trout. These fish average between 16 and 18 inches, with much larger fish caught. Last stocked in the early 1980s, the browns have had more than 30 years to acclimate to the Delaware system. With a rich and diverse forage base, these fish grow quickly and stoutly in a relatively short period of time. The vast amount of food also makes them very selective, as they can afford to be picky in regard to what they eat. Browns can be found in virtually every type of water, from the fastest of riffles to the slowest of pools. While they readily come to the surface to feed on adult insects, these are the apex predators of the river, and will not pass up an opportunity to eat any baitfish or other prey available to them.

➤ **Hatches:** The Delaware boasts what is perhaps the greatest number of mayfly hatches east of the Mississippi, and arguably the country. In addition to the famous spring hatches such as the Hendricksons (*Ephemerella subvaria*) and Green Drakes (*Ephemera guttulata*) that draw anglers from all over the East, there are close to 40 other species of mayflies that hatch on the river. These start as early as mid-March with *Baetis* (*Baetis vagans*) and end in the late fall with Tiny Blue-winged Olives known as Pseudos (*Pseudocloeon*). Sulphurs (*Ephemerella dorothea*) start in late spring and continue into the fall, providing very productive summertime dry-fly fishing.

Caddis and stoneflies hatch throughout the year as well. Fish eagerly take caddis on the surface early in the year, but get more finicky as the season progresses. At times, clouds of caddis fill the air. The Apple Green Caddis hatch in the spring is one of the most popular. Stonefly hatches differ from those in other rivers, in that the insects tend to hatch in the middle of the night as opposed to midday, as is normal on other Eastern streams. Anglers willing to forgo sleep can have success skating large dry flies across the surface in the dark. At this time some rather large brown trout are caught. Nymph fishers using large, heavy flies also find success, as these insects have a two-year life cycle and are almost always present.

The trout on the Delaware do not attain their large sizes on a diet of insects alone. They get big on the rich bonanza of baitfish and other aquatic life, such as leeches and crayfish. Whenever the reservoirs that feed the East and West Branches overflow, large numbers of juvenile alewives are released into the river. The trout not only take notice, they stuff themselves to the gills with them. These events offer some of the most incredible streamer fishing opportunities found in the East. Some of the largest fish of the year are caught when the alewives enter the Delaware.

Baetis dun. John Miller

Whether you wade or float, there is plenty of room on the Delaware for you. While the Big D may be a dry-fly fishing Mecca, those who swing nymphs or throw big streamers will not be disappointed. The Delaware is truly one of a kind, and without a doubt one of the finest wild trout streams in the country.

➤ **Tackle:** A 9-foot 5-weight rod with a floating line is your best bet for the Delaware River most of the time. If you want to fish streamers, a 9-foot 6-weight or 7-weight with a fast-sinking sink-tip is your best option. Dry-fly fishing is best done with a 9-foot 4-weight, as you may need to drop to 6X to effectively fish smaller patterns such as Blue-winged Olives. While rods longer than 9 feet can work, especially for nymphing, rods shorter than 9 feet are not practical. Nine- to 15-foot leaders and tippets in the 3X to 6X range are good bets. Strike indicators should be large enough to float two flies and added weight. Flies should include Woolly Buggers, sculpin and smelt patterns; and all stages of mayflies, stoneflies, and caddis in a variety of sizes and colors.

BART LARMOUTH started his fly-fishing career at the Delaware River Club. He returned to the club in 2011 after spending time guiding in Jackson Hole, Wyoming, and managing Tailwaters Fly Fishing Company in Dallas, Texas. He writes the daily blog and river reports for the club, assists customers with fly and gear selection, and helps them find the best place to fish. He is also a Federation of Fly Fishers Certified Casting Instructor. Bart can be reached at flyfish@thedelawareriverclub.com.

CLOSEST FLY SHOPS

The Delaware River Club
1228 Winterdale Road
Starlight, Pennsylvania 18461
570-635-5880
www.thedelawareriverclub.com
flyfish@thedelawareriverclub.com

West Branch Resort
150 Faulkener Road
Hancock, New York 13783
800-201-2557
www.westbranchresort.com
reservations@westbranchresort.com

Border Water Outfitters
159 East Main Street
Hancock, New York 13783
607-637-4296
www.borderwateroutfitters.com
bwo@hancock.net

CLOSEST GUIDES/OUTFITTERS

Cross Current Guide Service & Outfitters
100 Laurel Acres Road
Milford, Pennsylvania 18337
914-475-6779
www.crosscurrentguideservice.com
crosscurrent@optonline.net

East Branch Outfitters
1471 Peas Eddy Road
Hancock, New York 13783
607-637-5451
www.eastbranchoutfitters.com
info@eastbranchoutfitters.com

CLOSEST LODGING

The Delaware River Club (see above)

West Branch Resort (see above)

Bass' Hancock House
137 East Front Street
Hancock, New York 13783
607-637-7100
www.newhancockhouse.com

Smith's Colonial Motel
23085 New York 97
Hancock, New York 13783
607-637-2985
www.smithscolonialmotel.com
smithscolonial@yahoo.com

Becky's Bed & Breakfast
2406 State Highway 268
Hancock, New York 13783
607-637-5499
www.beckysanderbandb.com

CLOSEST RESTAURANTS

River Run Restaurant
150 Faulkener Road
Hancock, New York 13783
607-467-5533
www.westbranchresort.com
reservations@westbranchresort.com

Lydia's Crosstown Tavern
6031 Hancock Highway
Starlight, Pennsylvania 18461
570-635-5926
www.facebook.com/pages/Lydias-Crosstown-Tavern

Koo Koose Grille
129 Front Street
Deposit, New York 13754
607-235-2817
www.kookoosegrille.com

Circle E Diner
369 East Front Street
Hancock, New York 13783
607-637-9905
www.facebook.com/Circle.E.Diner

Riverside Café
16624 County Highway 17
Roscoe, New York 12776
607-498-5305
www.riversidecafeandlodge.com

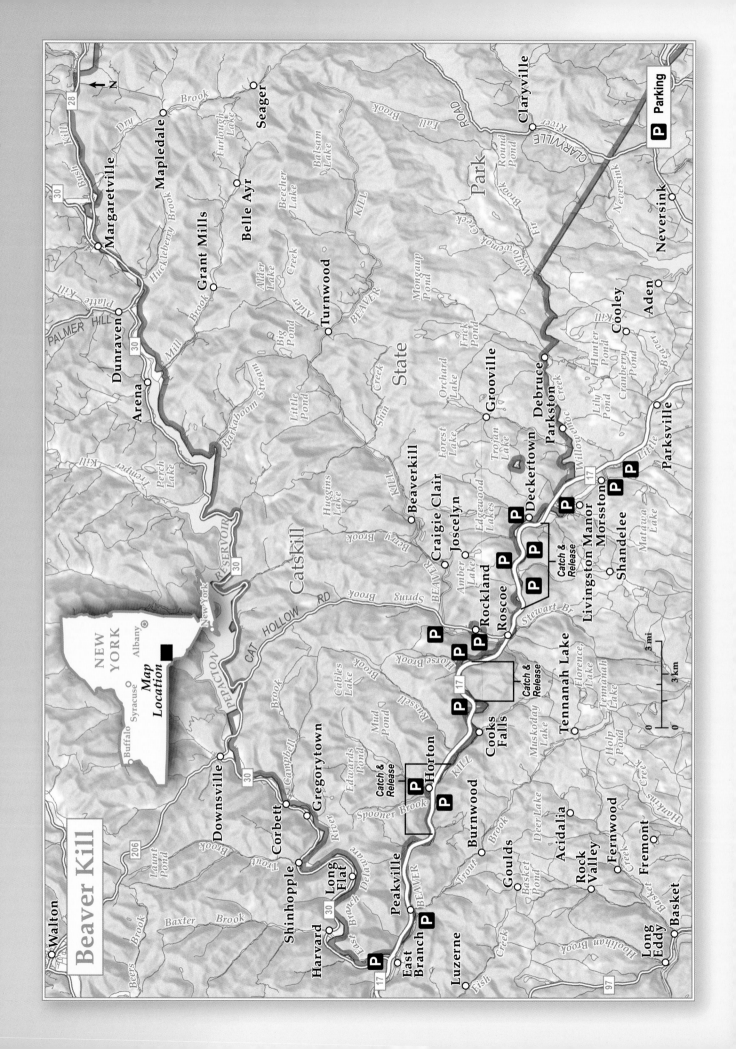

Beaver Kill

N

Walton

206

30

Margaretville

Dunraven

Arena

30

Downsville

Gregorytown

Corbett

Shinhopple

Harvard

30

Long Flat

Peakville

East Branch

17

Luzerne

Burnwood

Goulds

Rock Valley

Acidalia

Fernwood

Fremont

Basket

Long Eddy

97

Palmer Hill

Platte Kill

Bush Kill

Dry Brook

Huckleberry Brook

Mapledale

Grant Mills

Belle Ayr

Seager

Brook

Furlough Lake

Beecher Lake

Balsam Lake

Alder Lake

Turnwood

Big Pond

Little Pond

Perch Lake

Barkaboom Stream

Mill Brook

Alder Creek

BEAVER

KILL

Catskill

NEW YORK

Buffalo
Syracuse
Albany
New York

Map Location

PEPACTON RESERVOIR

30

CAT HOLLOW RD

Campbell Brook

Laurel Pond

Trout Brook

Beers Brook

Baxter Brook

Delaware River

East Branch

BEAVER KILL

Spooner Brook

Edwards Pond

Cables Lake

Mud Pond

Russell Brook

Horse Brook

Cooks Falls

Muskoday Lake

Tennanah Lake

Florence Lake

Tennanah Lake

Holp Pond

Trout Brook

Basket Pond

Deer Lake

Beaver Creek

Hoolihan Brook

Hankins Creek

Fish Creek

Catch & Release

Catch & Release

Huggins Lake

Berry Brook

Beaverkill

Craigie Clair

Joscelyn

Shin Creek

Spring Brook

Amber Lake

Rockland

Roscoe

Stewart Br

Catch & Release

Livingston Manor

Morsston

Shandelee

Mattawa Lake

Parksville

Little Beaver Kill

17

Edgewood Lakes

Trojan Lake

Forest Lake

Orchard Lake

Frick Pond

Grooville

Deckertown

Debruce

Parkston

Willowemoc Creek

Mongaup Pond

Round Pond

Fir Brook

Willowemoc Creek

CLARYVILLE ROAD

Claryville

Neversink River

Lily Pond

Hunter Pond

Cranberry Pond

Cooley

Aden

Neversink

State

Park

BEAVER

KILL

Fall Brook

P Parking

3 mi

3 km

0

0

29 · Beaverkill River

➤ **Location:** Southeastern New York, about a 2-hour ride from New York City; a 2-hour ride from Newark, New Jersey; a 3-hour ride from Hartford, Connecticut; and a 4-hour ride from Boston, Massachusetts. Full-service airports are available in all four cities.

The Beaverkill River is located in fabled Roscoe, New York. Roscoe is known as "Trout Town, U.S.A." or the "Fly-Fishing Capital of the East." The Beaverkill has been fished, and written about, for as long as fly fishing has been pursued in the United States. It is one of the most famous trout streams in the country, and has been since the early 1800s. Because it has been one of the East's premier trout fisheries for many generations, the Beaverkill's long-time fame may overshadow the outstanding fly-fishing opportunities it still offers today.

The Beaverkill River is sometimes referred to as the Beaver Kill. "Kill" means river in Dutch. It is a tributary of the East Branch of the Delaware River. The river is approximately 44 miles long, draining an area of roughly 300 square miles. By the mid-19th century, the native brook trout population had been decimated. This led to the establishment of hatcheries to try to bring back the fishing. Beginning in the 1880s, nonnative brown trout replaced the brook trout.

To say that the angling history associated with the Beaverkill is significant would be an understatement. Many fly-fishing innovations that originated in the United States began in the Catskills region of New York, and on the Beaverkill specifically. Given this rich literary history and high profile, you may not always be able to find a secluded pool on the Beaverkill. But you can still walk the same banks, and stalk the same pools and riffles, that some of the most celebrated anglers in the history of the sport have fished.

Fortunately, the Beaverkill is not a place you fish just for historic purposes. The Beaverkill has seen limited development. In fact, it is located in a region that really has not changed much—especially when you consider that it is just a couple of hours from New York City. Although the upper reaches of the river are mainly in private hands and inaccessible to average anglers, thanks to the efforts of the State of New York and concerned citizens, the lower Beaverkill offers some of the best public access you will find. The introduced brown trout have created an excellent, challenging, and nationally known fishery in the river's lower sections.

Upper Beaverkill. John Miller

The Beaverkill is a classic freestone river, with a steep gradient by Eastern standards. It is fed by mountain runoff and cold springs in its upper reaches. There are pools, runs, and plenty of pocketwater that accommodate all types of fly-fishing methods. The Beaverkill is located in a mountainous region with less permeable soil than that found in many other areas. This nonporous soil channels water and results in minimal loss to the watershed, but also limited buffering against seasonal high-water events.

Horton Bridge. Evan Lavery, Beaverkill Angler

Rainbow trout, brook trout, and brown trout are all present in good numbers on the Beaverkill. Brown trout and rainbow trout average between 12 and 16 inches. Larger fish, some over 20 inches, are encountered. Brook trout run smaller. While brown trout are the predominant species, spring offers some solid fishing for rainbow trout. Brook trout are found primarily in the numerous tributaries.

The Beaverkill is a wading river. Many anglers consider it the one of the best wading rivers in the region. Under normal flows, most of the river is accessible to wading anglers. While flows are constantly changing, rarely is the river unfishable. Flows run from 100–800 cfs. There are typically a few high-water events each year. Although the river runs off-colored during high-water periods, it tends to recover quickly, often within just a few days. High water is usually found in the spring. Low water is usually found in the summer and fall. The ideal flow for fly fishing is between 300 and 600 cfs.

What the Beaverkill is truly famous for is its dry-fly fishing. There are plenty of pools and flats that allow for sight casting to rising fish. Although the fish do feed on the surface in the fast water, it is the placid tailouts and famous pools that excite the dry-fly aficionado. While this brings throngs of fly fishers to the area, those willing to walk a bit can still find some level of solitude.

By mid-March, the Beaverkill is usually fishable. At this time both trout and insects become active. Peak fishing starts in the middle of April and runs though the beginning of July. Depending on rainfall and air temperatures, there can be excellent summer fishing as well. By late spring or early summer, the river warms up, limiting angling to early mornings or just before dark. As on many fisheries, fall brings a resurgence of insect activity. Due to the fact that this coincides with the beginning of the salmon season and the fall striper migration, traffic on the river is often much lower at this time of year than it is in the spring.

➤ **Regulations:** The Beaverkill is open to fishing from April 1 through November 30. There is a five-fish daily bag limit and a 9-inch minimum length limit. There are no tackle restrictions. There are two catch-and-release sections on the Beaverkill. Both are open to year-round fishing. Tackle here is restricted to artificial lures and flies only. The upper catch-and-release section runs from the Sullivan County line downstream 2½ miles. The lower catch-and-release section runs from 1 mile above, and 1.6 miles below, the Iron Bridge in Horton. From the Iron Bridge to the Route 17 bridge, the river is closed to angling from July 1 through August 31 to protect heat-stressed fish.

➤ **Hatches:** One aspect of the Beaverkill that draws fly fishers from all over the East is its robust and diverse hatches. Both mayflies and caddis are present. Spring hatches can last months. Hendricksons, Sulphurs, and Blue-winged Olives are all represented. There are also larger insects, such as March Browns and Green Drakes. With over a dozen significant mayfly hatches and a variety of caddis species, a thorough and accurate hatch chart is always helpful. For a helpful online chart, visit: planettrout.files.wordpress.com/2013/06/beaverkill-hatch-chart.jpg.

Large Beaverkill brown trout. John Miller

Beaverkill rainbow trout. John Miller

➤ **Tackle:** A 9-foot 5-weight rod with a floating line is your best bet for the Beaverkill River most of the time. A 9-foot 6-weight or 7-weight is a good option for streamer fishing from a boat. Dry-fly fishing is best done with a 9-foot 4-weight, as you may need to drop to 6X tippet to effectively fish smaller patterns such as BWOs. While rods longer than 9 feet can work, especially for nymphing, rods shorter than 9 feet are not practical. Strike indicators should be large enough to float two flies and added weight. Flies should include Woolly Buggers, sculpin patterns; and all stages of mayflies, stoneflies, and caddis, in a variety of sizes and colors.

EVAN LAVERY owns and operates The Beaverkill Angler in Roscoe, New York. He can be reached at 607-498-5194, mail@beaverkillangler.com, or www.beaverkillangler.com.

CLOSEST FLY SHOPS

The Beaverkill Angler
62 Stewart Avenue
Roscoe, New York 12776
607-498-5194
www.beaverkillangler.com
info@beaverkillangler.com

Baxter House River Outfitters
2012 Old Route 17
Roscoe, New York 12776
607-290-4022
www.baxterhouse.net
bhoutfitters@aol.com

Catskill Flies
6 Stewart Avenue
Roscoe, New York 12776
845-434-4473
www.catskillflies.com
flyshop@catskillflies.com

Dette Trout Flies
68 Cottage Street
Roscoe, New York 12776
607-498-4991
www.detteflies.com
joe@dettetroutflies.com

CLOSEST LODGING

Baxter House River Outfitters
2012 Old Route 17
Roscoe, New York 12776
607-290-4022
www.baxterhouse.net
bhoutfitters@aol.com

Roscoe Motel
2054 Old Route 17
Roscoe, New York 12776
607-498-5220
www.roscoemotel.com

Downsville Motel
6964 River Road
Downsville, New York 13755
607-363-7575
www.downsvillemotel.com

Reynolds House
1394 Old Route 17
Roscoe, New York 12776
607-498-4422
www.reynoldshouseinn.com

Creekside Cabins
703 Hazel Road
Roscoe, New York 12776
607-498-5873
www.creeksidecabins.com
gofish@creeksidecabins.com

CLOSEST RESTAURANTS

Riverside Café
16624 County Highway 17
Roscoe, New York 12776
607 498-5305
www.riversidecafeandlodge.com

Roscoe Diner
1908 Old Route 17
Roscoe, New York 12776
607-498-4405
www.theroscoediner.com

Spiro's Countryside Restaurant
179 Rockland Road
Roscoe New York, 12776
607-498-4419
www.spiroscountryside.com
comments@spiroscountryside.com

Raimondo's Restaurant & Pizzeria
Stewart Avenue
Roscoe, New York 12776
607-498-4702

Rockland House
159 Rockland Road
Roscoe, New York 12776
607-498-4240
www.rocklandhouse.com

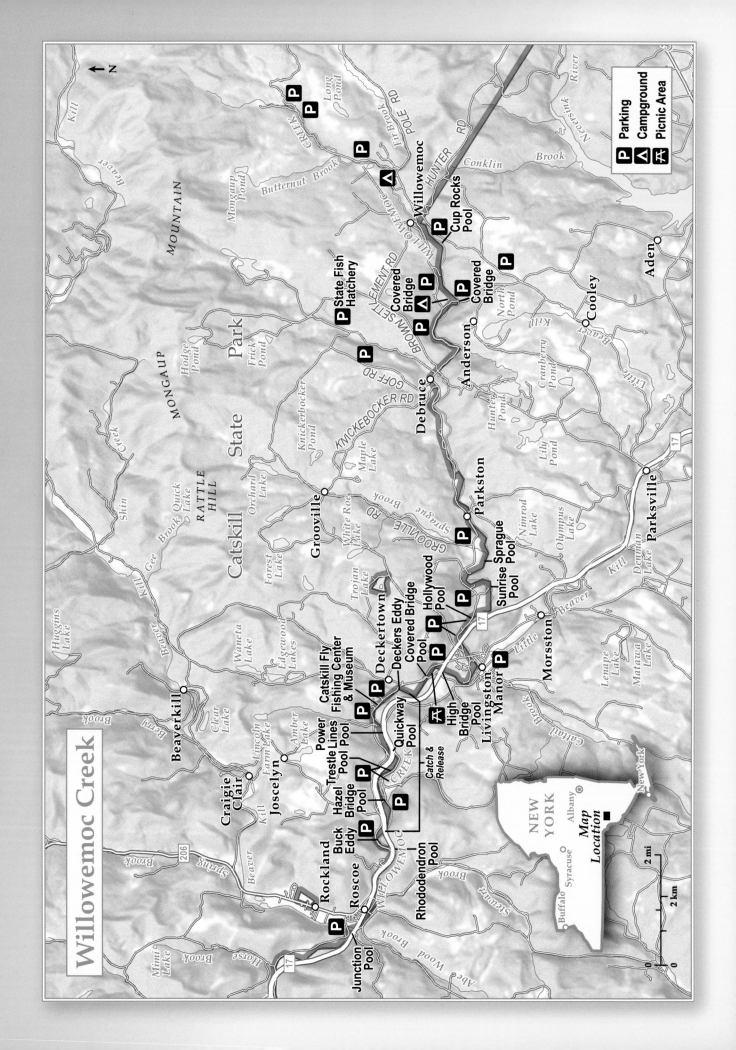

30 · Willowemoc Creek

➤ **Location:** Southeastern New York, about a 2-hour ride from New York City; a 2-hour ride from Newark, New Jersey; a 3-hour ride from Hartford, Connecticut; and a 4-hour ride from Boston, Massachusetts. Full-service airports are available in all four cities.

Willowemoc Creek is a tributary of the Beaverkill River and part of the Upper Delaware watershed. It shares the same prolific hatches, healthy trout populations, and stunning beauty. Unfortunately, the reputations of the other rivers in the area—including the Delaware, its two branches, the Neversink, the Esopus, and the Beaverkill—often overshadow the quality fly fishing found in the Willowemoc.

The Willowemoc has a rich fly-fishing history. Author George M. L. LaBranche cast his first dry fly on the creek at its confluence with Mongaup Creek. Theodore Gordon (of Quill Gordon fame), well-known Catskill fly tier Rube Cross, and authors Alfred W. Miller (aka Sparse Grey Hackle), Ed Van Put, and Edward R. Hewitt all frequented the Willow. The Dette, Darbee, and Kuttner fly shops overlooked the creek. It is home to the Catskill Fly Fishing Center & Museum, which is located along the catch-and-release section. There are two covered bridges over the stream: Vantran Covered Bridge in Livingston Manor and Willowemoc Covered Bridge in Willowemoc, both built in 1860.

This picturesque Catskill Mountain stream flows 27 miles before terminating at the Beaverkill in Roscoe, New York. The Willowemoc accounts for roughly 60 percent of the water in the Beaverkill's famed Junction Pool. Throughout its length, it is largely undeveloped, with the exception of the last 5 miles between Livingston Manor and Roscoe. The stream is mostly open to the public, with the exception of about 4 miles in the middle section. Countless easements and state-owned lands were purchased long ago to ensure access.

The Willowemoc starts on the southern slopes of the Beaverkill Range in the Big Indian Wilderness Area. Above its junction with Fir Brook, the Willowemoc is quite small, from a couple of feet wide to no more than 10 feet at its widest point. In this section, brook trout reign supreme. These jewels of the Catskills, wild native Eastern brook trout, are small, often no longer than 8 inches. Anything 10 inches or more is considered a trophy. In addition to the abundant brook trout, there are some wild and stocked brown trout. On occasion, large resident browns are caught, but they are few and far between and quite elusive.

Below Fir Brook in the town of Willowemoc, the stream transforms into a small river between 10 and 20 feet wide. In this area, brown trout become the predominant species, although brook trout are still quite numerous. The widening

Downstream of Hazel Bridge. Evan Lavery

of the stream opens up the canopy, making casting easier. To many, this is the most beautiful section of the creek. While access is still good, the creek is farther from the road than it is in other sections. This offers a bit of solitude.

In the town of Livingston Manor, the Willow makes another transformation. At its junction with the Little Beaver

131

Joe Fox with large brown trout. Christian Stathis

Kill and Cattail Brook, the flow increases significantly. Here the river widens to 30 to 40 feet. In this section, the brook trout population is noticeably smaller, and brown trout predominate. Wild rainbows populate the faster water—their numbers have increased over the years. Fish size increases here as well. Trout between 12 and 16 inches are quite common. Fish between 17 and 20 inches are not uncommon. However, fish over 20 inches are admittedly rare. This section also boasts the best public access.

From Livingston Manor to Roscoe, the Willowemoc is a large stream. This lower section is also greatly affected by runoff, quick to rise and become off-colored, but also quick to clear. Although there is no flow gauge on the Willowemoc, the USGS has a gauge downstream on the Beaverkill in Cooks Falls that can be used to ascertain the conditions. Wading is best in the lower section when the flows are between 200 and 800 cfs. Ideal conditions are between 300 and 600 cfs. Above Livingston Manor, the stream is much slower to rise and quicker to return to normal. The upper section can be waded as long as the gauge is at or below 2,000 cfs. During high-water periods, the upper Willow is often the only fishable water in the area.

➤ **Hatches:** Dry-fly fishing has long been the draw for anglers fishing the Willowemoc. Hatches start in mid-April with Blue Quills, Quill Gordons, and Hendricksons. This is followed in early May by the extremely prolific apple caddis and shad caddis hatches. Late May brings March Browns and

Grey Foxes. By June, the creek sees Green Drakes, Brown Drakes, *Isonychia*, Sulphurs, Cahills, and Blue Sedge Caddis. In the summer, *Isonychia*, Sulphurs, Yellow Drakes, Golden Drakes, Cahills, and Tricos are present. Come fall, Tiny Blue-winged Olives start to come off and remain on the water through the end of November. Winter hatches are limited to the occasional Blue-winged Olive, midge, or Tiny Black Stone hatch.

From Parkston Bridge upstream is open from April 1 though October 15. Between Parkston Bridge and the fabled Junction Pool at the Beaverkill, the stream is open from April 1 through November 30. The catch-and-release section starting roughly 1,200 feet above Elm Hollow Brook and running downstream 3½ miles to the second-to-last Route 17 bridge above Roscoe is open year-round. Tackle is restricted to artificial lures only here.

Willowemoc Creek is not just for the dry-fly purist. It has a variety of water types, and those willing to nymph, fish streamers, or swing wet flies will do well. Strike indicator nymphing tends to be most effective in runs and at the heads of pools, while straight-line nymphing can be quite effective in the riffles. When the water is high and off-colored, streamer fishing with large sculpin patterns can be an effective way to catch a big brown. A multi-fly rig of colorful wet flies is still a popular way to target brook trout in the upper sections.

The Willow, as the regulars call it, offers a rich history, beautiful scenery, quality fishing, and prolific hatches, providing anglers with everything they could want from a Catskill Mountain stream.

➤ **Tackle:** A 9-foot 5-weight rod with a floating line is your best bet for the Willowemoc most of the time. If you want to fish streamers, a sink-tip is a good idea. Dry-fly fishing is best done with a 9-foot 4-weight or 5-weight, as you may need to drop to 6X to effectively fish smaller patterns such as Blue-winged Olives. Rods longer than 9 feet can work, especially for nymphing. Lightweight rods (2- or 3-weight) shorter than 9 feet are preferred in the upper reaches. Strike indicators should be large enough to float two flies and added weight. Leaders should be between 9 and 15 feet—the longer the better for drys. Tippet should be between 4X and 7X—with 6X preferred for drys. Flies should include Woolly Buggers, streamer patterns, and all stages of mayflies, stoneflies, and caddis in a variety of sizes and colors.

Eighteen-inch brown trout caught by Joe Fox. Dette Trout Flies

Upper river. Shane Becker

JOE FOX owns and operates Dette Trout Flies in Roscoe, New York with his grandmother Mary Dette. His great-grandparents, Walt and Winnie Dette, opened the shop in 1928. Joe is an accomplished fly tier. His flies have appeared in several books. Joe can be reached at 607-498-4991, joe@dettetroutflies.com, or www.detteflies.com.

CLOSEST FLY SHOPS

Dette Trout Flies
68 Cottage Street
Roscoe, New York 12776
607-498-4991
www.detteflies.com
joe@dettetroutflies.com

Beaverkill Angler
62 Stewart Avenue
Roscoe, New York 12776
607-498-5194
www.beaverkillangler.com
info@beaverkillangler.com

Catskill Flies
6 Stewart Avenue
Roscoe, New York 12776
845-434-4473
www.catskillflies.com
flyshop@catskillflies.com

Baxter House River Outfitters
2012 Old Route 17
Roscoe, New York 12776
607-290-4022
www.baxterhouse.net
bhoutfitters@aol.com

CLOSEST GUIDES/OUTFITTERS

Dick Smith
16 Park Avenue
Roscoe, New York 12776
607-498-6024
darbee1@juno.com

CLOSEST LODGING

Roscoe Motel
2054 Old Route 17
Roscoe, New York 12776
607-498-5220
www.roscoemotel.com
roscoemotel@gmail.com

Reynolds House
1394 Old Route 17
Roscoe, New York 12776
607-498-4422
www.reynoldshouseinn.com
host@reynoldshouseinn.com

Creekside Cabins
703 Hazel Road
Roscoe, New York 12776
607-498-5873
www.creeksidecabins.com
gofish@creeksidecabins.com

DeBruce Country Inn
982 DeBruce Road
DeBruce, New York 12758
845-493-3900
www.debrucecountryinn.com

Baxter House River Outfitters
2012 Old Route 17
Roscoe, New York 12776
607-290-4022
www.baxterhouse.net
bhoutfitters@aol.com

CLOSEST RESTAURANTS

Madison's Main Street Stand
46 Main Street
Livingston Manor, New York 12758
845-439-4368
www.madstand.com

Riverside Café
16624 County Highway 17
Roscoe, New York 12776
607-498-5305
www.riversidecafeandlodge.com

Roscoe Diner
1908 Old Route 17
Roscoe, New York 12776
607-498-4405
www.theroscoediner.com

Spiro's Countryside Restaurant
179 Rockland Road
Roscoe New York, 12776
607-498-4419
www.spiroscountryside.com
comments@spiroscountryside.com

Rockland House
159 Rockland Road
Roscoe, New York 12776
607-498-4240
www.rocklandhouse.com

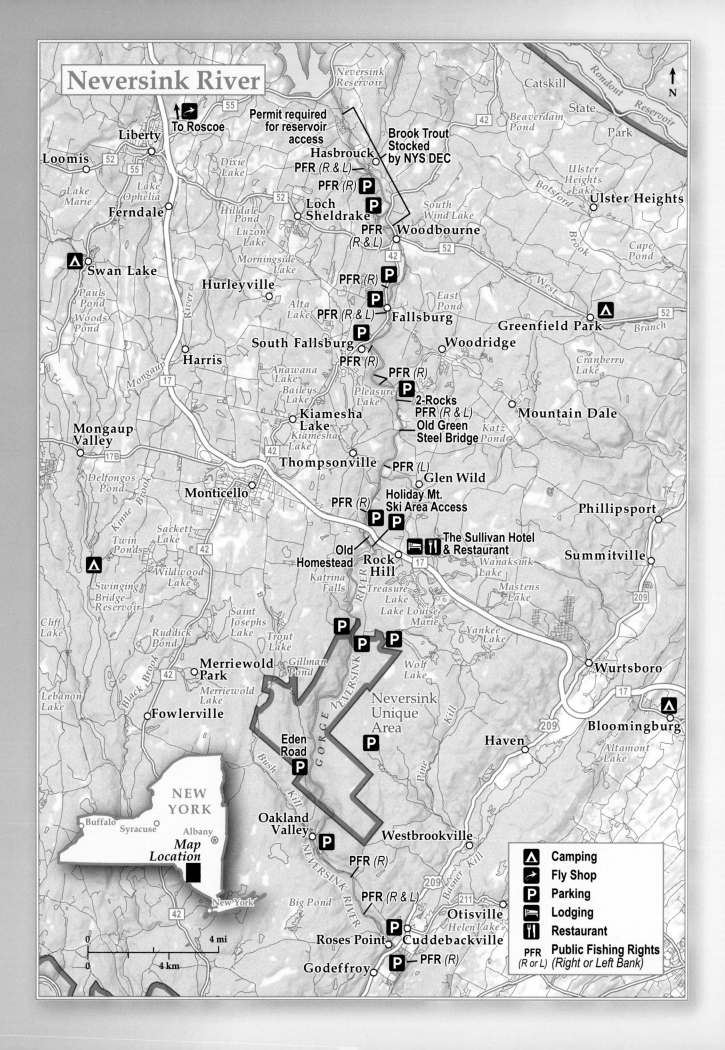

Neversink River

To Roscoe

Liberty

Loomis

Ferndale

Lake Marie

Lake Ophelia

Swan Lake

Hurleyville

Dixie Lake

Hilldale Pond

Luzon Lake

Morningside Lake

Pauls Pond

Woods Pond

Harris

Mongaup River

Permit required for reservoir access

Neversink Reservoir

Hasbrouck

PFR (R & L)

PFR (R)

Loch Sheldrake

PFR (R & L)

Brook Trout Stocked by NYS DEC

Woodbourne

South Wind Lake

PFR (R)

PFR (R & L)

Fallsburg

Alta Lake

South Fallsburg

PFR (R)

Pleasure Lake

PFR (R)

2-Rocks PFR (R & L)

Old Green Steel Bridge

East Pond

Woodridge

Katz Pond

Catskill

Rondout Reservoir

State

Park

Beaverdam Pond

Ulster Heights Lake

Botsford

Brook

West

Branch

Cape Pond

Ulster Heights

Greenfield Park

Cranberry Lake

Mountain Dale

Mongaup Valley

Anawana Lake

Baileys Lake

Kiamesha Lake

Kiamesha Lake

Thompsonville

PFR (L)

Glen Wild

Phillipsport

Monticello

Delfongos Pond

Sackett Lake

Twin Ponds

Wildwood Lake

Swinging Bridge Reservoir

Cliff Lake

Lebanon Lake

Kinne Brook

Black Brook

Ruddick Pond

Saint Josephs Lake

Trout Lake

Merriewold Park

Merriewold Lake

Fowlerville

Gillman Pond

Bush Kill

Eden Road

Oakland Valley

PFR (R)

Neversink River

PFR (R & L)

Big Pond

Roses Point

Godeffroy

PFR (R)

Holiday Mt. Ski Area Access

Old Homestead

Rock Hill

Katrina Falls

River

Gorge

Neversink

The Sullivan Hotel & Restaurant

Treasure Lake

Lake Louise Marie

Wanaksink Lake

Mastens Lake

Neversink Unique Area

Wolf Lake

Pine Kill

Yankee Lake

Haven

Westbrookville

Basher Kill

Otisville

Helen Lake

Cuddebackville

PFR (R)

Summitville

Wurtsboro

Bloomingburg

Altamont Lake

NEW YORK

Buffalo

Syracuse

Albany

Map Location

New York

0   4 mi

0   4 km

⛺	Camping
↗	Fly Shop
P	Parking
🛏	Lodging
🍴	Restaurant
PFR	Public Fishing Rights
(R or L)	(Right or Left Bank)

31 · Neversink River

➤ **Location:** Southeastern New York, about a 1½-hour ride from New York City; a 2-hour ride from Newark, New Jersey; a 3-hour ride from Hartford, Connecticut; and a 4-hour ride from Boston, Massachusetts. Full-service airports are available in all four cities.

The Catskill Mountains are an hour and a half north of New York City. Within this mountain range, seven great trout rivers are born. The proximity to this very large metropolitan area allows large numbers of fly fishers to enjoy some of the finest trout fishing in the United States.

The Neversink River is located just east of Roscoe, New York—Trout Town, U.S.A.—near the towns of Liberty and Monticello. Along with the Beaverkill and Willowemoc; East Branch, West Branch, and main stem of the Delaware; and Esopus Creek, the Neversink is in the heart of what is arguably the largest concentration of blue-ribbon trout water east of the Mississippi.

The Neversink begins in the highest peaks of the Catskills. The name means Mad River in Algonquian. It runs 55 miles before emptying into the Delaware River. The West Branch of the Neversink starts near the small town of Big Indian—near the headwaters of Esopus Creek. The East Branch of the Neversink originates near Slide Mountain, the highest peak in the Catskills. The two rivers converge near the small hamlet of Claryville, where they form the main stem of the Neversink River.

Many consider the Neversink to be the birthplace of American dry-fly fishing. It the late 19th century, Theodore Gordon used fur and feathers to create flies that matched the insects he found on the river. This style of dry flies is still used today. In fact, they are still referred to as Catskill-style dry flies.

Much of the upper Neversink is located on private land, some of which has been in the same families for generations. Some is managed as private fishing clubs, requiring membership to fish. There is, however, some access to the upper river on state-owned land. This section is primarily a brook trout fishery. There are a few browns mixed in as well.

The section of river of most interest to fly anglers is below the dam at Neversink Reservoir, just north of Hasbrouck. Local legend has it that the ghost of Theodore Gordon is seen fishing here. Public access is good. Cool water released from the dam helps keep temperatures at a range conducive to trout as far down as Bridgeville, a distance of roughly 15 miles. From Hasbrouck to below Fallsburg, the Neversink is a series of long pools. It transitions from a tailwater to a classic freestone stream here. This section is stocked with brown trout. There is also a good population of wild brown trout. Due to the topography of the river, floating is not an option. There are large boulders, and small falls, that can catch the unsuspecting floater by surprise. There are well-marked public access sites between Woodbourne and Fallsburg. Between Fallsburg and Bridgeville, there is a mix of public and private water.

Another popular spot is the Neversink River Recreational Area, better known as the Gorge. The State of New York purchased the land surrounding the Gorge from a private landowner. This is an especially scenic section of river; it is a

Solid Neversink brown trout. Ray Ottulich

Above the gorge in Bridgeville. John Miller

Neversink wild brown trout. John Miller

good idea to bring your camera to capture the views. The upper end of the gorge is located off Katrina Falls Road in Rock Hill. The hike to the water takes about 30 minutes. Going in (read, "downhill") is easy; coming out (read, "uphill") is not. Wearing a pair of hiking boots and carrying your waders and wading boots is the best way to access this section. I recommend using your wading staff for added security as well. The lower end of the Gorge can be accessed from Eden Falls Road. Due to its rugged location, the Gorge gets limited

fishing pressure. This offers the solitary fly fisher an experience you are unlikely to find anywhere else in the Catskills.

The river here is catch-and-release only. Tackle is restricted to artificial lures and flies. There is no stocking in the Gorge. There is a healthy population of wild brown trout, and some wild brook trout. Trout average 14 inches. Much larger fish are often encountered. This section of the Neversink also has the most significant population of stoneflies of any river in the Catskills. The water quality is excellent, and there are good populations of caddis and mayflies as well.

Trout on the Neversink are as wary as those found on any other Catskills river. A good presentation and a long leader are required to fool them consistently. During the hatches, it is important that you fish a fly that matches the natural insects in size, profile, and color. Paying attention to what stage of insect trout are feeding on is critical as well.

The Neversink exits the gorge in the Cortland Valley. From there it runs to its termination at the Delaware River in Port Jervis. This stretch is best fished early and late in the season, as the water warms rapidly. This section of river does, however, get a spring run of rainbows and shad from the Delaware River.

The Neversink River is one of the most famous trout fisheries in the country. It is the home water of Theodore Gordon. It is also located in a beautiful and rugged place—the Catskill Mountains of New York. Its location makes it easily accessible to about 20 percent of the nation's population.

➤ **Hatches:** Hatches vary from season to season. Small Blue-winged Olives are very important, as are caddis. Hendricksons, Grey Foxes, Light Cahills, Sulphurs, *Isonychias*, Tricos, and *Potamanthus* are all present. The gorge has the most prolific *Isonychia* hatches on the Neversink. In the summer, trout feed on terrestrials—especially beetles. For a detailed hatch chart, please visit www.flyfishingconnection.com/neversink.html.

➤ **Regulations:** The Neversink is open to fishing from April 1 through October 15. Fishing improves as water temps rise, and the insects become active. By May things are usually well on their way. The Gorge section of the Neversink River is managed under a strict catch-and-release regulation. Tackle is restricted to flies and artificial lures. Barbless hooks are recommended to protect the wild fish.

➤ **Tackle:** A 9-foot 5-weight rod with a floating line is your best bet for the Neversink River most of the time. If you want to fish streamers, a 9-foot 6-weight with a fast-sinking sink-tip is your best option. Dry-fly fishing is best done with a 9-foot 4-weight, as you may need to drop to 6X to effectively

The Stair Steps. Ray Ottulich

fish smaller patterns such as BWOs. While rods longer than 9 feet can work, especially for nymphing, rods shorter than 9 feet are not practical. Strike indicators should be large enough to float two flies and added weight. Flies should include Woolly Buggers, sculpin and minnow patterns; and all stages of mayflies, stoneflies, and caddis in a variety of sizes and colors.

DENNIS KARKA owns and operates Catskill Flies in Roscoe, New York. He can be reached at 607-498-6164, flyshop@catskillflies.com, or www.catskillflies.com.

CLOSEST FLY SHOPS

Catskill Flies
6 Stewart Avenue
Roscoe, New York 12776
845-434-4473
www.catskillflies.com
flyshop@catskillflies.com

Beaverkill Angler
52 Stewart Avenue
Roscoe, New York 12776
607-498-5194
www.beaverkillangler.com
mail@beaverkillangler.com

Baxter House River Outfitters
2012 Old Route 17
Roscoe, New York 12776
607-290-4022
www.baxterhouse.net
bhoutfitters@aol.com

CLOSEST GUIDES/OUTFITTERS

Neversink River Outfitters
PO Box 95
Forestburgh, New York 12777
914-799-4752
www.neversinkriver.com

Cross Current Guide Service & Outfitters
100 Laurel Acres Road
Milford, Pennsylvania 18337
914-475-6779
www.crosscurrentguideservice.com
crosscurrent@optonline.net

CLOSEST LODGING

Reynolds House
1394 Old Route 17
Roscoe, New York 12776
607-498-4422
www.reynoldshouseinn.com
host@reynoldshouseinn.com

Downsville Motel
6964 River Road
Downsville, New York 13755
607-363-7575
www.downsvillemotel.com

Baxter House River Outfitters
2012 Old Route 17
Roscoe, New York 12776
607-290-4022
www.baxterhouse.net
bhoutfitters@aol.com

Creekside Cabins
703 Hazel Road
Roscoe, New York 12776
607-498-5873
www.creeksidecabins.com
gofish@creeksidecabins.com

CLOSEST RESTAURANTS

Riverside Café
16624 County Highway 17
Roscoe, New York 12776
607 498-5305
www.riversidecafeandlodge.com

Spiro's Countryside Restaurant
179 Rockland Road
Roscoe New York, 12776
607-498-4419
www.spiroscountryside.com
comments@spiroscountryside.com

Roscoe Diner
1908 Old Route 17
Roscoe, New York 12776
607-498-4405
www.theroscoediner.com

Raimondo's Restaurant & Pizzeria
Stewart Avenue
Roscoe, New York 12776
607-498-4702

Rockland House
159 Rockland Road
Roscoe, New York 12776
607-498-4240
www.rocklandhouse.com

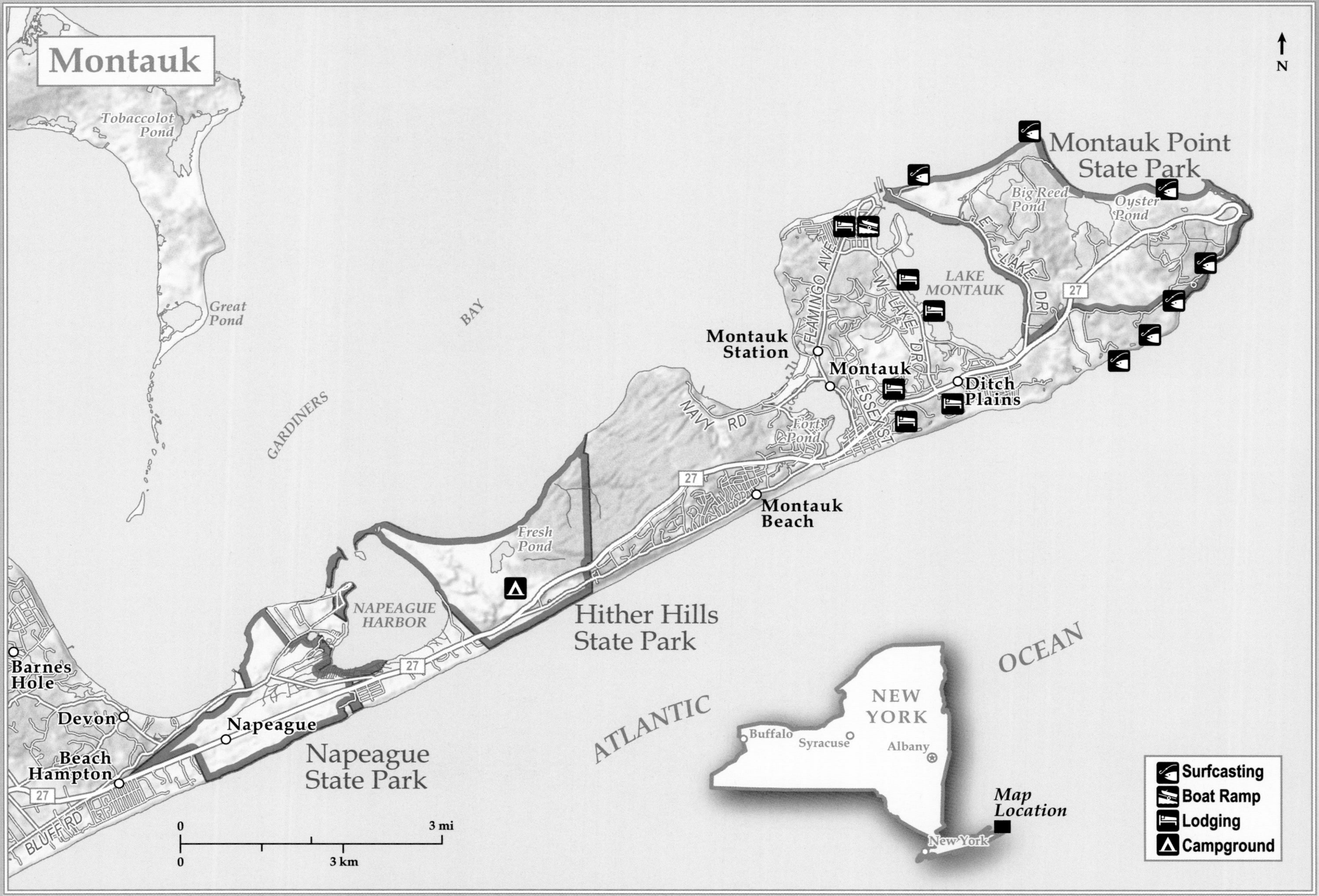

Montauk

N

Surfcasting
Boat Ramp
Lodging
Campground

Montauk Point
State Park

Oyster
Pond

Big Reed Pond

LAKE DR

E LAKE DR

LAKE
MONTAUK

W LAKE DR

FLAMINGO AVE

Ditch
Plains

Montauk

ESSEX ST

Fort
Pond

Montauk Station

Montauk Beach

NAVY RD

BAY

GARDINERS

Great
Pond

Tobaccolot Pond

Hither Hills
State Park

Fresh
Pond

NAPEAGUE HARBOR

Napeague
State Park

Napeague

OCEAN

Map
Location

New York

NEW YORK

Albany

Syracuse

Buffalo

New York

ATLANTIC

Barnes
Hole

Devon

Beach
Hampton

BLUFF RD

0   3 mi

0   3 km

➤ **Location:** Eastern tip of Long Island, New York, about a 3-hour ride from New York City; and a 3-hour ride—partly via ferry—from Boston, Massachusetts. Full-service airports are available in both cities.

The town of Montauk, at Long Island's easternmost point, is rich in fishing lore and history. Fly fishing is just the latest in its centuries-old recreational angling and commercial fishing history. Not only is Montauk the biggest commercial fishing port in New York, it is by far the largest saltwater recreational fishery in the Northeast.

Starting in May and running through November, Montauk Point and its treacherous, yet fish-friendly tide rips and currents attract gamefish in numbers not seen in many other places in the world. It is a complex ecosystem with its foundation in migrations of baitfish, gamefish, butterflies, birds, and not least, recreational and commercial anglers. The wildlife migrations are regional; the anglers come from all over the world.

Although Long Island Sound is 25 miles to the north and west, its effect on Montauk Point is significant. There are more than 100 miles of baitfish spawning and rearing creeks, bays, rivers, and estuaries that eventually flow past the George Washington–commissioned lighthouse at Montauk Point. Some say it represents up to five trillion gallons of seawater. The estuaries of Long Island Sound stretch all the way west to New York City, and as far east as Watch Hill, Rhode Island. It is this fact, and the forage that it produces, that creates the fish-so-thick-you-could-walk-on-them blitzes that Montauk is famous for.

Striped bass, or stripers, are the main attraction at Montauk. But both bluefish and false albacore are also pursued, making great additions to what is already a great fishery. Striped bass are a migratory species. Their native range is from Maine to the Carolinas. Two-thirds of the striped bass

population comes from the Chesapeake Bay. One-third of the population comes from the Hudson River. At some point during their north-to-south—and south-to-north—migrations, the striped bass have to pass Montauk Point. As a result of the ample baitfish supply found at Montauk, the stripers often stay around here longer than they do in most, if not all, other areas.

May is the beginning of the striper season in Montauk. This coincides with their northern migration. June sees the

Montauk Point blitz. Brendan McCarthy, Urban Fly-Guides

largest fish of the year caught by fly fishers. Surface fishing to large stripers is at its best at this time. Bluefish make an appearance in June as well, and will hang around until late October. July and August is generally a time for deepwater fishing, as the surface temperatures rise and fish feed on the surface only in early mornings, evenings, and on overcast days. This time of year brings the arrival of the false albacore and bonito, which appear toward the end of the summer.

September and October is when Montauk really shines. As the days get shorter, the bay anchovies show up in huge masses as they drop out of the bays and creeks, and migrate past the tip of Long Island on their way out to the Atlan-

Fishing the blitz at Montauk Point. Brendan McCarthy, Urban Fly-Guides

flies fished on an 8-weight rod with floating line are the preferred rigs for this style of fly fishing. Blue skies and calm winds at this time of year make it all the more enjoyable. Other fly-fishing opportunities in Montauk include offshore tuna, marlin, and sharks from June through October.

Montauk is a thriving tourist town, with all the amenities you would expect of a coastal community. There is every level of lodging, food, and services, from casual, to family, to luxury, to ultra-luxury. There are myriad non-fly-fishing activities as well. Surfing, sailing, horseback riding, water sports, and boat rentals are all available. There are also a number of art galleries, along with a robust retail infrastructure. Montauk is also very close to The Hamptons, for those days when the weather keeps you off the water, or for your nonfishing companions. Finally, Montauk is the most famous saltwater fly-fishing destination in the Northeast.

➤ **Tackle:** A 9-foot 9-weight rod with an intermediate line is your best bet for Montauk most of the time. If you are targeting false albacore, a 9-foot 10-weight is your best option. Fast-loading rods are recommended for long, accurate casts to fast-moving fish. The heavier rods also help land the larger fish without overplaying them. Ten-weight rods should be rigged with fast-sinking lines in the 450- to 550-grain range to help get the fly down in the fast currents. Flies should include rain bait patterns for false albacore. Clouser- and Deceiver-style flies are best for striped bass. Leaders should be in the 20-pound range. High-capacity reels with at least 250 yards of backing and reliable drags are a must.

tic Ocean. Massive schools of literally acres of striped bass, bluefish, and false albacore congregate to bust through these balls of baitfish in search of an easy meal. This is also the time when there can be hundreds of boats looking to take advantage of this amazing phenomenon. Add party boats, and wire line and surf fishers to the mix, and it is a scene unmatched anywhere else. Many people feel it is worth whatever it takes to witness one of the biggest fish migrations on earth.

The baitfish that occupy these waters run the gamut from ½-inch rain bait or bay anchovies to 2-pound menhaden. There is a strong squid run in June. Mullet run in August. Herring run in November and December. Tinker and Boston mackerel, butterfish, snapper bluefish, silversides, cinder worms, and sand eels are all present at one time or another. The appearance of any of these baitfish or other foods can trigger amazing fly fishing. The flies to match these baitfish and other foods are too numerous to count, but mostly they are variations on the Lefty's Deceiver or Clouser Minnow, matched in size and color, with a healthy dose of poppers, sliders, and Crease Flies thrown in.

Most fly fishing in and around Montauk is done in water from 4 to 60 feet deep. But I would be remiss if I didn't mention what many feel is the best fly fishing of the year: sight fishing the flats for striped bass. From early May and running well into July, within a short distance of Montauk, and even in the town proper, guides and anglers set out in Florida-style flats boats to pole the shallow, clear waters of Peconic and Gardiners Bays in search of stripers. This is some of the most challenging and rewarding, fishing a fly rodder can do anywhere. Wary fish that can run up to 30 pounds cruise around in a foot of crystal-clear ocean water over a white sand bottom in search of food. Sand eel or crab

Montauk Point striper. Brendan McCarthy, Urban Fly-Guides

Capt. Brendan McCarthy with big striper.
Brendan McCarthy, Urban Fly-Guides

CAPT. BRENDAN MCCARTHY owns and operates Urban Fly-Guides out of Brooklyn, Greenport, and Montauk, New York. He can be reached at 917-847-9576, info@urbanfly-guides.com, or www.urbanflyguides.com. Follow him at www.twitter.com/urbanfly-guide and www.facebook.com/mctrout.

CLOSEST FLY SHOPS

Paulie's Tackle of Montauk
4 Edgemere Street
Montauk, New York 11954
631-668-5520
www.pauliestackle.com

Tight Lines Tackle
53 Bay Street
Sag Harbor, New York 11963
631-725-0740
www.tightlinestackleinc.co
ken@tightlinestackleinc.com

Camp-Site Sport Shop
1877 New York Avenue
Huntington Station, New York 11747
631-271-4969
www.campsitesportshop.com

CLOSEST GUIDES/OUTFITTERS

Capt. Brendan McCarthy
Urban Fly-Guides
Brooklyn and Montauk, New York
917-847-9576
www.urbanflyguides.com
info@urbanflyguides.com

Capt. Paul Dixon
Dixon's To the Point Charters
East Hampton, New York 11937
516-314-1185
www.flyfishingmontauk.com
CaptainPaulDixon@mac.com

Capt. Andrew Derr
Long Island on the Fly
Greenport, New York 11944
212-495-9062
www.LIonthefly.com
Derrbott@gmail.com

CLOSEST LODGING

Snug Harbor Hotel (rooms/docking)
Star Island Drive
Montauk, New York 11954
613-668-2860
www.montauksnugharbor.com

Montauk Yacht Club (luxury rooms/resort)
32 Star Island Drive
Montauk, New York 11954
631-668-3100
www.igy-montauk.com
info@montaukyachtclub.com

The Harborside Hotel
362 West Lake Drive
Montauk, New York 11954
613-668-2511
www.montaukharborside.com
harborside@peconic.net

Hither Hills Campground (RV/tent sites)
164 Old Montauk Highway
Montauk, New York 11954
631-668-2554
www.nysparks.com/parks/122/details.aspx

CLOSEST RESTAURANTS

West Lake Chowder House and Marina
352 West Lake Drive
Montauk, New York 11954
631-668-5600
www.westlake-marina.com
info@westlake-marina.com

The Coast
41 South Euclid Drive
Montauk, New York 11954
631-668-3212
www.thecoastmontauk.com

Johnny's Pancakes
721 Main Street
Montauk, New York 11954
613-668-2383

V · MASSACHUSETTS

Downstream of Hoosac Tunnel. Harrison Anglers

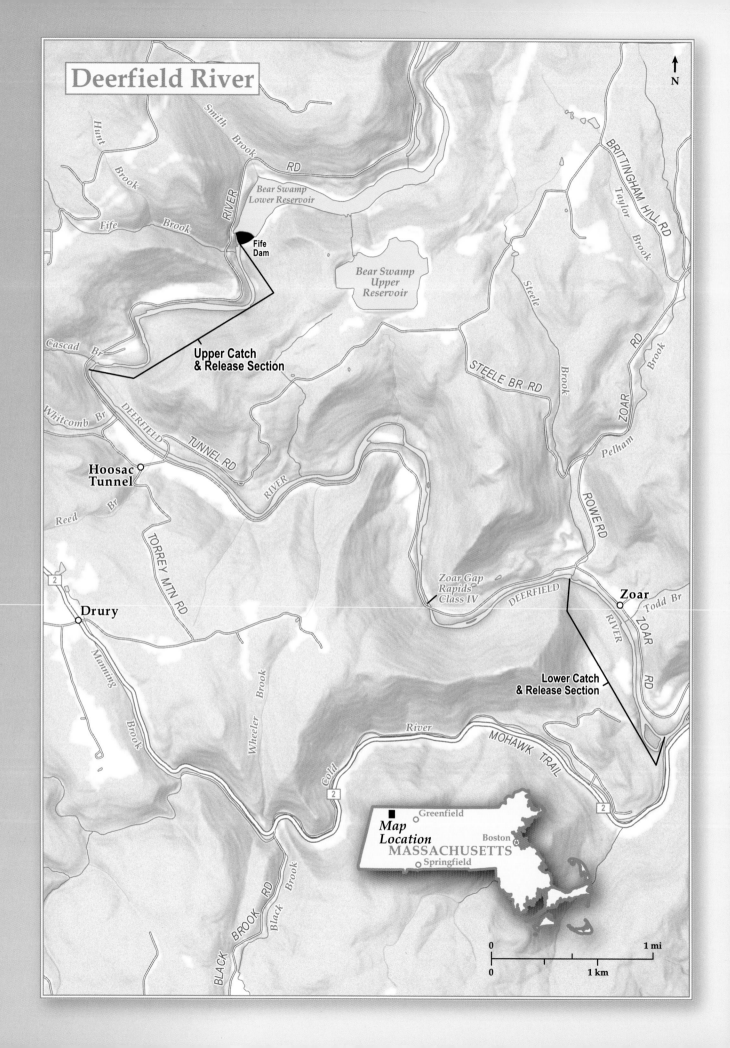

Deerfield River

Hunt Brook

Fife Brook

Smith Brook

RIVER RD

Bear Swamp
Lower Reservoir

Fife
Dam

Bear Swamp
Upper
Reservoir

BRITTINGHAM HILL RD

Taylor Brook

Steele Brook

STEELE BR RD

Pelham Brook

ZOAR RD

Upper Catch
& Release Section

Cascad Br

Whitcomb Br

DEERFIELD

TUNNEL RD

RIVER

**Hoosac
Tunnel**

Reed Br

TORREY MTN RD

ROWE RD

Zoar Gap
Rapids
Class IV

DEERFIELD

Zoar

Todd Br

ZOAR RD

RIVER

Lower Catch
& Release Section

2

Drury

Manning Brook

Wheeler Brook

Cold River

MOHAWK TRAIL

2

BLACK BROOK RD

Black Brook

2

**Map
Location**

Greenfield

Boston

MASSACHUSETTS

Springfield

N

0   1 mi

0   1 km

33 · Deerfield River

➤ **Location:** Northwestern Massachusetts, about a 2-hour ride from Boston; a 1½-hour ride from Hartford, Connecticut; and a 3-hour ride from Manchester, New Hampshire. Full-service airports are available in all three cities.

Nicknamed the "hardest-working river in New England," the Deerfield River in Massachusetts has long suffered from the demands of commerce. Although a majority of the riverbanks are owned and controlled by the railroad, the state, and the power companies, there is virtually no shoreline development, and much of the riparian zone remains undisturbed. In spite of the abuse, the Deerfield is one of the finest trout rivers in the Northeast.

Beginning in southern Vermont, the Deerfield flows 75 miles through four large reservoirs and six small impoundments on its way to the Connecticut River. In Vermont, the river's Central, West, and North Branches meet to create the main stem. From here it enters western Massachusetts. Along its path, there are century-old top-flow dams, large bottom-release dams, a mountaintop pump storage reservoir, "the glory hole," which resembles a massive sink drain, and miles of man-made diversion canals. Although the Deerfield is a blueprint for what not to do to a river, the trout are thriving.

The Deerfield is a success story—albeit something of an accidental one. Dams are part of the reason. High water temps in the summer seem to be the biggest challenge to most New England rivers. The tailwater effect from the dams on the Upper Deerfield watershed creates a coldwater fishery that will reach the mid-60s on a hot summer afternoon, but never "cook" like other rivers in the region. The decommissioning of the Yankee Atomic Plant in Rowe also impacted the trout fishery. This resulted in a 15-degree drop in the water temperature. This in turn helped a growing wild brown trout population in the upper river, and a wild rainbow trout population in the middle river. Rainbows average 12 to 15 inches, with occasional

fish over 20 inches—especially in the lower river. Browns are similar in size, but you have a better shot at a 20-plus-inch brown on the upper river.

Public access on the Deerfield is very good. Much of the upper river can be accessed from Zoar Road, which parallels the river from Route 2 to Fife Dam. There are two catch-and-release sections on the upper Deerfield. The first runs from Fife Brook Dam to the Hoosac Tunnel—a roughly 5-mile engineering marvel that took the lives of almost 200 workers. This 1.6-mile stretch may be the best on the river, especially in the winter months. The second catch-and-release section runs from Pelham Brook to just above Route 2, and is rough-

Bardwell Ferry Bridge on lower Deerfield. Harrison Anglers

ly 2.2 miles long. There are many good access points along Route 2 all the way to Shelburne Falls. As the river flows through Shelburne, three small impoundments offer match-the-hatch dry-fly fishing.

Below the #2 dam in Shelburne—#1 was planned but never constructed—is about 8 miles of river before it flows under Interstate 91 in Stillwater. This section of river has only two good public access points—Bardwells Ferry and Stillwater Bridges. There is a healthy population of wild and stocked rainbows and browns. The river here flows unim-

Downstream of Hoosac Tunnel. Harrison Anglers

*Above, Tom Harrison on a warm winter day and below,
Tom Harrison with a winter brown trout. Harrison Anglers*

peded to the Connecticut River, allowing American shad to access the Deerfield from April to July. Sight fishing for "poor man's salmon" can be excellent at times. Large smallmouth bass and the occasional Atlantic salmon are present as well.

The Deerfield is a tale of two rivers. At low water it flows at 125 to 150 cfs—resembling a small stream more than a river. When water is released to generate power, the river rises to 800 to 1,000 cfs. These releases are usually two to three hours in duration in midsummer, but can run 24 hours a day in spring and when there is an abundance of rainwater or snowmelt. At low water, wade fishing is the preferred method. Float fishing is preferred at high flows. The release schedule is posted daily on the website www.H2oline.com.

Both wade and float fishers have ample opportunities to experience the Deerfield. The trick is to be on the right stretch of river at the right time. Although most of the river can be waded during low flows, checking the flow forecast can make or break your trip. Many waders have found themselves stuck on the wrong side of the river. As a general rule, water released from the dam moves about 2 miles an hour, reaching Route 2 in about 4 hours. The release works its way downstream and hits the lower river in the late evening. This allows for low-water fishing most of the day downstream of the North River confluence. Though most locals fish the river at low water, midday releases give anglers access to larger feeding trout that would not normally be active during daylight hours.

The river from Fife Brook Dam down can be floated with a raft. The two most popular floats are from Fife down, and from the Bardwells Bridge to Route I-91. Drift boats are not recommended due to changing water levels and poor accesses. There is a Class III+ drop located at Zoar Gap. Inexperienced rowers or those unfamiliar with the river should *not* attempt to run Zoar Gap. During high-water periods, anglers share the water with kayakers, whitewater canoeists, and commercial rafts filled with thrill-seekers. On warm summer days, tubers also use the river. Those wishing to avoid

the recreationists can always find a place where lack of access keeps the crowds down.

➤ **Hatches:** Trout in the Deerfield feed on minnows, crayfish, insects, and eggs. The predominant minnows are dace and sculpins. Insects include stoneflies, mayflies, caddis, midges, and aquatic worms. Hatches are not what you would call prolific, but they are reliable. Midges are available year-round. Mayflies hatch from April through June, and in early fall. Caddis hatch most evenings. Stoneflies hatch throughout the season. The summer months offer good terrestrial fishing. The Deerfield is open to fishing year-round. While prime time may be April through November, you can catch fish all winter if you pick your days. Large Buggers, sculpin patterns, and many large attractor nymphs will take large browns in the colder months.

➤ **Tackle:** A 9-foot 5-weight rod with a floating line is your best bet for the Deerfield River most of the time. If you want to fish streamers, a 9-foot 6-weight rod with a fast-sinking line is your best option. Dry-fly fishing is best done with a 9-foot 4-weight, as you may need to use 6X tippet to effectively fish midge patterns. While rods longer than 9 feet can work, especially for nymphing, rods shorter than 9 feet are not practical. Strike indicators should be large enough to float two flies and added weight. Flies should include Woolly Buggers and sculpin patterns; all stages of mayflies, stoneflies, and caddis in a variety of sizes and colors; and worm and egg patterns.

TOM AND DAN HARRISON own and operate Harrison Anglers in Shelburne Falls, Massachusetts. They offer year-round float trips on the Deerfield and other western Massachusetts rivers. They can be reached at 413-222-6207, www.harrisonanglers.com, or tom@harrisonanglers.com.

Dan Harrison

Tom Harrison

CLOSEST FLY SHOPS

The Lower Forty
134 Madison Street
Worcester, Massachusetts 01610
508-752-4004
www.thelowerforty.com
lowerforty@verizon.net

Concord Outfitters
84 Commonwealth Avenue
West Concord, Massachusetts 01742
978-318-0330
www.concordoutfitters.com
andy@concordoutfitters.com

CLOSEST GUIDES/OUTFITTERS

Harrison Anglers
232 Old Vernon Road
Northfield, Massachusetts 01360
413-222-6207
www.harrisonanglers.com
tom@harrisonanglrs.com

GSOutfitting
Greenfield, Massachusetts
617-697-6733
www.gsoutfitting.com
eric@gsoutfitting.com

CLOSEST LODGING

Oxbow Resort Motel
1741 Mohawk Trail
East Charlemont, Massachusetts 01370
413-625-6011
www.oxbowresortmotel.com
info@oxbowresortmotel.com

Giovanni's Red Rose Motel
1701 Mohawk Trail
Charlemont, Massachusetts 01339
413-625-2666
www.redrosemotel.com

Warfield House B&B
200 Warfield Road
Charlemont, Massachusetts 01339
413-339-6600
www.warfieldhouseinn.com
info@warfieldhouseinn.com

Hawk Mountain Lodge
7 Main Street
Charlemont, Massachusetts 01339
413-339-8597
www.hawkmountainlodge.com
info@zoaroutdoor.com

Mohawk Park Campground
(riverside tent and RV sites)
Route 2 (just west of Zoar Road)
Charlemont, Massachusetts 01339
413-339-4470

CLOSEST RESTAURANTS

West End Pub
Lunch and Dinner Menu
16 State Street
Shelburne Falls, Massachusetts 01370
413-625-6216
www.westendpubinfo.com
westendpub16@yahoo.com

Gypsy Apple (gourmet dining)
65 Bridge Street
Shelburne Falls, Massachusetts 01370
413-625-6345
www.facebook.com/pages/GypsyApple-Bistro

The Bluerock Restaurant & Bar
10 Bridge Street
Shelburne Falls, Massachusetts 01370
413-625-8133
www.thebluerockrestaurant.com
eat@thebluerockrestaurant.com

Otters Restaurant
(breakfast, lunch, and dinner menu)
1745 Route 2
East Charlemont, Massachusetts 01370
413-625-2450
www.ottersrestaurant.com

Mohawk Park Pub & Restaurant
(lunch and dinner menu)
Route 2 (just west of Zoar Road)
Charlemont, Massachusetts 01339
413-339-4470

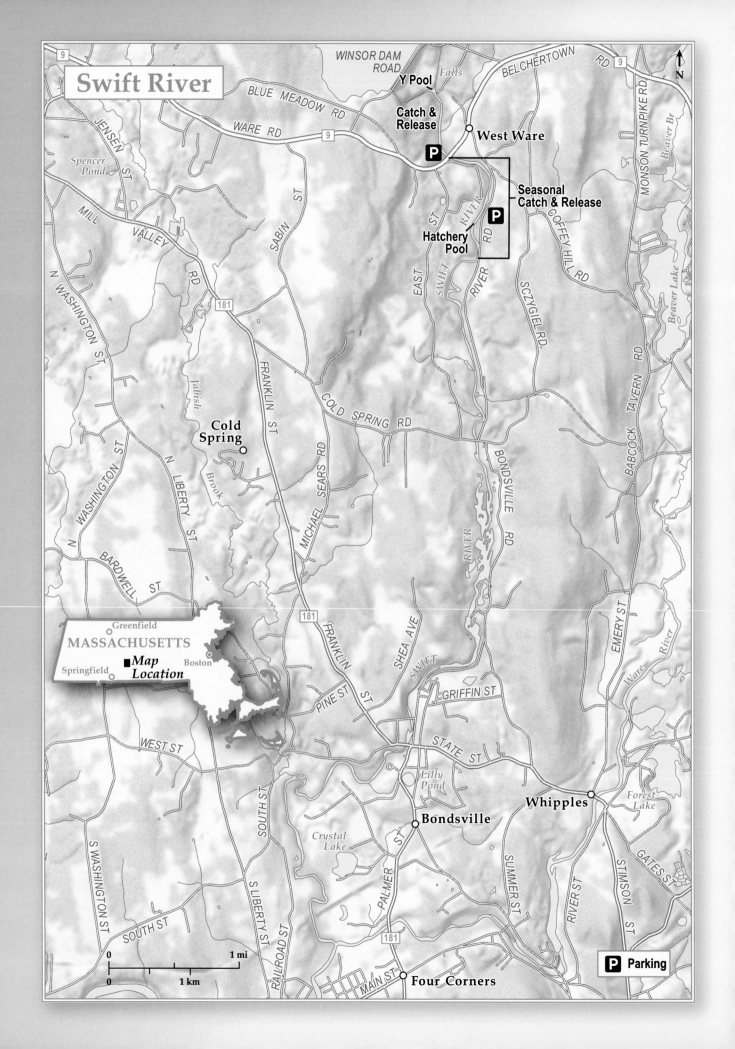

34 · Swift River

➤ **Location:** Central Massachusetts, about a 1½-hour ride from Boston; a 1-hour ride from Hartford, Connecticut; a 2-hour ride from Albany, New York; and a 2-hour ride from Manchester, New Hampshire. Full-service airports are available in all four cities.

Covering more than 25,000 acres, with a maximum depth of over 150 feet, Quabbin Reservoir in central Massachusetts serves as the public water supply for greater Boston. Construction of Windsor Dam, opened in 1939, created the reservoir while inundating several small towns. Old farm roads disappear into the depths of the reservoir, telling a story of a time when life in the upper Swift River Valley was far different than it is today. In recent times, the area around the reservoir has played a critical role in the reintroduction of bald eagles.

Two branches of the Swift River—East and West—flow into Quabbin. Both contain wild brook trout. One also serves as spawning habitat for the lake's landlocked salmon. It is here that the Swift begins its transformation from a small freestone stream into a unique tailwater fishery. Most Northeast rivers referred to as tailwaters do not fit the classic definition. The Swift is the exception, with the year-round cold, clear, water and plant and insect life you would expect to find. These conditions support a robust trout population, with some specimens growing to trophy size.

At the base of the 295-foot Windsor Dam, the Swift exits a power station through what is known as the bubbler. Water released from the dam runs between 38 and 55 degrees, depending on the time of year. Average flows run in the 40 to 60 cfs range. High flows can reach 600 cfs. There is also an overflow channel, known as the spillway, which releases water from the top of the reservoir when it is at capacity.

Below the dam, the Swift meanders through mature forest in 1,500-acre Herman Covey Wildlife Management Area. It terminates at the Ware River, roughly 10 miles downstream.

Two small dams interrupt the river in Bondsville. From Windsor Dam to Route 9, the Swift is arguably the most popular wade fishery in Massachusetts. This includes the famous Y Pool, where the dam's bubbler channel and overflow channel converge. Like all Massachusetts waters, it is open year-round to fishing. This section is restricted to fly fishing only, and managed for catch-and-release. It also just happens to be one of the most challenging stretches of water in the Northeast.

From Route 9 to Cady Lane—a distance of roughly 1 mile—the Swift is managed under a seasonal catch-and-release regulation. Harvest is prohibited from the beginning of July through the end of December. During this time, tackle

Early morning below Cady Lane. Harrison Anglers

is restricted to artificial lures and flies. There are abundant riffles, and a couple of large pools created by the remnants of old mill dams. This section holds many trout. Below the USGS Gauging Station, water is siphoned for use in the McLaughlin Fish Hatchery. The outflow from the hatchery, known as the pipe, is one of the most popular pools on the river. This is because trout congregate here to feed on food the hatchery fish miss.

Below Cady Lane, the Swift slows, widens, and deepens. There is approximately 4 miles of river before the first dam.

149

Kacie Breeds landing a brook trout. Casey Breeds

Bob Mallard with fall brook trout from catch-and-release section. John Vacca

This section has logjams and suspended weed beds that resemble those found in Western spring creeks. These provide excellent habitat for both insects and trout. There is also abundant tree canopy, which provides shade—and insects. Floating this section in the summer, while sight fishing to trout that are feeding on terrestrials, is a great way to catch trout at a time of year when many other fisheries have slowed down. The last mile is called the Swift River Reservoir. This is basically a stillwater. However, it holds a good number of large trout, including landlocked salmon from Quabbin that

Casey Breeds with rainbow trout. Casey Breeds

enter the river via the spillway during high water. This section receives very little pressure due to limited access, and the fact that it is difficult to wade. It is, however, a great float fishery for those willing to hire a guide.

Between the two dams, there is about ½ mile of riffle water. As the Swift nears the second dam, it becomes an impoundment. This section puts up some very large rainbows. Below the second dam is 3 miles of riffles, runs, and pocketwater. Brook, brown, and rainbow trout are found here. They are easy to miss for all but those with the sharpest eyes. This stretch sees even less pressure than the upper section. It has a lot of wade-friendly water, but access is difficult. The last 1½ miles before the Swift empties into the Ware are mostly deep, slow pools and runs, with logs and trees lining the banks. This is another section that is best fished from a boat.

The Swift River boasts both numbers of fish and large fish. It also offers the best sight fishing in the region, due to its crystal-clear water. It is a year-round fishery, and one of the finest winter fisheries in the Northeast. When you walk, or float, along the Swift, you are constantly looking at trout. Oftentimes the best thing to do is to pick a single fish, and work it until it eats, or flees.

➤ Hatches: Midge hatches are very consistent, and almost daily events. Mayflies include Blue-winged Olives and Sulphurs. Caddis are present as well. There are also stoneflies. The ever-present canopy provides a constant source of terrestrials, especially ants. Oftentimes a fish that just refused every size 22 midge in your box presented on 8X tippet, will inhale a terrestrial drifted over its head. Aquatic worms are present. While minnow life is sparse, trout will take streamers in the right places, at the right times.

Fly fishers who view the Swift River as beginning at Windsor Dam and ending at Route 9 are missing some very productive trout water. Those who venture down as far as Cady Lane are still only seeing the tip of the iceberg. To fully understand what a spectacular fishery the Swift River is, you need to float the lower end with a guide who knows the river well. I can assure you that you will not be disappointed.

➤ **Tackle:** A 9-foot 5-weight rod with a floating line will work on the Swift River most of the time. If you want to fish dry flies in the upper section, an 8- to 9-foot, 2- to 4-weight will help protect the 6X to 8X tippet you will need to catch fish consistently. If you want to fish streamers on the lower river, a 9-foot 6-weight with a fast-sinking line is your best bet. Rods longer than 9 feet can be used for nymphing. Strike indicators should be large enough to float two flies and added weight. Flies should include Woolly Buggers, sculpin patterns, and smelt patterns for the upper river; and all stages of mayflies, stoneflies, and caddis in a variety of sizes and colors. Summer terrestrials should include hoppers, beetles, spiders, and ants.

ERIC GASS owns and operates GSOutfitting in Greenfield, Massachusetts. He can be reached at 617-697-6733; Eric@gsoutfitting .com; or www.gsoutfitting.com.

CLOSEST FLY SHOPS

Lower Forty Outfitters
134 Madison Street
Worcester, Massachusetts 01610
508-752-4004
www.thelowerforty.com
lower40@verizon.net

Concord Outfitters
84 Commonwealth Avenue
West Concord, Massachusetts 01742
978-318-0330
www.concordoutfitters.com
andy@concordoutfitters.com

Bear's Den
34 Robert Boyden Road
Taunton, Massachusetts 02780
508-977-0700
www.bearsden.com
scott@bearsden.com

CLOSEST GUIDES/OUTFITTERS

GSOutfitting
Greenfield, Massachusetts
617-697-6733
www.gsoutfitting.com
eric@gsoutfitting.com

Harrison Anglers
232 Old Vernon Road
Northfield, Massachusetts 01360
413-222-6207
www.harrisonanglers.com
info@harrisonanglers.com

Marla Blair's Fly Fishing Guide Service
18 Letendre Avenue
Ludlow, Massachusetts 01056
413-583-5141
www.marlablair.com
marlablair@yahoo.com

CLOSEST LODGING

Lord Jeffery Inn
30 Boltwood Avenue
Amherst, Massachusetts 01002
413-256-8200
www.lordjefferyinn.com
reservations@lordjefferyinn.com

Holiday Inn Express
400 Russell Street
Hadley, Massachusetts 01035
413-582-0002
www.hiexpress.com

Bird Song Bed & Breakfast
815 South East Street
Amherst, Massachusetts 01002
413-256-0433
www.birdsongofamherst.com
BirdsongofAmherst@comcast.net

Hartman's Herb Farm
1026 Old Dana Road
Barre, Massachusetts 01005
978-355-2015
www.hartmansherbfarm.com
hartmansherb@hotmail.com

The Mucky Duck Bed and Breakfast
38 Park Street
Belchertown, Massachusetts 01007
413-323-9657

CLOSEST RESTAURANTS

Pinocchio's
2054 Bridge Street
Three Rivers, Massachusetts 01080
413-284-0202
www.pinocchiosristorante.com

The Grapevine Grill (Greek cuisine)
62 Turkey Hill Road
Belchertown, Massachusetts 01007
413-323-4117
www.grapevinegrill.com
GVgrille@hotmail.com

Roadhouse Café (breakfast)
176 Federal Street
Belchertown, Massachusetts 01007
413-323-6175
www.roadhousecafe.net
info@roadhousecafe.net

Mexicali Fresh Mex Grill
146 West Street
Ware, Massachusetts 01082
413-277-0925
www.mexicalisfreshmex.com

Hawley's Family Restaurant
151 North Main Street
Belchertown, Massachusetts 01007
413-323-7686

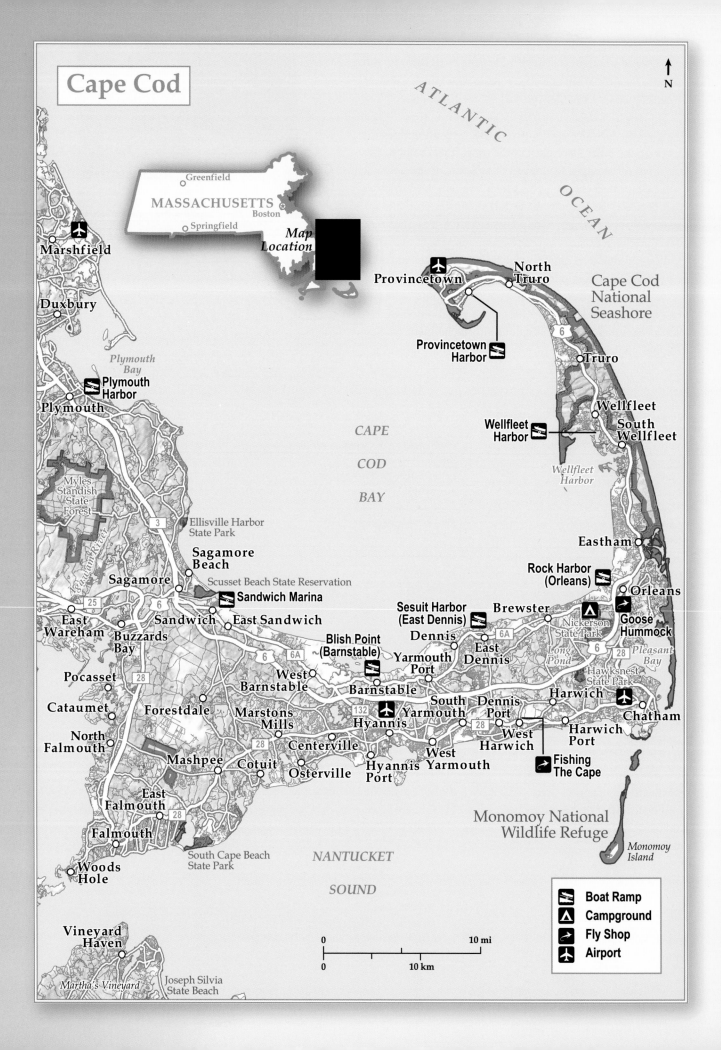

Cape Cod

N

ATLANTIC OCEAN

Greenfield

MASSACHUSETTS
Boston
Springfield

Map Location

Marshfield

Provincetown
North Truro

Cape Cod National Seashore

Duxbury

Plymouth Bay

Plymouth Harbor
Plymouth

Provincetown Harbor

Truro

Wellfleet
South Wellfleet

Wellfleet Harbor

Wellfleet Harbor

CAPE

COD

BAY

Myles Standish State Forest

Ellisville Harbor State Park

Eastham

Sagamore Beach

Scusset Beach State Reservation

Rock Harbor (Orleans)

Orleans

Sagamore

Sandwich Marina

Sesuit Harbor (East Dennis)
Brewster

Nickerson State Park

Goose Hummock

East Wareham
Sandwich
East Sandwich

Dennis

East Dennis

Long Pond

Pleasant Bay

Buzzards Bay

Blish Point (Barnstable)
Yarmouth Port

Hawksnest State Park

Harwich

Pocasset

West Barnstable

Barnstable

South Yarmouth
Dennis Port

Harwich Port

Chatham

Cataumet

Forestdale

Marstons Mills

Hyannis

West Harwich

North Falmouth

Centerville

West Yarmouth

Fishing The Cape

Mashpee

Cotuit

Osterville

Hyannis Port

East Falmouth

Monomoy National Wildlife Refuge

Falmouth

South Cape Beach State Park

NANTUCKET

Monomoy Island

Woods Hole

SOUND

Vineyard Haven

	Boat Ramp
	Campground
	Fly Shop
	Airport

0   10 mi
0   10 km

Martha's Vineyard
Joseph Silvia State Beach

35 · Cape Cod Bay (stripers)

➤ **Location:** Eastern Massachusetts, about a 1-hour ride from Boston; a 2-hour ride from Manchester, New Hampshire; a 2½-hour ride from Hartford, Connecticut; and a 4½-hour ride from New York City. Full-service airports are available in all four cities.

Picture this: It is high noon on a hot, hazy, sunny day and you are standing in water just above your knees. You have your fly rod in hand and the fish are swimming right past you, some even bumping into your shins. Your cast is perfect, even if it is a little short, because once again—fish on!

Or this. You are standing barefooted on the white fiberglass deck of a Florida-style flats boat, wearing your polarized sunglasses and floppy sun hat, with fly rod ready to cast. The sky is clear, the water is a shade considered tropical, and you can see all the details of the sandy bottom. You scan the water, and spot large, gray undulating pods of bait, and look a little harder to see that they are being pushed and herded by big fish.

Are you on a vacation in Florida, the Bahamas, Turks and Caicos, or Los Roques? The Seychelles, perhaps? No—this a summer day on a Cape Cod Bay sand flat.

Cape Cod is famous for its saltwater fishing. Charter boats with crusty captains are a common sight at all Cape Cod harbors. Filled with tourists, the boats escort anglers to find striped bass, bluefish, and bluefin tuna. Sonar is the key, coupled with lead-core lines that are dragged all over the bay, producing happy fishermen with big fish for dinner.

Fly fishing has traditionally been the domain of Chatham's famous Monomoy Island, with its ubiquitous sand flats. However, the recent influx of seals—and now great white sharks—has rendered Monomoy more popular for seal tours than for fly fishing.

My fly-fishing expertise is Cape Cod Bay, the body of water formed by the arm that is Cape Cod. Cape Cod Bay offers shallow-water and deepwater fishing from the Cape Cod Ca-

nal to the tip of Provincetown. Shallow water and sand flats line almost the entire coastline. The bay's 10- to 12-foot tides coupled with New England's ever-changing weather, provide fluctuating conditions all day.

The most sought-after fish are striped bass and bluefish. Stripers, with their languid slurping style, are more coveted, however, the toothy bluefish actually give the best fight. These two species are often found together, feeding on the same pods of bait. They say that the largest stripers hang below the blues, enjoying the leftover bits of mutilated baitfish drifting down from the voracious blues. Nevertheless, don't be surprised to witness stripers pursuing the bait in a flurry of fins and tails of both blues and stripers.

Avery Revere with striper. Salty Fly Cape Cod

The best part of fly fishing Cape Cod Bay is that it can be done by foot, kayak, or boat. A satellite map will give you the lay of the land. Look for sandy flats that abut channels. Seek out contours, structure, rocks, and weed beds. When fishing by foot or kayak, find public access and start walking, or launch your kayak. There are public boat ramps from Sandwich to Provincetown.

Whether you are wading, kayaking, or boating, always pay close attention to tides. Cape Cod Bay tides can drop or rise as much 6 inches every 15 minutes. When wading, it is easy to become stranded. In a boat, you could spend several

End of the day. Avery Revere, Salty Fly Cape Cod

hours high and dry. As always when you're on the water, it is imperative that you keep an eye on the weather. Cape Cod is notorious for strong southwest winds that can make paddling home difficult. Add a couple of knots of current and you could be late for dinner.

On the flats, the trick is to cast early and get the fly to bottom in front of the oncoming fish. As always, be prepared with your own favorite striper fly. Just because the Clouser works for me does not necessarily mean it's the best pattern for you—definitely try your luck with your own choice fly.

How to work the fly is another important factor. I tell my clients to vary their retrieve when blind casting. Everybody has his or her own rhythm; if the fish aren't biting, change the rhythm. When fishing the flats, try twitching the fly intermittently between strips. When the fish are busting bait on the surface, tie on a popper and work it along the surface. Bluefish will go wild.

Cape Cod Bay striped bass feed primarily on sand eels. However they also eat spring herring, squid, and mackerel, as well as clams and small shrimp. Fall brings pods of men-

Striper on the flats. Avery Revere, Salty Fly Cape Cod

haden. Nevertheless, my experience is that it is the sand eel that stripers crave. The Cape Cod Bay sand eel feeds not only the striped bass, but also it is also the food of choice for the bluefin tuna, and the whales that are found near Provincetown.

Spring, summer, and fall are the best times to fish Cape Cod Bay. Striped bass and bluefish are both migratory species. Generally, the striped bass arrive before the bluefish. However, in recent years this has not been the case. The behavior of these fish varies by season. In the spring, you will find the stripers milling around the estuaries and the surrounding marshes. In late spring and early summer, the fish move to the flats and into the bay. Diving gannets and terns mark their feeding blitzes. By midsummer, they are generally difficult to find without the aforementioned sonar, so fly fishing requires late-night stealth or predawn excursions. By August, they ball up on the flats, and the first signs of fall are pods of menhaden and the accompanying bobbing terns.

The striper fishery has an amazing history, including a strong comeback after a decade of scarcity in the 1970s. There are many theories about the trends of the striper fishery. Organizations such as Stripers Forever, and publications like *Fly Fishing in Salt Waters* help to keep one abreast of this fishery.

➤ **Regulations:** The Massachusetts Department of Fish & Game now requires that all saltwater anglers buy a fishing license. For further details, visit www.mass.gov/dfwele. Regulations require that a striped bass be at least 28 inches long to be kept. All others must be released so they can breed.

➤ **Tackle:** A 9-foot 9-weight fly rod is your best all-around choice for Cape Cod Bay. Eight-weight rods can work as well—especially for schoolie stripers. Intermediate lines are the best option—I recommend the clear or clear-tipped lines. A reel designed for saltwater use is recommended. Leaders should be 9 feet long and 12-pound test. Flies should include Clousers, Deceivers, and sand eel patterns. Patterns in white, white and yellow, and white and olive seem to work best. Small Clousers can be used to imitate sand eels. Barbless hooks are suggested.

CAPT. AVERY REVERE owns and operates Salty Fly Cape Cod Fishing Charters. She can be reached at 508-362-5482, saltyflycapecod@comcast.net, or www.saltyflycapecod.com.

CLOSEST FLY SHOPS

Fishing The Cape
16 Route 28
West Harwich, Massachusetts 02671
508-432-1200
www.fishingthecape.com
info@fishingthecape.com

Goose Hummock
15 Massachusetts 6A
Orleans, Massachusetts 02653
508-255-0455
www.goose.com

CLOSEST GUIDES/OUTFITTERS

Salty Fly Cape Cod
Capt. Avery Revere
Cape Cod, Massachusetts
508-362-5482
www.saltyflycapecod.com
saltyflycapecod@comcast.net

CLOSEST LODGING

Ashley Manor
3660 Main Street
Barnstable, Massachusetts 02630
508-362-8044
www.ashleymanor.net
stay@ashleymanor.net

The Captain Freeman Inn
15 Breakwater Road
Brewster, Massachusetts 02631
508-896-7481
www.captainfreemaninn.com
info@captainfreemaninn.com

Land's End Inn
22 Commercial Street
Provincetown, Massachusetts 02657
508-487-0706
www.landsendinn.com
info@landsendinn.com

Ambassador Inn and Suites
1314 Main Street
South Yarmouth, Massachusetts 02664
508-394-4000
www.goambassadorinn.com

CLOSEST RESTAURANTS

Hemisphere Waterfront Dining
98 Town Neck Road
Sandwich, Massachusetts 02563
508-888-6166
www.hemispherecapecod.com

Mattakeese Wharf Waterfront Restaurant
273 Millway Road
Barnstable, Massachusetts 02630
508-362-4511
www.mattakeese.com

The Brewster Fish House
2208 Main Street (Route 6A)
Brewster, Massachusetts 02631
508-896-7867
www.brewsterfishhouse.com

The Mews Restaurant & Café
429 Commercial Street
Provincetown, Massachusetts 02657
508-487-1500
www.mews.com

Capt. Bob Hines at Barberville Dam. John Halnon

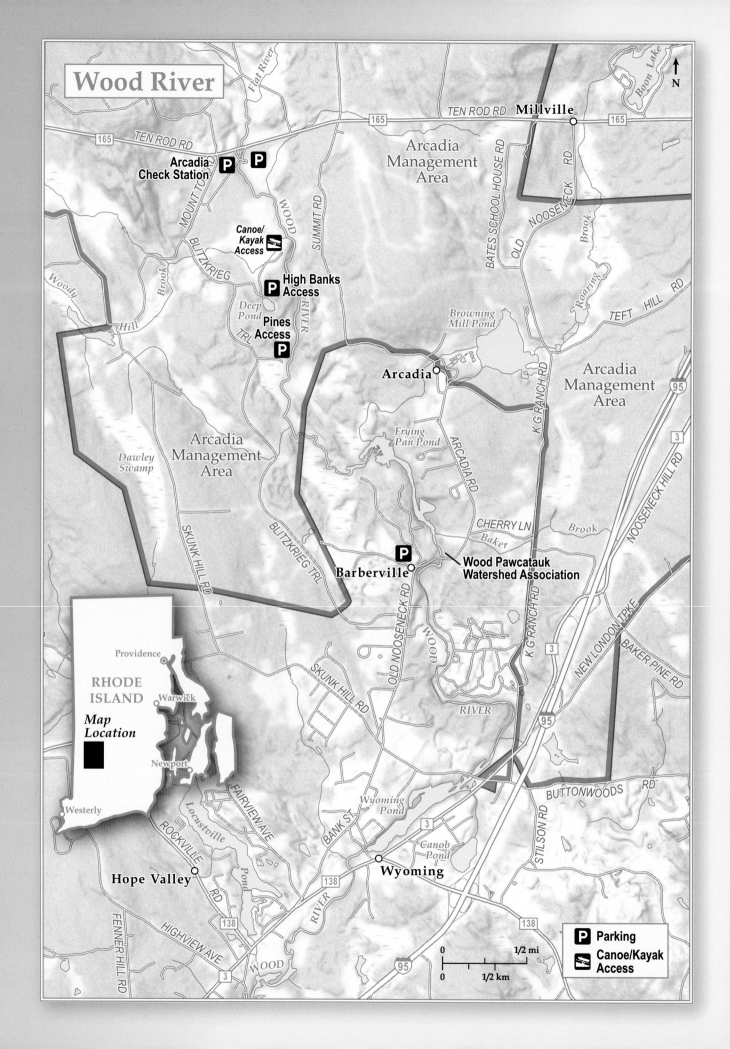

Wood River

N

Millville

TEN ROD RD

165

Arcadia
Management
Area

TEN ROD RD

165

**Arcadia
Check Station**

P P

BATES SCHOOL HOUSE RD

OLD NOOSENECK RD

Boon Lake

Canoe/
Kayak
Access

WOOD

SUMMIT RD

MOUNT TOM RD

BLITZKRIEG

Brook

Woody

Hill

RIVER

**High Banks
Access**

P

Deep
Pond

**Pines
Access**

P

Browning
Mill Pond

Roaring

Brook

TEFT HILL RD

95

3

Arcadia

Arcadia
Management
Area

K G RANCH RD

NOOSENECK HILL RD

Frying
Pan Pond

ARCADIA RD

Dawley
Swamp

Arcadia
Management
Area

SKUNK HILL RD

BLITZKRIEG TRL

CHERRY LN

Baker   Brook

P

Barberville

**Wood Pawcatauk
Watershed Association**

OLD NOOSENECK RD

WOOD

K G RANCH RD

3

95

BAKER PINE RD

NEW LONDON TPKE

STILSON RD

BUTTONWOODS RD

RHODE
ISLAND

Providence

Warwick

**Map
Location**

Newport

Westerly

Locustville Pond

ROCKVILLE RD

FAIRVIEW AVE

SKUNK HILL RD

RIVER

Wyoming
Pond

BANK ST

3

Canob
Pond

Wyoming

Hope Valley

FENNER HILL RD

HIGHVIEW AVE

138

WOOD

RIVER

138

95

0   1/2 mi

0   1/2 km

P Parking

Canoe/Kayak
Access

36 · Wood River

➤ **Location:** Southern Rhode Island, about a 1-hour ride from Providence; a 2-hour ride from Boston, Massachusetts; a 3-hour ride from Manchester, New Hampshire; and a 3½-hour ride from Portland, Maine. Full-service airports are available in all four cities.

The Wood River is undoubtedly Rhode Island's—and one of southern New England's—premier trout streams. That this river is found in the smallest state in the country, and a state that has some of the highest population densities in the country, is a real testimony to those charged with managing and preserving this resource.

The Wood River valley is considered one of the coldest locations in Rhode Island. This is due its low-lying and flat geography. Anglers fishing the Wood find themselves among majestic pines, oaks, and maples. During the fall, the foliage rivals anywhere found in New England. Located along the Rhode Island–Connecticut border, the Wood is the primary tributary of the Pawcatuck River. The river has eight dams along its length. The topography is a mix of riffles, placid runs, pools, and undercut banks. This provides a wide variety of conditions for those seeking specific types of water to fish. The Wood is easily accessible, with numerous public access points. These include, but are not limited to, the Deer Check Station on Route 165, the dam at Wyoming Pond, and several sites within the Arcadia Wildlife Management Area.

The source of the Wood River is in the swamps northeast of Potters Pond in Sterling, Connecticut. From here the river flows southeast into Rhode Island. Once in Rhode Island, the Wood flows southeast past Escoheag Hill, and over Stepstone Falls, before receiving the Flat River. After it merges with the Flat River, the Wood heads southward through the Arcadia Wildlife Management Area. From here it flows into the towns of Richmond and Hopkinton.

The Wood River within the Arcadia Wildlife Management Area is of most interest to fly fishers. Here fly fishers can pursue stocked brown trout, brook trout, and rainbow trout, along with a small population of wild native brook trout. The fish within the confines of the management area are sheltered by the heavy tree canopy, and undercut banks that provide protection from the sun. These help keep the water temperature cool during the summer months. This area is also used by hikers, bikers, and hunters pursuing upland game and deer. Be sure to check the Rhode Island Department of Environmental Management website for rules in regard to safety and fishing during hunting season.

The Wood River is stocked several times annually, mostly with rainbow trout and brown trout. It is also periodically stocked with brook trout in certain stretches of the river. The Wood is float stocked by the Narragansett, Rhode Island Chapter of Trout Unlimited and the Rhode Island Division of Fish & Wildlife. This helps disburse fish and lessen the initial mortality due to predation by otters, mergansers, stocking truck chasers, and so on often associated with high concentrations of freshly stocked fish.

➤ **Regulations:** The Wood River is open to fishing from the second Saturday in April through the end of February. There are no tackle restrictions. There is a five-fish limit from the season opener through November 30. The limit drops to

Capt. Bob Hines at Barberville Dam. John Halnon

Left. Capt. Bob Hines with a fine brook trout. John Halnon
Above. Capt. Bob Hines at Big Bend Pool. John Halnon

two fish from December 1 through the end of the season. Between Route 165 and the Barberville Dam, there is a two-fish limit from May 11 through the end of the season.

➤ **Hatches:** Prime time on the Wood River is from May through October. During this period the river experiences what could be called prolific hatches. Beginning in mid- to late April, the river fishes well with streamers, attractor patterns, and nymphs. The first significant hatch is the Black Quills. This is followed by Hendricksons and March Browns. These spring mayfly hatches continue throughout the month of May. Prior to the hatch, fly fishers do best using subsurface flies such as Hare's-ears, Pheasant-tails, and various mayfly emergers in sizes 12 and 14. As the spring days get longer and water temperatures increase, mayfly hatches become more prolific. Insects start to hatch in the late morning and continue until dusk. Black Quills, Adams, and Tan Caddis, in sizes 16 and 14, are your best bets.

With the arrival of early summer, hatches begin to overlap. Consequently, the trout become more selective as they key in on a certain species of insects. Fly fishers must pay close attention to the riseforms, how the trout are feeding, and what they eating. Sulphurs ranging from size 16 to 20, and Light Cahills in size 14, are abundant at this time.

The month of July brings one of the Wood River's most exciting mayfly hatches, the *Hexagenia limbata,* or Hex as it is referred to locally. Warming water temperatures trigger the emergence of this mayfly on steroids. These flies are by far the largest species of mayflies that hatch on the river all season. The hatch starts at dusk, and sometimes lasts well into the dark. Be sure to have a flashlight on you when you fish the Hex hatch. During this time, trout move from their sheltered undercut banks and stage up to feed on the drifting duns. The hits are explosive. As it gets dark, you may need to set the hook based on sound, not sight. This is as fun as fly fishing gets. Patterns tied on size 6 long-shank hooks, with calftail wings and elk hair extended bodies work well. Large, bright, and high-floating are the keys to success.

By approximately the second week of August, the Wood River becomes a great terrestrial fishery, with plentiful black

Capt. Bob Hines with rainbow trout. John Halnon

ants, inchworms, beetles, and even a few hoppers. By this time, many of the local fly fishers have abandoned the river to pursue striped bass and false albacore in the salt. This means that the river sees less traffic than it does at other times of year.

Trout also feed on minnows such as sculpin, dace, and fallfish. Crayfish are also present. There are also leeches.

Having been fortunate enough to fly fish all the major Western trout streams and spring creeks, I am pleased to call the Wood River my home. I believe you would be as well.

➤ Tackle: A 9-foot 5-weight rod with a floating line is your best bet for the Wood River most of the time. If you want to fish streamers a 9-foot 6-weight with a fast-sinking sink-tip is your best option. Dry-fly fishing is best done with a 9-foot 4-weight, as you may need to drop to 7X to effectively fish smaller patterns such as BWOs. While rods longer than 9 feet can work, especially for nymphing, rods shorter than 9 feet are not practical. Strike indicators should be large enough to float two flies and some level of added weight. Flies should include Woolly Buggers; sculpin and minnow patterns; and all stages of mayflies, stoneflies, and caddis in a variety of sizes and colors.

CAPT. BOB HINES owns and operates Fly Fish Rhode Island Guide Service in Smithfield, Rhode Island. He guides both freshwater and saltwater anglers. Bob can be reached at 401-949-5021, www.flyfishri.com, or flyfishri@aol.com.

Middle River. Rich Strolis, Catching-Shadows

VII ❧ CONNECTICUT

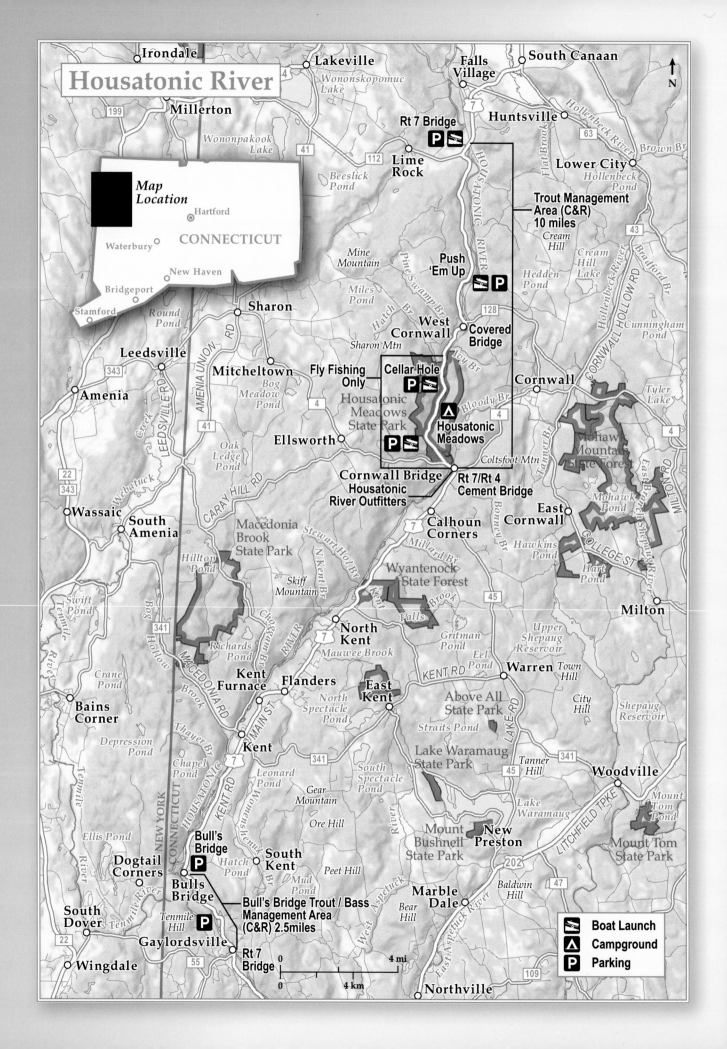

37 · Housatonic River

➤ **Location:** Northwestern Connecticut and southwestern Massachusetts; a 1-hour ride from Hartford, Connecticut; a 3-hour ride from Boston, Massachusetts; and a 2-hour ride from New York City. Full-service airports are available in all three cities.

"There is no tonic like the Housatonic."
—*Oliver Wendell Holmes, Sr.*

The Housatonic is one of the finest trout fisheries in New England. It is also one of the most popular. In addition to trout, the river holds smallmouth bass, pike, and carp. Pike are the only species that are indigenous to the river—all others are introduced. The Housatonic is 142 miles long. It begins in Pittsfield, Massachusetts, and terminates in Long Island Sound.

Prior to the 1700s, the Housatonic River supported runs of anadromous salmon, shad, and striped bass. Due to a fast-growing population and development of the iron industry during the Revolutionary War, numerous dams and furnaces were erected on the river. The dams negatively affected the migratory fish. Much of this infrastructure still exists—especially on the tributaries. George Black's book, *The Trout Pool Paradox,* is an excellent source for history on this region.

The upper Trout Management Area (TMA) starts at Falls Village and extends roughly 10 miles to Cornwall Bridge. Route 7 parallels the river, offering numerous parking areas. It encompasses the covered bridge in West Cornwall—one of the most photographed in the country. It contains one of the first catch-and-release areas in New England, with 3½ miles restricted to fly fishing only. The catch-and release came about as a result of decades of PCB contamination. Thanks to the efforts of state and organizations such as Trout Unlimited, the Housatonic Fly Fishermen's Association, The Rainbow Club, the Connecticut Department of Energy & Environmental Protection, the Housatonic Valley Association, and local fly shops, the river is being managed to protect and enhance the fishery. There is a 2½-mile TMA located at Bulls Bridge, approximately 15 miles downstream. It is not as accessible as the upper TMA, and offers a level of solitude. The deeper holes hold some of the largest fish in the river.

Natural flow was implemented as part of the relicensing of the Falls Village Dam. This improved the habitat. The Housatonic can get quite warm in the summer. The consistent flows, along with the fact that the river flows over miles of limestone, result in some of the most prolific and varied hatches in the East. The river also has a robust population of baitfish, crustaceans, amphibians, and other foods. This helps trout grow up to 4 inches per year.

Late spring at covered bridge in West Cornwall, Connecticut. Torrey Collins

➤ **Hatches:** Hatches start with stoneflies in late February or early March. Classic Eastern mayflies such as Hendricksons and Blue Quills follow in April. By mid- to late spring, stoneflies, caddis, Sulphurs, Cahills, Blue-winged Olives, and *Isonychia* hatch. Summer brings White Flies and flying ants. *Isonychia* reappear in September, followed by Blue-winged Olives and midges.

The Housatonic offers superb dry-fly fishing. I have been on the river on spring evenings when ten different species of mayflies were hatching, along with some caddis. Things can

Left. April sunset over the covered bridge in West Cornwall, Connecticut. Ian Ingersoll

Above. Torrey Collins with 21-inch nymph-caught brown trout. Mandy Sanasie

get frustrating when one fish is honed in on Rusty Spinners, another on Cahill emergers, and another on skittering caddis. On a good night you may have 2 or 3 used flies on your vest—on a more challenging evening, you may have 20 or more, and still not know what the fish are feeding on. Thomas Ames, Jr., author of *Hatch Guide for New England Streams*, *Fishbugs*, and *Caddisflies*, did a majority of his research and photography on the Housatonic River. If you like hatches, drive no farther.

The Connecticut Department of Energy & Environmental Protection stocks 18,000 trout annually in the upper TMA. Stockings occur in the spring and the fall. Rainbow and brown trout ranging from 6 to 18-plus inches are stocked. In addition our fly shop, Housatonic River Outfitters, raises money to stock up to 2,000 Kamloops rainbows ranging from 15 to 24 inches. These are more heat-tolerant and do better during the warm summer months. If we get one or two cool summers and ample rainfall, the river is full of large holdover trout that test your skill and terminal tackle.

The TMAs are open year-round. The best trout fishing is in the spring and fall. Torrey, my store manager, catches some of his biggest trout of the year nymphing in March. Spring evenings are magical—you should spend as much time on the water as you can. Nymphing the heads of the pools and runs prior to and during hatches can be productive. Trout will also rise willingly to insects on the surface. Fish continue to feed into the evening on spinners and adult stoneflies. If you are here on an overcast day, Blue-winged Olives will be on the water nearly all day.

Fall is the most beautiful time of year to fish the Housatonic. Trout are rising to ants, Blue-winged Olives, and *Isonychia*. The mountains look like a painter brushed them with the colors of a campfire. If the trout are not rising, nymphing can be quite productive. I like to fish large streamers in hopes of hooking one of the trophy trout that inhabit the river. Fish over 30 inches have been caught on streamers, especially at night.

When the river heats up, trout move into thermal refuge areas—tributary mouths and spring holes. These areas are closed to fishing. At this time, the Housatonic becomes one of the best smallmouth bass and pike fisheries in the state. Pike over 3 feet long are fairly common—50 smallmouth in a day is not uncommon. While the Housatonic is famous for its trout fishing, its warmwater fishery is highly underrated.

The Housatonic is a large river. It is surrounded by the southern tip of the Berkshire Mountain Range. It is littered with large boulders, and resembles the Clearwater or Nez Perce Rivers in Idaho. These rocks can make wading difficult. The Housatonic can be fished from a drift boat or pontoon boat. This gives you access to fish that are not accessible to wading fly fishers.

The fly shops and guides in the area will be glad to spend the day showing you around our beautiful and productive river.

➤ **Tackle:** A 9-foot 5-weight rod with a floating line is your best bet for the Housatonic River most of the time. If you want to fish streamers, a 9-foot 6-weight with a fast-sinking sink-tip line is your best option. Dry-fly fishing is best done with a 9-foot 3-weight or 4-weight, as you may need to drop to 6X to effectively fish smaller patterns such as Blue-winged Olives. While rods longer than 9 feet can work, especially for nymphing, rods shorter than 9 feet are not practical. Strike indicators should be large enough to float two flies and added weight. Flies should include Woolly Buggers and sculpin patterns; and all stages of mayflies, stoneflies, and caddis in a variety of sizes and colors.

Mike Simoni with large rainbow trout. Alain Barthelemy

HAROLD MCMILLAN, Jr. owns and operates Housatonic River Outfitters in Cornwall Bridge, Connecticut. He can be reached at 860-672-1010, www.dryflies.com, or hflyshop@aol.com.

CLOSEST FLY SHOPS

Housatonic River Outfitters
24 Kent Road
Cornwall Bridge, Connecticut 06754
860-672-1010
www.dryflies.com
hflyshop@aol.com

Upcountry Sport Fishing
352 Main Street
Pine Meadow, Connecticut 06061
860-379-1952
www.farmingtonriver.com
upcountrysports@gmail.com

CLOSEST GUIDES/OUTFITTERS

Housatonic Anglers
26 Bolton Hill Road
Cornwall, Connecticut 06753
860-672-4457
www.housatonicanglers.com
housangler@yahoo.com

CLOSEST LODGING

Cornwall Inn
270 Kent Road
Cornwall Bridge, Connecticut 06754
860-672-6884
www.cornwallinn.com
info@cornwallinn.com

The Inn at White Hollow Farm
558 Lime Rock Road
Lime Rock, Connecticut 06039
860-435-8185
www.whitehollowfarm.com

Hitching Post Country Motel
Route 7 South
Cornwall Bridge, Connecticut 06754
860-672-6219
www.cthitchingpostmotel.com
anjupatel84@gmail.com

Breadloaf Mountain Lodge & Cottages
13 Route 7
Cornwall Bridge Connecticut 06754
860-672-6064
www.breadloafmountainlodge.com
info@breadloafmountainlodge.com

CLOSEST RESTAURANTS

The Wandering Moose Café
(breakfast, lunch, and dinner)
421 Sharon Goshen Turnpike
West Cornwall, Connecticut 06796
860-672-0178
www.thewanderingmoosecafe.com

Fife 'n Drum (lunch and dinner)
53 Main Street (Route 7)
Kent, Connecticut 06757
860-927-3509
www.fifendrum.com
info@fifendrum.com

Kent Pizza Garden
Lunch & Dinner
17 Railroad Square
Kent, Connecticut 06757
860-927-3733
www.kentpizzagarden.com
info@kentpizzagarden.com

Wasabi Japanese Cuisine
24 South Main Street
Kent, Connecticut 06757
860-927-0048

Cornwall General Store & Deli
Breakfast & Lunch
25 Kent Road
Cornwall Bridge, Connecticut 06754
860-672-6578

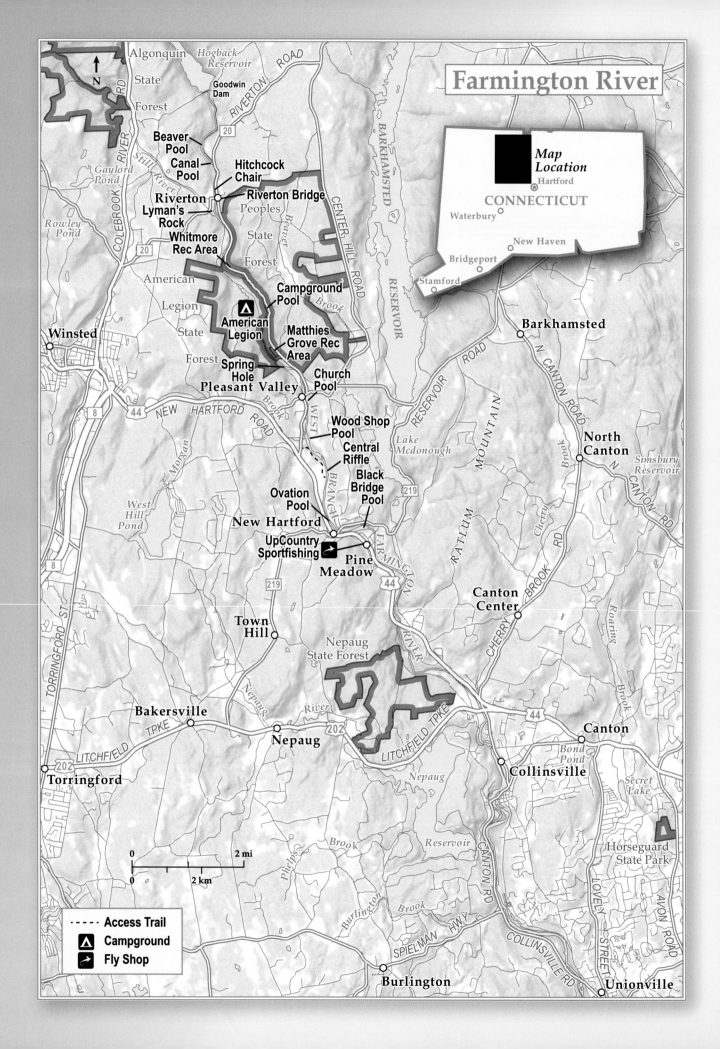

38 · Farmington River

➤ **Location:** Northwestern Connecticut, about a 30-minute ride from Hartford; a 2-hour ride from Boston, Massachusetts; and a 2-hour ride from New York City. Full-service airports are available in all three cities.

Amazingly enough, what is arguably the finest wade-in trout fishery in New England, and one of the finest in the Northeast, lies not in Maine, Vermont, or New Hampshire, but in heavily populated Connecticut. How can that be? Sound fisheries management, that's how. Sure, a bottom-release dam that feeds in cold water year-round helps, but take away the protective regulations and the Farmington River would be just another underutilized and underachieving put-and-take river. The best news is that Connecticut Fish and Game is not resting on its laurels, but continues to tweak the rules to better protect the fishery, and provide more quality fishing opportunities.

The Farmington is roughly 81 miles long. It begins in western Massachusetts and ends where it enters the Connecticut River in the town of Windsor. The watershed encompasses roughly 610 miles and well over 384,000 acres. The Farmington is a classic freestone river. It is made up of riffles, runs, pocketwater, and pools. Coldwater releases from Hogback Dam provide year-round trout fishing. The Farmington is a wading river. Average flows in the Pleasant Valley and New Hartford area range from 250–600 cfs. This is the best wading level. High flows in the 600–1,000 cfs range can make it difficult to wade in some sections. But, as is often the case, high water can make the fishing a bit easier. It is rare to see watercraft used for fishing. This is due to the river's small size and the fact that it is heavily waded. There is also abundant public access on the river. Formal parking areas and streamside trails make it easy to get around. What sets the Farmington apart from its neighbors is the fact that while other rivers get warm in the

summer months, the Farmington River stays cold all season and remains an outstanding trout fishery during even the hottest months. These conditions have made the Farmington a favorite with fly fishers all across the Northeast.

A strong strain of hatchery brown trout with a level of genetic diversity that rivals wild fish, and a progressive management plan that protects fish have created a trout fishery that is unmatched in the area, and well known throughout the Northeast. The Farmington is heavily stocked with brown trout every year. It is also stocked with rainbow and

Middle River. Rich Strolis, Catching-Shadows

brook trout. Although the upper reaches are managed primarily for brown trout, there are strong numbers of stocked, holdover, and wild rainbow trout, as well as both wild and stocked brook trout. The fish-per-mile counts are very high by Northeast standards. The Farmington boasts an annual holdover rate of anywhere between 25 and 55 percent. This varies to some degree from year to year, based on conditions, fishing pressure, and other factors. In addition, there are increasing numbers of wild brown trout in the river. Trout in the upper reaches average between 14 and 16 inches, with fish in the 20-inch range very common. Fish up to 24 inches are encountered.

The section of Farmington most popular with fly fishers is the 21-mile stretch from the base of the Hogback Dam in Hartland downstream to the town of Unionville. This is arguably the best trout water on the river. This section contains a year-round Trout Management Area approximately 4 miles long. Catch-and-release and barbless hooks only are mandatory. There are no tackle restrictions. The special-regulations area starts at the old abutment at the tail of Whittemore Pool, and ends at the Route 219 Bridge in New Hartford. A seasonal Trout Management Area extends from here to the end of the 21-mile section at the Route 177 bridge in the town of Unionville. This section is managed under the same regulations noted above from September 1 through the third Saturday in April. From the third Saturday in April through the last day of August, the regulations are two fish, with a 12-inch minimum length limit.

➤ **Hatches:** If dry-fly fishing is your cup of tea, few if any rivers in the Northeast offer more consistent hatches. There is something coming off the water nearly every day of the year, if you know where to look. Hatches are both bountiful and diverse. Complex and masking hatches are common, with multiple insects coming off the water at the same time during peak months. Most of the typical Northeastern hatches are found on the Farmington. There are myriad sizes and color variations of Blue-winged Olives, Quill Gordons, Hendricksons, Slate Drakes, and Sulphurs. Stoneflies are well represented, with Golden Stones, Yellow Sallies, and Brown

Rich Strolis with BWO-caught brown trout above Church Pool. Rich Strolis, Catching Shadows

and Black Winter Stones all present. Caddis hatches are especially strong, and last throughout the season. Midges are also present. The closer you get to Hogback Dam, the longer the duration of the hatches. This is due to the cold water released from the bottom of the dam. If you plan accordingly, you can fish the Hendrickson hatch for 4 to 6 weeks as it progresses up the watershed toward the dam. If you stayed in one spot, the duration of the hatch would be closer to 10 to 14 days. For some reason, hatches on the Farmington are often one to two sizes smaller than they are on other nearby rivers. The fish clearly know this.

In addition to the robust insect population, there are sculpins, darters, blacknose dace, and crayfish. Baitfish numbers increase as you get farther from the dam. These provide a

Hitchcock Chair Factory in Riverton.
Rich Strolis, Catching Shadows

Inset. Torrey Collins with 23-inch rainbow trout. Mandy Sanasie

reliable year-round food source for some of the larger fish in the river. This means that the Farmington can be a good streamer river when the conditions are right. If you want to fish streamers, concentrate on low-light periods and times when the water is high or off-colored. The Farmington is also a great nymphing river with high fish counts, concentrations of fish, and well-defined runs.

The Farmington River is one of the most popular wade fisheries for trout in the Northeast—and for good reason. Lots of fish, large fish, strong and diverse hatches, generous public access, and miles of well-regulated water makes the Farmington a great place to cast a line.

➤ Tackle: A 9-foot 5-weight rod with a floating line is your best bet for the Farmington River most of the time. If you want to fish streamers a 9-foot 6-weight or 7-weight with a fast-sinking sink-tip is your best option. Dry-fly fishing is best done with a 9-foot 3-weight or 4-weight, as you may need to drop to 6X to effectively fish smaller patterns such as BWOs. While rods longer than 9 feet can work, especially for nymphing, rods shorter than 9 feet are not practical. Strike indicators should be large enough to float two flies and added weight. Flies should include Woolly Buggers and sculpin patterns; and all stages of mayflies, stoneflies, and caddis in a variety of sizes and colors.

RICH STROLIS owns and operates Catching-Shadows Custom Flies. His custom flies include several patterns that he designed exclusively for the Farmington River. Rich guided on the Farmington River for 10 years, and plans to guide there again in the near future when his two girls get a bit older. Look for Rich's upcoming book, *The Creative Fly Patterns of Rich Strolis,* from Stackpole Books. He can be reached at 860-309-4795, rstrolisflyguy@gmail.com, or www.catching-shadows.com.

CLOSEST FLY SHOPS

Upcountry Sport Fishing
352 Main Street
Pine Meadow, Connecticut 06061
860-379-1952
www.farmingtonriver.com
upcountrysports@gmail.com

Orvis Avon
380 West Main Street
Avon Marketplace
Avon, Connecticut 06001
860-678-7900
www.orvis.com/avon

Housatonic River Outfitters
24 Kent Road
Cornwall Bridge, Connecticut 06754
860-672-1010
www.dryflies.com
hflyshop@aol.com

CLOSEST LODGING

Pine Meadow House
398 Main Street
New Hartford Center, Connecticut 06057
860-379-8745
www.pinemeadowhousebb.com
pressmanfly@charter.net

Hillside Motel
671 Albany Turnpike
Canton, Connecticut 06019
860-693-4951
www.hillsidemotel44.com
info@hillsidemotel44.com

Torringford Manor B & B
1440 Torringford Street
Torrington, Connecticut 06790
860-201-5459
www.torringfordmanorbandb.com

Residence Inn Hartford Avon
55 Simsbury Road
Avon, Connecticut 06001
1-860-678-1666
www.marriott.com/hotels/travel/bdlha-residence-inn-hartford-avon

CLOSEST RESTAURANTS

Portobello's Restaurant
107 Main Street
New Hartford, Connecticut 06057
860-693-2598
www.portobellosct.com

Chatterley's Restaurant
2 Bridge Street
New Hartford, Connecticut 06057
860-379-2428
www.chatteleysct.com

Saybrook Fish House
460 Albany Turnpike
Canton, Connecticut 06019
860-693-0034
www.saybrookfishhousecanton.com

Log Cabin Restaurant
110 New Hartford Road
Barkhamsted, Connecticut 06063
860-379-8937
www.theloghouserestaurant.com
logrestaurant@sbcglobal.net

Wild brown trout. Outcast Anglers

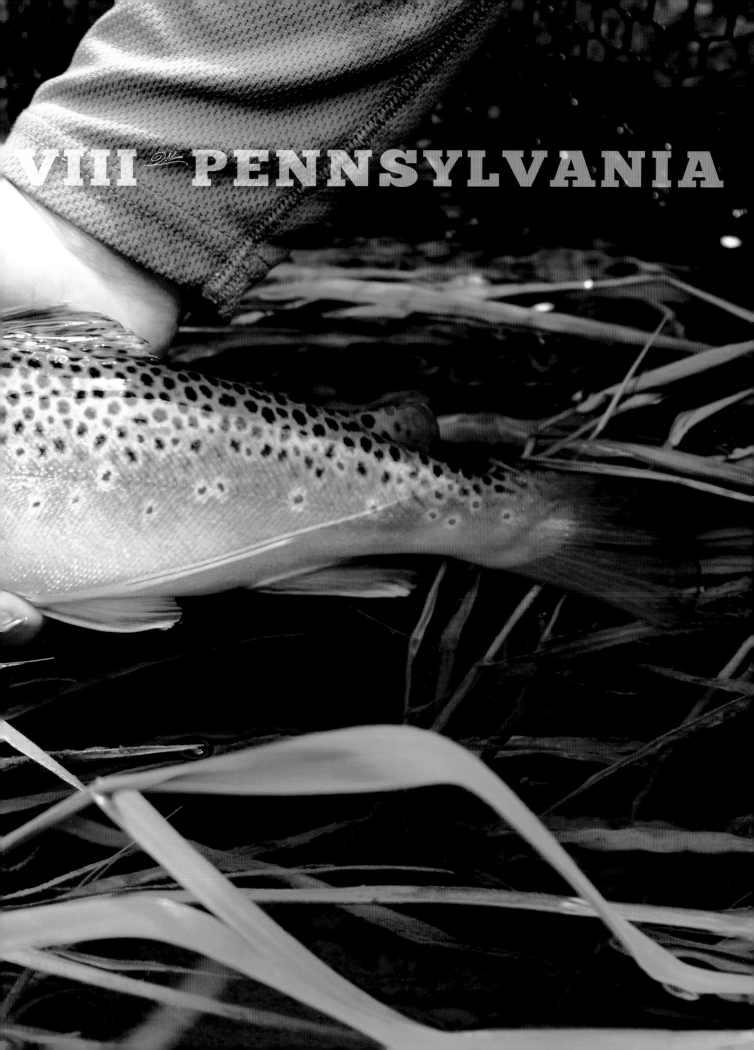

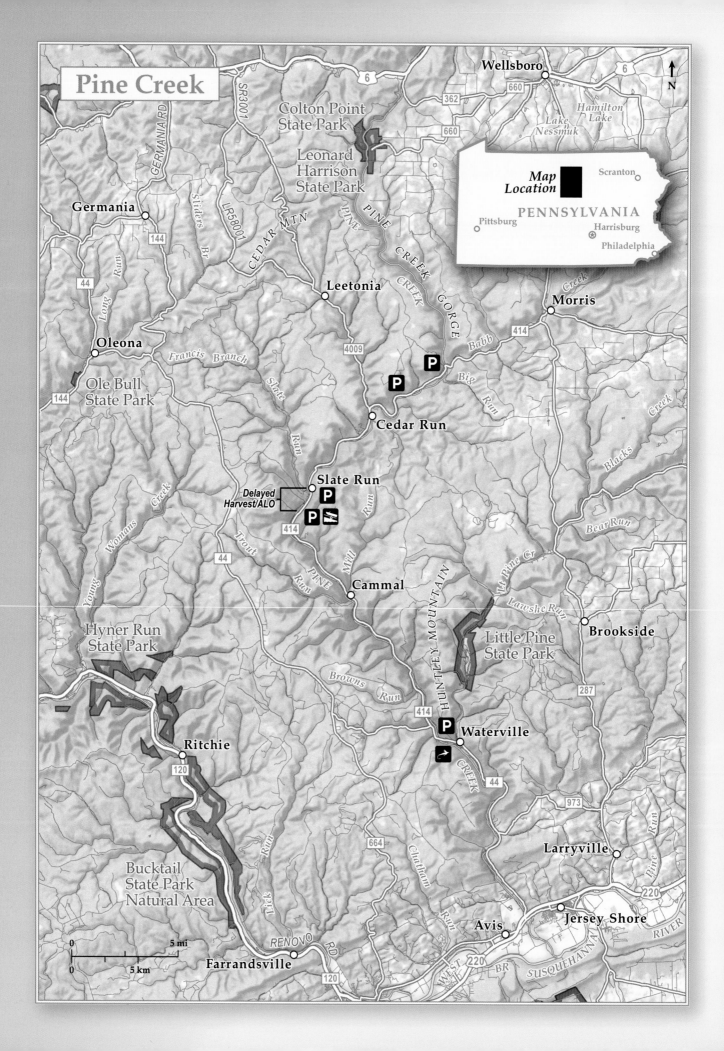

39 · Pine Creek

➤ **Location:** North-central Pennsylvania, about a 1-hour ride from State College, a 2-hour ride from Harrisburg, a 3½-hour ride from Philadelphia; and a 3½-hour ride from New York City. Full-service airports are available in all four cities.

The South, Middle, and West branches of Pine Creek converge near the town of Galeton to form Pine Creek, sometimes referred to as Big Pine Creek. The creek enters what is often referred to as the Grand Canyon of Pennsylvania near the town of Ansonia. Here it is paralleled by the Pine Creek Rail Trail. From here the stream travels due south to the town of Blackwell. Routes 414 and 44 parallel the creek for the rest of its length. The stream ends at its confluence with the West Branch of The Susquehanna River near Williamsport—home of Little League Baseball.

The Iroquois called this stream *Tiadaghton*, or "The River of Pines." It is the longest creek in the United States, at over 85 miles. The watershed covers more than 975 square miles. The creek drops 1,900 feet in elevation over its length. There are four major tributaries: the West Branch of Pine Creek, Marsh Creek, Babb Creek, and Little Pine Creek.

From the late 1800s to the early 1900s, demand for timber by the shipbuilding industry left the Pine Creek Valley a barren wasteland. The debris the loggers left behind fueled massive wildfires that led to extensive erosion and siltation. This left Pine Creek a lifeless stream. The forest was eventually reclaimed, and today the area is an inviting recreational area with stands of trees over a hundred years old. The streams have cleansed themselves and now host populations of wild brook trout, brown trout, rainbow trout, smallmouth bass, and walleye.

In 1992 Pennsylvania opened the Pine Creek Rail Trail, considered one of the top ten rail trails in the world. The trail parallels Pine Creek for 62 miles. This includes 47-mile Pine Creek Gorge in Leonard Harrison State Park, Colton Point State Park, and Tioga State Forest—a National Natural Landmark. The gorge is part of 12,000-acre Pine Creek Gorge Natural Area. It is also designated as a Pennsylvania Scenic River. Pine Creek was one of only 27 rivers originally listed as eligible for National Wild and Scenic River designation. It reaches depths of nearly 1,000 feet.

Pine Creek is a large freestone stream. There are places where the stream is 200 to 250 feet wide. There are pools 12 to 15 feet deep. Some riffles are nearly a mile long. Wading staffs and belts are recommended. The United States Geological Survey gauging station located at Cedar Run provides current and historic flow data. Levels between 2 feet and 2.8 feet are the most common, and considered safe for wading. At these levels, fly fishers can access most of the creek. Levels over 2.8 feet are considered high and not recommended for wading. Levels below 1.8 feet are ideal for wading, as anglers can reach almost everything—including the opposite banks. In the early season, the stream can sometimes be floated with drift boats, but the floating season is short-lived. Levels above 2.4 feet are recommended for floating.

Late spring on Pine Creek. Rick Nyles, Sky Blue Outfitters

Pine Creek Canyon. Nick Raftas, Sky Blue Outfitters

Pennsylvania State Representative Mike Hanna with Little Pine brown trout. McConnell's Country Store & Fly Shop

➤ **Regulations:** There is generous parking and public access along Pine Creek. Three sections on Pine Creek and its tributary Little Pine Creek are open to year-round fishing. They are managed under what are called delayed-harvest, artificial-lures-only regulations. These sections of stream are very popular with fly fishers. From Little Pine Creek upstream, Pine Creek is classified as trout water. It is stocked annually by the state with brook, brown, and rainbow trout. The stream is also stocked by local clubs, businesses, anglers, and two fly shops in the area, who pay their own money to do so. The rest of the stream is open under standard seasons and regulations.

While much of Pine Creek can get quite warm in the summer, there are two sections on Pine, and one on Little Pine, that remain cool due to influxes of cold water. These are where the delayed-harvest, artificial-lures-only regulations apply. The first one is a mile long. It runs from Darling Run to just downstream of the confluence with Owassee Slide Hollow. The second is just over a mile long. It runs from Slate Run to just upstream of Naval Run. The latter is the more popular due to the stocking of large brown trout. Slate Run, Little Slate Run, Naval Run, and a spring seep at School House Riffle all contribute cold water to the creek. There is a 1-mile section on Little Pine Creek that runs from Otter Run to the confluence of Schoolhouse Hollow. Large browns and rainbows are stocked here. Trout from 15 to 16 inches are common—fish over 20 inches are caught.

➤ **Hatches:** Pine Creek has a good population of baitfish. Crayfish are present as well. Spring hatches can be epic. Mayflies, caddis, and stoneflies are all present. Mayflies include Hendricksons, Grey Foxes, March Browns, Green Drakes, Sulphurs, and Cahills. Caddis hatches are very strong and diverse. As with most streams, Pine Creek has a signature hatch, in this case the March Brown. This is one of the largest mayflies found in the area. They start hatching near the end of April and continue for 3 to 4 weeks. Because of their size, they are often mistaken for Brown Drakes. March Browns on Pine Creek run a size or two larger than those found elsewhere.

For the fly fisher, Pine Creek offers a multitude of opportunities. The state-sponsored stocking program, along with fish stocked by private groups, ensure that fish numbers remain strong throughout the season. The special regulations, in conjunction with the size of the stream, mean that some large fish will be caught. The diverse minnow and insect life makes it even more interesting. The ample public access is a bonus as well. Add to this the unrivaled scenic beauty of the Pine Creek Valley and surrounding mountains of the Allegheny Plateau, and Pine Creek is an enjoyable place to fish.

➤ **Tackle:** A 9-foot 5-weight rod with a floating line is your best bet for Pine Creek most of the time. If you want to fish streamers, a 9-foot 6-weight with a fast-sinking sink-tip is your best option. Dry-fly fishing is best done with a 9-foot 4-weight, as you may need to drop to 6X to effectively fish smaller patterns such as Blue-winged Olives. While rods longer than 9 feet can work, especially for nymphing, rods shorter than 9 feet are not practical. Strike indicators should be large enough to float two flies and added weight. Flies should include Woolly Buggers; sculpin and crayfish patterns; and all stages of mayflies, stoneflies, and caddis in a variety of sizes and colors.

A healthy Pine Creek brown trout.
Rick Nyles, Sky Blue Outfitters

GLENN MCCONNELL owns and operates McConnell's Country Store & Fly Shop in Waterville, Pennsylvania. He is a licensed fishing guide who has fished throughout Pennsylvania, New York, Montana, the Atlantic Coast, and New Brunswick. Glenn can be reached at 570-753-8241, glenn@mcconnellscountrystore.com, or www.mcconnellscountrystore.com.

CLOSEST FLY SHOPS

McConnell's Country Store & Fly Shop
10853 North Route 44
Waterville, Pennsylvania 17776
570-753-8241
www.mcconnellscountrystore.com
glenn@mcconnellscountrystore.com

Slate Run Tackle Shop
Route 414
Slate Run, Pennsylvania 17769
570-753-8551
www.slaterun.com
info@slaterun.com

CLOSEST GUIDES/OUTFITTERS

Lance Wilt's Outcast Anglers
Tylersville, Pennsylvania 17747
570-660-0285
www.outcastangler.com
guide@outcastangler.com

Salmo Trutta Enterprises
Dave Rothrock
70 Main Road
Jersey Shore, Pennsylvania 17740
570-745-3861

Sky Blue Outfitters
212 Deysher Road
Fleetwood, Pennsylvania 19522
610-987-0073
www.skyblueoutfitters.com
skyblue@dejazzd.com

An Irish Angler, Inc.
Mike O'Brien
2943 Northway Road Ext.
Williamsport, Pennsylvania 17701
570-220-0391
info@flyfish-pa.com

CLOSEST LODGING

The Hotel Manor
392 Slate Run Road
Slate Run, Pennsylvania 17769
570-753-8414
www.hotel-manor.com
htlmanor@kcnet.org

Cedar Run Inn
281 Beulahland Road
Cedar Run, Pennsylvania 17727
570-353-6241
www.cedarrunpa.com
cri@epix.net

Pine Creek Inn
645 North Route 44
Jersey Shore, Pennsylvania 17740
570-865-6471
pinecreekinn@yahoo.com

Gamble Farm Inn & Suites
311 North Main Street
Jersey Shore, Pennsylvania 17740
570-398-1981
www.gamblefarminn.com
info@gamblefarminn.com

Little Pine State Park
(cabins and RV & tent sites)
4205 Little Pine Creek Road
Waterville, Pennsylvania 17776
570-753-6000

CLOSEST RESTAURANTS

The Waterville Tavern (casual dining)
10783 North Route 44
Waterville, Pennsylvania 17776
570-753-5970
watervilletavern@yahoo.com

The Venture Inn (casual dining)
1896 N Route 44
Jersey Shore, Pennsylvania 17740
570-753-5188

The Hotel Manor
(casual dining; reservations recommended)
392 Slate Run Road
Slate Run, Pennsylvania 17769
570-753-8414
www.hotel-manor.com
htlmanor@kcnet.org

Cedar Run Inn
(fine dining; reservations required)
281 Beulahland Road
Cedar Run, Pennsylvania 17727
570-353-6241
www.cedarrunpa.com
cri@epix.net

Gamble Farm Inn & Suites (casual dining)
311 North Main Street
Jersey Shore, Pennsylvania 17740
570-398-1981
www.gamblefarminn.com
info@gamblefarminn.com

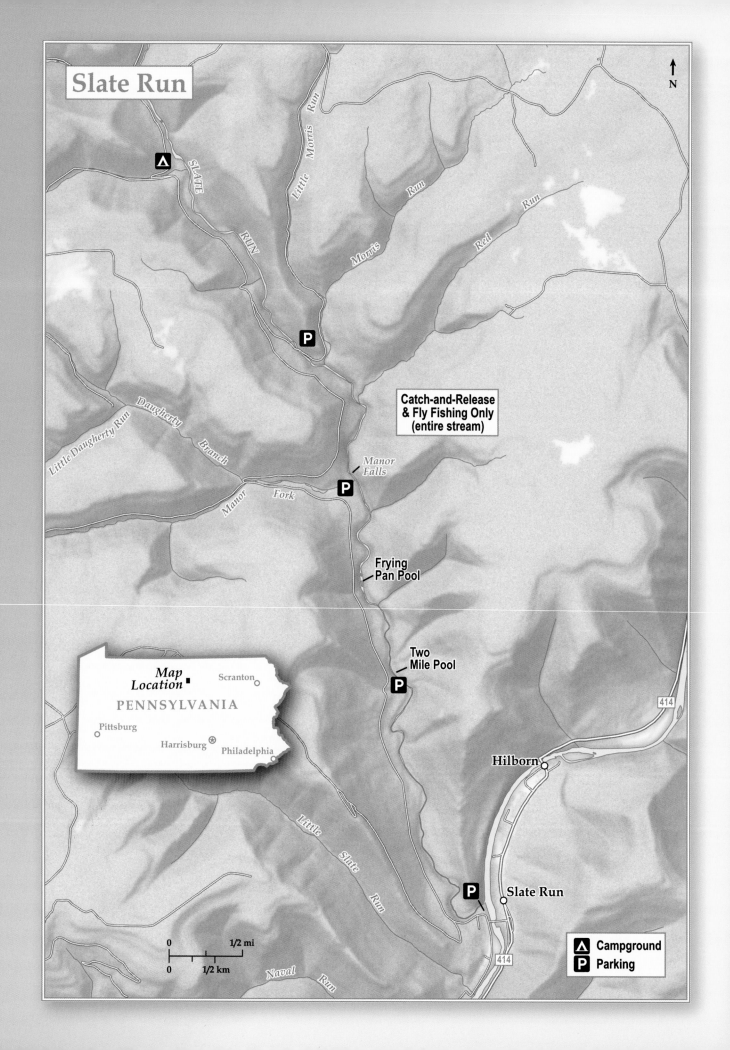

Slate Run

N

Catch-and-Release & Fly Fishing Only (entire stream)

Little Morris Run

Morris Run

Red Run

SLATE RUN

Little Daugherty Run

Daugherty Branch

Manor Fork

Manor Falls

Frying Pan Pool

Two Mile Pool

Hilborn

Little Slate Run

Naval Run

Slate Run

414

Map Location ■

PENNSYLVANIA

○ Scranton

○ Pittsburg

Harrisburg ✪

Philadelphia ○

0   1/2 mi

0   1/2 km

△ Campground

P Parking

40 · Slate Run

➤ **Location:** North-central Pennsylvania, about a 1½-hour ride from State College, a 4-hour ride from Philadelphia or Pittsburgh; a 4-hour ride from New York City; and a 5-hour ride from Washington D.C. Full-service airports are available in all five cities.

Slate Run is located in the rugged mountains of northern Pennsylvania. The stream is named for its layers of slate outcroppings that stairstep downward from its high source to its mouth at Pine Creek. Slate Run flows through a deep gorge with forest-covered slopes. The steep gradient, plus layers of slate, facilitate the formation of rocky pools, riffles, pockets, and underwater ledges inhabited by trout.

The first European settler in the Slate Run area was Jacob Toomb. He built a home, along with a sawmill and a gristmill, at the stream's mouth in the late 1700s. Other pioneers arrived soon afterward and homesteaded in the Pine Creek Valley. By the mid-1800s, the village of Slate Run included a general store, hotel, post office, and churches. A few decades later it evolved into a busy logging community—a far cry from its current status as a haven for recreational activities.

Slate Run is classified by Pennsylvania as a Class A wild trout stream. To recognize the stream as such in a state known for world-class limestone water speaks volumes. The Pennsylvania Fish and Boat Commission restricts angling at Slate Run to catch and release and fly-fishing only. Trout Unlimited has ranked Slate Run as one of the top 100 trout streams in the United States. The stream flows entirely through public land, including two state forests, providing excellent access for the fly fisher.

Slate Run originates at the confluence of Francis Branch and Cushman Branch. After tumbling 7½ miles through a canyon, it empties into Pine Creek near the village of Slate Run. It gathers additional water from several major tributaries—Red Run, Morris Run, and Manor Fork. These freestone brooks are home to native brook trout and some wild browns. For the most part, the stream is paralleled by a road. In the case of many Eastern streams, such a road would provide easy access to the water. However, this is not the case with regard to Slate Run. While the road will get you into the mountains here, it is often hundreds of precipitous feet above the streambed. This makes access to much of Slate Run rather difficult.

The best way to reach remote sections of the stream is to utilize the angler paths accessible from a number of pull-offs on the road. Some of the easier access points are found at the Hotel Manor near the mouth of Slate, at the Two-Mile

David Peress on a misty morning. Bill Dyla

pull-off, at the Manor Lodge, and at the Morris Run Bridge (a dead-end road that's suitable for four-wheel drive). Anglers should note that climbing back up to the roadway following a long day on the stream can be a challenge, so plan accordingly. During late spring and summer, timber rattlesnakes are always a possibility. While they are seldom a problem, pay attention and always give them plenty of room. Due to the rugged terrain and the wild nature of the gorge, it is never a bad idea to fish with someone else.

Manor Run Falls. Walt Franklin

The upper section of Slate Run is a narrow mountain stream lined with boulders, evergreens, and deciduous forest. It consists of pocketwater, riffles, and small pools. Native brook trout are the predominant species here. An occasional fish may reach 12 inches long. Wild browns are also present, but are smaller than their counterparts in the lower run. Slate's upper section receives less angling pressure than the lower stream, so the fishing may be more relaxing and the solitude more complete.

The lower half of Slate Run is primarily brown trout water, with fish generally larger than those encountered above. Browns in excess of 20 inches are caught each year. During the summer, Pine Creek gets too warm for trout. At this time, many of its fish migrate into Slate Run in search of thermal refuge. These are mostly browns, but the occasional rainbow trout will show up as well. These summer visitors settle into the lower stream and add to the resident fish population. Here the stream is wider and has longer pools and riffles, making it more hospitable to fly casters. Areas close to Pine Creek may reach 30 feet or more in width.

The cool temperatures and fertile water found at Slate Run result in abundant hatches of mayfly, stonefly, and caddis. Even during the summer months the water temperature remains cool enough for trout. When other streams have become too warm for trout, fishing on Slate Run continues to hold up providing summer recreation for the fly fisher. The stream can be productive in any season, but winter fishing is not usually recommended due to the potential hazard of ice.

➤ **Hatches:** Mayfly hatches on Slate Run include Blue Quills, Quill Gordons, Hendricksons, March Browns, Green Drakes, Blue-winged Olives, Sulphurs, Cahills, and Slate Drakes. A variety of caddis hatch prolifically throughout the

warmer months. Stoneflies are important as well. During the summer, terrestrial fishing can be very good. A Black Ant, beetle imitations, or a Green Weenie (a local favorite) are effective patterns.

It is best to wear drab or camouflage clothing when you fish Slate Run. If you use a wading staff, a rubber cap on the bottom is recommended to muffle the noise produced by metal. Stalk your quarry like a heron, and use an upstream approach. Walk slowly and minimize your profile and your shadow on the stream. Cast to the nearest trout first before wading to the head of a pool. The low, clear water requires stealth and the use of long, light leaders. Enjoy your catch but, unlike that premier fisher, the heron, give your trout a quick release.

Slate Run is a wild trout stream. The fish here are not the cookie-cutter stocked trout found in many other streams and rivers. These fish rely on instincts to evade predators such as otters, herons, and human beings. You may not catch as many fish on Slate as you might on some heavily stocked waters, but these trout are beautiful and wild.

➤ **Tackle:** An 8- to 9-foot rod, in a 4- or 5-weight with a floating line is your best bet for Slate Run under most conditions. Rods shorter than 8 feet are best in the upper sections. Rods longer than 9 feet can be useful for nymphing in the lower sections. Strike indicators and split-shot are helpful. Flies should include attractor drys and nymphs; all stages of mayflies, stoneflies, and caddis; terrestrials; and sculpin and baitfish imitations.

Slate Run brown trout. Walt Franklin

Wild brookie. Walt Franklin

WALT FRANKLIN is an active member of the Slate Run Sportsmen, an influential organization working to preserve Slate Run and its fly-fishing heritage. He has fished New York and Pennsylvania extensively for decades. A writer, naturalist and educator, Franklin has published numerous books, including *River's Edge* (Wood Thrush Books, 2008). He has recently refished Slate Run in its entirety and written of it in his blog, called *Rivertop Rambles* (www.rivertoprambles.wordpress.com).

CLOSEST FLY SHOPS

Slate Run Tackle Shop
Route 414
Slate Run, Pennsylvania 17769
570-753-8551
www.slaterun.com
info@slaterun.com

McConnell's Country Store & Fly Shop
10853 North Route 44
Waterville, Pennsylvania 17776
570-753-8241
www.mcconnellscountrystore.com
glenn@mcconnellscountrystore.com

CLOSEST GUIDES/OUTFITTERS

Lance Wilt's Outcast Anglers
Tylersville, Pennsylvania 17747
570-660-0285
www.outcastangler.com
guide@outcastangler.com

Salmo Trutta Enterprises
Dave Rothrock
70 Main Road
Jersey Shore, Pennsylvania 17740

Sky Blue Outfitters
212 Deysher Road
Fleetwood, Pennsylvania 19522
610-987-0073
www.skyblueoutfitters.com
skyblue@dejazzd.com
570-745-3861

An Irish Angler
Mike O'Brien
2943 Northway Road
Williamsport, Pennsylvania 17701
info@flyfish-pa.com

CLOSEST LODGING

The Hotel Manor
392 Slate Run Road
Slate Run, Pennsylvania 17769
570-753-8414
www.hotel-manor.com
htlmanor@kcnet.org

Cedar Run Inn
281 Beulahland Road
Cedar Run, Pennsylvania 17727
570-353-6241
www.cedarrunpa.com
cri@epix.net

Black Forest Inn
15 Black Forest Acres
Lock Haven, Pennsylvania 17745
570-769-6070
www.blackforestbar.com
information@blackforestbar.com

Pine Creek Inn
5645 North Route 44 Highway
Jersey Shore, Pennsylvania 17740
570-865-6471
pinecreekinn@yahoo.com

Little Pine State Park
(cabins and RV & tent sites)
4205 Little Pine Creek Road
Waterville, Pennsylvania 17776
570-753-6000

CLOSEST RESTAURANTS

The Hotel Manor
(casual dining; reservations recommended)
392 Slate Run Road
Slate Run, Pennsylvania 17769
570-753-8414
www.hotel-manor.com
htlmanor@kcnet.org

Black Forest Inn (casual dining)
15 Black Forest Acres
Lock Haven, Pennsylvania 17745
570-769-6070
www.blackforestbar.com
information@blackforestbar.com

Cedar Run Inn
(fine dining; reservations required)
281 Beulahland Road
Cedar Run, Pennsylvania 17727
570-353-6241
www.cedarrunpa.com
cri@epix.net

Mountain Top Inn
17333 Coudersport Pike
Lock Haven, Pennsylvania 17745
570-769-6238
www.facebook.com/pages/Mountain-Top-Inn
schenck.mttop@gmail.com

181

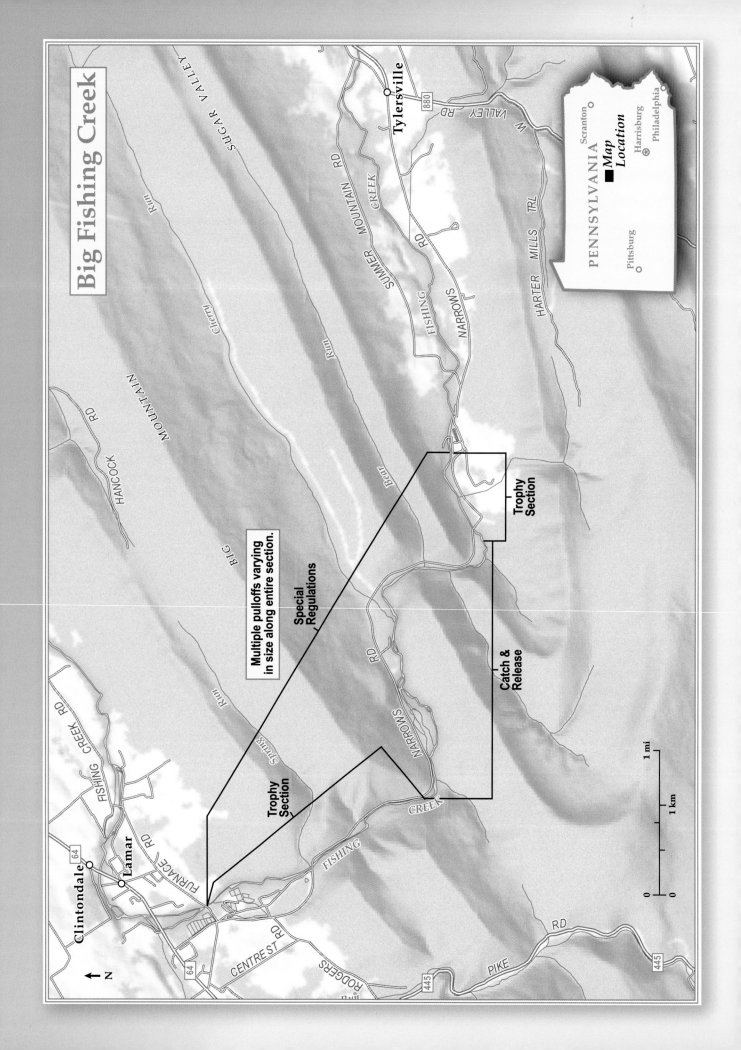

Big Fishing Creek

PENNSYLVANIA

Scranton
Map
Location
Harrisburg
Philadelphia
Pittsburg

Tylersville

Clintondale

Lamar

Trophy
Section

Multiple pulloffs varying
in size along entire section.

Special
Regulations

Catch &
Release

Trophy
Section

N

1 mi

1 km

0
0

41 · Big Fishing Creek

➤ **Location:** Central Pennsylvania, about a ½-hour ride from State College, a 3-hour ride from Philadelphia or Pittsburgh; a 3½-hour ride from New York City; and a 4-hour ride from Washington, D.C. Full-service airports are available in all five cities.

There is probably a stream named "Fish" or "Fishing" in every county in Pennsylvania.

As a result, things can get really confusing when talking about either. The "Fishing Creek" covered in this chapter is locally known as Big Fishing Creek. It is located in Lamar, near the fly-fishing mecca of State College. This creek supports a healthy population of brown and brook trout, along with the occasional tiger trout—a brook-brown hybrid. There are good numbers of fish in the 14- to 16-inch range.

Having fished and guided in Pennsylvania, Montana, and Patagonia, I have had the opportunity to fish many remarkable rivers, streams, and lakes. Most of these support impressive populations of wild trout. While many of these yield greater numbers of fish, and some larger fish, to the average angler, few rival the natural beauty and overall productivity of Big Fishing Creek.

Big Fishing Creek shares the characteristics of both limestone and freestone streams. It harbors robust insect life and offers a diversity of angling that is second to none. Big Fishing Creek begins as a small freestone stream near the town of Carroll. It flows westward through Sugar Valley. From its headwaters to the town of Eastville, it is what is called an intermittent stream. The creek disappears into sinkholes and limestone caverns. It mysteriously reappears farther downstream, forced to the surface by some unseen underground obstruction. Marginal habitat and inconsistent flows prevent the stream from supporting healthy populations of trout between Tylersville and the headwaters. As the stream enters an area known as The Narrows, it collects water from multiple springs near the Pennsylvania Fish and Boat Commission's Fish Culture Station.

These springs contribute 10,000 to 15,000 gallons of 50-degree water per minute. Trout thrive throughout the year under these conditions. It is here that Big Fishing Creek is transformed into a world-class trout fishery.

State Route 2002 parallels much of Big Fishing Creek from the Tylersville Fish Hatchery downstream to Fleming's Bridge. It is strictly managed. There is a catch-and-release section sandwiched between two Trophy Trout sections. The limit on the trophy sections is two fish, with a minimum length limit of 14 inches. There is public access at Pennsylvania State Game Lands #295 located near The Narrows. Pay attention to the posted regulations signs. Much of the land adjacent to SR2002 is owned by the Big Fishing Creek cabin association. This coalition of cabin owners has been generous enough to keep certain portions of the stream open

Winter fishing. Outcast Anglers

to public access. This section encompasses approximately 2 miles of special-regulations waters. It is closed to access on Sundays, and when the cabin is occupied.

Trout habitat varies drastically along Big Fishing Creek. Each bend and riffle presents a new set of challenges. Ranging in width from 20 to 40 feet wide, Big Fishing Creek is a medium-size stream. This allows anglers to prospect

The Braids. Outcast Anglers

every inch of river—and they should. Trout can be found just about anywhere. But the fishing is not easy—the trout here are earned, not won. The water is clear. Downed trees and low-hanging foliage make casting difficult. Land and airborne predators keep the trout wary. This is place where you *hunt* as much as you *fish*. Regulars stalk their quarry, read the water, and make every cast count. They leave no stone unturned, hitting every possible lie. This is the best way to succeed on Big Fishing Creek.

➤ **Hatches:** A plethora of insect hatches can be found on Big Fishing Creek. Starting in March and running through October, you can expect to see a wide array of insects. Oftentimes there are compound hatches where multiple species of insects are hatching at once. Midges, Blue-winged Olives, grannom caddis, and Hendricksons hatch in April. These are followed by March Browns, Sulphurs, and Green Drakes in May. Tricos, Blue Quills, and multiple species of stoneflies hatch throughout the summer. Slate Drakes and October Caddis hatch in the fall.

In spite of its spectacular dry-fly fishing opportunities, Big Fishing Creek is primarily a subsurface fisherman's stream. As a rule, regulars ply the waters with nymphs and streamers,

viewing surface activity as icing on the cake. A brace of wet flies or nymphs fished using high-sticking or indicator methods is productive. However, the former is often the more effective way to cover the water. Plus, many locals in this very traditional area view indicator fishing as sacrilegious. Indicators do, however, allow you to reach fish that will not tolerate a high-sticking angler who is mere feet away. During the summer, terrestrials can produce great topwater action. This requires long, accurate casts over clear water.

Presentation is considered far more important than imitation. A well-presented reasonable imitation will outfish a poorly presented exact imitation in almost all cases. One exception is during a heavy emergence, when fish are likely to key on a certain stage of a specific insect. At this time, an exact imitation is required—and a good presentation helps. Actively swimming an appropriate nymph or emerger imitation during periods of insect activity can fool even the most wary trout in the stream, even when a dead-drifted imitation fails.

Sculpins, dace, crayfish, and minnows are all present. These provide food for fish of all sizes—and especially large ones. While smaller patterns are typically the most effective in regard to numbers, larger patterns will often catch the biggest fish. Natural colors seem to be the most effective. Fishing these patterns along the bottom will often entice strikes from fish that are not interested in anything else. Streamer action is typically best in the early spring.

Big Fishing Creek has served as a home base for the training of the U.S. Youth Fly Fishing Team because it is a difficult place to fish and a great place to hone your skills. If you measure success strictly by numbers of fish caught, you may be disappointed. If, however, you appreciate a challenge, this is the place for you.

➤ **Tackle:** A 9-foot 4- or 5-weight rod with a floating line can work for Big Fishing Creek under most conditions. Longer rods up to 10 feet are strongly recommended, as they can help anglers keep more line off the water. Strike indicators should be large enough to support some added weight. Flies should include attractor drys and nymphs; all stages of mayflies, stoneflies, and caddis; and sculpin and baitfish imitations.

Wild brown trout. Outcast Anglers

Spring sucker spawn. Outcast Anglers

LANCE WILT owns and operates Outcast Anglers. He can be reached at 570-660-0285, fish.central .pa@gmail.com, or www.outcastangler.com.

CLOSEST FLY SHOPS

TCO Fly Shop
2030 East College Avenue
State College, Pennsylvania 16801
814-689-3654
www.tcoflyfishing.com
tcoflyshop@tcoflyshop.com

Flyfisher's Paradise
State College, Pennsylvania 16801
2603 East College Avenue
814-234-4189
www.flyfishersparadise.com
sywensky@aol.com

The Feathered Hook
516 Main Street
Coburn, Pennsylvania 16832
814-349-8757
www.thefeatheredhook.com
Jonas@thefeatheredhook.com

CLOSEST OUTFITTERS/GUIDES

Lance Wilt's Outcast Anglers
Tylersville, Pennsylvania 17747
570-660-0285
www.outcastangler.com
guide@outcastangler.com

Dennis Charney
Bellefonte, Pennsylvania 16823
814-280-3171
www.dennischarney.com
dcharney@gotmc.net

CLOSEST LODGING

The Guesthouse at Longmeadow
21 Longmeadow Lane
Loganton, Pennsylvania 17747
570-725-2603
www.theguesthouseatlongmeadow.com
theguesthouse@longmeadow.com

Centre Mills Bed and Breakfast
461 Smullton Road
Rebersburg, Pennsylvania 16872
814-349-8000
www.centermills.com
centremills@gmail.com

Hampton Inn at Lamar
24 Hospitality Lane
Mill Hall, Pennsylvania 17751
570-726-3939
hamptoninn3.hilton.com

The Feathered Hook Bed & Breakfast
516 Main Street
Coburn, Pennsylvania 16832
814-349-8757
www.thefeatheredhook.com
Jonas@thefeatheredhook.com

CLOSEST RESTAURANTS

Browns Hill Tavern & Motel
717 Browns Hill Road
Mill Hall, Pennsylvania 17751
570-726-3090
www.brownshilltavern.com
brownshilltavern@yahoo.com

Elk Creek Café
100 West Main Street
Millheim, Pennsylvania 16854
814-349-8850
www.elkcreekcafe.net

The Hublersburg Inn & Family Tavern
449 Hublersburg Road
Howard, Pennsylvania 16841
814-383-2616
www.hublersburginn.com
innkepper@hublersburginn.com

The Cottage Restaurant
5833 Nittany Valley Drive
Mill Hall, Pennsylvania 17751
570-726-3985

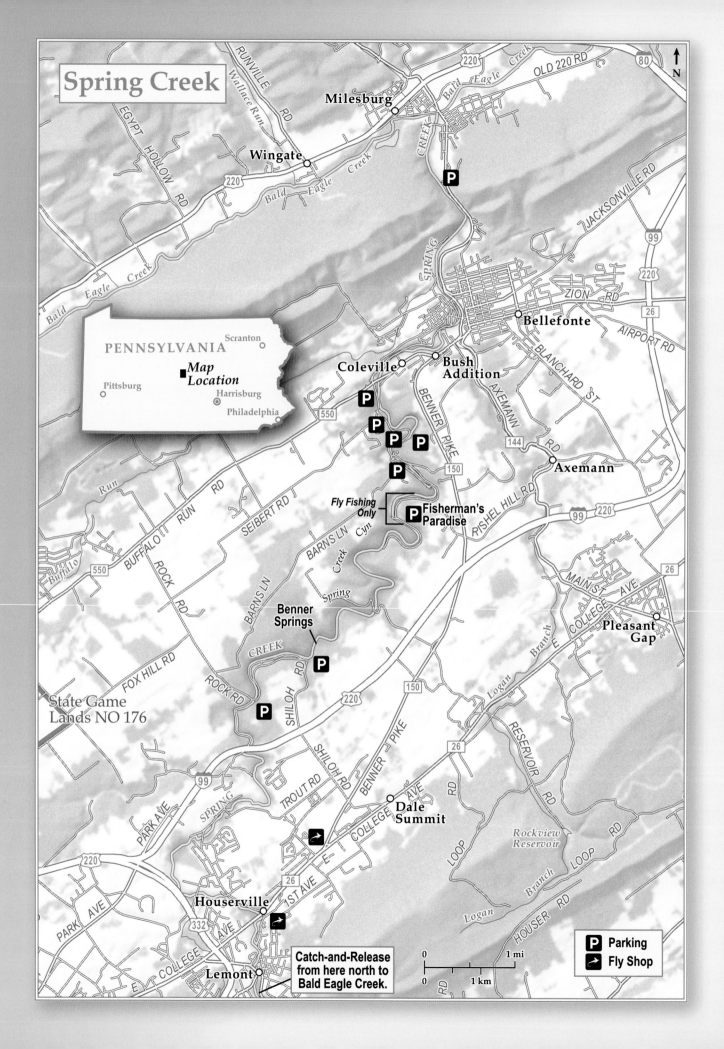

Spring Creek

Milesburg

Wingate

RUNVILLE RD

WALLACE RUN

EGYPT HOLLOW RD

OLD 220 RD

220

80

PENNSYLVANIA

Scranton

Map Location

Pittsburg

Harrisburg

Philadelphia

Bellefonte

JACKSONVILLE RD

99

220

26

ZION RD

AIRPORT RD

Coleville

Bush Addition

BLANCHARD ST

AXEMANN RD

144

Axemann

150

550

Fly Fishing Only

Fisherman's Paradise

RISHEL HILL RD

99

220

26

RUN RD

SEIBERT RD

BARNS LN

Creek Cyn

Spring

Benner Springs

BENNER PIKE

BUFFALO RUN RD

ROCK RD

CREEK

ROCK RD

SHILOH RD

220

150

26

LOGAN BRANCH

COLLEGE AVE

MAIN ST

Pleasant Gap

RESERVOIR RD

FOX HILL RD

State Game Lands NO 176

99

SHILOH RD

TROUT RD

BENNER PIKE

COLLEGE AVE

Dale Summit

LOOP RD

Rockview Reservoir

LOGAN BRANCH LOOP

HOUSER RD

PARK AVE

SPRING

26

E 1ST AVE

Houserville

332

PARK AVE

COLLEGE AVE

Lemont

Catch-and-Release from here north to Bald Eagle Creek.

0   1 mi

0   1 km

P Parking

Fly Shop

42 · Spring Creek

➤ **Location:** Central Pennsylvania, about a 1-hour ride from Harrisburg; a 2½-hour ride from Pittsburgh; and a 3-hour ride from Philadelphia. Full-service airports are available in all three cities.

Spring Creek is arguably the finest wild trout stream in Pennsylvania. It is designated as a Class A fishery throughout its entire length. It is also managed for catch-and-release throughout its entire length. The famous Fisherman's Paradise section is designated fly fishing only. The Paradise, as it is known locally, was the first special-regulations fishery in the country. Harvest limits, special passes, and separate fishing areas for women and children were all part of the early special regulations. Eventually, catch-and-release regulations were put in place.

Spring Creek is roughly 22 miles. It starts near the town of Boalsburg. It passes through a gap in Bald Eagle Mountain before joining Bald Eagle Creek at Milesburg. The first roughly 10 miles are mostly private. The section most popular with fly fishers is from the Route 26 bridge downstream to Milesburg. Spring Creek is a multi-use resource, with hiking, biking, and even a kayak and canoe slalom training center located in Bellefonte.

In the 1930s, Spring Creek was heavily stocked. The Fisherman's Paradise section was well known for producing large fish on a regular basis. At that time, in addition to an abundance of fish, the stream experienced prolific insect hatches. This resulted in a lot of fishing pressure. During the 1950s, human population growth began to have an increasingly negative impact on the health of Spring Creek. Over the coming years, sewage, poor farming practices, industrial pollution, and accidental releases of chemicals such as Kepone, Mirex, and cyanide took a heavy toll on the trout population. These had an even more devastating effect on the insect life. In 1981, recognizing that it could no longer endorse the consumption of fish from

Spring Creek, Pennsylvania ceased stocking the stream and imposed a catch-and-release restriction.

In time, Spring Creek's trout population rebounded. Soon it exceeded the 36 pounds of trout per acre required to qualify as a Class A trout fishery. Some sections of Spring Creek meet these criteria many times over. The stream is no longer stocked. Its population is comprised primarily of wild brown trout with the occasional rainbow trout. The rainbow trout population is in part a result of hatchery escapees. The lower reaches of Spring Creek contain stocked rainbows that

Fish Commission property below Fisherman's Paradise. Dennis Charney

migrate up into it from Bald Eagle Creek. Each year sees an increase in the population of wild rainbow trout as well.

➤ **Hatches:** Unfortunately, the insects have not recovered as well as the trout have. Spring Creek no longer supports Green Drakes, Hendricksons, or March Browns. However, Blue-winged Olives, Sulphurs, Cahills, Blue Quills, and Tricos have returned in healthy numbers. The Sulphur hatch is the most popular hatch on Spring Creek. It provides

Upper Fisherman's Paradise. Brett Damm

great dry-fly fishing during the month of May, and well into June. Caddis, crane flies, and midges are present as well. Terrestrials become important as the hatches fade, and can provide surface action all summer long.

Several major springs influence the overall condition of Spring Creek. They are located all along its length and provide a source of cool and nutrient-rich water. There are countless smaller springs and seeps found throughout the system as well. This, along with the year-round protective regulations, keeps Spring Creek fishing well regardless of the time of year. Subsurface fishing with cress bugs, scuds, nymphs, and midge pupae is effective all season long.

Spring Creek offers the visiting angler generous public access and easy wading along most of its length. Most of the stream is open to the public. There are only a few small parcels that are posted to trespass. From the Benner Springs access downstream to where Spring Creek terminates at Bald Eagle Creek, there are several clearly marked public parking areas. Most of the stream is knee- to waist-deep. The shallow depth and relatively gentle flow make the stream very easy to wade for fly fishers of all levels of experience and physical ability.

As you work your way down Spring Creek, you will find that the water volume increases and water temperature decreases. In the town of Bellefonte, the largest of the springs contributes a constant burst of cold water to the stream. Logan Branch is another local spring creek that enters at the town of Bellefonte. This, along with the spring, results in the last few miles of Spring Creek being the coldest stretch of the stream.

When the area gets hit with heavy rain, Spring Creek is the last stream to muddy up and the first to clear up. This is important to know, as it can be a trip saver. If your plans had you on another body of water at this time, you may want to check out Spring Creek before giving up. However, others know this, so you will not be alone. At these times, fishing pressure on Spring Creek can become quite heavy.

Nymphing is often the most productive tactic on Spring Creek. However, there are periods when there are good dry-fly opportunities. Sulphurs, Blue-winged Olives, Tricos, caddis, and terrestrials are all present. Streamer fishing can be productive at times, especially during high-water events and in the fall. The predominant baitfish are dark olive to black sculpins. Cress bugs, scuds, worms, and midges are important as well. Spring Creek usually runs relatively clear. As a result, drab patterns tend to be more productive than bead-head or flashy patterns.

Spring Creek flows just outside State College, the home of Pennsylvania State University. This area has one of the best concentrations of trout water in the East. There are lodging and dining options in a wide range of prices for visiting fly fishers. This also provides non-fly fishers with the opportunity to enjoy everything that a college town has to offer. There are sporting events, shows, shopping, dining, and pubs, all within minutes of where you can get your boots wet. This does, however, come with a price. At times, football games and the occasional NCAA tournament can make lodging hard to secure.

➤ **Tackle:** A 9-foot 5-weight rod with a floating line is your best bet for Spring Creek most of the time. Dry-fly fishing is best done with a 4-weight, as you may need to drop to 6X tippet to effectively fish smaller patterns such as BWOs and midges. Rods longer than 9 feet can work—especially for nymphing. Strike indicators should be large enough to float two flies and added weight. Flies should include Woolly Buggers and sculpin patterns; all stages of mayflies, stoneflies, caddis, and midges in a variety of sizes and colors; and scuds, worms, and a selection of terrestrials for fishing during the summer months.

Wild rainbow trout. Rick Nyles, Sky Blue Outfitters

Wild brown trout. Sam Galt

DENNIS CHARNEY has been fly fishing for over 25 years. He owns and operates Dennis Charney Guide Service in Bellefonte, Pennsylvania. He offers fly-tying and fly-fishing instruction. Dennis has been a staff instructor for the Wulff School of Fly Fishing for a decade. He can be reached at 814-280-8171 or www.dennischarney.com.

CLOSEST FLY SHOPS

Flyfisher's Paradise
2603 East College Avenue
State College, Pennsylvania 16801
814-234-4189
www.flyfishersparadise.com
sywensky@aol.com

TCO Fly Shop
2030 East College Avenue
State College, Pennsylvania 16801
814-689-3654
www.tcoflyfishing.com
tcoflyshop@tcoflyshop.com

The Feathered Hook
516 Main Street
Coburn, Pennsylvania 16832
814-349-8757
www.thefeatheredhook.com
Jonas@thefeatheredhook.com

CLOSEST GUIDES/OUTFITTERS

Dennis Charney
Bellefonte, Pennsylvania 16823
814-280-8171
www.dennischarney.com
dcharney@gotmc.net

Lance Wilt's Outcast Anglers
Tylersville, Pennsylvania
570-660-0285
www.outcastangler.com
guide@outcastangler.com

Sky Blue Outfitters
212 Deysher Road
Fleetwood, Pennsylvania 19522
610-987-0073
www.skyblueoutfitters.com
skyblue@dejazzd.com

CLOSEST LODGING

Spring Creek House
1088 West Water Street
Bellefonte, Pennsylvania 16823
814-353-1369
www.springcreekhouse.com
mikegruendler@hotmail.com

The Atherton Hotel
125 South Atherton Street
State College, Pennsylvania 16801
814-231-2100
www.athertonhotel.net
info@athertonhotel.net

The Limestone Inn
490 Meckley Road
State College, Pennsylvania 16801
814-234-8944
www.limestoneinn.com
kpatzer@psualum.com

Best Western Inn & Suites
115 Premiere Drive
State College, Pennsylvania 16801
814-234-8393
www.bestwestern.com/bestwestern/US/PA/
State-College-hotels

CLOSEST RESTAURANTS

Otto's Pub
2235 North Atherton Street
State College, Pennsylvania 16801
814-867-6886
www.ottospubandbrewery.com

Gigi's
2080 Cato Avenue
State College, Pennsylvania 16801
814-861-3463
www.gigisdining.com
info@gigisdining.com

Kimchi Korean Restaurant
1100 North Atherton Street
State College, Pennsylvania 16801
814-237-2096
www.kimchistatecollege.com
kimchistatecollege@gmail.com

Olde New York
2298 East College Avenue
State College, Pennsylvania
814-237-1582
www.oldenewyork.net
info@oldenewyork.net

Brothers Pizza
253 Benner Pike
State College, Pennsylvania
814-234-4200

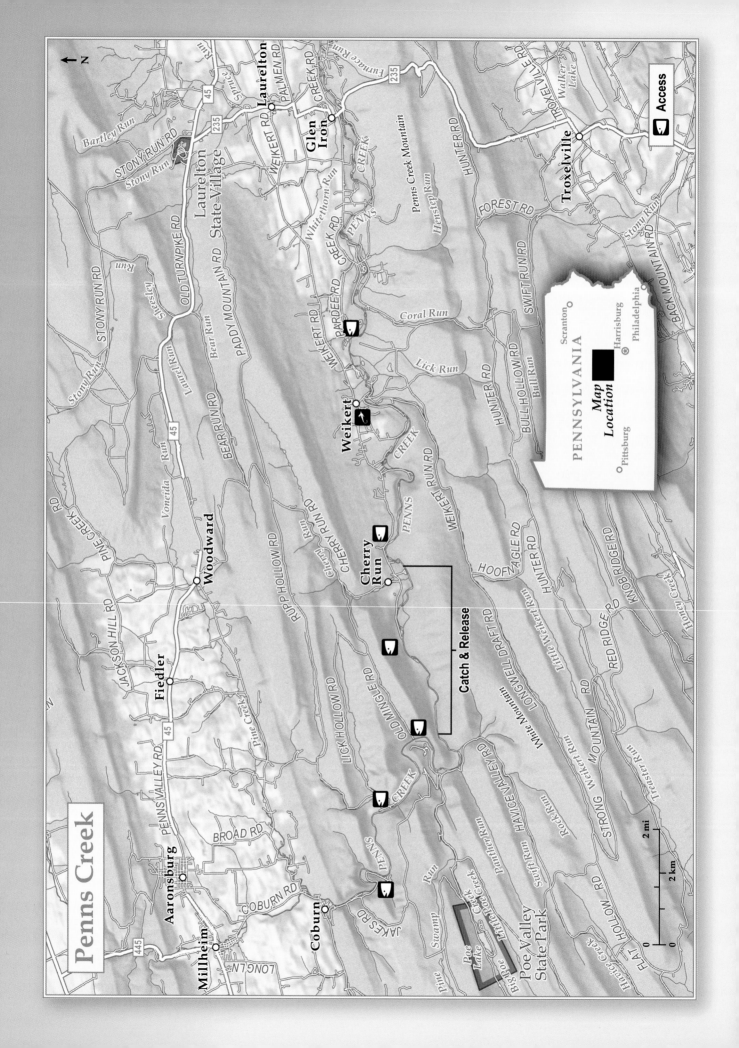

43 · Penns Creek

➤ **Location:** Central Pennsylvania, about a 1-hour ride from Harrisburg; a 3-hour ride from Philadelphia; a 3½-hour ride from Pittsburgh; and a 4½-hour ride from New York City. Full-service airports are available in all four cities.

Penns Creek has a history of cultivating some of the country's finest anglers and writers. Charles M. Wetzel authored several books in the 1940s and 1950s that include fly-fishing and insect information specific to Penns Creek. Other notable Penns Creek regulars are George Harvey, Joe Humphries, and Charles Meck. All have written books on fly fishing. Sadly, George is no longer with us. He leaves a legacy of teaching fly fishing to more than 36,000 students at Penn State University and other venues.

During the late 1800s, Penns was a working creek, transporting agricultural products and logs downstream to the Susquehanna River, and then to Harrisburg and beyond. Along the river were scores of mills and the dams that powered them. Fortunately, all but one of the dams have since been removed. Some of the old mills remain, adding a level of character to the creek.

Penns Creek emanates at Penns Cave, a limestone cavern located near Spring Mills. The cave releases approximately a million gallons of water per day. Most of the upper 7 miles of creek is private. There are, however, a few small sections open to the public. The slow, gentle currents provide classic spring creek conditions. The dry-fly fishing is exceptional from here to the only dam on the creek. The dam is located about 7 miles downstream of Spring Mills. This area holds some very large wild rainbow and brown trout. The hatches are what you would expect to find on a spring creek.

A stocked section runs from the dam to where Elk Creek enters Penns Creek in the town of Coburn. This section is roughly 2 miles long. This is a park-and-fish area, perfect for anglers looking for easy access. The creek here is about 15 to 20 feet wide. The flow is moderate. Nymphs, wets, and dries all work here. In addition to the stocked fish, there are some wild fish that migrate up from below Elk Creek.

➤ **Regulations:** An All Tackle Trophy Trout section starts below Elk Creek. Elk provides cold, limestone-influenced water, doubling the size of Penns to 30 to 40 feet. From Elk Creek downstream 7 miles, Penns is open to fishing year-round. From Opening Day—the second Saturday in April—until Labor Day, there is a two-fish limit. The minimum

Lower river. Bruce Fisher, Penns Creek Angler

length limit is 14 inches. The first 2 miles offers easy access. The flow quickens, with riffles, runs, and pools. Wading can be tricky. The fishing here can be very good. Below this, the rest of this section can be accessed only on foot. There are 5 additional miles of All Tackle Trophy Trout water. An old railroad bed provides access to the creek.

This is where the Penns Creek really comes into its own. The fact that you have to walk lessens traffic. The farther you go, the fewer anglers you will see. As you walk along the railroad bed, you are surrounded by mountains. The hatches are epic and prolific.

Inset. Nice dry fly-caught brown trout.
Bruce Fisher, Penns Creek Angler

Below the catch-and-release section. Bruce Fisher, Penns Creek Angler

The Canyon is my favorite place to fish. This starts below the All Tackle Trophy Trout section. For 3.8 miles, Penns is managed for catch-and-release and year-round fishing. This is referred to as The Project and is located downstream of Poe Paddy State Park. The easiest way to reach the upper end is to walk through the railroad tunnel at Poe Paddy. The lower end can be accessed from a small parking lot off Weikert Road—the catch-and-release section is about a mile upstream. This is a very remote area. You are surrounded by mountains. Penns doubles in size, increasing to 60 to 80 feet wide. Wildlife, including deer, grouse, bears, and waterfowl. The creek in this area has riffles, runs, and pools. Hatches on this section can be so thick it is hard to see your fly among the naturals. Streamers and terrestrials work well. A brace of wet flies can be especially effective. This method of fishing goes back well over a hundred years, and rarely fails. Large Golden Stonefly nymphs are also effective. Fish run in the 14- to 18-inch range, but much larger fish are always possible. These trout can be quite picky. They have been educated by some of the finest anglers in the country. The longer the season goes on, the harder they are to catch. The best flows for fishing are between 250 and 1,000 cfs. Above 1,000 cfs, wading becomes dangerous. Large boulders fall from the mountains every year, and there are many loose rocks. A wading staff should be carried at all times.

Much of Penns Creek can be accessed from Route 45, and the many side roads that parallel the river for most of its length. Public access is very good from Elk Creek downstream. You will see signs inviting fishermen to park and access the water. Most read: *Catch-and-release is appreciated.* Please respect the landowners who allow access to the river. Without their cooperation and generosity, much of Penns Creek would be inaccessible.

The catch-and-release section ends about 600 yards below where Cherry Run enters the creek. Below this, Penns is a large river by any standards. In many places it is over 100 feet wide. There is good fishing for the next 7 miles, ending at a bridge in the town of Glen Iron. This area is stocked with brown, rainbow, and brook trout. This area can be fished from the second Saturday in April through February.

➤ **Hatches:** Trout in Penns Creek feed on minnows, insects, and crayfish. The predominant minnows are sculpins, fallfish, suckers, and shiners. Insects include hellgrammites, stoneflies, mayflies, and caddis. The most significant hatches are grannoms, Blue Quills, Hendricksons, Grey Foxes, March Browns, Sulphurs, Green Drakes, Golden Drakes, Blue-winged Olives, and midges. Hatches are predictable, and start in mid-February, running through the end of July. By mid-October, the caddis, Blue-winged Olives, and Slate Drakes appear, providing great dry-fly fishing into November.

Penns Creek is one of the finest trout fisheries in the nation. It has been for generations, and it still is today.

➤ **Tackle:** A 9-foot 5-weight rod with a floating line is a good choice for Penns Creek most of the time. If you want to fish streamers, a 9-foot 6-weight with a floating line or intermediate line is your best option. Dry-fly fishing is best done with a 9-foot 4-weight, as you may need to drop to 6X tippet to effectively fish smaller patterns such as Blue-winged Olives. Strike indicators should be large enough to float two or three flies and added weight. Flies should include Woolly Buggers, Muddlers, and sculpin patterns; and all stages of mayflies, stoneflies, and caddis in a variety of sizes and colors.

Brook trout from catch-and-release section.
Bruce Fisher, Penns Creek Angler

BRUCE FISHER owns and operates Penns Creek Angler. He is also the president for the nonprofit organization Total Outdoors (www.totaloutdoors.org), which helps military families learn fly fishing. Bruce has fly fished for more than 35 years. He can be reached at info@pennscreekangler.com, or www.pennscreekangler.com.

CLOSEST FLY SHOPS

Penns Creek Angler
5540A Weikert Road
Weikert, Pennsylvania 17885
570-922-1053
www.pennscreekangler.com
info@pennscreekangler.com

The Feathered Hook
516 Main Street
Coburn, Pennsylvania 16832
814-349-8757
www.thefeatheredhook.com
Jonas@thefeatheredhook.com

TCO Fly Shop
2030 East College Avenue
State College, Pennsylvania 16801
814-689-3654
www.tcoflyfishing.com
tcoflyshop@tcoflyshop.com

Flyfisher's Paradise
2603 East College Avenue
State College, Pennsylvania 16801
814-234-4189
www.flyfishersparadise.com
sywensky@aol.com

CLOSEST GUIDES/OUTFITTERS

Outcast Anglers
Tylersville, Pennsylvania 17747
570-660-0285
www.outcastangler.com
fish.central.pa@gmail.com

Dennis Charney
Bellefonte, Pennsylvania 16823
814-280-3171
www.denischarney.com
dcharney@gotmc.net

Penns Creek Guides
415 Lower Georges Valley Road
Spring Mills, Pennsylvania 16875
814-364-9142
www.pennscreekguides.com
pennscreekguides1@yahoo.com

CLOSEST LODGING

Mifflinburg Hotel
264 Chestnut Street
Mifflinburg, Pennsylvania 17844
570-966-5400
www.mifflinburghotel.com
mifflinburghotel@dejazzed.com

Penns Creek Angler (streamside lodging house)
Weikert, Pennsylvania 17885
www.pennscreekangler.com
info@pennscreekangler.com

Penns Creek Mountain Lodge
868 Penns Creek Road
Mifflinburg, Pennsylvania 17844
570-966-4528
www.pennscreekmountainlodge.com
info@pennscreekmountainlodge.com

The Feathered Hook Bed & Breakfast
516 Main Street
Coburn, Pennsylvania 16832
814-349-8757
www.thefeatheredhook.com
Jonas@thefeatheredhook.com

CLOSEST RESTAURANTS

La Primavera
2593 Old Turnpike Road (Route 45)
Lewisburg, Pennsylvania 17837
570-523-1515
www.laprimaverarist.com
laprimavera2000@yahoo.com

Scarlet D/Mifflinburg Hotel
264 Chestnut Street
Mifflinburg, Pennsylvania 17844
570-966-5400
www.mifflinburghotel.com
mifflinburghotel@dejazzed.com

The Barnyard Restaurant
14605 Old Turnpike Road
Millmont, Pennsylvania 17845
570-922-0055
www.barnyardrestaurant.com

Union County Sportsman's Club
50 Sportsmen's Club Lane
Millmont, Pennsylvania 17845
570-922-1128
www.ucspca.com

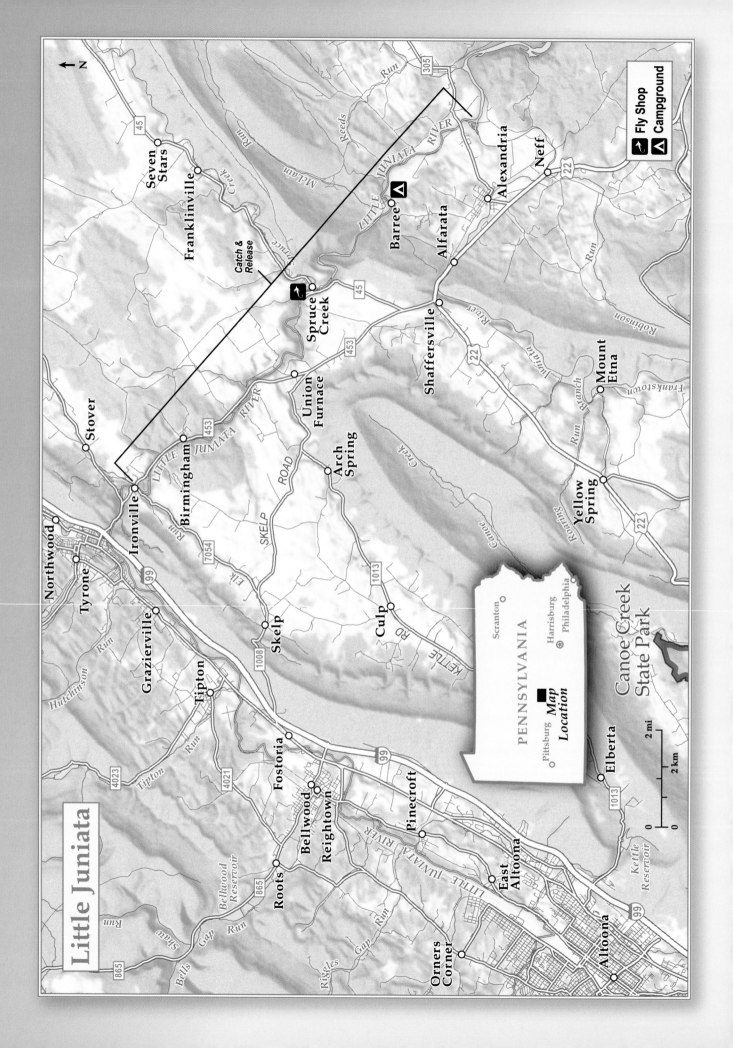

Little Juniata

N

Fly Shop
Campground

Seven Stars

Franklinville

Stover

Ironville

Northwood

Tyrone

Grazierville

Tipton

Fostoria

Bellwood

Reightown

Roots

Pinecroft

East Altoona

Elberta

Altoona

Orners Corner

Skelp

Culp

Arch Spring

Union Furnace

Birmingham

Spruce Creek

Catch & Release

Barree

Alfarata

Shaffersville

Yellow Spring

Mount Etna

Neff

Alexandria

45

305

22

45

453

453

7054

1008

1013

1013

865

99

4023

4021

865

99

22

Little Juniata River

Little Juniata River

Little Juniata River

Spruce Creek

Melchin Run

Reeds Run

Canoe Creek

Robinson Run

Frankstown

Juniata River

Run Branch

Roaring Run

Kettle Creek

Shade Gap Run

Bells Gap Run

Riggles Gap Run

Tipton Run

Hutchinson Run

Bellwood Reservoir

Kettle Reservoir

Elk Run

SKELP ROAD

KETTLE RD

Canoe Creek State Park

PENNSYLVANIA

Scranton

Pittsburg

Map Location

Harrisburg

Philadelphia

2 mi

2 km

0

0

44 · Little Juniata River

➤ **Location:** Central Pennsylvania, about a 1-hour ride from Harrisburg; a 2½-hour ride from Pittsburgh; and a 3-hour ride from Philadelphia. Full-service airports are available in all three cities.

Though located in the heart of central Pennsylvania's trout country, and in the midst of such famous fisheries as Cedar Run, Fishing Creek, Penns Creek, Pine Creek, Slate Run, Spring Creek, and Spruce Creek, the Little Juniata has no real fly-fishing heritage. That is because prior to 1970, the "J," as it is referred to locally, was little more than an open sewer. Upstream towns—including Altoona, a city of 50,000—dumped raw sewage and industrial waste directly into the river. A large paper mill in Tyrone added color and foam to the mix. The Clean Water Act of 1972 brought about significant changes to the way we treated our rivers—including the Little Juniata. Within a few years, three modern wastewater treatment plants were built on the river, and the pulp mill was closed.

Then Hurricane Agnes flushed the watershed with an epic flood in 1972. When the floodwaters receded, the Little Juniata flowed clear and cold for the first time in over a hundred years. Wild brown trout living in the unpolluted tributaries, including Tipton Run and Spruce Creek, rapidly populated the once-barren Little Juniata from Tyrone to Barree. The brown trout from Spruce Creek are remnants from early stockings of fish obtained from Germany in the 1890s. Trout numbers grew fast in this big, newly hospitable river.

The Pennsylvania Fish and Boat Commission stocked the Little Juniata with hatchery trout fingerlings for all but a few years between 1975 and 2010, under the guise of supplemental stocking. At the request of the Little Juniata River Association, the Pennsylvania Fish and Boat Commission agreed to fin-clip the fingerlings stocked into the river for a period of 2 years. The goal was to conduct extensive electroshocking surveys after the fact to evaluate the effective-

Railroad bridge over upper river. Wet Fly Waterguides

ness of the stocking efforts. The results showed that the Little Juniata had what would be categorized by the Pennsylvania Fish and Boat Commission as a Class A population of wild brown trout, with more than 3,000 wild, stream-born trout per mile. This confirmed that, as suspected, stocking was no longer needed.

Of greatest interest to fly fishers is the 13-mile section of the Little Juniata downstream from Tyrone. Beginning at the Ironville bridge and extending to the junction with the Frankstown Branch, the Little Juniata is managed under a strict catch-and-release regulation. There are no tackle re-

strictions. For the first 7 miles, there is good public access. Below here, the fabled Spruce Creek enters the river. There is an area of this stream owned by Pennsylvania State University, and named after George Harvey, who founded the first college-level fly-fishing class for credit at the University.

Downstream from Spruce Creek, after a mile or so of private water, the river enters the Rothrock Gorge. Unless you float through, the only way to access the gorge and its 1½

Stone Arch Bridge. Bill Anderson

miles of public water is to drive to the small village of Barree and work your way upstream from there. In 2006, the Little Juniata River Association, with the assistance of Pennsylvania Fish and Boat Commission, initiated a program to preserve public fishing access on the Little Juniata. To date, $200,000 has been paid to landowners, thus guaranteeing that more than 5 miles of stream is permanently open for fishing and boating access. This includes the Green Hills Campground property, where fly fishers intermingle with campers from March to October. Access downstream of Green Hills is limited to the south bank only—there is a railroad bed on the north bank. Plans for a 10-car parking area at the end of the road are underway, and should be available soon. This will provide parking for approximately 2 miles of fishing at the Allison Public Fishing Access.

Small wild rainbow trout. Little Juniata Watershed Association

► **Hatches:** The Little Juniata is a veritable insect factory. The first hatch is the grannom caddis in mid-April. This is followed by Sulphur mayflies in May. Various other caddis hatch from April to late June. Tricos hatch in July and August. Hatches wind down with Slate Drakes in September. Add to this several sizes of Cahills, Crane Flies, Grey Foxes, midges, BWOs, and a few Green Drakes—found only below Spruce Creek—and you have reliable, match-the-hatch dry-fly fishing for much of the season.

In addition to the hatches, there is good midsummer terrestrial fishing. For most of its length, the river has a dense tree canopy consisting primarily of sycamores, oaks, maples, and black willows. Caterpillars, beetles, inchworms, and especially ants live in this canopy. The trout below wait eagerly for these insects to drop out of the trees, feasting on these high-protein meals from above. You will often need accurate, sidearm casts to get your offerings under the overhanging limbs. This is where the big trout lurk.

In addition to bountiful insect life, the Little Juniata has a healthy population of minnows. Sculpins, dace, common shiners, and suckers are all present. Crayfish, once extremely abundant throughout but reduced as a result of pollution, are making a comeback, especially in the lower river.

Float fishing on medium to high flows, while throwing large Woolly Buggers and streamers to the banks and side eddies, can be very productive for those who are here at the right time. Even boats as large as drift boats can be effectively used in flows over 500 cfs. However, float fishing in any type of watercraft, including one-man pontoons, at normal flows during May through October can result in frequent dragging over dry rocks. Any summer rain event can provide good flows for boaters for a few days.

Over the last 30 years, the Little Juniata River has been transformed from an open sewer to a Class A wild trout fishery. At 13 miles, the Little Juniata now boasts the longest stretch of catch-and-release water in Pennsylvania. Its wild brown trout, plentiful hatches, and beautiful setting—as it flows under historic stone arches and through steep limestone gorges—will challenge and satisfy even the most discerning of fly fishers.

► **Tackle:** A 9-foot 5-weight rod with a floating line is your best bet for the Little Juniata River most of the time. If you want to fish streamers, a 9-foot 6-weight with a fast-sinking sink-tip is your best option. Dry-fly fishing is best done with a 9-foot 4-weight, as you may need to drop to 6X to effec-

Upper river brown trout. Wet Fly Waterguides

tively fish smaller patterns such as BWOs and midges. While rods longer than 9 feet can work, especially for nymphing, rods shorter than 9 feet are not always practical. Strike indicators should be large enough to float two flies and added weight. Flies should include Woolly Buggers; crayfish, sculpin, and dace patterns; all stages of mayflies, stoneflies, and caddis in a variety of sizes and colors, and a selection of terrestrials for fishing during the summer months.

BILL ANDERSON is president of the Little Juniata River Association and operates Troutboomer Outfitters, specializing in fly-fishing instruction for beginners and families. He can be reached at 814-684-5922, or bjuniata@verizon.net. For information about LJRA, visit the website at: www.littlejuniata.org.

CLOSEST FLY SHOPS

Spruce Creek Outfitters
Route 45
Spruce Creek, Pennsylvania 16683
814-632-3071
www.sprucecreekoutfitters.org

TCO Fly Shop
2030 East College Avenue
State College, Pennsylvania 16801
814-689-3654
www.tcoflyfishing.com
tcoflyshop@tcoflyshop.com

Flyfisher's Paradise
State College, Pennsylvania 16801
2603 East College Avenue
814-234-4189
www.flyfishersparadise.com
sywensky@aol.com

CLOSEST OUTFITTERS/GUIDES

Troutboomers
326 Hobbit Hollow Road
Altoona, Pennsylvania 16601
814-684-5922
bjuniata@verizon.net

Outcast Anglers
Tylersville, Pennsylvania 17747
570-660-0285
www.outcastangler.com
fish.central.pa@gmail.com

CLOSEST LODGING

The Inn at Edgewater Acres
7653 Edgewater Acres Circle
Alexandria, Pennsylvania 16611
814-669-4144
www.edgewateracres.net
info@edgewateracres.net

The Atherton Hotel
125 South Atherton Street
State College, Pennsylvania 16801
814-231-2100
www.athertonhotel.net
info@athertonhotel.net

The Limestone Inn
490 Meckley Road
State College, Pennsylvania 16801
814-234-8944
www.limestoneinn.com
kpatzer@psualum.com

Comfort Suites
140 Stroehman Drive
Altoona, Pennsylvania 16601
814-942-2600

Hillendale Hunting and Fishing Clubstars
941 Morrow Road
Tyrone, Pennsylvania 16686
814-684-5015
www.hillendalehuntingclub.com

CLOSEST RESTAURANTS

Spruce Creek Tavern
5450 Isett Road
Spruce Creek, Pennsylvania 16683
814-632-3287
www.facebook.com/pages/Spruce-Creek-Tavern
sprucecreektavern@windstream.net

The Inn at Edgewater Acres *(see above)*
The Main Street Café
214 Main Street
Alexandria, Pennsylvania 16611
814-669-4494
www.mainstcafe.us
café@mainstcafe.us

Gigi's
2080 Cato Avenue
State College, Pennsylvania 16801
814-861-3463
www.gigisdining.com
info@gigisdining.com

Kimchi Korean Restaurant
1100 North Atherton Street
State College, Pennsylvania 16801
814-237-2096
www.kimchistatecollege.com
kimchistatecollege@gmail.com

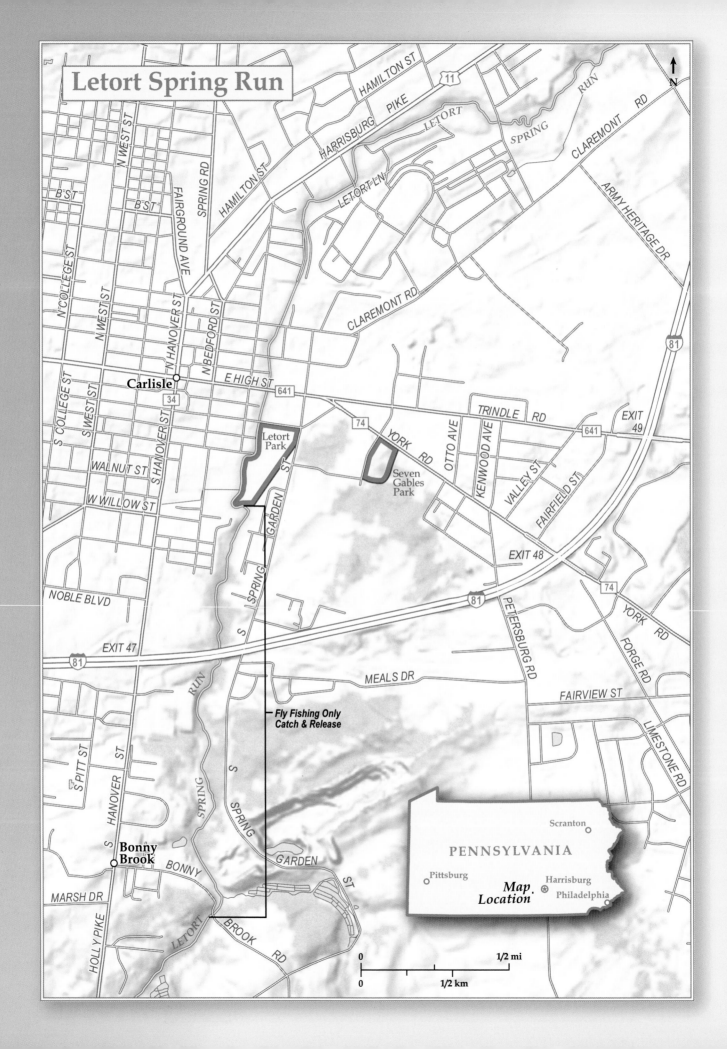

Letort Spring Run

Carlisle

Letort
Park

Seven
Gables
Park

Fly Fishing Only
Catch & Release

Bonny
Brook

N WEST ST
B ST
B ST
N COLLEGE ST
N WEST ST
S WEST ST
S COLLEGE ST
S WEST ST
FAIRGROUND AVE
SPRING RD
HAMILTON ST
N HANOVER ST
N BEDFORD ST
S HANOVER ST
E HIGH ST
WALNUT ST
W WILLOW ST
NOBLE BLVD
S PITT ST
S HANOVER ST
MARSH DR
HOLLY PIKE
GARDEN ST
SPRING
S SPRING
RUN
S SPRING
GARDEN
BONNY
LETORT
BROOK
RD
MEALS DR

HAMILTON ST
HARRISBURG PIKE
LETORT LN
LETORT
SPRING
RUN
CLAREMONT RD
CLAREMONT RD
ARMY HERITAGE DR

11
34
641
74
641
74
81
81

YORK RD
OTTO AVE
TRINDLE RD
KENWOOD AVE
VALLEY ST
FAIRFIELD ST
EXIT 49
EXIT 48
PETERSBURG RD
YORK RD
FORGE RD
FAIRVIEW ST
LIMESTONE RD

EXIT 47

PENNSYLVANIA

Scranton

Pittsburg

Harrisburg
Map
Location
Philadelphia

0   1/2 mi

0   1/2 km

45 · Letort Spring Run

➤ **Location:** South-central Pennsylvania, about a 1-hour ride from Harrisburg; a 2½-hour ride from Philadelphia; a 3-hour ride from Pittsburgh; and a 1½-hour ride from Washington, D.C. Full-service airports are available in all four cities.

Letort Spring Run is to fly fishing what Gettysburg is to the Civil War, Little Bighorn is to the Plains Indian Wars, and Bunker Hill is to the Revolutionary War—sacred ground. It is to Pennsylvania what the Batten Kill is to Vermont, the Neversink River is to New York, the Rapid River is to Maine, and the Madison River is to Montana. Being at the Letort just feels different—like something very important happened there. You can sense the presence of those who came before you more than anywhere else I have ever fished.

Fly-fishing legends such as Vince Marinaro, Charlie Fox, Ed Koch, Ed Shenk, Alfred Miller (aka Sparse Grey Hackle), and Lefty Kreh all honed their skills on Letort Spring Run. Mere mortals like the rest of us learn just how much our fly-fishing skills need honing on the Letort. To say that the Letort is a difficult stream to fish would be a gross understatement—like referring to Mount Everest as "a tough climb." I have fished such notoriously demanding fisheries as the three Paradise Valley, Montana, spring creeks: Railroad Ranch on the Henry's Fork in Idaho; Silver Creek in Picabo, Idaho; and Flat Creek in Jackson, Wyoming. I consider the Letort harder to fish than all of them.

The Letort was a hotbed for groundbreaking technical advances in fly fishing. At a time when delicate dry flies were king in the Catskills, and classic streamers were the rule in Maine, the Letort faithful developed odd-looking patterns to imitate terrestrials such as hoppers, crickets, beetles, jassids, and cicadas. They experimented with crane flies, midges,

scuds—referred to as sow bugs or cress bugs locally—and other previously overlooked trout foodstuffs. They lengthened their leaders to improve their presentations. They studied how trout responded to their surroundings. They watched fish feed and learned how best to catch them. They even experimented with relocating insects to establish hatches.

The Letort is what is referred to as a "limestone creek." Limestone creeks are to the East what spring creeks are to the West. They get their water primarily from underground

Matt Supinski below Bonney Brook Road. Laurie Supinski

springs. They flow cold and clear most of the year. Most true limestone creeks have few if any tributaries—and when they do they are often just smaller limestone creeks. The Letort is the most famous limestone creek in the country—and one of the most famous in the world. While some sections of other limestone creeks have been manicured right to the edge of water, much of the Letort lies within an unmaintained meadow. This means that you often have tall grass, trees or bushes right behind you. Add to this the slow clear water, spongy banks, muddy bottom, and wild fish, and most fly fishers will have their hands full.

Vince Marinaro and Charlie Fox memorial. Beau Beasley

The section of the Letort that is of most interest to fly fishers lies between Bonny Brook Road and the town of Carlisle. Here the stream is managed under strict barbless-hooks-only, fly-fishing-only, and catch-and-release regulations. This roughly 1½-mile section of stream also contains the fabled Marinaro Meadow—where local fly-fishing legends gathered to talk strategy, conditions, hatches, and techniques. Here the Letort is a small, meandering meadow stream. Rarely is it ever wider than the length of a car or two. Even then, when you eliminate the weed-choked sections, you are often left with just narrow channels a foot or so wide that are actually fishable. Getting a decent drift when your fly line is lying on a watercress bed is a real challenge—to say the least.

The Letort is a wild brown trout fishery. There are fish up to 4 pounds here—and maybe larger. These trout are as wily and wary as any fish you will ever encounter. One wrong move and they will stop feeding—or worse, flee for cover. I once made the mistake of stepping in the water—which is prohibited under the current regulations—to get a better angle on a rising fish. I immediately bumped a fish that shot upstream, and created a domino effect of bumped fish for a hundred or so feet above me. The silt I kicked up put down fish for a couple of hundred feet below me.

Brown trout caught during Isonychia *hatch.*
Nick Raftas, Sky Blue Outfitters

To effectively fish the Letort, you must stay out of the water and move stealthily along the banks—it's more like hunting than fishing. You must keep a low profile, avoid casting a shadow, stay away from the banks while moving around, and kneel when you are in position to cast. Blind casting is usually a bad idea—unless there is a chop on the water, or it is running high and off-colored due to rain, and you are prospecting with small streamers.

The trout in the Letort feed on minnows, insects, and crustaceans—scuds. Scuds and terrestrials are present much of the year. The predominant minnows are sculpins. The insects include a variety of mayflies and some caddis. Hatches on the Letort are rarely epic. Sulphurs, Blue-winged Olives, and Tricos are all present.

As they say, if you get skunked on the Letort, you are in good company. Even the most seasoned and skilled Letort fly fishers have days on the stream when nothing seems to go right. Expert fly anglers who are unfamiliar with the water are often humbled—or worse. Catches of one or two fish a day are considered a success. More than that is considered praiseworthy.

You might ask yourself, why would I bother going to all this trouble just to be humbled? Because Letort Spring Run is a great fishery. And because, as I wrote at the beginning of the chapter, the Letort is hallowed ground, and just as any Civil War buff should see the Gettysburg Battlefield, and any Plains Indian Wars aficionado should see the Little Bighorn Battlefield, any serious fly fisher should see—and fish—the Letort if they have the chance.

➤ **Tackle:** Any standard trout fly rod with a floating line will work on Letort Spring Run. However, many of the dedicated Letort anglers use short, light-line rods—as short as 6 feet and as light as 2-weight. There is no need for a sinking or sink-tip line, as the stream is small and relatively shallow. Most of your fishing will be done with drys, scuds, and smallish streamers. Nymphing terminal tackle should be small and light. Flies should include small Woolly Buggers and small sculpin patterns; all stages of mayflies and caddis in a variety of sizes and colors; a good selection of terrestrials; and some size 16 to 18 scuds in olive, tan, and light gray.

Overcast summer afternoon. Nick Raftas, Sky Blue Outfitters

Vince Marinaro, Charlie Fox, and friend. Lefty Kreh

BOB MALLARD has fly fished for over 35 years. He is a blogger, writer, and author; and has owned and operated Kennebec River Outfitters in Madison, Maine since 2001. His writing has been featured in newspapers, magazines, and books at the local, regional, and national levels. He has appeared on radio and television. Look for his upcoming books from Stonefly Press, *25 Best Towns: Fly Fishing for Trout* (winter 2014) and *50 Best Places: Fly Fishing for Brook Trout* (summer 2015). Bob is also a staff fly designer for Catch Fly Fishing. He can be reached at www.kennebecriveroutfitters.com, www.bobmallard.com, info@bobmallard.com or 207-474-2500.

CLOSEST FLY SHOPS

Yellow Breeches Outfitters
2 East 1st Street
Boiling Springs, Pennsylvania 17007
717-258-6752
www.yellowbreechesoutfitters.com
rowland@yellowbreechesoutfitters.com

CLOSEST GUIDES/OUTFITTERS

Mike Heck's Trout Guides
Orvis Endorsed Guide
1664 Malibu Drive
Chambersburg, Pennsylvania 17007
717-816-7557
www.fallingsprings.com
trout@mris.com

Sky Blue Outfitters
212 Deysher Road
Fleetwood, Pennsylvania 19522
610-987-0073
www.skyblueoutfitters.com
skyblue@dejazzd.com

CLOSEST LODGING

Pheasant Field Bed & Breakfast
150 Hickorytown Road
Carlisle, Pennsylvania 17013
877-258-0717
www.pheasantfield.com
stay@pheasantfield.com

Allenberry Resort Inn and Playhouse
1559 Boiling Springs Road
Boiling Springs, Pennsylvania 17007
800-430-5468
www.allenberry.com
aberry8@allenberry.com

Stardust Motel
1502 Holly Pike
Carlisle, Pennsylvania 17013
717-243-6058

Motel 6
1153 Harrisburg Pike
Carlisle, Pennsylvania 17013
717-249-7622

CLOSEST RESTAURANTS

Allenberry Resort Inn and Playhouse
1559 Boiling Springs Road
Boiling Springs, Pennsylvania 17007
800-430-5468
www.allenberry.com
aberry5@allenberry.com

Boiling Springs Tavern (fine dining)
1 East 1st Street
Boiling Springs, Pennsylvania 17007
717-258-3614
www.boilingspringstavern.net

Aya Japanese Steakhouse
235 South Spring Garden Street
Carlisle, Pennsylvania 17013
717-218-8000
www.ayasteakhiuse.com
ayajapanesesteakhouse@yahoo.com

Redd's Smokehouse BBQ (pub-style food)
109 North Hanover Street
Carlisle, Pennsylvania 17013
717-254-6419
www.reddssmokehousebbq.com

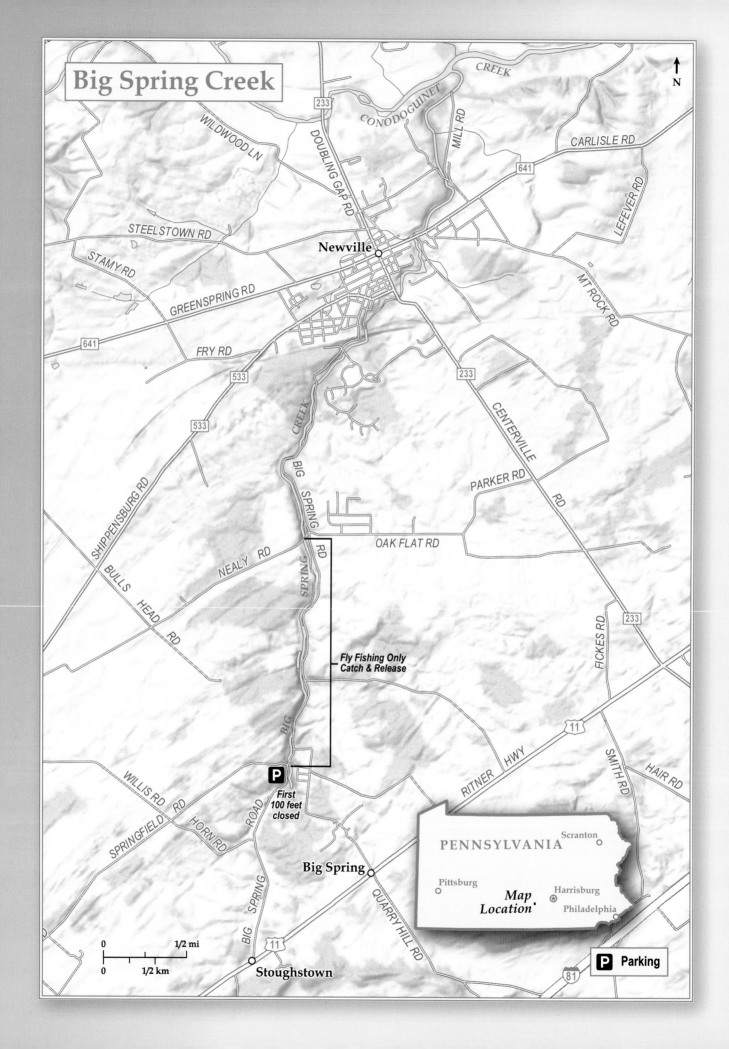

Big Spring Creek

N

CREEK

CONODOGUINET

CREEK

WILDWOOD LN

DOUBLING GAP RD

MILL RD

CARLISLE RD

233

641

STEELSTOWN RD

LEFEVER RD

ST AMY RD

Newville

GREENSPRING RD

MT ROCK RD

641

FRY RD

533

233

CENTERVILLE RD

533

PARKER RD

CREEK

BIG SPRING

OAK FLAT RD

NEALY RD

SPRING RD

BULLS HEAD RD

Fly Fishing Only Catch & Release

FICKES RD

233

BIG

11

WILLIS RD

RITNER HWY

SMITH RD

HAIR RD

P

First 100 feet closed

SPRINGFIELD RD

HORN RD

ROAD

PENNSYLVANIA

Scranton

Big Spring

Pittsburg

Harrisburg

BIG SPRING RD

QUARRY HILL RD

Map Location

Philadelphia

0   1/2 mi

0   1/2 km

11

Stoughstown

81

P Parking

46 · Big Spring Creek

➤ **Location:** South-central Pennsylvania, about a 1-hour ride from Harrisburg; a 2½-hour ride from Philadelphia; a 3-hour ride from Pittsburgh; and a 1½-hour ride from Washington, D.C. Full-service airports are available in all four cities.

Big Spring Creek is a "good news/bad news/good news" story. In fact, it may be that all-too-rare fish story with a happy ending.

While working in the Greater D.C. area, I was on an every-other-week, 3-day weekend stayover, to cut down on flights—and do some fishing. I was on a three-stream rotation among Letort Spring Run, Falling Springs, and Big Spring. It was also a three-species rotation among brown, rainbow, and brook trout, respectively. When you consider that limestone streams are best known for brown trout, this was an odd coincidence.

Big Spring is located near Newville. It runs roughly 5 miles before terminating at Conodoguinet Creek. The stream originates from a large spring. The gin-clear water runs in the low-50s range most of the year. It has the heavy weed growth typical of spring creek—and the insects and crustaceans. It is one of the most famous limestone creeks in the country. Big Spring was a favorite of Vince Marinaro, Charlie Fox, and the rest of the Fly Fishers' Club of Harrisburg faithful. It also has a history as a working stream, once powering several mills. Many early pictures show these historic buildings. Most of the buildings are gone—but you can still see the remnants of some old dams.

Big Spring is arguably the finest limestone creek brook trout fishery in the country. Being from New England, I am not easily impressed by brook trout—I see a whole lot of them, and some very large ones. But these brook trout impressed even me. I caught several that were as large as any I had caught outside Maine and Canada. They were as healthy and beautiful as any I had seen. Unlike most, these brook trout were difficult to catch—in fact, they were as selective as any trout I have ever fished for. This kept me coming back to Big Springs. There are also rainbow and brown trout, some of which grew to rather impressive sizes. One book I read showed an angler holding a nearly 2-foot rainbow. In June 1945, Don Martin caught a brown trout that was 31 inches in length, had a 20½-inch girth, and weighed 15½ pounds—a new state record. This was the good news.

The state of Pennsylvania built a fish hatchery on the headwaters of Big Spring Creek in 1971—it went live in 1972. This was the bad news. This started the downward spiral of

Barrel factory at headwaters of Big Spring Creek. Matt Supinski

the fabled brook trout population. A study done in the late 1990s determined that effluent from the hatchery was negatively impacting the brook trout. Unfortunately, we had traded a high-quality, unique, and famous wild trout population for a fish farm. By the early 2000s, local anglers had taken action to try to close the hatchery on Big Spring Creek. To their credit, the powers that be made the right decision, and the hatchery was decommissioned in 2001. This is the new good news.

Big Spring Creek in Newville, Pennsylvania. Nick Raftas, Sky Blue Outfitters

By the late 2000s, the upper section of Big Spring once again boasted a robust brook trout population. This returns Big Spring to its former place at the top of the limestone creeks in regard to brook trout, and makes it a wild native brook trout fishery of national significance. Recent electroshocking efforts have turned up brook trout up to 18 inches. Rainbows up to 24 inches have been seen. While fewer in number, brown trout even larger have been encountered, with fish close to 30 inches reported. The demise of the hatchery on Big Spring appears to have helped other aquatic life. There are reports that certain mayflies have seen an increase in numbers, and range expansion. This is a good sign, as the presence of these insects is an indication of overall stream health.

The part of Big Spring Creek that is of most interest to fly fishers runs from the headwaters at the site of the old hatchery, down roughly a mile or so. This includes the Heritage Trout Angling section. The spring itself, down roughly 100 feet, is closed to fishing. Below this lies "the ditch," a long, slow run where some of the largest fish in the stream live.

Native brook trout. Matt Supinski

While these fish may be easy to see, they are anything but easy to catch. From its headwaters to the Nealy Road Bridge it is open to year-round fishing, and managed under strict barbless-hooks-only, fly-fishing only, and catch-and-release regulations. There is no wading unless specifically noted. The regulations get less protective as you move downstream.

As on most limestone creeks, to effectively fish Big Spring you must stay out of the water, and move carefully and quietly along the banks. Keeping a low profile is always a good idea. Try to avoid casting a shadow over the water. Cast to fish you can see. Blind-cast only when there is a chop on the water, or the stream is running high or off-colored. The trout in the Big Spring feed on minnows, insects, and scuds—or cress bugs. Scuds are present year-round. Terrestrials are available in the spring and summer. There are sculpins. Insects include both mayflies and caddis. Hatches are rarely what you would call epic. Sulphurs are probably the most important insects.

The latest battle on Big Spring is in regard to rainbow trout. Post hatchery removal, the wild rainbow trout population has exploded. Conversely, the brown trout have dropped off. There are people who feel that the rainbow trout could negatively affect the brook trout—a legitimate concern. Brook trout will never get as large as the rainbow trout—no one is denying that. Anglers like big fish. It would also not be easy to eradicate the nonnative rainbow trout. Again, we are faced with a decision that pits what is *best* against what is *right*.

Big Spring Creek is a special place. It offers large, beautiful, and difficult-to-catch fish in an idyllic rural setting. There is always the chance of encountering a true trophy trout—in small water. Big Spring Creek is actually getting better and better. As I said in the beginning, a fish story with a happy ending.

➤ **Tackle:** Any standard trout fly rod with a floating line will work on Big Spring Creek. There is no need for a sinking or sink-tip line, as the stream is small and relatively shallow. Most of your fishing will be done with drys, scuds, and smallish streamers. Nymphing terminal tackle should be small and light. Flies should include small Woolly Buggers and small sculpin patterns; all stages of mayflies and caddis in a variety of sizes and colors; a good selection of terrestrials; and some size 16 to 18 scuds in olive, tan, and light gray.

Wyatt Dietrich with native brook trout. Bill Ferris

BOB MALLARD has fly fished for over 35 years. He is a blogger, writer, and author; and has owned and operated Kennebec River Outfitters in Madison, Maine since 2001. His writing has been featured in newspapers, magazines, and books at the local, regional, and national levels. He has appeared on radio and television. Look for his upcoming books from Stonefly Press, *25 Best Towns: Fly Fishing for Trout* (winter 2014) and *50 Best Places: Fly Fishing for Brook Trout* (summer 2015). Bob is also a staff fly designer for Catch Fly Fishing. He can be reached at www.kennebecriveroutfitters.com, www.bobmallard.com, info@bobmallard.com or 207-474-2500.

CLOSEST FLY SHOPS

Yellow Breeches Outfitters
2 East 1st Street
Boiling Springs, Pennsylvania 17007
717-258-6752
www.yellowbreechesoutfitters.com
rowland@yellowbreechesoutfitters.com

CLOSEST GUIDES/OUTFITTERS

Mike Heck's Trout Guides
Orvis Endorsed Guide
1664 Malibu Drive
Chambersburg, Pennsylvania 17007
717-816-7557
www.fallingsprings.com
trout@mris.com

Sky Blue Outfitters
212 Deysher Road
Fleetwood, Pennsylvania 19522
610-987-0073
www.skyblueoutfitters.com
skyblue@dejazzd.com

CLOSEST LODGING

Pheasant Field Bed & Breakfast
150 Hickorytown Road
Carlisle, Pennsylvania 17013
877-258-0717
www.pheasantfield.com
stay@pheasantfield.com

Allenberry Resort Inn and Playhouse
1559 Boiling Springs Road
Boiling Springs, Pennsylvania 17007
800-430-5468
www.allenberry.com
aberry8@allenberry.com

Stardust Motel
1502 Holly Pike
Carlisle, Pennsylvania 17013
717-243-6058

Motel 6
1153 Harrisburg Pike
Carlisle, Pennsylvania 17013
717-249-7622

CLOSEST RESTAURANTS

Allenberry Resort Inn and Playhouse
1559 Boiling Springs Road
Boiling Springs, Pennsylvania 17007
800-430-5468
www.allenberry.com
aberry5@allenberry.com

Boiling Springs Tavern (fine dining)
1 East 1st Street
Boiling Springs, Pennsylvania 17007
717-258-3614
www.boilingspringstavern.net

Aya Japanese Steakhouse
235 South Spring Garden Street
Carlisle, Pennsylvania 17013
717-218-8000
www.ayasteakhiuse.com
ayajapanesesteakhouse@yahoo.com

Redd's Smokehouse BBQ (pub-style food)
109 North Hanover Street
Carlisle, Pennsylvania 17013
717-254-6419
www.reddssmokehousebbq.com

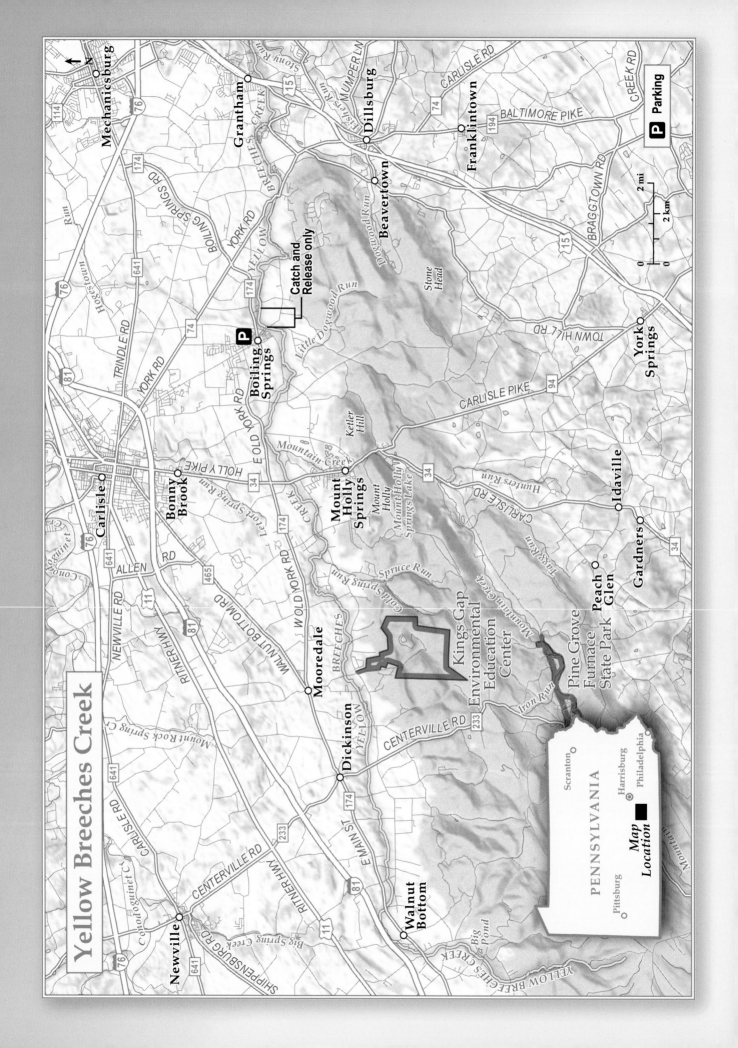

Yellow Breeches Creek

Parking 🅿

N ←

Mechanicsburg

Grantham

Dillsburg

Carlisle RD

Franklintown

BALTIMORE PIKE

CREEK RD

Beavertown

Catch and Release only

🅿 Boiling Springs

Stone Head

York Springs

Ketler Hill

CARLISLE PIKE

Bonny Brook

Mount Holly Springs

Mount Holly Springs Lake

Idaville

Gardners

Mooredale

Kings Gap Environmental Education Center

Peach Glen

Pine Grove Furnace State Park

Dickinson

Walnut Bottom

Newville

PENNSYLVANIA

Scranton

Harrisburg

Philadelphia

Map Location

Pittsburg

Big Pond

YELLOW BREECHES CREEK

2 mi

2 km

0   0

➤ **Location:** South-central Pennsylvania, about a ½-hour ride from Harrisburg; a 2-hour ride from Philadelphia; a 3-hour ride from Pittsburgh; and a 2-hour ride from Washington, D.C. Full-service airports are available in all four cities.

Yellow Breeches Creek was rightly chosen for inclusion in this book. It was home to some of the most legendary fly fishermen in history, such as Vince Marinaro, Charlie Fox, Ed Shenk, and Gene Utech. The Pennsylvania Fly Fishing Museum is located on the grounds of the Allenberry Playhouse, just a short walk from the stream. The Breeches, as it is called locally, has been visited by such luminaries as Baseball Hall of Famer Ted Williams, and Presidents Dwight D. Eisenhower and Jimmy Carter. Yellow Breeches Creek is approximately 40 miles long. Trout are stocked from Route 233 down to the Susquehanna River, a distance of about 30 miles.

Yellow Breeches Creek begins in the Michaux State Forest. Its headwaters are located on the northwestern side of South Mountain. Several small streams drain the area. The creek flows north through Walnut Bottom, before turning east toward the Cumberland Valley. The stream is paralleled by a railroad bed. It passes through Huntsdale, site of the Huntsdale State Fish Hatchery. Here it gets an influx of cold spring water. It is joined by Mountain Creek near the town of Mount Holly Springs. Old Town Run enters the creek just before it passes Boiling Springs to the north. The gin-clear water from the spring-fed lake cools the main creek. Dogwood Run pours in just below Williams Grove. It is then joined by Stony Run. Pippins Run joins the creek next. Cedar Run enters near the end of the creek. Yellow Breeches is designated by Pennsylvania as a Scenic River.

Yellow Breeches Creek is a large stream. It is as wide as 60 feet in some places. On average, the creek is roughly 25 to 40 feet wide. Yellow Breeches is stocked with brook trout, rainbow trout, brown trout, and the Pennsylvania version of the golden trout—actually a golden rainbow trout. In addition to both stocked and holdover trout, Yellow Breeches has a strong population of wild trout. Yellow Breeches Creek is one of Pennsylvania's finest fly-fishing trout streams. It is also one of the most heavily fished streams in the state.

The area of most interest to the fly fishers is the catch-and-release section located in the town of Boiling Springs. Tackle is restricted to artificial lures only. The catch-and-release section starts at the outlet from Boiling Springs, and extends down past Allenberry Resort Inn and Playhouse—a distance of roughly 1 mile. This section is easily accessible and very wadable. This area benefits from the cool limestone water coming out of Boiling Springs. This helps keep the stream at a constant temperature, which makes it year-round fishery.

Race Street Bridge. Maggie Grenier

There is good fishing found outside the catch-and-release area as well. The areas above the catch-and-release stretch are utilized by fly fishers on a regular basis. Pine Road, which is located right off Route 34, is a favorite spot for local anglers. This section of the Yellow Breeches boasts a population of wild brown trout. Downstream of the catch-and-release area, you will find what is referred to as William Grove. William Grove is the home of the Williams Grove Speedway. It was formerly home to the Williams Grove Amusement Park, which closed several years ago. This section of stream was one of Vince Marinaro's favorite spots. This area is known for

Above. Outlet from Boiling Springs. Maggie Grenier
Inset. Brown Trout. Joel LaMarco

its strong Trico, Sulphur, and White Fly hatches. It is, however, prone to warming, and is often too hot for trout in the summer months. However, you will find fish wherever cold water enters the creek from small feeder streams.

➤ Hatches: The Breeches has strong hatches. Hatches begin early and end late. By late February and early March, there is an emergence of Early Black Stoneflies. On cloudy warm days when the temperatures get above 40, you are likely to come across some small Blue-winged Olives or midges. By April, grannoms and Hendrickson mayflies become the flies of choice. Crane flies are also presented at this time. By mid-May the Sulphurs start to appear. This hatch can be epic in certain sections of the stream. This hatch starts near dusk and goes right into the dark. The Sulphurs last until mid-June, after which the stream experiences a light hatch of Light Cahills. During June the Tricos appear. This hatch attracts fly fishers from all over. You need to be at the stream by 6 A.M. to ensure that you get a spot. For the rest of the

summer and into the early fall, terrestrials are the ticket. In August, the stream experiences its famous White Fly hatch. This is one of the most popular hatches on the creek. This hatch can be prolific, and anglers gather closer together at this time than at any other time of year. The hatch starts with the emergence of the *Hexagenia* about 7:30 P.M. The White Fly comes off at about 8:30 P.M. This hatch will last until the first week of September. Caddis are important throughout the year. Caddis can be tan, brown, or green. Scuds, cress bugs, and sow bugs are present. Aquatic worms are also present.

The wet fly is making a comeback on the Breeches. Soft-hackles and traditional wets both work. The Light Cahill wet fly works wonders during the White Fly hatch. The Breeches is also a great nymphing river. Nymphing can save your day when everything else fails to produce fish. Midge pupae in a variety of colors can work very well. During high-water periods, do not be afraid to throw streamers and Woolly Buggers. During the winter, trout are caught with nymphs and streamers.

Yellow Breeches Creek is a great stream to fly fish. It has ample public access and good tourism infrastructure. While in the area, be sure to visit the fabled Letort Spring Run, Big Spring Creek, and Green Spring. Central Pennsylvania is a great place to fish.

Brown Trout. Joel LaMarco

➤ **Tackle:** Any standard trout fly rod with a floating line will work on Yellow Breeches Creek. There is no need for a sinking or sink-tip line, as the stream is relatively shallow. Most of your fishing will be done with dries, scuds, and smallish streamers. Nymphing terminal tackle should be small and light. Flies should include small Woolly Buggers; small sculpin patterns; all stages of mayflies and caddis in a variety of sizes and colors; and some size 16 to 18 scuds in olive, tan, and light gray.

ROWLAND E. HARRISON owns and operates Yellow Breeches Outfitters in Boiling Springs, Pennsylvania. He can be reached at 717-258-6752, www.yellowbreechesoutfitters.com, or Rowland@yellowbreechesoutfitters.com.

CLOSEST FLY SHOPS

Yellow Breeches Outfitters
2 East 1st Street
Boiling Springs, Pennsylvania 17007
717-258-6752
www.yellowbreechesoutfitters.com
www.info@yellowbreechesoutfitters.com

CLOSEST GUIDES/OUTFITTERS

Mike Heck's Trout Guides
Orvis Endorsed Guide
1664 Malibu Drive
Chambersburg, Pennsylvania 17007
717-816-7557
www.fallingsprings.com
trout@mris.com

Four Seasons Flyfishing Guide Service
Carlisle, Pennsylvania
717-713-8282
www.fourseasonsflyfishing.com
flyfisher9304739@aol.com

Sky Blue Outfitters
212 Deysher Road
Fleetwood, Pennsylvania 19522
610-987-0073
www.skyblueoutfitters.com
skyblue@dejazzd.com

CLOSEST LODGING

Allenberry Resort Inn and Playhouse
1559 Boiling Springs Road
Boiling Springs, Pennsylvania 17007
800-430-5468
www.allenberry.com
aberry8@allenberry.com

Pheasant Field Bed & Breakfast
150 Hickorytown Road
Carlisle, Pennsylvania 17015
877-258-0717
www.pheasantfield.com
stay@pheasantfield.com

Sleep Inn
5 East Garland Drive
Carlisle, Pennsylvania 17015
717-249-8863
www.sleepinn.com/hotel/pa055

Wingate By Wyndham
385 Cumberland Parkway
Mechanicsburg, Pennsylvania 17055
717-766-2710
www.hotelmechanicsburg.com

CLOSEST RESTAURANTS

Allenberry Resort Inn and Playhouse
1559 Boiling Springs Road
Boiling Springs, Pennsylvania 17007
800-430-5468
www.allenberry.com
aberry8@allenberry.com

Boiling Springs Tavern (fine dining)
1 East 1st Street
Boiling Springs, Pennsylvania 17007
717-258-3614
www.boilingspringstavern.net

Aya Japanese Steakhouse
235 South Spring Garden Street
Carlisle, Pennsylvania 17013
717-218-8000
www.ayasteakhiuse.com
ayajapanesesteakhouse@yahoo.com

Redd's Smokehouse BBQ (pub-style food)
109 North Hanover Street
Carlisle, Pennsylvania 17013
717-254-6419
www.reddssmokehousebbq.com

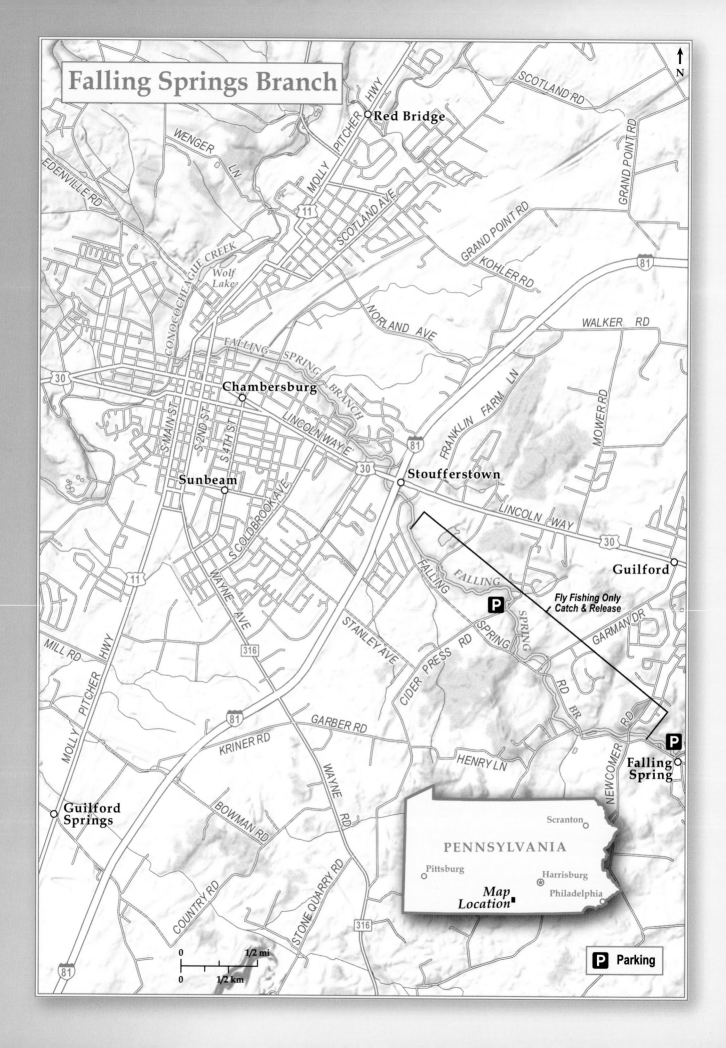

Falling Springs Branch

N

Red Bridge

SCOTLAND RD

WENGER LN

EDENVILLE RD

MOLLY PITCHER HWY

SCOTLAND AVE

11

GRAND POINT RD

GRAND POINT RD

KOHLER RD

81

WALKER RD

CONOCOCHEAGUE CREEK

Wolf Lake

NORLAND AVE

FALLING SPRING BRANCH

30

Chambersburg

LINCOLN WAY E

81

FRANKLIN FARM LN

MOWER RD

Stoufferstown

LINCOLN WAY

30

Guilford

S MAIN ST

S 2ND ST

S 4TH ST

Sunbeam

S COLDBROOK AVE

P

Fly Fishing Only
Catch & Release

FALLING SPRING

FALLING SPRING

GARMAN DR

11

WAYNE AVE

316

STANLEY AVE

CIDER PRESS RD

SPRING RD BR

MILL RD

MOLLY PITCHER HWY

81

GARBER RD

KRINER RD

WAYNE RD

HENRY LN

NEWCOMER RD

P

Falling
Spring

Guilford
Springs

BOWMAN RD

COUNTRY RD

STONE QUARRY RD

316

PENNSYLVANIA

Scranton

Pittsburg

Harrisburg

Philadelphia

Map
Location

0   1/2 mi

0   1/2 km

81

P Parking

48 · Falling Spring Run

Location: South-central Pennsylvania, about a 1-hour ride from Harrisburg; a 2½-hour ride from Philadelphia; a 3-hour ride from Pittsburgh; and a 1½-hour ride from Washington, D.C. Full-service airports are available in all four cities.

Falling Springs originates near the historic city of Chambersburg. Its crystal-clear waters flow through farmlands and grassy meadows outside of town. It winds and weaves its way through neighborhoods as it enters town. Once in town, it flows behind homes, through backyards, and eventually to its confluence with Conococheague Creek.

Falling Springs is one of the finest wild trout fisheries in Pennsylvania. It is also one of the few limestone creeks known for its rainbow trout. The creek was once heavily stocked. Stocking was discontinued, and the stream now boasts an abundant population of wild trout. Falling Springs has both rainbow and brown trout. Most of the rainbows are found above town. In town, while rainbow numbers are increasing, there are currently more browns. Both rainbow and brown trout can grow to impressive lengths. They average between 9 and 14 inches. Smaller trout are plentiful. Much larger trout are encountered.

The densest trout populations are found in the first 4 miles of the stream. This section is managed for fly fishing only and catch-and-release. Most of this stretch of stream flows through private property. It is, however, under a public easement program that allows access. Some of the meadows are owned by the Pennsylvania Fish and Boat Commission.

Below here the creek enters Chambersburg. The area is much quieter than you would think. When fishing the stream in town, fly fishers would never guess that they are in busy Chambersburg. This 1.1-mile stretch of stream is managed for Delayed Harvest and holds a fair number of holdover and wild browns.

Much habitat restoration work has been done along the length of the stream by Falling Spring Trout Unlimited, Falling Springs Greenway, Ecotone, Inc., and local landowners and businesses. They all deserve our thanks.

Falling Springs is a year-round fishery. The limestone waters remain cool all summer and ice-free during the winter. Trout can be found feeding on the surface all year. However, prime time for surface activity is from April through September.

Fish do not come easy on Falling Springs. However, fly fishers will have plenty of opportunities to catch trout. As on all spring creeks, the clear water, slow currents, aquatic vegetation, and wild fish make fishing a real challenge.

Parking for fly fishers is allowed at this private residence. Beau Beasley

Hatches: Falling Springs has a robust and diverse population of mayflies, caddis, and midges. These insects hatch throughout the year. As on most spring creeks, there are cress bugs and freshwater shrimp. These two crustaceans are

Keeping out of the water. Mike Heck Trout Guides

important food sources. Fly fishers should come equipped with a good selection of shrimp and cress bug patterns in size 18 through 14.

Blue-winged Olives and Black Stoneflies start the dry-fly season. They can start on any warm day in February, but really get going in March and April. Blue-winged Olives hatch from 10 A.M. into the afternoon. After a few days, trout will start to feed on the surface. A size 18 *Baetis* nymph works well before the hatch. Low-profile patterns such as Compara-duns work best during the emergence. These should be in the size 18 to 20 range. Blue-winged Olives also hatch in the fall. Trout occasionally feed on clumsy adult stoneflies as they skate across the surface. However, the real action is subsurface. This insect runs in the size 16 to 14 range.

By mid-April, there are heavy hatches of Black Caddis. Some trout feed on cripples, but most of the attention is focused on pupae and emergers. After several days, females return to the water at dusk to deposit their eggs. The dying caddis provide easy meals for the trout, but a tough challenge for the fly fisher. Trout can be very selective as they pick insects off the surface. Patterns in the size 18 to 20 range, and 6X tippet, are needed at this time.

The most anticipated hatch of the year is a pale yellow mayfly, locally known as the Sulphur. This starts around the third week of May. The hatch occurs during the evening, often right at dark. Sulphur duns, emergers, and parachutes in size 18 and 16 effectively match this hatch. Shortly after hatching, the duns molt, returning to the water as spinners. At this time a size 16 yellow/brown spinner is your best bet.

The last major hatch of the year is the Trico. It begins in July and lasts until the first frost—a period of up to sever-

Watercress provides cover for fish and insects. Beau Beasley

al months. When it is hot, male Tricos hatch at night and return to the creek to wait for the females. When it is cool, males and females will hatch at the same time—in the morning. After mating, the flies molt into spinners and fall into the creek. The exact time of the spinner fall depends on air temperature—the hotter the air, the earlier the spinner fall. Tricos are best imitated with a size 22 or 24 fly. The delicate 7X tippet required to effectively fish this hatch, along with the tiny flies, make for a challenging but rewarding experience.

In addition to the mayfly and caddis hatches, Falling Springs has year-round midge hatches. On most days, trout can be found rising to drifting midges.

Terrestrials become important food sources during the summer. Ants, beetles, leafhoppers, crickets, and grasshoppers all find a way to fall into the stream. These easy, high-protein meals are eagerly taken by waiting trout. A well-placed terrestrial along an undercut bank or structure can often lure out a good-size trout.

December through mid-February can be productive for those willing to work hard. At this time, cress bugs, shrimp, and a small olive nymphs are your best options. Small streamers in olive, black, and brown can work as well. Woolly Buggers can also be effective when fished along undercut banks and in the deeper runs.

Falling Springs is truly a treasure. The wild trout living in the cool, clear water are as beautiful as any you will ever encounter. The fishing is as challenging as any you will find anywhere.

➤ **Tackle:** Any standard trout fly rod with a floating line will work on Falling Spring Branch. There is no need for a sinking or sink-tip line, as the stream is small and relatively shallow. Most of your fishing will be done with drys, scuds, and smallish streamers. Nymphing terminal tackle should be small and light. Flies should include small Woolly Buggers; small sculpin patterns; all stages of mayflies and caddis in a variety of sizes and colors; a good selection of terrestrials; and some size 16 to 18 scuds in olive, tan, and light gray.

MIKE HECK owns and operates Mike Heck Trout Guides. He has authored several books, including *Spring Creek Strategies* (Headwater Books, 2008). Mike can be reached at 717-816-7557, trout@mris.com, or www.fallingsprings.com.

CLOSEST FLY SHOPS

Yellow Breeches Outfitters
2 East First Street
Boiling Springs, Pennsylvania 17007
717-258-6752
www.yellowbreechesoutfitters.com
rowland@yellowbreechesoutfitters.com

CLOSEST GUIDES/OUTFITTERS

Mike Heck's Trout Guides
Orvis-Endorsed Guide
Chambersburg, Pennsylvania 17202
717-816-7557
www.fallingsprings.com
trout@mris.com

CLOSEST LODGING

Craig Victorian Bed & Breakfast
756 Philadelphia Avenue
Chambersburg, Pennsylvania 17202
717-263-3371
www.craigvictorian.com
info@CraigVictorian.com

The Inn at Ragged Edge
1090 Ragged Edge Road
Chambersburg, Pennsylvania 17202
717-496-8372
www.theinnatraggededge.com
info@TheInnAtRaggedEdge.com

Best Western
211 Walker Road
Chambersburg, Pennsylvania 17202
717-262-4994
book.bestwestern.com

Four Points by Sheraton
1123 Lincoln Way East
Chambersburg, Pennsylvania 17202
717-263-9191
www.starwoodhotels.com

CLOSEST RESTAURANTS

The Orchards Restaurant
1580 Orchard Drive
Chambersburg, Pennsylvania 17202
717-264-4711
www.orchardsrestaurant.com

Rosalie's Fabulous Grill
1901 Scotland Avenue
Chambersburg, Pennsylvania 17202
717-262-4981
www.rosaliesfabgrill.com

Molly's Pub
253 East Chestnut Street
Lancaster, Pennsylvania 17602
717-396-0225
www.mollyspub.com

Mario's Italian Restaurant
831 Wayne Avenue
Chambersburg, Pennsylvania 17201
www.facebook.com/pages/Marios-Italian-Restaurant
mariosrestaurant1995@hotmail.com

Montezuma Mexican Restaurant
820 Wayne Avenue
Chambersburg, Pennsylvania 17201
717-709-1003
www.montezumamex.com
jmunoz@montezumamex.com

*Ken Lockwood Gorge Trout Conservation
Area in winter. Jim Holland*

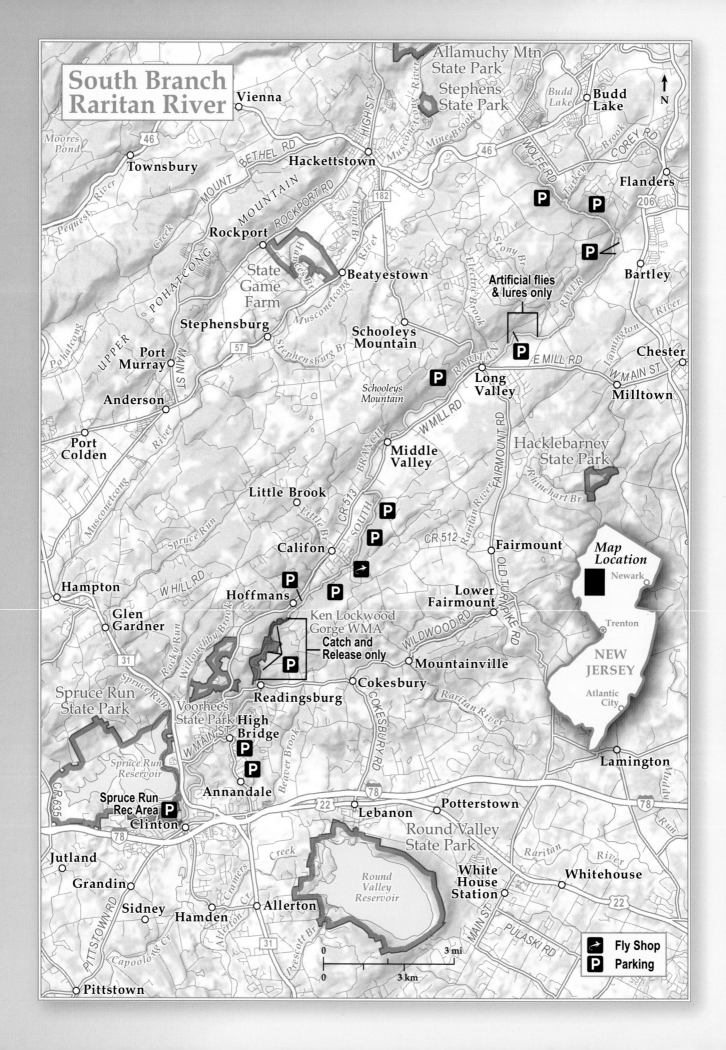

49 · South Branch Raritan River

➤ **Location:** Northwest New Jersey, about a 1-hour ride from Newark; a 1-hour ride from New York City; and a 1½-hour ride from Philadelphia, Pennsylvania. Full-service airports are available at all three cities.

The South Branch of the Raritan occupies a special place in the hearts of anglers living in the New York metropolitan area. Probably the most common sentiment expressed by visiting anglers is that they can't believe they are in New Jersey.

The South Branch originates at the outflow of Budd Lake a few miles northeast of Hackettstown. Here it is a small mountain stream. The river runs approximately 50 miles to its confluence with the North Branch of the Raritan in Branchburg. This area was called *Tucca-Ramma-Hacking* by the Lenape tribe. This means "the flowing together of water." It was originally called Two Bridges by the early European settlers due to two bridges built in the 1730s that met at a now-defunct small island on the North Branch. Today this area is referred to as The Confluence.

On its way to Long Valley, the river is fed by numerous tributaries that contain native brook trout. These fish have been here since the last Ice Age. It is indeed the geology that holds the key to the success of the river. The area is rich in limestone, providing numerous springs that buffer the pH. This makes the waters ideal for mayflies, caddis, and stoneflies, as well as wild trout. Average flows are in the 65–200 cfs range, making wading easy.

The upper 22 miles of the river is of the most interest to fly fishers. It has a reputation as being one of the finest year-round trout streams in the region. In addition to brook trout, brown trout and rainbow trout can be found throughout this section.

From Budd Lake to the Claremont Trout Conservation Area, the South Branch tumbles approximately 8 miles down Schooley's Mountain, through farmland, woods, and marsh. The river is small here. Public access is generous and well-marked. The 1¼-mile section known as the Claremont Tract is not stocked, but is managed as a wild fishery. Tackle is restricted to artificial lures and flies only. There is a one-fish limit. The minimum length limit is 15 inches.

From Long Valley to Califon, a distance of about 7 miles, the South Branch increases in size and widens into a medium-size trout river averaging 40 to 50 feet in width. In addi-

Ken Lockwood Gorge Trout Conservation Area in winter. Jim Holland

tion to numerous springs keeping temperatures cool, brush and trees shade the river, providing the trout with plenty of cover. The river here is composed mainly of glides and runs with an average depth of 2 to 4 feet. Just above Califon is a recently restored stretch of water that should provide additional angling opportunities for years to come. This area has some of the best hatches on the river. There are Hendricksons and Sulphurs in the spring. There are caddis after that. Slate Drakes offer action into the fall. While the hatch occurs at midday, the evening spinner fall can be memorable. This

217

Keith Gardner releasing "Bubba," a 26-inch brown trout. Zach Gardner

Rainbow trout. Jim Holland

area is also known for large fish—especially Kamloops rainbows, which are privately stocked and now reproducing in the river.

Less than 2 miles below Califon is the famed Ken Lockwood Gorge. This 2½-mile Trout Conservation Area was placed under catch-and-release regulations starting in January 2014. Tackle is restricted to artificial lures and flies only. The river drops steeply here as the mountains rise on either side. There is a great deal of pocketwater and fast runs. Several pools, notably the Ledge, Trestle, and Monument, offer excellent dry-fly action. But the area is better known for its productive nymph fishing. Euro-style nymphing with a pair of nymphs is a great way to probe the runs and pockets here. Skilled nymph fishers often use 10-foot 4-weight rods with an emerger behind a weighted nymph. Many anglers also employ a dry-dropper using a Stimulator with a small Beadhead Pheasant-tail or Hare's-ear roughly 18 inches beneath it. The Lake Solitude Fishing Club marks the downstream boundary of the Gorge. Some fish stocked by the club migrate upstream. Rainbow trout and brown trout between 16 and 20 inches are fairly common here. They do not, however, come easy, and landing one within the rocky confines of the Gorge is considered an accomplishment.

Below the Gorge the river continues through High Bridge, then on to Clinton and its famed Red Mill. Crowds of anglers gather at the falls here for Opening Day—it is quite the spectacle. The river is stocked here. However, it tends to warm up by Fathers Day, and the trout fishing slows down, but not before some great Sulphur hatches. There is, however, an emerging fishery for carp and northern pike here, as well a strong population of smallmouth bass.

The New Jersey Division of Fish and Wildlife closely monitors the health of the river with periodic electrofishing surveys. The Headwaters Raritan Association conducts an annual macroinvertebrate sampling of stream insects. More than 44,000 trout are stocked in the river every year. It is a very well-managed resource.

➤ Hatches: Typical Eastern hatches are found on the South Branch. Spring hatches begin in mid-February and run through the end of June. Fall hatches start in late August and run through November. Major hatches include Early Black Stoneflies; several varieties of grannoms; Spotted Sedges and Green Sedges; mayflies including Quill Gordons, Hendricksons, Blue Quills, March Browns, Sulphurs, and Summer Sulphurs (*vitreus, hebe,* and *varia*), Blue-winged Olives, Light Cahills, *Isonychias, Baetis*; and Yellow Sally stoneflies. There are even some large *Hexagenia* mayfly hatches in late August. October Caddis hatch in September. There is excellent terrestrial fishing in the summer as well—ants and beetles provide the best action.

Trout in the South Branch of the Raritan average a foot in length. However, much larger fish are caught. Special regulations, particularly catch-and-release and artificial lures and flies only, add to the overall experience while ensuring that the fishery is allowed to prosper. The South Branch of the Raritan River is a very special place within an easy drive of the masses.

➤ Tackle: A 9-foot 5-weight rod with a floating line will work for most situations encountered on the South Branch Raritan. Longer rods up to 10 feet can be helpful for nymphing. If you want to fish streamers, a 9-foot 6-weight with a fast-sinking sink-tip is your best option. Dry-fly fishing is best done with a 9-foot 4-weight, as you may need to drop to 6X to effectively fish smaller patterns such as Blue-winged Olives. While rods longer than 9 feet can work, especially for nymphing, rods shorter than 9 feet are not practical. Strike indicators should be large enough to float two flies and added weight. Flies should include Woolly Buggers; minnow and sculpin patterns; and all stages of mayflies, stoneflies, and caddis in a variety of sizes and colors.

JIM HOLLAND co-owns and operates Shannon's Fly & Tackle in Califon, New Jersey. He can be reached at 908-832-5736, shannonsfly@gmail .com, or www.shannonsflytackle.com.

CLOSEST FLY SHOPS

Shannon's Fly and Tackle
74B Main Street
Califon, New Jersey 07830
908-832-5736
www.shannonsflytackle.com
shannonsfly@gmail.com

Ramsey Outdoors
281 Route 10 East
Succasunna, New Jersey 07876
973-584-7798
www.ramseyoutdoor.com
customerservice@ramseyoutdoor.com

CLOSEST GUIDES/OUTFITTERS

Rise Form Guides
281 Route 10 East
Succasunna, New Jersey 07876
973-584-7798
www.riseformstudio.tv
mcawful@riseformstudio.tv

CLOSEST LODGING

The Raritan Inn
528 County Road 513
Califon, New Jersey 07830
908-832-6869
www.raritaninn.com
innkeeper@raritaninn.com

Califon Bed & Breakfast
16 Academy Street
Califon, NJ 07830
877-778-8298
www.califonbnb.com
info@galifonbnb.com

Courtyard Lebanon by Marriott
300 Corporate Drive
Lebanon, New Jersey 08833
908-236-8500
www.marriott.com

Hampton Inn
16 Frontage Drive
Clinton, New Jersey 08809
908-713-4800
www.hamptoninn3hilton.com

Neighbor House
143 West Mill Road CR 513
Long Valley, New Jersey 07853
908-876-3519
www.neighborhouse.com
neighborhouse@comcast.net

CLOSEST RESTAURANTS

Long Valley Brew Pub
1 Fairmount Road
Long Valley, New Jersey 07853
908-876-1122
www.restaurantvillageatlongvalley.com
Andrea.RestaurantVillage@gmail.com

The Tewksbury Inn
55 Old Turnpike Road
Oldwick, New Jersey 08858
908-439-2641
www.thetewksburyinn.com
tewksburyinn@gmail.com

Tony's Bistro
419 County Road 513
Califon, New Jersey 07830
908-832-5272
www.facebook.com/TonysBistroCalifon

Circa
37 Main Street
High Bridge, New Jersey 08829
908-638-5560
www.circa-restaurant.com

The Clinton House
2 West Main Street
Clinton, New Jersey 08809
908-730-9300
www.theclintonhouse.com
theclintonhouse@comcast.net

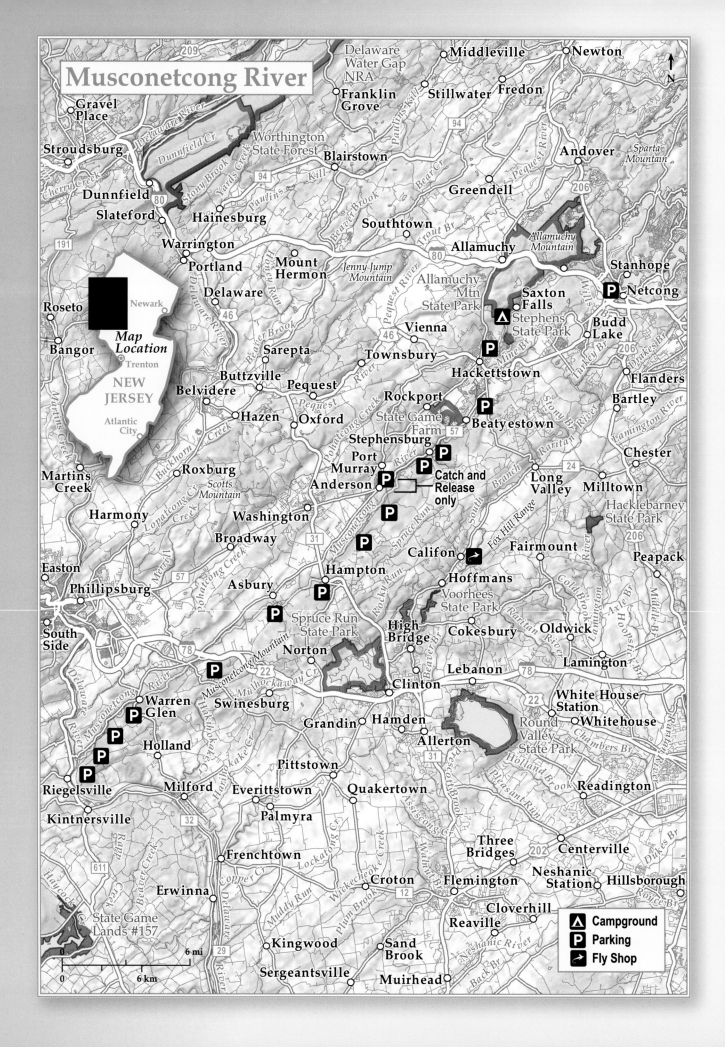

Musconetcong River

Campground
Parking
Fly Shop

50 · Musconetcong River

➤ **Location:** Northwestern New Jersey, about a 1-hour ride from Newark; a 1-hour ride from New York City; and a 1½-hour ride from Philadelphia, Pennsylvania. Full-service airports are available at all three cities.

The Musconetcong River, or the Musky as it is known locally, is New Jersey's longest trout stream. It is also arguably the most popular.

Indigenous people have inhabited the Musconetcong Valley for more than 10,000 years. The Plenge Site on the lower river is one of only two major Paleoindian archaeological sites in New Jersey, and one of the most significant in the Northeast. The Leni Lanape tribe named the Musconetcong, which means "river that flows from two lakes." The river begins at the dam at Lake Hopatcong at the Morris County–Sussex County border and flows through Lake Musconetcong. The Musky is roughly 42 miles long, about 25 miles of which is designated as a federal Wild & Scenic River.

The Musky has benefited from the efforts of Trout Unlimited and other parties who have worked to restore and protect the river. To date, six obsolete dams have been removed. This provides passage for trout and anadromous fish, such as American shad and striped bass in the lower river. There has also been significant channel restoration throughout the watershed. This benefits both trout and insects. More restoration work is planned.

The Musky leaves developed and congested Hackettstown and flows through farm country for the rest of its length. As it flows southwest toward its termination at the Delaware River, it mixes with water from the limestone aquifer and cools down. The best trout habitat is actually in the lower two-thirds of the river. This runs from Mansfield Township down to Riegelsville. As a result of the limestone aquifers cooling and improving water quality in the lower river, it is known as an upside-down watershed.

The Musky is home to native brook trout and nonnative browns. Both species reproduce in the watershed. There are wild fish in the many tributaries along the 42-mile length of river as well. The state stocks the river with brook, brown, and rainbow trout. There is a certain level of private stocking as well.

Access is very good with town-, county-, and state-owned lands along much of the river. Many landowners allow fishing on their property as well. Most of the bridges along the Musky offer public access. There are actually very few that do not, and these are well marked as private lands. Anglers should pay special attention to the section of river

Anglers fish the Hendrickson hatch on the lower Musky. Brian Cowden

between Asbury and Bloomsbury. Much of this is owned by or under easement to private clubs. There is, however, public access on state-owned lands along Asbury Bloomsbury Road above Route 78.

There is good public access on the upper river. However, trout fishing here is primarily seasonal, with the exception of some wild fish found near tributaries upstream of Beatystown in Mansfield Township. Warm summer temperatures between Lake Hopatcong and the Saxton Falls dam force the trout downstream in search of cooler water.

There is public water on the middle river at the Shurts Road bridge, the Route 31 bridge, Shoddy Mills, Changewater, and Butler's Park. These hold good populations of trout. They also support strong hatches. Public access is very good. This is where the limestone influence becomes obvious, with springs and small, watercress-lined streams entering the river. Near Penwell in Mansfield Township, you will find the Point Mountain Trout Conservation Area. Here you will find some of the best water on the river. This special-regulations section is managed for trophy trout and is open to fishing year-round. The hatches are strong and diverse. The Cliffdale Inn property is held in public trust and was the recipient of channel restoration work in the winter of 2011. This enhanced the habitat and benefited both wild and holdover fish.

Cadillac Rock in fall in Musky Gorge. Brian Cowden

The lower river can be easily accessed from the Interstate 70 corridor. Here the river is large. It stays cool right through the summer. Below County Route 519, you will encounter wild trout that enter the river from the Delaware, especially during the fall. There are also holdover fish and some large wild browns. In addition to the standard nymphs and dries, streamers stripped through deep holes and along undercut banks and submerged trees can produce some large fish. You should focus on the state-owned land around Cyphers Road Bridge. Fish downstream until you hit the Delaware River.

In this section, Trout Unlimited, along with partners in the Musconetcong River Restoration Partnership removed two wood cofferdams dating to the late 1800s, lowered a stone dam dating back to 1790, and removed the concrete Finesville Dam entirely, greatly improving the habitat. These projects also opened up the lower river to spawning anadro-

Brian Cowden with big brown trout. Brian Cowden

mous fish. Above Route 519 lies the spectacular Musconetcong Gorge. Here you will find wild browns accessible only to the angler willing to hike in. Trout Unlimited and its partners are working to remove a large dam that currently blocks another mile of narrow gorge pocketwater.

➤ Hatches: The Musky boasts prolific caddis hatches. There are also solid mayfly hatches, with most of the major Eastern species represented. The late winter–early spring Black Stonefly hatch is one of the best in the region. This provides reliable surface action on warmer days in late winter and early spring. After this the caddis and mayflies begin to hatch in earnest. The best fishing occurs during the Sulphur hatch, which begins by mid-May and lasts into July in some years. This small yellow mayfly seems to get every trout in the river looking up. The early morning Trico hatch in late summer and early fall is another important event. Scuds make up a significant portion of the aquatic insect biomass and should not be overlooked.

The Musky is a wading river. It is best fished at flows below 350 cfs. There is a USGS flow gauge at the Bloomsbury station. Flows over 500 cfs can make wading difficult and even dangerous in some spots, but can be fished if you stay out of the faster water. Summer flows as low as 125 cfs or less are not uncommon.

➤ Tackle: A 9-foot 5-weight rod with a floating line will work for most situations encountered on the Musky. Longer rods up to 10 feet can be helpful for nymphing. If you want to fish streamers, a 9-foot 6-weight with a fast-sinking sink-tip is your best option. Dry-fly fishing is best done with a 9-foot 4-weight, as you may need to drop to 6X to effect-

Brian Cowden releasing a nice brook trout. Brian Cowden

ively fish smaller patterns such as Blue-winged Olives. While rods longer than 9 feet can work, especially for nymphing, rods shorter than 9 feet are not practical. Strike indicators should be large enough to float two flies and added weight. Flies should include Woolly Buggers, minnow and sculpin patterns; scuds; and all stages of mayflies, stoneflies and caddis in a variety of sizes and colors.

BRIAN COWDEN is the Trout Unlimited Coordinator for the Musconetcong River Initiative. He also guides for Shannon's Fly and Tackle in Califon, New Jersey. Brian can be reached at 201-230-3383, BCowden@tu.org, or www.tu.org.

CLOSEST FLY SHOPS

Shannon's Fly and Tackle
74B Main Street
Califon, New Jersey 07830
908-832-5736
www.shannonsflytackle.com
shannonsfly@gmail.com

Ramsey Outdoors
281 Route 10 East
Succasunna, New Jersey 07876
973-584-7798
www.ramseyoutdoor.com
customerservice@ramseyoutdoor.com

CLOSEST GUIDES/OUTFITTERS

Rise Form Guides
281 Route 10 East
Succasunna, New Jersey 07876
973-584-7798
www.riseformstudio.tv
mcawful@riseformstudio.tv
973-584-7798
www.ramseyoutdoor.com
customerservice@ramseyoutdoor.com

CLOSEST LODGING

The Raritan Inn
528 County Road 513
Califon, New Jersey 07830
908-832-6869
www.raritaninn.com
innkeeper@raritaninn.com

Hampton Inn
16 Frontage Drive
Clinton, New Jersey 08809
908-713-4800
www.hamptoninn3hilton.com

Neighbor House
143 West Mill Road CR 513
Long Valley, New Jersey 07853
908-876-3519
www.neighborhouse.com
neighborhouse@comcast.net

Holiday Inn
111 West Main Street
Clinton, New Jersey 08809
888-233-9450
www.holidayin.com

Comfort Inn
1925 State Route 57
Hackettstown, New Jersey 07840
908-813-8860
www.comfortinn.com

CLOSEST RESTAURANTS

Long Valley Brew Pub
1 Fairmount Road
Long Valley, New Jersey 07853
www.restaurantvillageatlongvalley.com
Andrea.RestaurantVillage@gmail.com
908-876-1122

The Tewksbury Inn
55 Old Turnpike Road
Oldwick, New Jersey 08858
908-439-2641
www.thetewksburyinn.com
tewksburyinn@gmail.com

Tony's Bistro
419 County Road 513
Califon, New Jersey 07830
908-832-5272
www.facebook.com/TonysBistroCalifon

Circa
37 Main Street
High Bridge, New Jersey 08829
908-638-5560
www.circa-restaurant.com

The Clinton House
2 West Main Street
Clinton, New Jersey 08809
908-730-9300
www.theclintonhouse.com
theclintonhouse@comcast.net

John McGeehan on Yellow Breeches. Joel LaMarco

Philanthropy

We at Stonefly Press feel that it's important to view ourselves as a small part of a greater system of balance. We give back to that which nourishes us because it feels natural and right.

Stonefly Press will be donating a portion of our annual profits to conservation groups active in environmental stewardship. We encourage all our readers to learn more about them here, and encourage you to go a step further and get involved.

American Rivers
(americanrivers.org)

Bonefish & Tarpon Trust
(bonefishtarpontrust.org)

California Trout
(caltrout.org)

Coastal Conservation Association
(joincca.org)

Friends of the White River
(friendsofwhiteriver.org)

Riverkeeper
(riverkeeper.org)

Trout Unlimited
(tu.org)

Western Rivers Conservancy
(westernrivers.org)

Index

Bradford Camps, Munsungan Lake, Maine. Bob Mallard